# The University and Civil Society

# THE UNIVERSITY AND CIVIL SOCIETY

BY

# Jonathan F. Fanton

 New School for Social Research
NEW YORK

Copyright 1995 by Jonathan F. Fanton

All rights reserved.

New School for Social Research
66 West 12 Street
New York, NY 10011

Designed by Levavi & Levavi, Inc
Manufactured in the United States of America

Library of Congress Cataloging-in-Publication Data
Fanton, Jonathan F.
  The University and Civil Society

Library of Congress catalogue number 95-67519
ISBN: 0-9645074-0-4

# CONTENTS

INTRODUCTION 1

ACKNOWLEDGMENTS 13

PART I
**THE SPECIAL MANDATE
OF THE NEW SCHOOL 17**

1. INAUGURAL ADDRESS 19
*(November 16, 1982)*

## A. Foundation and Aims of the New School

2. AN INSTITUTION OF ITS TIME 31
*(Selected from Annual Report, 1986)*

3. THE TRANSFORMING ENERGY OF MODERNISM 35
*(Selected from Commencement, May 1987)*

4. IDEAS MATTER 38
*(Commencement, May 1985)*

5. CONNECTING PUBLIC AND INTELLECTUAL DISCOURSE  41
*(Commencement, May 1986)*

6. THE NEW SCHOOL: THE QUINTESSENTIAL NEW YORK CITY INSTITUTION  45
*(Annual Report, 1988)*

7. RESPONDING TO THE INTERDEPENDENCE OF THE MODERN WORLD  51
*(Selected from Annual Report, November 1989)*

8. UNDERGRADUATE EDUCATION AT THE NEW SCHOOL  59
*(Selected from Annual Report, 1987)*

9. ART AND SOCIAL TRANSFORMATION  63
*(Commencement, Parsons, May 1987)*

10. A WORK IN PROGRESS  66
*(Convocation, September 1994)*

## B. Reflections on Education

11. NURTURING OPTIMISM  73
*(Commencement, May 1992)*

12. TEXT AND CONTEXT  79
*(Selected from Welcoming Remarks, September 1986)*

13. FREEDOM CARRIES RESPONSIBILITIES  81
*(Commencement, Parsons, May 1990)*

14. ESTABLISHING A NETWORK FOR COLLECTIVE INFLUENCE  85
*(Commencement, Parsons, May 1992)*

## Part II
## FREEDOM AND DIVERSITY 91

### A. Academic Freedom and Freedom of Expression

15. THE UNIVERSITY IN EXILE 95
*(Selected from Fiftieth Anniversary Convocation, April 1984)*

16. ADDRESSING APARTHEID: THE QUESTION OF OFFICIAL VIEWS 99
*(Letter to the University Community, May 1985)*

17. THE MATSUNAGA EXHIBIT AND FREEDOM OF EXPRESSION 104
*(Letter to the University Community, November 1989)*

18. A SANCTUARY OF NONREPRESSION 112
*(Selected from Aims of Education Convocation, September 1990)*

19. REAFFIRMING THE COMMITMENT TO FREEDOM OF EXPRESSION 116
*(Remarks to the Independent Committee on Arts Policy, March 1991)*

20. THE MULTIPLE MEANINGS OF POLITICAL CORRECTNESS 123
*(Selected from Aims of Education Address, September 1991)*

21. ARE FREEDOM OF EXPRESSION AND FREEDOM FROM INTOLERANCE MUTUALLY EXCLUSIVE? 131
*(Letter to the Editor, New York Times, December 13, 1989)*

## B. Democracy, Pluralism, and the University

22. REPRESENTATION FOR THE UN(DER)REPRESENTED  137
*(Annual Report, 1990)*

23. THE DEMOCRATIC EXPERIMENT: HAVE WE SUCCEEDED?  144
*(Selected from Commencement, May 1990)*

24. AGE OF FRAGMENTATION ... OR PLURALISM?  148
*(Commencement, May 1993)*

PART III
# ART AND SOCIETY  155

## A. The New School and the NEA Challenge

25. SAYING NO TO THE OBSCENITY CONDITION  159
*(Statement on New School NEA Litigation, May 1990)*

26. A CONDITIONAL VICTORY  164
*(Statement on the Reauthorization of the NEA, November 1990)*

27. A TRUCE WITH THE NEA  166
*(Memorandum to the University Community, February 1991)*

## B. Support for the Arts: Where Does It Come From?

28. IS PUBLIC FUNDING COMPATIBLE WITH ARTISTIC FREEDOM?  171
*(Commencement, Parsons, May 1991)*

29. LOOKING AT THE EUROPEAN MODEL 175
*(Selected from Commencement, Parsons/Paris,
May 1993)*

30. ON ESTABLISHING A NATIONAL ARTS POLICY 179
*(Commencement, Mannes, May 1993)*

## PART IV
## THE CHALLENGE OF MAINTAINING INDEPENDENT INSTITUTIONS 183

31. THE ERODING SUPPORT FOR PRIVATE INSTITUTIONS 185
*(Commencement, May 1991)*

32. THE IMPORTANCE OF THE TUITION ASSISTANCE PROGRAM 189
*(Report to New York State Civic and Professional Leaders, March 1986)*

33. HIGHER EDUCATION'S FALL FROM GRACE 192
*(June 1987)*

34. MAKING THE CASE FOR FUNDING 195
*(Remarks to New York State Division of the Budget as Chair, Commission on Independent Colleges and Universities, November 1989)*

35. PEER REVIEW AND MAINTAINING EXCELLENCE 209
*(Annual Report, November 1991)*

36. SUSTAINING THE SENSITIVE ECOLOGY OF THE UNIVERSITY 215
*(Annual Report, November 1992)*

PART V
# HELSINKI WATCH AND THE STRUGGLE FOR HUMAN RIGHTS AND DEMOCRACY 231

37. NOTES FROM WENCESLAS SQUARE 233
*(Prague, October 1989)*

38. A FRAGILE HOLD ON THE FUTURE: PRAGUE AND SOFIA, 1989 238
*(Memorandum to the Board of Trustees, November 1989)*

39. LIVING WITH UNCERTAINTY: MOSCOW 1990 253
*(Memorandum to the Board of Trustees, June 1990)*

40. A NEW HISTORY FOR ROMANIA? 271
*(Memorandum to the Board of Trustees, January 1990)*

41. BUCHAREST REVISITED: REALITY SETS IN 287
*(Notes on a Visit to Bucharest, July 1990)*

42. THE STRUGGLE CONTINUES: GERMANY 1990 298
*(Memorandum to the Board of Trustees, August 1990)*

43. A FLUID MOMENT FOR YUGOSLAVIA 305
*(Memorandum to the Board of Trustees, June 1991)*

44. THE CHOICE BETWEEN REFORM AND REPRESSION IN ESTONIA, LATVIA, AND LITHUANIA 319
*(Memorandum to the Board of Trustees, February 1991)*

45. A WATERSHED MOMENT  338
*(Report on a Trip to Turkey,
January 1992)*

46. REFLECTIONS ON BULGARIA  354
*(Memorandum to the Board of Trustees,
June 1992)*

47. ALBANIA: A FIRST GLIMPSE  368
*(Memorandum to the Board of Trustees,
November 1992)*

48. LAST TRIP TO CZECHOSLOVAKIA/UPDATE
ON HUNGARY  382
*(Memorandum to the Board of Trustees,
December 1992)*

49. TROUBLE IN THE CAUCASUS  403
*(Memorandum to the Board of Trustees,
July 1993)*

50. THE SPECIAL CASE OF TRNAVA UNIVERSITY  433
*(Democracy Seminar Conference, Prague,
July 1993)*

51. AMERICAN BUSINESS SHOULD CONSIDER HUMAN RIGHTS
BEFORE INVESTING  444
*(New York Times Op-Ed Article with Kurt R. Soderlund,
July 1993)*

52. ADVANCING REFORM IN HIGHER EDUCATION
IN EASTERN AND CENTRAL EUROPE  447
*(Annual Report, 1993)*

53. SOUTH AFRICA: THE CASE FOR CAUTIOUS AND COMPLEX OPTIMISM  456
*(Memorandum to the Board of Trustees, March 1994)*

54. THE "GREAT GAME" REVISITED: PROBLEMS AND POTENTIAL IN CENTRAL ASIA  475
*(Memorandum to the Board of Trustees, July 1994)*

NEW SCHOOL CHRONOLOGY AND STATISTICAL PROFILE  503

INDEX  509

# INTRODUCTION

When I came east from the University of Chicago to be interviewed for the presidency, I knew very little about the New School for Social Research. As I struggled through rush-hour traffic from LaGuardia Airport, I thought about turning around and going home. I am glad I did not. My meeting with the Student-Faculty Advisory Committee to the search was a transforming experience. The diversity, raw energy and intelligence, the evident caring and commitment to the New School impressed me deeply. They told me a tale of rapid growth and change, of the need to build a university from schools with quite separate histories, of a desire to maintain the traditional character of the New School while adapting to the reality of its expanded size and scope. I heard the challenge, liked the people, and felt comfortable for reasons I could not then explain. I left the interview wanting to come to the New School and had no hesitation about accepting the offer when it came.

I hope this collection of my speeches and essays, issued on the occasion of the New School's seventy-fifth anniversary, will be useful to my successors and to the Trustees, faculty, and students of the New School in appreciating their duties as stewards of this special place.

The New School is an unusual institution, important beyond its size and years to the world of ideas and the search for liberal democracy. It is not an easy institution to comprehend, especially given the dramatic changes which have occurred over the past three decades during which John R. Everett and I have been privileged to serve as its President. Much of what I have said and written seeks to remind us that changes in size and scope do not alter the fundamental character or mission of the New School. I have tried to thicken the history, tradition, and culture of our distinctive institution, much as our first President, Alvin Johnson, sought to define it in the first instance.

Painfully aware of how thin are the New School's archives, and, save Johnson's own memoir, how spare the institutional history, I have labored consciously to build a record of reason for all our major decisions. I also wanted to share my work more widely with the hope that it would advance an understanding of the nature of universities and their role in building liberal democratic societies, a role also played by the human rights movement. The final section of this volume mainly derives from my work as chair of the Helsinki Watch Committee, a division of Human Rights Watch.

While I do not pretend to have a carefully honed philosophy which guides my every act, I do hope the reader will discern the beliefs and principles that provide my moral compass. Because the views expressed in my work depend so much on those beliefs and principles, I would like to indulge in a few personal reflections which may help the reader understand what follows. This exploration of the people, ideas, books, and experiences which influenced my intellectual development and administrative style owes its inspiration to a marvelous book by Kai Erikson, *Encounters*, which traces such interactions with grace and insight.

I am very much a product of my environment: a Connecticut Yankee, a Protestant from a Republican family, educated at the Choate School and Yale University. I am an historian by training, and an old-fashioned one at that, interested more in the narrative that tries to reveal what happened and why than in grand theories of human nature. I majored in American history at Yale College and at its graduate school, where I wrote my dissertation on Robert Lovett, a gifted investment banker and public servant who influenced national security policy from World War II through the Korean conflict and beyond. I was fortunate to be at Yale during a stellar era for its history department. Five professors made special contributions.

Norman Pollack, who taught my freshman history section, was the first Marxist I ever met—and I liked him. His take on

American history shook my settled Republican middle-class notions about right and wrong and introduced me to issues of race, class, and gender; and for a time, he persuaded me that the Populists embodied the best hope for America. His next-door neighbor in the corner office in Silliman College was Hans Frei, a professor of religion, whose seminar on the interaction between philosophy and public life raised questions of morals and meaning on which I am still reflecting.

My decision to become an historian rather than a lawyer or architect owes much to Edmund Morgan, Howard Lamar, and John Morton Blum. Morgan's undergraduate colonial history course was of particular interest because I identified strongly with the aspirations of the Founders of our country. My own family came to America in the 1680s, settling in Connecticut not far from where I still live. His course introduced me to the excitement of using original sources. My term paper, examining how democracy first took root in America, caught Morgan's attention and it was he who first suggested I become a professional historian. That suggestion found reaffirmation through my work with Howard Lamar on my senior thesis, a history of the National Youth Administration, which, to my astonishment, won the Porter prize for the best student history paper in 1965.

But Morgan's advice would not have taken were it not for the inspiration and patient mentorship of John Morton Blum, whose course on twentieth-century politics and culture touched my spirit. There for the first time I understood how history could not only make the past comprehensible but also offer useful lessons for the present. Later, when I went back to graduate school after a stint in the Yale administration, it was Blum who encouraged me to complete the Ph.D. and did his best to teach me to write clearly. Style, of course, relates to substance, and Blum's insistence that the word "inevitable" has no place in historical writing yielded a valuable lesson. I do think people make a difference in events large and small. I do not accept any outcome as inevitable, although I do understand the concept of odds and the fact that some victories may come at too high a price.

Some of my historical heroes would not please my paternal grandfather, Willard Fanton, a lifelong Republican and first selectman of Weston, Connecticut. Thomas Jefferson, James Madison, and Abraham Lincoln he would gladly embrace, probably Theodore Roosevelt and Nelson Rockefeller as well. But Franklin and Eleanor Roosevelt, Harry Truman, Robert Kennedy, and Martin Luther King would be over the line. I have always admired people who faced genuine crisis with courage, who could surmount the limits of their own background to see the world in a fresh way, and who were—in the words of Dean Acheson—"present at the creation" of a new nation or movement. I have been drawn to practical people who made a difference and, I suppose, that is what I have tried to be.

Having already confessed the absence of a coherent philosophy of life, I nevertheless lay claim to a sense of history that has infused purpose into my work and influenced my administrative style. I continue to draw on the lessons of historical works, some read over 30 years ago. Here is a sample.

Edmund Morgan's *Birth of the Republic* illuminates the importance of equality as the essential issue over which the American Revolution was fought. I have interpreted that to mean not merely equality of opportunity but equality of outcome, a notion made much clearer to me through Michael Walzer's concept of "complex equality" in his *Spheres of Justice*. Morgan's biography of John Winthrop, *A Puritan's Dilemma*, helped me understand my own ancestors and why they insisted that every individual had the obligation to fulfill, even stretch, his or her potential. I have taken considerable comfort from Winthrop's diary entry explaining that recreation was necessary in preparing the body and spirit to work harder and with greater creativity.

Kenneth Stampp's *And the War Came* brought home to me with historical force the fact that wars are not inevitable and that different actions by individuals up to the last minute can change the course of events.

Frederick Jackson Turner's *The Frontier in American History* together with David Potter's *People of Plenty* and

Alexis de Tocqueville's *Democracy in America* got me thinking about distinctive American traits, about the question of national character, its uses and limitations. My understanding of civil society and passion for maintaining a vigorous not-for-profit sector, including private higher education, owe much to their insight.

Richard Hofstadter's *The Age of Reform* originally piqued my interest in social change, as did de Tocqueville's *The Old Regime and the Revolution*. Hofstadter's theory of the status squeeze and de Tocqueville's warnings about the danger of rising expectations offered insights upon which I have often drawn.

John Blum's *The Republican Roosevelt* tutored me in the use of power, especially the value of appearing to want an objective which in the end can be compromised in pursuit of a more important goal. Arthur Schlesinger's trilogy on the New Deal provided a useful insight into the importance of timing and the transformational power of Franklin Roosevelt's confidence and optimism; it also illuminated the virtues and pitfalls of management by competitive assignment of tasks to more than one person. C. E. Lindblom's essay "Muddling Through" made me feel better about incremental gains—the only gains most of us are able to achieve in our administrative work—and helped me realize there is a difference between good and bad incrementalism.

John F. Kennedy's *Profiles in Courage*, which I read in junior high school, has on occasion helped me take on fights that I thought were right in the face of long odds. Indeed, I have told myself that I should take on such battles every so often just to be sure my tendency to compromise and conciliate has not overwhelmed my commitment to principle.

C. Van Woodward's *The Strange Career of Jim Crow* touched me in the 1960s as I became involved in the civil rights movement. At first I saw the race problem as Southern but gradually came to understand that racism was a national disease that knew no sectional boundaries. My activism in picketing against Jim Crow laws in Maryland in 1961 thus gave way to a decade of work in opening educational opportunities for minority students through the Ulysses S. Grant Foundation, an undergraduate tutoring program at Yale, the Transitional Year Program, Project Upward Bound, and others.

Henry Stimson's *On Active Service in War and Peace* and Elting Morrison's masterful Stimson biography, *Turmoil and Tradition*, introduced me to a group of patriotic public servants, many Yale-trained, whom I greatly admired and who inspired me with their dedication to the public interest, their integrity, their intelligence and hard work. Stimson and his circle, including Robert Lovett, shared a faith in the potential of America to lead the quest for a more just, humane, and peaceful world, a faith undiminished by the horrors of two world wars. I have always admired Stimson's injunction against cynicism.

The reader may very well be thinking that the influences I cite are very narrow, and so they are: America, New England, Choate, and Yale. What breadth I can claim comes from my involvement with the civil rights movement and Helsinki Watch.

When I interviewed for the New School presidency, a Trustee took me aback when he asked why I would want to be President of the New School. Where was the fit? "A square peg in a round hole" was the image he offered. On the surface he was right. Although I was no longer a Republican, my brand of independent centrism seemed at odds with the leftist image of the New School. My narrative style of American history hardly seemed appropriate for a cosmopolitan faculty for whom theory was all important. My small-town Protestant upbringing seemed off-key for a tough urban university with strong Jewish roots. And my experience at Yale and Chicago, two elite research universities, seemed oddly matched to this institution with adult education at its core.

I replied to that good question that I had three criteria for my next job: I wanted an institution which was very different from Yale and Chicago, not one which sought to be like them. I wanted an institution which aspired to be first-rate at what it did and had a reasonable chance to succeed. And I wanted a challenge, an institution which had problems to be fixed. I did not want to have it said at the end of the day that I merely had sustained the status quo. The New School met all three criteria.

As I took up my duties as President of the New School, two people for whom I had worked were constantly on my mind: Kingman Brewster, President of Yale, and Hanna Gray, Provost of Yale and later President of the University of Chicago. Brewster had an uncanny sense of timing and a capacity to anticipate a political threat and to grasp an educational opportunity. He framed questions and issues creatively, always starting with the big picture and usually illuminating complexity that had eluded most of his colleagues. He gave people a chance, the benefit of the doubt, until their words or deeds proved them foolish or untrustworthy. That openness encouraged students and faculty to express their views freely and constructively. And his manner evoked from all those around him their civil and reasoned behavior. He picked first-rate people and got the best out of each through a talent for delegation coupled with high standards and quiet oversight. Most of all, he understood people psychologically, their foibles and insecurities as well as their principles and strengths.

That quality he had in common with Hanna Gray, who knew what motivated people better than they knew themselves. These two leaders taught me the value of analyzing what events in people's lives, both professionally and personally, might affect their ability to do their job and condition their interaction with their colleagues and me. Brewster and Gray shared an unbending commitment to quality, a determination to strengthen every part of the university. I have never known two people who worked harder or with more complete dedication to their institutions.

From Gray I learned how to plan, how to use my history training to frame the questions that shaped the reality of the institution, and how to face difficult issues directly and the sooner the better. My time at Chicago was a growing-up period where I gained confidence that my administrative talents were not limited to the one setting I had known as an adult. I also learned something about transitions by watching the patience with which Gray slowly assembled her team and the respect she accorded deans and officers whom she had inherited.

Three other individuals influenced my administrative style: Arthur Singer, senior vice president of the Sloan Foundation (who nominated me to the New School), introduced me to the world of public policy and the imperative of asking the right questions and seeking the best expert advice; Joel Fleishman, for whom I worked at Yale in the early days, bore witness to the power of energetic optimism tempered with hard-nosed realism; and Joseph Califano, for whom I worked briefly at the Department of Health, Education, and Welfare, was a model of how to be compassionate and tough, fair and demanding, romantic and practical in fruitful tension.

The speeches and essays which make up this volume reflect who I am and what people, reading, and experiences have shaped me. They also reveal, I hope, a congruence of spirit and purpose between me and the New School for Social Research. The New School's commitment to intellectual and artistic freedom, its willingness to challenge inherited orthodoxies, its belief that reasoned discourse and education lead to human progress, and its conviction that education should be open to all on the basis of merit resonate powerfully with values I have always respected and tried to reflect.

Indeed, I have seen it as my role to preserve the basic character of the New School in the face of radical changes in its size and scope and in the composition of its student body. I have sought to find language to describe our present mission in ways which reinforce our traditions. And I have tried to use the New School's experiences to illuminate the problems and possibilities for American higher education more generally. The final section of this volume chronicles a fresh chapter in the New School's concern for scholars in peril and societies in search of liberal democracy.

The New School first started as an adult evening school and later expanded to include part-time graduate students seeking master's and Ph.D. degrees in the social sciences. By

1994 it enrolled nearly 6,000 degree students (half of them undergraduates), who provide 80 percent of the tuition income. No longer limited to social research, the university is now one of the largest sources for arts education in the country with Parsons School of Design, Mannes College of Music, and a new theater program with the Actors Studio. Our service to the professions, principally for our home city of New York, has expanded with the Graduate School of Management and Urban Policy, and graduate programs in media studies, architecture, and teacher training. The humanities are well represented in our new undergraduate college, named for trustee Eugene Lang, and the committees on historical studies and liberal studies in the Graduate Faculty. My essay "Rooted in Academic Freedom" (1985) articulates the principles that have guided this growth, while my annual report "An Institution of its Time" (1986) outlines the characteristics that still make the New School distinctive: its penchant for innovation, its search for special niches, its commitment to meeting unmet needs, its determination to be independent and protect artistic and intellectual freedom, and its critical stance to mainstream social science.

It is essential to understand that a university is not a nation state governed by majority rule. The Trustees are by law a self-perpetuating group of governors not bound to respond to the will of the administration, faculty, students, or alumni. A university by design is not a democratic institution, even though Trustees have delegated broad authority to the President, who in turn has delegated primacy to the faculty in such matters as academic standards, curriculum, and faculty appointments.

Yet the Trustees are obliged to set the long-term course of the university—deciding, for example, to absorb Parsons and Mannes, to start an undergraduate liberal arts college, and to subsidize the Graduate Faculty because of its importance to intellectual life here and abroad.

The Trustees also have the obligation to protect the ability of individual members of the community to advocate controversial and unpopular positions. Their ability to do so depends on keeping the university neutral on issues not directly related to higher education. Otherwise, their "official" view might exercise undue influence on the intellectual life of the university, a danger I discuss in "Addressing Apartheid" (1985), a letter to the university community on the issue of racial separatism in South Africa.

Another internal threat to intellectual freedom comes from peer pressure to conform, sometimes known as "political correctness." My feeling that the media's formulation of those pressures is too simplistic gave rise to my convocation address, "The Multiple Meanings of Political Correctness" (1991). I believe the New School has been freer than most universities of both internal and external abridgement of artistic and intellectual freedom. We rightly pride ourselves on the intellectual tension we have produced by encouraging the clash of divergent viewpoints and controversial speakers. Encouragement and protection of artistic and intellectual freedom have been at the top of my agenda as President of the New School. Our challenge to the National Endowment for the Arts (NEA), over its inclusion of what we took to be unconstitutional conditions on a small grant, was motivated by the protection of artistic freedom. So was my defense of the Matsunaga exhibit, which contained images offensive to African-Americans, women, and others. Our strong freedom of expression policy and our vigorous steps to protect the right of controversial speakers are tangible evidence of that commitment.

The perception that universities are no longer sanctuaries for free and independent thought has resulted in a slow but steady erosion of public support for higher education. We depend on that support for our tax exempt status and monies for research and scholarship programs. I have wanted the New School to take the lead in reminding the public of the central role played by universities in maintaining a healthy civil society. Our challenge to the NEA, our vigorous insistence on the rights of controversial speakers and provocative exhibitions to appear on campus, and our steadfast resistance to intellectual conformity are all part of that endeavor.

In my work as chair of the New York Commission on Independent Colleges and Universities, I sought to make the case for private universities in the public service. Private universities are in fragile shape these days; not all of them will survive. And those that do will prosper only if their mission is clear and their quality high. My testimony to the New York State Division of the Budget—"Making the Case for Funding" (1989)—is addressed to those matters.

One important role for private higher education, strongly embraced at the New School, is the provision of educational opportunity on the basis of merit, not family circumstance.

America's charter documents set forth a radical view of a democratic society with equality and openness as fundamental principles. The commitment to receive people from around the world and the legacy of slavery and segregation have tested that vision and called into question early twentieth-century notions of the melting pot. We are now struggling for a more complicated conception of a society which respects cultural differences while seeking to preserve elements of a common culture as well.

I have wanted the New School to lead in this project both by building a diverse faculty and student body and by creating a climate comfortable for diversity. I have encouraged the New School faculty to take the lead in revising our curriculum so that it reflects the many different cultures that have enriched America. Our ambition is to be the most diverse high-quality private institution in the country. With 21% of its students from abroad and many students from families which recently immigrated to America, the New School has achieved admirable ethnic diversity. But it has not done well enough in including African-Americans and Latinos, two groups underrepresented in higher education. I have long feared that if universities like the New School cannot be inclusive and make American pluralism work, then there is little hope for the larger society.

Our concern for maintaining a healthy liberal democracy committed to pluralism in America finds a parallel in our concern for the transition to democracy in Eastern and Central

Europe. One feature of the New School's tradition I have sought to revive and broaden stems from Alvin Johnson's dramatic rescue of scholars facing repression and worse in Europe during the 1930s and 1940s. The creation of the University in Exile, now called the Graduate Faculty of Political and Social Science, saved the lives and careers of 167 scholars, forever changing the nature of the New School and, in many ways, American intellectual life in general. This concern for scholars in peril found fresh expression in the New School's Eastern and Central Europe project, which sponsored the underground Democracy Seminar network in Poland, Hungary, and elsewhere during the Soviet period. After the revolutions of 1989, the project came above ground to help universities in fourteen countries rebuild fields—sociology, political science, philosophy, among them—which had been banned or politicized during the Soviet period. My own interest in this project was strengthened by my active work in the region as chair of the Helsinki Watch Committee.

The final section of this volume contains several reports describing trips I took jointly for Helsinki Watch and the New School, a natural link because so many of the New School's Democracy Seminar members were also human rights activists. The pieces are written in a journalistic style—which means they are dated—but I hope they remain interesting as historical documents nonetheless. Taken together, they affirm that courageous individuals can make a difference in resisting repression and provoking change. They also reveal something of the scholar's role in building civil society.

While the New School's historical ties have been to Europe, our scholarly interest in transition to democracy and free markets knows no geographical boundaries. We are building strength in Latin America and Africa to enrich our comparative perspective. My trip to South Africa in the winter of 1994, for example, opened the way for a parallel African project which will help balance our European perspective.

# Acknowledgments

Many of the pieces in this volume have benefited from a back-and-forth with close colleagues, most of all Richard Rogers, who served as Secretary of the Corporation for 12 years. Our lively debates about principles and purposes sharpened my thinking. And his capacity to find a relevant quote, to add a clarifying transitional paragraph, to chop out repetition and diversion, has enriched many an essay. In the early years Steve White of the Sloan Foundation helped hone my message, and in the later period Kurt Soderlund of the New School brought his talent for clear and orderly presentations to my assistance. Jeri Laber, the director of Helsinki Watch, is a gifted writer and editor whose skills improved many of my human rights reports. Finally, my wife Cynthia has deepened my appreciation for literature and history beyond America. So the gradual appearance of allusions beyond my own field reflect the reading she has given me. Her own polymathic grasp of life and literature has deepened my understanding of people and my perspective on history.

Cynthia, Kai Erikson, Ira Katznelson, Richard Rogers, and Kurt Soderlund have provided valuable insight which sharpened this introduction. Gail Kinn did a marvelous and sensitive job in editing the main body of my work, and Grace Lichtenstein and Al Landa have helped bring it to print. I am grateful to Dan and JoAnna Rose, Vera List, Aso Tavitian, and Bill Green for funds which supported my foreign travel.

# The University
# and
# Civil Society

# PART I

# The Special Mandate of the New School

# Inaugural Address

(NOVEMBER 16, 1982)

I accept this symbol of office and the trust you have placed in me with a sense of exhilaration and gratitude. To the Trustees of the New School, and especially their gifted chairman, my deep thanks. Thanks too are in order for those who have participated in today's ceremony, to those who have helped plan it, and to you who have come here to celebrate with us.

Samuel Johnson remarked once that it was wonderful how the prospect of being hanged concentrated the mind. I am not about to suggest that becoming president of a university is quite the same as being hanged, although there were moments in the late 1960s which invited the comparison. But the occasion does concentrate the mind, and to that I can bear witness.

A familiar name is likely to be taken for granted, and I found it required a certain effort to look upon the words "New School for Social Research" as if I were meeting them for the first time. Certainly they were not casually chosen. I went back to the sources, as historians will, and most particularly to *Pioneer's Progress*, the autobiography of Alvin Johnson, the New School's first president. The school's name, it turns out, was much debated. But "after trying all sorts of names," he wrote, "we accepted as a compromise the 'New School for Social Research.' Mitchell"—economist Wesley Clair Mitchell—"claimed that it was I who invented the name. If that is true, I deserve to be punished for it."

We can't be sure today just how or why the name offended him. Madison, I think, would have been his preference. "School" may have bothered him, or even "social research." But judging by what he did while he was president, I'm inclined to believe he would have positively insisted on "new."

Taken at its face value, "new" can be elusive and misleading. If we insist on being literal, we have to be aware that it constantly threatens to become a deceit. These days, when everything in the world rushes past, "new" loses its meaning almost as soon as it is spoken. Indeed, the very word "new" can become a certificate of that which is venerable. I need hardly remind you that New College, at Oxford, was founded in 1379; and the Pont Neuf, not too far from our own outpost in France, is after all the second oldest bridge in Paris and clearly shows its age. And we have recently seen a nostalgic campaign to restore interest in art nouveau.

Few words can be taken in their literal meaning, and "new" is not one of them. For this school, for more than 60 years the word has been construed as a challenge. It defies us to defend its presence and we can accomplish that in one way and one way only: by a constant process of renewal.

We can look back on our past with satisfaction, perhaps, but never with complacency. Shakespeare had a phrase for an institution concealed in its past: "monumental mockery," he called it. We want none of that.

Our name embodies concepts of time and perspective. It implies a capacity to discern authentic innovation and to distinguish it from mere novelty. It calls forth the courage to judge what is old and should be discarded, what is old and must be honored, and what is old and must be rejuvenated. It invokes leadership that will both comprehend and engage the future. And it symbolizes, above all, a fundamental element in the American character: the respect for timeless principles joined by the determination to apply those principles to new conditions as new conditions arise.

The word compels our attention and releases our native optimism. Whatever is described as "new" has been imbued with a kind of magic for Americans. In this century alone, we have had The New Nationalism, The New Freedom, The New Deal, The New Frontier, and even The New Federalism. Our country is known as The New World, and when it was no more than a group of colonies its potential moved Hector St. John Crèvecoeur to pose this famous question: "What then is the American, this new man?" We can do no better than echo him today: What then is the University, this New School?

It began, under Alvin Johnson, as an institution of continuing education; it was created explicitly for that purpose. But during the 1930s Johnson himself made a home here for the University in Exile, at once meeting a desperate human need, by rescuing almost 200 European scholars and their families from persecution abroad, asserting the timeless principle of academic freedom, and establishing in our city a center of intellectual ferment and creativity second to none.

Another period of renewal began in the 1960s led by John R. Everett, my distinguished predecessor. Under his stewardship, the New School became a true urban university with the founding of a Graduate School of Management and Urban Professions, the merger with the Parsons School of Design and later the Otis Art Institute, and the emergence of a liberal arts college.

Parsons, which became part of this university in 1970, was a new and permanent reflection of a spirit which had been manifested from the earliest beginnings. A catalogue in the 1920s noted that "most of the work of the New School is cultural." The word "cultural" was used broadly, and it embraced the dance of Martha Graham, the art of Thomas Hart Benton, the music of Aaron Copeland, the poetry of Robert Frost. Cultural clearly meant something more than the social sciences; the school was attracting to its adult courses those who recognized the central importance and the personal satisfaction afforded by the arts.

For the New School, these years constituted a period of great growth, but it was not mere growth alone that made them so satisfying. Rather, it was the awareness that the New School retained the capacity to be ever new, as its founders had intended.

To be "new" has been, as it turns out, to depart from some of the assumptions and practices of our founders. For example—and it is an important example—our founders believed that their mission was directed to the service of mature, adult citizens. Today, when higher education is seen as a birthright, there is no valid reason why the extraordinary resources and energies of the New School should be arbitrarily limited to any "constituency" defined by age or experience.

Higher education is designed for *all* those who seek to examine the world and its ways in an informed, dispassionate, and responsible fashion. The New School is committed to a realistic encounter with this challenge. The desire to study and to learn is the sole criterion for acceptance. Those who possess that desire are welcome, certified or not by secondary school. The preface to the very first course announcement, in 1919, said tersely that the New School had been brought into being "to meet the needs of intelligent men and women interested in the grave social, political, and economic problems of the day." Those words speak as well to the present purposes of the New School, especially the Adult Division, as to the days when they were first set down.

The old needs remain, not very much altered with the passage of time. Many of those who come to the New School are here because the sheer delight in education is alive in them, and is not fulfilled in their workaday rounds. Others have devoted their lives to specialized activities and see in the New School the opportunity to explore wider horizons.

As it happens, almost all have secondary school certificates, and some have certificates to burn; no one asks to see them. The New School remains the country's only university with an unqualified commitment to continuing education, and surely will always honor that commitment, which has so far served more than 1.5 million men and women. The Adult Division will expand its reach as we explore the manifest implications of the cable, the cassette, and the computer.

Our mission also has been extended by a necessary concern for undergraduate education. There is no university better placed to reach out for the intelligent and the concerned young, and we would be derelict if we did not do so. Our undergraduate college is small and of excellent quality: that must not change. But now let us test the hypothesis that we should expand our present college to perhaps 1,000 very able students, drawn primarily from the New York metropolitan area. To that end I have appointed a distinguished commission of scholars and educators, chaired by Professor

Robert Heilbroner and drawn from within the New School and from other institutions. The commission will consider the feasibility, shape, and substance of a highly selective liberal arts college, closely tuned to the times and speaking to the needs of the intellectually gifted whenever they are ready to enter college. This will be no easy task, for it will require a substantial amount of curricular invention if the College is to have the academic integrity and vitality characteristic of the New School.

Any expansion of our involvement with undergraduate education calls for a deeper commitment to the Graduate Faculty. We have already embarked upon a course that will strengthen the Graduate Faculty by permanent and visiting appointments which reinforce our distinctive traditions. We shall reach out, as always, to those who ask truly new questions, who are not bound by artificial disciplinary lines, who perceive the appropriate links between research and action, and who represent the highest levels of international scholarship in the social sciences, philosophy, and history. All serious universities look to their graduate faculties for guidance and sustenance. Indeed, in view of the caliber of students we wish to attract to the undergraduate college, the boundary between graduate study and the later years of the undergraduate curriculum is not, and should not be, always clearly discernible.

That alone would be reason enough for the New School to devote increased attention to its Graduate Faculty. But there are intellectual and historical reasons as well. Our founders—Charles Beard, Thorstein Veblen, James Robinson—and the scholars of the University in Exile—Adolph Lowe, Hans Staudinger, Emil Lederer—conducted radical inquiries into social conditions. These inquiries challenged the status quo. They went to the roots and invoked our fundamental strength: the power of reason. The determination to pursue such examinations has never been more needed than now.

If our curiosity is formulated entirely in technical terms, it is likely to be satisfied sooner or later. But the technical solutions tend to create massive, unanticipated, and intractable problems which technologists do not address but which profoundly concern the social scientist and the humanist. No problem is solved if its solution generates graver problems of human conduct and understanding.

The New School was born in the social ferment whose roots lay in industrialism and urbanization. The Graduate Faculty was determined to define and animate alternatives to fascism and Stalinism in the turmoil leading to and from World War II. Final solutions to the problems of war and peace, poverty amid plenty, racism and repression within a democratic society have been elusive. Even the notion of progress seems exhausted and offers no comfort as the end of this century of hope approaches. As a consequence of that disillusionment, there is a worldwide questioning of the utility of the social sciences. Broken dreams, broken promises, and skepticism replace the robust hope that once powered social research. Some might argue that a Graduate Faculty devoted principally to the social sciences would feel this burden with special force.

Let me say now as clearly as I can that the New School rejects this counsel of despair. Our special tradition, our special approach to the social sciences and philosophy, give us rich potential for constructive service. The New School has been identified with no single ideology, but chiefly with a process of inquiry marked by a ruthless integrity.

So past searches and present disappointments carry no imperative for the vitality of the New School as it addresses the issues central to the political economy of postindustrial societies. There is a fresh intellectual agenda in the making here: new questions to be formulated, new orthodoxies to be challenged, new alternatives to be framed and explored. And, as we help refurbish the agenda for all concerned people everywhere, we must also reforge the bond between adult education and graduate training that has served this institution so well in the past.

All this flows, I believe, from a respect for the name bestowed upon us by our founders. But from that name one important element is missing. The name is long enough as it is, I suppose, which may explain the absence of any reference to the city of which it is so distinctly a part. It would challenge the most graceful stylist among us to find a name that contained the word "new" twice repeated and did not, at the same time, give some vague impression that something had gone wrong.

But the New School is, and has always been, a New York City institution. Its founders believed strongly in the link between thought and action, and much of the action for which they looked was action in behalf of the community in which the school made its home. From the very beginning, inspired largely by one of its founders, Herbert Croly, the New School offered professional education in a program of courses and fieldwork for those interested in urban planning and in the problems of unions and industrial relations.

That early start led in 1964 to what is now called the J. M. Kaplan Center for New York City Affairs, the first university institute devoted to the study and improvement of a single major metropolis. The Center matured rapidly to include graduate programs in policy analysis and ultimately a full-fledged Graduate School of Management and Urban Professions, with emphasis on the emerging professions indigenous to New York.

I need hardly say that the relationship between the city and the New School cuts both ways. A good deal of the character of the New School is drawn from the city itself, and especially from Greenwich Village.

Most universities in our country display an envy for Oxford and Cambridge, with their intimations of a life of quiet contemplation among green meadows and gray towers. To be sure, the image in America is often sadly shattered during these Saturday afternoons in autumn, but even when great cities spread out to swallow such universities up, the flavor of Oxbridge somehow clings.

The New School resembles far more nearly the great universities of the European continent, proudly and self-confidently sharing the hurly-burly of the capital cities; indeed, very much a part of that hurly-burly. There is contemplation in abundance to be found in those universities, but their studies look out on the turmoil of the city. The university spills out into the streets, and those streets and all that concerns them become a part of the university.

A good many years ago Oliver Wendell Holmes the younger wrote: "I think that as life is action and passion, it is required of a man that he should share the action and passion of his time, at peril of being judged never to have lived." A university set in a great city cannot hope to escape the action and passion of its time even if it should choose to do so. The New School is just such a university, seeking those students who will put it to the test. We dare not fail that multitude of talented, eager, and acute men and women, young and old, to be found within a few miles of our lecture halls and seminar rooms.

As we now receive this university, this New School, we recognize an expanded sense of time: undergraduate education in both Parsons and the College ... advanced training in the Graduate Faculty and the School of Management ... continuing education in the Adult Division. These embrace a lifetime of education for those citizens who are, at the same time, scholars. Yet they are components in a single enterprise. This is a unity which must be recognized and sustained so that the strengths of each element will buttress one another. None will lead, none will follow; all will rise as one. I can conceive of no definition of our task that is more engrossing, more demanding, and in the end more rewarding.

And as long as we remember, as our founders always remembered, that we are the New School, we are not likely to fail. Our life will be exciting, but it will not be easy. I, for one, do not expect it to be easy.

Having reflected a good deal about the meaning of the word "new," I should like to conclude by referring to a very old book. When, almost 400 years ago, the translators who produced the King James version of the Bible spoke about their own efforts, they had this to say in their message to the reader:

> Zeal to promote the common good, whether it be by devising anything ourselves, or revising that which hath been

laboured by others, deserveth certainly much respect and esteem, but yet findeth but cold entertainment in the world. It is welcomed with suspicion instead of love, and with emulation instead of thanks, and if there be any hole left for cavil to enter (and cavil, if it do not find an hole, will make one) it is sure to be misconstrued, and in danger to be condemned.... For was there ever anything projected, that savoured in any way of newness or renewing, but the same endured many a storm of gainsaying, or opposition?

They were wise men, and we will do well to heed their warning. With your help, I will serve the New School for Social Research as I believe you would wish it to be served: by pledging myself to newness and renewing.

# Foundation and Aims of the New School

# An Institution of Its Time

(SELECTED FROM ANNUAL REPORT, 1986)

The New School is very much an institution of its time, a university of the twentieth century. Founded in a period of extraordinary artistic, intellectual, and educational ferment worldwide, it has sought to mirror the cultural and social concerns of its times. It thus has changed and redefined itself in concert with the remarkable changes of this century. Yet, just as twentieth-century history has been punctuated by frequent returns to fundamental values and searches for institutional and conceptual anchors in the midst of change, so too the New School has continually returned to the questions of identity. We have a responsibility to measure how our daily activity corresponds to the university's deeper sense of mission and purpose.

This is not an easy task, in part because the New School is so eclectic and in part because we have thought of ourselves as a university for only a short time. The question of identity, of fundamental character and purpose, is too complex to be addressed adequately in a few paragraphs. Besides, in so diverse an institution the process of reflecting on our identity should engage the entire New School community.

So I would like to share my own thoughts on five characteristics which are at the heart of the New School. I also offer these ideas as a stimulus to a wider discussion in which I hope you will join.

*1.* The New School, by its very nature, is an innovator. We seek to identify unmet educational needs and underserved populations and to design educational programs to respond to those needs. These efforts sometimes result in new programs in existing fields, but often they represent forays into new fields and disciplines. The past year alone provides some examples: the B.F.A. program in jazz; the joint master's program with Palmer School of Library Science of Long Island University; the master's program in architecture and design criticism at Parsons and the Graduate Faculty; the proposed master's program in historical studies at the Graduate Faculty; several certificates in health services, gerontological services, and human resources at the Graduate School; the certificate in alcoholism counseling in the Adult Division; and a new Graduate School branch campus at Wilton Development Center.

2. Consonant with this commitment to innovation, the New School does not attempt to encompass all realms of knowledge. We choose the university's disciplinary foci carefully. In each field we enter, whether in art and design or social theory or aspects of the humanities, the New School and Parsons help shape those fields. Professor Charles Tilly offers the following assessment of the New School which, while addressed to the Graduate Faculty, represents the kind of identity each of our schools strives for:

> The New School for Social Research stands out from all other universities in its commitment to critical assessment of contemporary social life and institutions; its strong orientation to historical and comparative analysis; its effort to integrate North American and European social thought; its skepticism and catholicity with respect to methods of social inquiry; its awareness of the philosophical foundations of social research; and its zeal to direct the social sciences toward major political, moral and esthetic choices faced by today's citizens and power holders.

3. The New School combines both quality and openness. Gaining entrance to most of our programs is relatively easy, since we are used to working with older people and people of all ages who are not on traditional academic tracks. Often people who apply cannot produce a conventional record or set of test scores. Such a circumstance rarely presents a problem at the New School, since we are willing to give people a chance. At the same time, our courses—be they for credit or not—are serious and demanding. Degree requirements are high, and those who graduate are well trained in their professions or disciplines. The New School is committed to the

notion that learning is a lifelong process and that, through education, value can be added to all human beings at any stage in their lives. The "value added" test is the principal measure of our success.

4. The New School is passionately connected to the world in which it exists and committed to the belief that the application of knowledge, aesthetic judgment, and reason can produce a better, fairer, more humane, and more peaceful world. It is equally committed to freedom of expression and has no institutional view on how that better world should be achieved. Rather, its classrooms, studios, and lecture halls are open to all points of view, on the very faith that ongoing dialogue among differing views is the surest route to progress. A recent ad hoc faculty committee on freedom of expression, chaired by Ira Katznelson, has reaffirmed and elaborated the university's commitment to academic and intellectual freedom.

5. The New School draws strength from and seeks to contribute to New York City. It is, as Mayor Edward Koch once said, the "quintessential New York institution." That is true in the continuing education opportunities we offer to adult New Yorkers through the original New School and Parsons School of Design, the midcareer training programs offered by the Graduate School of Management, the effort by Eugene Lang College to bring a small, high-quality liberal arts program to students primarily in the metropolitan area, the higher-education opportunity program of Parsons, and the Master of Arts in Liberal Studies at the Graduate Faculty designed for part-time adult New Yorkers. Through graduate research projects, undergraduate internships, or special training programs, the university faculty and students are deeply connected to the life of the city.

These five characteristics are meant to be descriptive of what the New School is and what, in some sense, it has always been. But I also suggest them as a set of standards for judging the university's well-being and its adherence to its responsibility and mission. We are performing well if, in pursuing our daily activities of building faculty, academic programs, a financial base, and buildings, it can be said that we are:

- Innovating and meeting unmet educational needs
- Helping to define the boundaries of the fields in which we teach and do research
- Expanding educational opportunity and "adding value" to the 40,000 students who study here every year
- Deepening our connections to the world outside our academic walls and protecting complete freedom of inquiry and expression within
- Making a contribution to New York City

These five criteria may not correspond to each individual's conception of the New School. An institution as protean as this one will naturally call out many understandings of function and purpose. Those wanting a single, precise, and neat definition will find the New School forever frustrating. But those many more who find exhilaration in ambiguity will continue to be attracted to this university. I would welcome discussion of these characteristics and the many others which might be cited. I am certain of one thing, however. While we may agree on a set of principles, the concrete manifestations of those principles will change over time. Our very name, a name which I think carries great power, makes this almost obligatory.

The New School is hard to place in the hierarchy of American higher education. That we would dare to be both democratic in our admissions and demanding in our standards puzzles those who seek to rank the New School. We should delight in this inability to be categorized. For the public perception to be that the New School is first-rate and an interesting intellectual and artistic center should, I think, be enough.

# THE TRANSFORMING ENERGY OF MODERNISM

(SELECTED FROM COMMENCEMENT, MAY 1987)

The New School for Social Research, most people agree, is a funny name for a university with such a heavy emphasis on the arts and humanities. The name has been the subject of debate from the very beginning as the founders considered what to call their new enterprise. Alvin Johnson had proposed Adam Smith University, or David Hume, or James Madison, or Thomas Jefferson, but his ideas were vetoed by Charles Beard, Wesley Clair Mitchell, James Harvey Robinson, and the others. That debate revealed differences among our founders about the purpose of the New School. Some saw it primarily as a research institute. It would address political, social, and economic issues arising out of the industrial and urban growth of America. Others like Alvin Johnson had the notion of an advanced school of adult education on the model of what Albert Mansbridge had created in England.

The New School began in 1919 with this question unresolved, and within 4 years the effort to meet both objectives proved financially unsound. In 1923, the New School faced the first of many financial crises that would threaten its existence. Alvin Johnson became director that year and was soon approached by a group of students led by Clara Mayer, later Dean of the New School. They offered financial help and ideas for a curriculum with broader public appeal. By the next fall Johnson and Mayer had expanded the New School's curriculum beyond its original social science and policy focus by adding courses in psychology, philosophy, literature, art, and architecture. Henceforth, the New School pledged to offer "whatever seriously interested persons of mature intelligence" wanted to study. "Most of the work of the New School," the 1927 catalogue reported, "is cultural.... The students...come to the New School primarily to satisfy purely intellectual needs." Clearly, Johnson's vision of "an institution for the continued education of the educated," as he put it, had taken hold.

Most of the original faculty had by then returned to conventional research universities. In their place came an extraordinary array of artists and intellectuals offering lectures on myriad cultural themes. Listen to some of the names: Roscoe Pound and Felix Frankfurter on jurisprudence, poet Robert Frost, art historian Meyer Schapiro, painter Thomas Hart Benton, writer Thomas Mann, Lewis Mumford on architecture and planning, composers Aaron Copland and Virgil Thomson, dancers Doris Humphrey and Martha Graham, philosophers Bertrand Russell and Sidney Hook, anthropologists Franz Boas and Margaret Mead, psychiatrist Erich Fromm, photographer Berenice Abbott, painter Stuart Davis, and muralist José Orozco.

What a fantastic epoch in the life of this institution, of any institution! Those who taught here in the 1920s and 1930s saw themselves in the vanguard of a new, more rational, and egalitarian society. In a word, the New School embodied the transforming energy of modernism. Johnson and Mayer saw a unity in their increasingly eclectic curriculum. The original focus of the New School, the study of urban, industrial America, found expression in art, architecture, and literature. Social research, broadly conceived, included both music composition and wage and price studies. Modern art, music, dance, and architecture helped the general public understand the complexities of contemporary reality.

New School philosopher Horace Kallen perhaps best made the link between the aspirations of the New School's founders and the artistic explosion that occurred at the New School and in the larger society between the wars. In his book *Art and Freedom*, he argued that without art human freedom and dignity could not exist: "Art ... conforms nature to man and advances a frontier of freedom against the compulsions of the cosmos." The themes that animated the original New School shaped the degree programs that have been added over the years, perhaps best symbolized by the joint programs between the Graduate Faculty and Parsons today.

John Dewey, one of the New School's founders, wrote, "It is a commonplace to say that education should not cease when one leaves school. The point of this commonplace is that the purpose of school education is to insure the continuance of education by organizing the powers that insure growth." I hope that each of you, in the process of earning your degree here, has organized the powers that ensure growth. Like Dewey, I speak of the kind of growth which will lead you to seek knowledge that is now unfamiliar to you; a growth which signifies an ever-broadening appreciation of culture and of human diversity. To be well educated and to continue to be well educated, you must cultivate the habit of being versatile.

That versatility will be more than just an opportunity for personal enrichment. It also will help fulfill another, perhaps greater, objective of the New School: the strengthening of our democratic society. Our founders saw an informed citizenry, but even more a thoughtful citizenry, as the best protection of freedom. It still is. So, as you leave us today, I offer not a farewell, but rather the encouragement to come back soon. And, until we see you again, I wish you all the best.

# IDEAS MATTER

(COMMENCEMENT, MAY 1985)

If there is one common thread in the diverse fabric of the New School, it is a respect for theory, a belief that ideas matter. From the seminar in the College, to the laboratory at the Graduate School of Management and Urban Professions, to the lecture course in the Adult Division, to the conceptual focus of the Media Studies programs, to the pro-seminar at the Graduate Faculty, the common thread has been the search for understanding—understanding which makes sense of the disparate facts and events of our history and experience. Abstract, elusive, sometimes frustrating, theory is the essential tool in building that understanding.

Theory has played a more important role in your education than it has for students at most other universities. John Maynard Keynes, writing some years ago, commented on the importance of theory:

> The ideas of economists and political philosophers, both when they are right and when they are wrong, are more powerful than is commonly understood. Indeed, the world is ruled by little else. Practical men, who believe themselves to be quite exempt from intellectual influences, are usually the slaves of some defunct economist. Mad men in authority, who hear voices in the air, are distilling their frenzy from some academic scribbles of a few years back.

If there is any doubt of the wisdom of Keynes' remark, one need look no further than his own work to see the power of theoretical influence. Economic history in the past 50 years is dominated by Keynes' "academic scribblings." Or consider other towering theoretical minds of the twentieth century and how the practical work of government, high technology, mental health, education, and child rearing have been transformed by their efforts. I am thinking of Marx, Einstein, Freud, Dewey, and Piaget; there are many more.

At times, it seems the power of theory is not quite what it once was. We live in an era and in a country which is obsessed with everyday, practical concerns. We believe as an article of faith that every problem has an immediate solution even though a mountain of false starts and failures, both at home and abroad, argues to the contrary. Our society places less value than we used to on basic research, provides less money for it, and gives less support to the universities which have nurtured fundamental inquiry and social theory. To some extent, ironically, universities have helped create this situation. As they have pursued federal dollars and corporate largesse, they have let themselves be lured toward the world of applied research and overpromised practical solutions and away from the theoretical inventions which are fundamental to the progress of the human race.

Your university has never wavered from its commitment to teaching, training, and research that emphasizes theoretical, philosophical, and historical dimensions. The very name "New School" suggests an openness to change, an optimism that new social arrangements could be better than old orthodoxies and that new approaches emerge only from minds encouraged to think broadly and freely. Einstein said it best: "The formulation of a problem is often more essential than its solution.... To raise new questions, new problems, to regard old problems from a new angle, requires creative imagination and marks real advance in science." Those words could well be this university's credo. At the New School we frame the questions that others seek to answer, we fashion the theories that others embrace and confront, and we have a passionate belief that ideas matter. Over the years, this community has never sacrificed the chance for an enduring insight in exchange for the fleeting satisfaction of momentary influence.

Let me make explicit one other point implicit in what I have already said. Theory is not just for the geniuses who put their marks on entire historical epochs. Theoretical thinking is for *all* of us. Reflect on those seminars, laboratories, lectures, and pro-seminars, on what you read, what you heard, what you said. Try to distill the capacity for critical thinking that you achieved in those settings. Those moments need not and should not be seen as a drug-induced high point of insight never again to be reached without external stimulation. Rather, they represent a finely honed new skill for use in the diverse settings you are about to enter. And, like all skills, the capacity to think analytically and to search for the theoretical underpinnings beneath the surface of situations needs exercise to keep its edge.

"There are not many," Keynes concluded, "who are influenced by new theories after they are twenty-five or thirty years of age, so the ideas that civil servants and politicians, and even agitators apply to current events are not likely to be the newest." I assume some who graduate today are or will be civil servants, politicians, and agitators. But your presence here, especially those of you over 30, proves Keynes wrong. You must never be satisfied with mindless applications of old ideas and theories. That is not what you learned here. Rather, you will be among those who constantly search for fresh approaches, who believe there are new theories to explain social, economic, and political phenomena and to reconcile conflict, and some of you will invent them.

# Connecting Public and Intellectual Discourse

(COMMENCEMENT, MAY 1986)

Each year, as this commencement ceremony approaches, I find myself somewhat bemused by the words "social research" in our name. We persist with our original identification even though I am about to confer degrees in a wide variety of fields—the liberal arts, social sciences, management, media, art and design.

Now, perhaps it has not occurred to you, as you have been earning these degrees, to ask, "What am I doing at a university dedicated to social research?" Or perhaps for some of you it is clear, and for others of no concern. But I find myself thinking about the term "social research." It seems to address two realms—society and the academy, or the public and the intellectual—and it suggests that these realms are closely intertwined. Yet the more common perception these days is that public discourse and intellectual discourse are very different and quite separate.

That perception is certainly not new. Aristotle, in the *Politics*, asked a question which posed a similar distinction. "Which life," he wondered, "is more desirable, the life of participation in the work of the state ... or one like a foreigner's, cut off from the association of the state ... that is, the contemplative life?" Over the centuries, a line has often been drawn between these two pursuits.

The founders of the United States rejected Aristotle's choice, and none of them represented the unity of Aristotle's two lives more so than did Thomas Jefferson; rarely in history have the political and intellectual communicated so intimately, and with such power, as they did within that one mind. Jefferson was both scholar and leader. But he revealed his own sense of what is most important in the epitaph he chose for his tombstone. It describes him as "author of the

Declaration of American Independence, of the statute of Virginia for religious freedom, and father of the University of Virginia." He overlooked being President of the United States. The exercise of authority was not what counted for him. What mattered was, on the one hand, shaping public affairs to respect and preserve fundamental human rights and, on the other, enriching the life of the mind. These were inseparable.

To some extent, I suppose, you who graduate today possess the two casts of mind which Jefferson employed so abundantly and to our lasting benefit. But more generally in our society, we allow those two ways of thinking to be represented by different groups of people. And we constantly ask ourselves how to bring public and intellectual discourse together as naturally as they were fused in Jefferson. He and his generation of founders set a standard for how we would have our society work, even though the history of the United States displays a drift away from that ideal.

Those who established the New School, in the early years of this century, set out to correct that drift. It was no accident that our first president, Alvin Johnson, took Thomas Jefferson as his model and even considered naming this new institution in Jefferson's honor. Johnson and his colleagues were deeply aware of the growing separation between public and intellectual life, and they, like Jefferson's generation, refused to make Aristotle's choice. Their notion of social research affirmed that this separation could be bridged, that the society and the academy, for the sake of civilization's future, must come together.

This did not mean—nor does it mean today—that universities as institutions should take official views on public issues, become active politically, or even be direct agents of social change. Quite the contrary. The burden and the pleasure of public discourse must rest with the people within the institution—the faculty and students. That discourse is heightened and strengthened to the extent that all points of view can find free expression on a university campus. Before intellectual life can influence public discourse, there must be engagement, not a priori rejection, of unpopular views. This test is not being met at a time when leaders of our own—or any government—are not invited or, if invited, not permitted to speak freely at our universities. I hope and believe this community shares our founders' commitment to hearing all points of view.

But the quality of public discourse has a more subtle, more elusive, more fundamental dimension for those of us within universities. We need to ask whether scholars and intellectuals are helping pose the questions which in turn shape and illuminate the public agenda. The sociologist Robert Bellah offers a despairing assessment. He recently said, "The university is no longer the place for the training of leadership and public service in a free society. The university as it is organized at present isn't set up to engage in the public dialogue that would provide moral leadership or even encourage it." In this view, it seems, Aristotle's division between the public and contemplative life has reached an extreme in universities. Alas, I too fear that much of academic life today is so absorbed in ever narrowing questions that the connection between intellectual and public discourse is almost impossible—and would be so even if the times were more sympathetic. I hope and believe we at the New School are an exception.

Let me cite an example of what I mean. Many believe that a problem exists in this country about how Presidents are chosen, how political parties work. There is a veritable industry studying the technical structure of party systems, the impact of the media on politics, the interaction of economic and sectional issues with party alignments, and much more. All good questions, worthy of pursuit. But does any one of them alone or in aggregate hold the key to what ails, for example, the Democratic Party? Or is a more telling insight to be found at a second level of questions, which frame and address the issues that Jefferson joined, such as the conflict between the basic values of freedom and equality?

Though the present reality is far from the promise of full equality, how do we achieve that equality while still respecting individual freedom? I would like to think the social research practiced here—and not only by social scientists—

illuminates the theoretical and philosophical foundations of issues in ways which make them accessible to public discourse, public leaders, and indeed the public itself. That has been our chosen responsibility since the beginning, and what matters most to us here today is whether the university has fulfilled this responsibility for you, our graduates. This is really why the words "social research" attract my attention. I think the founders put them in our name to remind their successors that one of the fundamental purposes of this institution is to support and sustain the public dialogue, to bring intellectual perspectives and insights to it, and, in so doing, to encourage morally reasoned leadership.

If we are meeting this responsibility, then those of you leaving the University's degree programs will venture upon new pursuits, or return to old ones, with a broader vision. Of course, you are more knowledgeable. You have new and more finely honed skills, and your abilities to analyze, to be critical, and to understand have grown. But you are also, I suspect, more sensitive to the complexities of the world we live in, more attuned to public issues and to the public interest, more aware of the contributions that intellectual inquiry can make to the public debate, and more ready to use those contributions or make them yourselves.

The public and intellectual realms will probably always remain somewhat separate. If so, the vital and necessary bridge between them will be individuals who, like Thomas Jefferson and Alvin Johnson, can blend the public and intellectual in their own thought processes. In these last years, at a university devoted to "social research" in its best sense, you have been doing just that. I hope it has become a habit. Moreover, I hope that, in the spirit of this university, you will see it as a stimulating and provocative personal responsibility.

# THE NEW SCHOOL: THE QUINTESSENTIAL NEW YORK CITY INSTITUTION

(ANNUAL REPORT, 1988)

The American system of higher education is a unique blend of public and private institutions. No other country has so many private institutions with so diverse a set of missions. But this system is at some risk. In the past decade numerous private institutions have closed or been merged, and there are pressures drawing colleges and universities toward conformity. Although private institutions have the freedom to be different, that freedom is infrequently exercised these days. The more institutions look alike, the harder it will be for them to survive and prosper and the less vigorous will be this nation's system of higher education.

Against this background, we have sought to preserve— even sharpen—the distinctive qualities of the New School for Social Research. For some, the New School is a quintessential New York institution, while for others its roots are distinctly European. Both are right. The New School is at once focused on New York and intensely international in its outlook. In this way it is like the city itself, concerned with local matters but also recognized as a leading international center. This essay will explore the New School's deepening commitment to New York City and to New Yorkers.

The New School was formed, as its first announcement stated, to allow "intelligent men and women" to address themselves to "the grave social, political, economic, and educational problems of the day." The process of education was intended not only to inform and expand the minds of individuals, but also to help ameliorate the difficulties that society faced. By focusing on an adult population, our founders meant to drive academic inquiry and instruction beyond the comfortable and self-satisfied confines of campus walls and into the daily life and debate of the general public.

The sources of this socially responsible approach to higher education were numerous and varied. One of them, most certainly, was the milieu in which the idea of the New School was conceived. One wonders if the New School could have grown up in any American city other than New York.

Only here—in our nation's most eclectic and worldly urban center—could an institution like the New School take hold and thrive. Throughout the history of this university, the city has raised our sights beyond the self-limiting bounds of the parochial, and toward a more inclusive way of seeing, knowing, and acting. The effort that would epitomize the New School as a socially responsible, outward-looking institution—the establishment of the University in Exile—would not have been possible without New York's atmosphere of intellectual freedom and ferment, and its welcome embrace of immigrants from around the globe.

The New School experience, in its own way, has always testified to the possibilities and responsibilities of life in an urban environment and the special joys and challenges of a great metropolis. The city has nourished the New School intellectually, and in turn the New School has always acknowledged an obligation to devote its educational energy to the needs of the city. While maintaining a cosmopolitan world view, the New School has never forgotten its origins in the urban landscape.

The New School's concern for the city found expression in its earliest years. In 1923, Lewis Mumford gave a series of lectures that all but created urban affairs as a topic for scholarly study. There quickly followed a series of courses examining every aspect of urban life, such as Alexander Goldenwieser's Racial Groups in Greater New York, Paul Blanshard's The Politics and Government of New York City, and Frieda Wunderlich and Julie Meyer's The Union Situation in New York City. In 1939 at the New School, Charles Abrams established the first program for the study of urban housing in the United States. Twenty-five years later, these ongoing concerns coalesced into a full-scale research and teaching program when Robert MacIver launched the Center for New York City Affairs, the first such center devoted to the study of a single city.

Under the leadership of Henry Cohen, the Center—subsequently named for a New School trustee, the late Jacob M. Kaplan—quickly came to embody the ideals of service, responsibility, and practical solutions to social problems envisioned by the New School's founders. Its research division, headed by Blanche Bernstein, became a leader in the study of demography, welfare, and urban poverty. In 1965, the Center began the Metropolitan Information Service, a catalog of city affairs that was the forerunner of the *City Almanac*, the quarterly journal of urban issues. Three years later, responding to the report of the Kerner Commission on Civil Disorder, the center established the path-breaking Urban Reporting Project in conjunction with the New York Urban Coalition. The project provided workshops and training for black and Hispanic journalists and, from 1969 to 1971, operated the influential Community News Service, which spotlighted events in the minority community for the city's major media.

In the early 1970s, the Kaplan Center spawned the Graduate School of Management and Urban Professions, dedicated to training professionals for service in the public, private, and nonprofit sectors. The Graduate School soon created a Master of Arts program in Urban Policy Analysis to educate policy analysts and managers for city government and other settings. The Graduate School's service to the city continued in the years that followed, most notably with the introduction of the highly respected *Fiscal Observer.*

While the Graduate School is our most tangible link to New York, the New School's other academic divisions are also deeply connected to the city. Let me offer some illustrations and suggest a few ideas for enhancing our service to the city.

Like the New School, Parsons School of Design draws its energy from New York and is intertwined with both its cultural and commercial life. Of the nearly 600 graduates that Parsons produces every year, 75 percent choose to remain in the city to pursue their careers. Parsons alumni play leading roles in a host of New York's most important industries—notably fashion, and retailing, advertising, graphic design, architecture, interior design, and illustration. Like the Graduate School of Management and Urban Professions, Parsons has a long history of service to the city. Over the years, Parsons students and faculty members have designed banners to decorate the street lights on 42nd Street, produced a design impact study of low-income housing, designed model cells for the Department of Corrections on Rikers Island, and, during August Heckscher's tenure as City Parks Commissioner, produced a design study of the Central Park Zoo.

The Graduate Faculty, though always international in focus, has strong links to the city and urban life. Building on the early New School's contributions to urban studies, Graduate Faculty scholars have pioneered in the formulation of historical stages of urban development and in community studies. A new research center on lower Manhattan is now in the planning stages. With the Graduate School of Management, Rutgers University, and the Graduate Center of the City University of New York, the Graduate Faculty sponsors an influential, metropolitan-wide workshop on urban affairs. And Dean Ira Katznelson, whose own scholarship has focused on questions of race, class, and inequality in New York and other urban centers, currently chairs the Social Science Research Council's Committee on New York City.

No part of this university has touched the lives of more New Yorkers than the original New School Adult Division. We estimate that nearly 1.5 million people have studied at the New School, a number that grows by 25,000 annually. Historically, the New School's continuing education students have been overwhelmingly white and middle class. That remains true today. But the city's demographic profile has changed dramatically, and the New School should reach out to new populations. The expansion of an English as a Second Language (ESL) program is one promising example. The arrangement with District Council 37, through which its members can complete a baccalaureate at the New School, is another. Still, we must do more to meet the educational needs of New York's minority population.

The New School has traditionally served people clustered between ages 25 and 55, yet we know the population is aging. With the single exception of the Institute for Retired Professionals, the New School has little programming designed for senior citizens. The expansion of our offerings for older people is an important goal for the period ahead.

As we seek to serve new populations, we should experiment with off-campus programs elsewhere in the city of New York. We draw few students from upper Manhattan, the Bronx, Queens, or outer Brooklyn.

Another opportunity for service arises from our initiatives to help improve the public school system. In the New School's Adult Division, there are already several examples. Under the auspices of the Chancellor's New School Fellowship Program, the university annually awards free noncredit courses to approximately fifty outstanding public school students and teachers. In addition, by virtue of an agreement with the United Federation of Teachers, all teachers are eligible for a one-third tuition reduction for one noncredit course per semester at the New School.

Between now and the end of the century, a large percentage of New York City teachers will retire. As a result, New York will face a shortage of properly trained teachers. The New School is exploring the possibility of devising fresh ways of training teachers for our schools.

In our most ambitious program, still in the planning stages, we propose to affiliate with six high schools in our neighborhood. Our students would tutor in those schools, while the most gifted high school students could take college-level courses at the university. Teachers from those schools could enroll in adult or graduate-level courses to update their knowledge in their discipline or learn new skills such as computing. Administrators could study at the Graduate School of Management. Parents who wished to complete an undergraduate degree could do so on a significant scholarship in the

New School's baccalaureate program for adults. Our decision to concentrate on six schools reflects our judgment that an effective school improvement effort must involve teachers, administrators, students, and their parents.

Eugene Lang College is ideally suited to take the lead in these arrangements. It is the only small, private, high-quality liberal arts college specifically designed for students graduating from New York City public high schools. Moreover, its curriculum is intended not only to enable Lang students to learn about the city, but also to help them learn from it through field courses, urban research projects, internships, and community service programs. The College offers instruction at a modest price, has scholarship funds designated for graduates of New York City public high schools, and especially welcomes students who are the first generation of their families to attend college.

These are but the latest possibilities in a mission that stretches back to the founding of the university and has guided it through its evolution. The New School for Social Research has developed and changed along with the city. It has derived much of its energy and intellectual and artistic strength from the city. Inevitably, the New School and New York have become intimately identified with each other. The sense of social responsibility that has guided the New School is also very much in harmony with this urban center, which has been a laboratory for great social challenges.

As New York City undergoes the rapid change that has always contributed to its vitality, the New School must respond to this change by expanding its own sights while opening its imagination to new needs and its doors to new students. As we celebrate the twenty-fifth anniversary of the Kaplan Center, I call on the faculty and students of the New School to seek new avenues for service to this city. I look forward to joining with city officials and citizens in a renewed effort to make New York a better and more humane place.

# Responding to the Interdependence of the Modern World

(SELECTED FROM ANNUAL REPORT, NOVEMBER 1989)

It is commonplace to observe that the world is becoming smaller and smaller under the influence of rapid transportation, instant communication, and intertwined economies. The students we now educate will live and work in a world that will place a premium on an ability to speak several languages, a familiarity with diverse cultures, and an understanding of the current political economies of many peoples and states.

We think the New School prepares its students well for the interdependent nature of modern civilization. Our very location in America's most international city is a magnet for students and faculty who grasp the future. Our founders, too, were alive to this potential. Charles Beard, Thorstein Veblen, James Harvey Robinson, John Dewey, Herbert Croly, Alvin Johnson, and others met in the offices of the *New Republic* in 1918 to plan their new school. From those conversations came a paper entitled "A Proposal for an Independent School of Social Sciences for Men and Women." The paper consciously placed the proposed new school in a European tradition as it envisioned an institution that could become "as powerful in modern life as some of the great universities were in the middle ages."

Almost from the beginning, the New School offered the general public access to scholars from abroad. New School President Alvin Johnson's work with the *Encyclopedia of the Social Sciences* gave him broad exposure to the best scholars in the social sciences, philosophy, and history throughout Europe. In the 1920s, historian Gaetano Salvemini, Freud student Fritz Wittels, editor of the *New Leader* Henry Bailsford, political theorist Harold Laski, philosopher Bertrand Russell, and economist John Maynard Keynes, among others, lectured at the New School.

The international outlook of those early years was indelibly imprinted on the identity of the New School with the founding of the University in Exile in 1933. Alvin Johnson took the lead in organizing a rescue mission that saved 170 scholars and their families from the perils of the totalitarian regimes of Hitler and Mussolini. While most were placed at leading universities throughout the United States, a number remained here to found the Graduate Faculty of Political and Social Science. The special quality of mind brought to the New School by the refugee generation gave our social science teaching and research a character distinct from the dominant American approach to those disciplines.

The Graduate Faculty came to represent a continental outlook in the social sciences, emphasizing a philosophical, historical and comparative point of view. As a consequence, our faculty may well be better known in Europe and the developing world than in the United States. That familiarity is invigorated by extensive ongoing contacts with the European academic community through a number of faculty exchanges—for instance, the Heuss Professorship established by the Federal Republic of Germany, which each year brings a distinguished German scholar to the New School; the University in Exile Professorship funded by the Berlin Senate; the visiting faculty program made possible by the Volkswagen Foundation; and scholars brought from East Central Europe by the Open Society Fund and by fellowships provided by members of our Board of Trustees.

The international dimension of the Graduate Faculty is not limited to the infusion of perspectives brought by academicians from abroad. The legacy of the University in Exile is apparent in the international and interdisciplinary nature of recent faculty scholarship as well. While it is impossible to list all the research questions being explored, a few examples are illustrative:

- Class and state formation in Europe
- Language, ethnicity, and immigration across Europe, North America, and Africa
- The impact of the changing international situation on contemporary social and economic policy in the Western democracies
- The relationship of culture, politics, and democratic institutions in Eastern Europe and the Western democracies
- Technological unemployment in Europe and the United States
- Structural change and contention in Britain and France
- The American interventionist state
- The role of Islam in the emergence of a new world economic order from the fourteenth to sixteenth centuries
- Rural and urban change and social transformation in Latin America

While we might expect to find international topics being studied at most research universities, it should be remembered that at the Graduate Faculty such work occurs within a relatively small—only seventy scholars—and well-integrated collegium. The shared orientation to international themes across disciplines gives the Graduate Faculty a dominant international character. At a time when American social science tends to be focusing on indigenous American subjects and problems, the Graduate Faculty's approach continues to be distinctive, counter to popular trends, and deeply responsive to global challenges and needs.

While the university's internationalism is readily apparent in our programs in the social sciences and philosophy, it is no less significant in our extensive programs in the arts. As a form of communication and expression, the arts inherently transcend national boundaries. In this spirit, Parsons School of Design has made an aggressive effort to offer its students an education in the arts that reaches beyond our own traditions.

The Mannes College of Music shares Parsons' international outlook and is extremely cosmopolitan in its faculty and student body. Members of its faculty have been trained and have performed in all the major capitals of the world. Almost half of the student body comes from countries other than the United States. Mannes alumni also regularly give performances in concert halls on every continent. From the standpoint of musical scholarship, Mannes presents an historical analog to the Graduate Faculty and the University in Exile. In the 1930s, David Mannes brought to the United States two renowned musicologists, Felix Salzer and Hans Weisse, both proponents of the revolutionary musical theory of the Austrian scholar Heinrich Schenker. That European approach to musical analysis was thus transplanted to the United States, where, at Mannes, it became a salient force in musical theory in both this country and Europe.

The original New School, with its strong international emphasis, continues to fulfill our founders' vision. Last year, the Adult Division enrolled 3,400 people in foreign language studies and another 1,300 in sixty-six courses about the literature, history, art, politics, and cultures of other countries. These courses ranged from explorations of profound and timeless themes to exposure to aspects of everyday life in other milieus, such as culinary practices and manners.

In recent years scholarly conferences and lectures at the university spanned the world. Among the highlights were In Time of Plague—The History and Social Consequences of Lethal Epidemic Disease; Escape from Violence: Social Conflict and Refugees in the Contemporary Third World; First World Charity?: "Live Aid" and the Famine in Africa; Adam Michnik and Human Rights; Gorbachev: Changes in the U.S.S.R—Changes in Eastern Europe?; Palestinian Refugees Conflict Management in Divided Cities; State Power and Class Power in Developing States; and The Education of the Artist in the United States and the U.S.S.R.

As you might expect, the New School is a congenial place for foreign students. At last count, 800 students from eighty-six other countries were taking courses for credit at the New School—14 percent of our degree students. Our faculty is also a diverse group, representing as it does scholars from Western and Eastern Europe, Asia, Africa, and Latin America, as well as Americans who received their training abroad. Many universities have exchange programs and international relations departments, but few are enriched by such a cosmopolitan collection of faculty and students.

It is fair to ask whether enough of our students take full advantage of the opportunities available at the New School to broaden their perspectives. What does it mean to be properly educated in matters international? At the New School, believing as we do that education does not stop with the acquisition of a formal credential, our answer involves study over a lifetime.

The purposes of knowing more about the world seem to me to be threefold. First, it is an *obligation of citizenship* in a democratic society that we be well informed and thus able to make sensible choices in public policy and public leaders. We have learned a painful lesson in the second half of this century about the dangers of leaving foreign policy decisions to a core of elite experts. Congress has insisted on a full partnership with the executive branch in foreign affairs, and thus the responsibility of ordinary citizens is increased. A second purpose involves *individual growth*, satisfaction, and pleasure. Much of the world's cultural riches lie outside our borders, even beyond the English-speaking areas of the world. A well-educated person will derive deeper insight and understanding of human nature and experience through travel abroad informed by a study of the history and culture of other countries. Finally, a person sensitive to the wider world is bound to have more *professional opportunities* in an era in which almost everything is internationalized.

While the university is already well equipped to help students of all ages deepen their knowledge of the world, we will be expanding our commitment to providing such educational opportunities. Let me mention five ways.

*1.* The new Rose and Irwin Wolfson Center for National Affairs has increased the university's offerings in domestic public policy for adults. We should now focus our attention on a parallel effort in international affairs. We need to quicken our capacity to respond to important developments as they occur. The New School should be recognized as *the* place for adult New Yorkers to turn in order to understand the wider world. Among the issues our curriculum should address are recent developments in China, the Soviet Union, and East Central Europe; the obligations of the developed world to redress global inequity; America's military role in the world; the future of the Strategic Defense Initiative; the implications of an economy for trade policy and for domestic labor arrangements; immigration and refugee policy; global environmental questions; international debt and the future of democracy in Latin America; how foreign policy is made and implemented in the United States; and the status of human rights around the world. These, of course, are illustrations drawn from a rich menu of possible courses and lectures, some of which are already available at the New School.

2. Travel and study abroad programs are fruitful ways to deepen our understanding of different parts of the world. Parsons already operates summer programs in seven countries, and I would like to see others added—for example, in China, the Soviet Union, Latin America, and northern Europe. Most of our schools make study abroad possible; in fact, last year 1,100 students were involved in such programs. Still, I would like to see virtually all our undergraduate students enrolled in some formal study abroad during their time at the university. This will require a significant expansion of our programs around the world. I also hope that a resumption of travel and study programs for adults will be part of that expansion.

Conversely, the presence of international students greatly enriches the educational environment of the university. I would like to increase the number of such students and, more important, be sure that students from less developed parts of the world have access to the New School. Only 30 percent of our present group of international students come from such countries. The university needs to increase scholarship funds available to international students who are not eligible for federal or state loan and grant monies. I ask that the capital campaign for each of our schools contains gift opportunities for endowed scholarships for international students.

3. Since the fiftieth anniversary commemoration of the University in Exile in 1984, we have intensified our concern for intellectual freedom and human rights in East Central Europe. Those efforts have been directed to Poland, Hungary, Czechoslovakia and now will expand to the Soviet Union. Last year, for example, we had visiting faculty members from Poland, Hungary, and Czechoslovakia, and now will expand to the Soviet Union. Also, under the guidance of Professor Jeffrey Goldfarb, we have sponsored a Joint Seminar on Democracy and Democratization in New York, Warsaw, and Budapest, with common reading lists and an exchange of scholarly papers. Prague will soon be added to this undertaking. Our journal *Social Research* has published a special issue dedicated to bringing the work of younger scholars in the region to the West and will soon offer another special edition of young scholars in the Soviet Union.

We want to broaden all these exchange programs, send more visiting lecturers to the region, increase the flow of Western journals and books, and open new initiatives in the Soviet Union and the more difficult-to-enter countries such as Bulgaria and Romania.

A significant expansion of these activities will give new life and a modern definition to the tradition of the University in Exile as the New School should again take the lead in helping intellectuals who are enduring repression.

4. For historical reasons, the university's international programs have had a European face, and our comparative advantage will continue to rest there. But in a more complicated world an emphasis on Europe, unbalanced by greater attention to Asia, Africa, Latin America, and the Middle East, will yield a distorted perspective for our students. Parsons has already pioneered programs in these other regions. Next, we need to enhance our research strength in at least one other part of the world, most likely Latin America, given the interests of existing members of the Graduate Faculty. In addition, the curriculum in all our schools should be reviewed and sup-

plemented to strengthen our attention to continents other than Europe.

5. Finally, the New School needs to be more responsive to the changing international nature of our own hometown. As new immigrant populations arrive in the city and merge into its economic, social, and cultural life, we have an obligation to identify and address ourselves to the educational needs they present. Being a "quintessential New York institution" will in the coming years mean being more eclectic than ever, more skeptical of settled assumptions about learning, and more deeply and fundamentally international.

All these ideas resonate with traditions of the New School that reach back to its founding and to the creation of the University in Exile. The rapid rate of change in the world around us—think of the Soviet Union, East Central Europe, China—places a premium on a capacity to understand the politics and cultures of other societies. This is so whether to enhance one's professional life or simply to discharge responsibly the obligations of citizenship in a democracy. The university that equips all its students, regardless of their field, to see perceptively beyond a country's borders is bound to be stronger than one that continues to consign matters international to the ghetto of area studies. The New School for Social Research seeks to infuse its international perspective across every facet of its curriculum. Only then can we say that we have educated our students—undergraduate, graduate, and adult—as broadly as possible.

# Undergraduate Education at the New School

(SELECTED FROM ANNUAL REPORT, 1987)

The New School first opened its doors to undergraduates in 1944. At that time, its purpose was to educate veterans returning from World War II and adult women who had been denied the opportunity of a college education. Over the years some 4,000 older students have attended and 1,250 have graduated from the New School's B.A. program. Its alumni include sculptor Leonard Baskin, American historian Gerda Lerner, publisher Gilbert Kaplan, and actor Peter Falk. This distinctive program—taught primarily in the evenings and open to students who have already had a year of college—has attracted many talented people who found conventional colleges unappealing or who were barred from attending them by their circumstances. The flexible curriculum, the adult environment, the energy and ferment of Greenwich Village—all these things have combined to make the New School an ideal place for mature and independent-minded students. In the 1980s, the B.A. program continues to attract highly motivated students and is growing. We are placing a major emphasis on older students returning to earn a degree and expect this program to grow from its present size of 220 to 750 students by the mid-1990s.

The university ventured ambitiously into the education of conventional-age undergraduates in 1970 when it absorbed Parsons School of Design.

One of Parsons' distinguishing features is its international character. Since the curriculum, methodology, and standards are similar at each of its locations, students can move easily within the Parsons system to experience the cultural and artistic perspectives of three major centers of art and design. Additional programs in Japan, France, West Africa, Israel, and other locations further enlarge the range of possibilities.

In preparing students for careers in art and design, Parsons seeks to integrate the visual arts with society. That objective is met in two ways. First, the Parsons faculty in all three locations includes senior practicing professionals attuned, through their work, to immediate social currents and needs. Second, using the liberal arts resources of the New School, Parsons students study the relationship between their work and the social, cultural, and political environment in which they live. As Dean David Levy has said, Parsons

> must accept a responsibility that goes far beyond the mere transmission of data or professional skill....We believe that the quality of contemporary life is profoundly affected by the practices of visual and design disciplines. Painters, sculptors, graphic designers, fashion designers, architects transform our environment in ways that contribute to our psychological as well as our physical well-being. Thus, to preserve and foster a culture that can describe itself as "civilized"...we must recognize our obligation to nurture new generations of creative and well-educated young people.

Parsons, then, produces students well-grounded in the basics of the fine arts and sharply honed in particular design disciplines who also are liberally educated. Nowhere is Parsons' commitment to the liberal arts better illustrated than in the new 5-year joint program with Eugene Lang College in which a student earns both a B.A. and a B.F.A.

The New School's experience with the liberal arts for students in the 18-22 age group began in the 1970s with the Freshman Year Program, which allowed gifted New York high school students the opportunity to study at the New School in lieu of their senior year of high school. As expected, all of them entered colleges elsewhere after their time here. Somewhat unexpectedly, many of the freshman year students were eager to continue at the New School as degree candidates. In response to a growing demand for a 4-year college founded on the principles of the Freshman Year Program, the New School began in the late 1970s to transform that program into a 4-year, degree-granting college that came to be known as the Seminar College.

In 1984, largely through the generous financial support of Trustee Eugene M. Lang, that process was dramatically accelerated. The Trustees approved a plan to expand the curriculum and the student body. Their decision was prompted by four factors: (1) the need in New York City for a high-quality, small liberal arts college in a university setting, with a distinctive curriculum, available at a modest price; (2) the opportunity to knit together the disparate parts of the New School into an integrated university through the development of an undergraduate college; (3) the rapid increase in teaching resources generated by the rebuilding of the Graduate Faculty; (4) the underuse of the New School's many classrooms in the daytime.

In view of New York's vast resources, it is somewhat surprising that the city does not have the benefit of a small, highly selective liberal arts college. The New School is filling that void.

Eugene Lang College is intended for students committed to serious intellectual work. It makes no pretense of offering the range of amenities and extracurricular activities found at typical residential colleges. Instead, Lang College draws its special character from a distinguished faculty and a highly individualized approach to education—an approach founded on small seminars as the primary mode of instruction. The curriculum is especially strong in areas in which the New School as a whole has been traditionally anchored: political philosophy and social criticism, public policy and urban studies, the performing and visual arts, and the humanities, especially writing.

The college's rich academic offerings are immeasurably enhanced by its location in New York's Greenwich Village, one of the city's most vibrant neighborhoods. Students are encouraged to experience the unparalleled cultural, intellectual, and artistic diversity of this great city in as many ways as possible. The college offers its students New York City internships that are closely related to their academic interests and thus provides a practical dimension which reinforces their academic pursuits. Above all, the college seeks to exemplify the distinctive traditions of the New School: an innovative curriculum, sensitivity to the important social and cultural issues of our time, and a student body which reflects the rich diversity of New York City.

The college feels a particular obligation to extend educational opportunity to the full range of New York City's citizens, especially those of limited means. We foresee that many of our students will be the first in their families to enroll in college. A large proportion will receive scholarship assistance, and a good number will be from minority groups.

In the years ahead, undergraduate education will be increasingly important to the life of the university. Though our commitment to adult and graduate education remains as strong as ever, our greatest challenges and opportunities are at the undergraduate level. The future health of the university depends in large measure on how well we provide for our growing undergraduate population.

The New School of the near future, then, will be a university that values equally continuing, graduate, and undergraduate education. With the emergence of a strong undergraduate presence will come temptations toward conformity with traditional universities. We must resist those undercurrents and hold fast to our own special character. The intellectual and artistic ferment and freedom in the classroom or studio—those qualities that the university both celebrates and manifests—are inextricably linked to the vibrancy, hardship, and challenge of New York City life. The New School's mission has always been to respond to these challenges in new and imaginative ways. We are being tested now more than ever. Yet the resilience and vision that this institution has shown over its 68-year history offers confidence for the future.

# Art and Social Transformation

(COMMENCEMENT, PARSONS, MAY 1987)

This is an important moment for you and for Parsons, and I want to reflect briefly on what makes you and Parsons so special.

One could start with some simple observations. Parsons, it is widely acknowledged, offers the highest-quality training and education of any art and design school in the country. Anyone who has seen the senior departmental exhibitions this year, as I have, must agree that your artistic achievement is remarkable. That you and Parsons are the best certainly makes you special. But it does not explain why.

There are many insights one might offer, but two aspects of your training stand out. As it happens, both have deep roots in the history of Parsons and the New School.

What strikes me in looking at your senior projects is that you all are well grounded in the underlying fundamentals, learned painfully, no doubt, in your Foundation Year. You draw well, use color sensitively, control texture, and capture light, and you appreciate the architecture of form and space. In short, you have mastered the skills that are at the heart of all artistic endeavor. A Parsons education stresses the elements of the fine arts in every discipline. It rejects any tension between the fine and applied arts.

This stance harks back to Parsons' early years. Its progenitor, the Chase School, founded in 1896, was devoted to painting and sculpture. It was not then very different from other schools—not until the influence of Frank Alvah Parsons began to be felt. In 1909, the Chase School became the New York School of Fine and Applied Arts, and a year later Frank Parsons became president. He was among the first American educators to grasp the relationship between the visual arts and the industrial march of society. "Industry is this nation's life," he wrote, "art is the quality of beauty in expression; and industrial art is the cornerstone of our national art." Quickly,

Parsons transformed the school's character by adding interior architecture and decoration, fashion design, and advertising art to the purely fine arts curriculum. And thus, this institution —renamed Parsons School of Design in 1940—took essentially its present character and philosophy in the years prior to World War I. Fine arts and design were irrevocably united. Each informed the other, as they do today at Parsons, and as your work so clearly shows.

At about the same time another institution was also taking shape in this city, the New School for Social Research. That leads me to the second aspect of your education that is distinctive. You are not only exquisitely trained in your chosen disciplines; but you are also well educated in the liberal arts. Parsons values the liberal arts deeply—a belief that is reinforced strongly by its place within a university whose heritage extends back to the same era as Parsons.

Those years when Parsons and the New School began and grew were a fertile period in American history. Theodore Roosevelt and Woodrow Wilson were the dominant national leaders; the progressive movement was at its zenith. Putting nineteenth-century determinism behind, Americans of that era were imbued with a sense of optimism and hope about the prospect for the good society. The individual could make a difference, and collectively the electorate could shape the destiny of the country. Conflicts and tensions, whether between city and country, native Americans and newcomers, or business leaders and workers, could be resolved. Economic growth need not erode traditional American values; the products of industry, material things, could also be beautiful.

Art was a central part of this great social transformation. Art, in fact, transformed the New School. Its movement from the social sciences to a more encompassing cultural curriculum was advanced by a growing preoccupation with the arts. Many distinguished artists and critics came to the New School—among them, Lewis Mumford, Berenice Abbott, Thomas Hart Benton, and Stuart Davis. New School philosopher Horace Kallen provided the intellectual link between the social sciences and the arts when he argued that both were substantially committed to the same goal: human liberation. The links between art and social science, between the fine arts and liberal arts, were graphically affirmed when Parsons joined the New School in 1970. They are an inherent part of your education, and the aims they represent are deeply embedded in the traditions of Parsons and the New School. We hope you will carry those aims—human liberation and freedom—into the future with you.

The aims of education now broaden into the aims of life. Education will not cease but takes on a new character, less the sole focus and more integrated into everyday living. You are setting out down a road on which you will create your own freedom. I am sure you will face difficult challenges, encounter joys and sadness, face struggle and achievement. I hope that your experience at Parsons and the New School will lead you to think often of how to make the most of that freedom. You certainly have a full background in art to sustain that reflection.

# A Work in Progress

(CONVOCATION, SEPTEMBER, 1994)

The New School, true to its name, is a work in progress. Our university has enlarged its size and scope dramatically over the past 25 years. We hope the seventy-fifth anniversary will help the outside world understand that we are not new, we are not a school, and we do a good deal more than social research. And those of us within the university should think hard about what the university has become, and be sure that the flow of information and the channels for participation in decision making are adequate to the present-day reality. I want to talk with you for a few moments about the university's historical development and an opportunity you will have to shape its future. You are here at a moment of historical transition. You are the first generation of students to look upon the university as a residential community.

Alvin Johnson and his colleagues who founded the New School—John Dewey, Thorstein Veblen, Charles Beard, among others—would be surprised at the subject of these remarks. Indeed, the very setting of a convocation for new and returning degree students would seem odd to them given their express intention of establishing an institution where adults would take courses for personal enrichment, not for credit. But institutions change, and from 1933, when Johnson established the University in Exile, now the Graduate Faculty, the New School was on course to becoming a university.

When the New School marked its fiftieth anniversary, it consisted of the original Adult Division and the Graduate Faculty. There were only 80 undergraduates seeking degrees here in 1969; the New School had only 90 full time faculty and staff; the alumni body numbered a mere 4,000. All activities were contained in two buildings.

The watershed moment in the New School's modern history came in 1970, the year it rescued Parsons School of Design from bankruptcy. When Parsons joined the New

School, the age of expansion began in earnest. In rapid succession the Center for New York City Affairs became the Graduate School of Management and Urban Policy* in 1975, the master of arts degree in Media Studies was first offered that same year, the Seminar College was founded in 1977, and the Parsons Paris campus was reopened in 1981.

The Seminar College grew into Eugene Lang College in 1985. The Mannes College of Music joined us in 1989. Bachelor's programs have been added in jazz and design marketing; and new master's programs were created in historical studies, architecture, psychoanalytic studies, gender studies and feminist theory, political economy, teacher education, and just this fall, the dramatic arts. The original New School non-credit programs now account for only 20 percent of tuition income. More than half of our nearly 6,000 degree students are undergraduates. The full-time faculty and staff now number 650, and the alumni body has swelled to 30,000. Our physical plant includes eleven buildings encompassing nearly 1 million square feet.

We have become a complex urban university that depends on common services like libraries, computer centers, dormitories, and a health center. At least 1,000 students a year take courses in schools other than their academic home divisions. Common policies on freedom of expression, sexual harassment, and discriminatory harassment apply to all parts of the university. The development of central services and policies has been in some tension with the decentralized tradition of the university. And the university's rapid growth in size and scope has diminished the sense of informality and even intimacy which characterized earlier times. Our objective now must be to have the best of both worlds: to enjoy the benefits of a large institution with opportunities for study in many fields, but also to restore the easy communication and sense of participation present when the place was smaller and less complex.

In pursuit of that goal, last spring students expressed

---

*This school was originally called the Graduate School of Management and Urban Professions.

strong interest in having more information and in being heard on issues that affect all of us. This is a healthy sign which we welcome: it is a landmark in our evolution as a university community that wants to maintain its artistic and intellectual distinctiveness but also enjoy forms of community life typical of more traditional universities.

We all want to preserve the New School's defining characteristics: its penchant for innovation, its search for special niches, its commitment to meeting unmet needs, its determination to be independent and to protect artistic and intellectual freedom, and its critical stance to mainstream social science and policy. I suspect you were attracted to your academic program by these qualities and by the distinctive profile of your school or department. The energy, imagination, and passion which drive this place flow from the autonomy that our schools have enjoyed under the New School umbrella. Local initiative and flexibility are great strengths which must be encouraged.

The creation of a university community which respects the special nature of each of our schools requires us to be clear about what universities are and are not. They are not nation states. Members of university communities do not exercise their political rights as citizens through the university. Universities as institutions do not take formal positions on policy issues nor do they directly intervene in social matters except through the important medium of education. Their mission is the discovery and transmission of knowledge and the training of students for a life of moral reflection and useful work.

Our university is an independent institution chartered by the State of New York, which vests complete authority for its affairs in fifty Trustees. A primary responsibility of the Trustees is to create an environment which protects intellectual and artistic freedom. Indeed, one reason that states grant universities certain privileges, such as tax exemption, is in the belief that a healthy society benefits from artistic and scholarly activity free to advocate unpopular and controversial positions. While the university as an institution is neutral on issues unrelated to education, that very neutrality protects the opportunity for you and your faculty to speak freely on any topic and to challenge the established order.

And while the Trustees have all the legal power within the university, they have delegated authority over academic matters to the President, who in turn cedes primacy in faculty appointments, admission standards, and the curriculum to the faculties of each school. The faculty, in turn, involves students in decisions on curricular issues, faculty evaluations, and the like.

There are deep, enduring reasons that universities are stronger when they encourage such involvement:

- Learning about how organizations work, including the constraints they face and their complexity, is an important part of a student's education.
- Fuller communication and participation reaffirm a shared understanding of the university's mission, which at its core remains constant, but which benefits from periodic reinterpretation.
- Widespread consultation enables the university to serve its faculty and students better, to be more responsive to community concerns, and to make sounder decisions.
- Understanding the needs of the university tempers the demands and expectations placed upon the university by all its members and inspires alumni and others who care about it to offer financial support.

The issue that the New School faces today is how to increase significantly participation and communication in a way that respects the traditions, special character and autonomy of each of the university's academic divisions. In the last couple of years, the modes for participation in university affairs have expanded exponentially, for the faculty, for lay advisers, for the alumni. But our concern here is for student involvement. Committee work may be the last thing on your minds today as you grapple with the mix of anxiety and anticipation which is natural as you begin your studies. But soon you will feel at home here and will care about making this a better place. Here are some ways you can help.

Since many of the decisions that affect you directly are made in your individual schools, you should consider service on one of the 30 local divisional committees needing some 150 student members. And at the university level, there are 16 committees seeking student members—committees on the libraries, the academic computing center, honorary degrees, student life, and diversity, for example. And there are all-student advisory committees on essential services such as health care, financial aid, and the registrar and bursar function. This is not to suggest that the only way to have your views heard is to serve on a formal committee. You should feel free to talk with your teachers, your dean, and the student life staff—indeed, with anyone on this stage, including me. Our job is to make your experience at the university as good as it can possibly be.

The modes of communication and participation that we fashion this year will shape the nature of the university over its next 75 years. In Dean Acheson's phrase, you are "present at the creation" of a new sense of this university, at a moment when we are working together to strengthen the bonds of community.

The New School has always attracted socially aware students, people who care about making the world better. We are a community of activists who believe the application of information and reason can bring social progress. Let us apply those convictions to making our own university stronger. I urge you to begin this year, this term, taking an active interest in the affairs of your school, program, or department.

From all of us, I wish you an exciting and fulfilling academic and artistic experience this year and every year you are with us.

# Reflections on Education

# Nurturing Optimism

(COMMENCEMENT, MAY 1992)

At the end of his long career in public service, Secretary of War Henry Lewis Stimson wrote: "The only deadly sin I know is cynicism." At age 80, Stimson counseled the younger generation around President Truman not to plunge prematurely into a cold war, but rather to temper skepticism with trust lest unchecked it turn into cynicism.

Now, nearly half a century later at the Cold War's end, we have another opportunity for fresh thinking about forms of government and relations among nations. In the United States we also face an important election this fall, one which could change the direction of our domestic policy. What are the prospects for a vigorous national debate on the issues and what should our role be, yours and mine, in healing the ills of our political process? How can we escape the trap of cynicism which leads to what Robert Reich calls the "secession of the successful"?

It is a painful irony that the first blossoms of democracy in Eastern and Central Europe coincide with rising doubts about its effectiveness here in America. There is a real danger that a loss of confidence in our political leaders will turn into a loss of confidence in democracy itself. Skepticism about those in positions of power can lead to alienation from the political process, enervating pessimism, and even cynicism.

How do we explain why in the last presidential election only 51 percent of those eligible actually voted? That means our President was chosen by only a little more than a quarter of our adult citizens. Voter participation has been dropping steadily, a trend likely to continue given the turnout in this year's primaries. Only 31 percent of registered voters expressed a preference on Super Tuesday.

Those numbers tell us that something is dreadfully wrong. So does the record number of members of Congress who are quitting in frustration. Another sign is the pervasive mistrust of our leaders. A 1991 Harris survey showed that only 21 percent of those questioned had "a great deal of confidence" in the White House. Congress fared worse with an anemic 9 percent. Not that other professions scored very well either. University presidents came in at 21 percent, the press at 14 percent, and business leaders at 15 percent. When you listen to the President, the governor, the mayor, or other leaders, do you find yourself starting with the assumption that they are not telling the truth, at least not the whole truth? A disturbingly large number of citizens believe that people in power routinely lie.

The Harris poll's alienation index stands at an all-time high, with fully 66 percent of those surveyed feeling alienated. This is quite a jump from 29 percent when the survey began in 1966.

That was about the time I graduated from college, and I remember believing that participation in the political process could make a difference, and that our leaders could be trusted. Was that an unusual attitude at the time? I don't think so. Would it be atypical today? Clearly, and sadly, the answer is yes. What caused this change? Let me hazard a few observations.

The conventional wisdom, I suppose, settles on the double whammy of the Vietnam War and Watergate. The deception that accompanied the undeclared and probably illegal war in Vietnam shocked people of all ages and across the political spectrum. And surely the sordid details of life in the Oval Office revealed by the Watergate tapes sapped respect and dignity from the presidency. But the war and Watergate are now almost a generation past. So what other factors fuel the rising doubts about our government and its leadership?

The first is the quality of our leaders themselves. Let's be blunt. We are experiencing a drought in leadership, not simply in terms of competence, but in terms of ethical behavior as well. And it is not only among political leaders. In business, law, philanthropy, religion, and higher education too, we are seeing an appalling degree of irresponsibility, self-interest, and even venality among people in positions of authority.

It is tempting to conclude that inept and corrupt political leadership is now the norm. But a fair reading of our history points to previous periods of weak leadership. Ask yourself, for example, about the Presidents between Andrew Jackson and Theodore Roosevelt, with the obvious exception of Abraham Lincoln. A pretty bleak 65 years. And in our own century the only quality between the two Roosevelts was Woodrow Wilson. While we have faced uninspiring choices in recent years, they are not inevitable, and we should not accept them. Indeed, we need to take responsibility as citizens for promoting better candidates and for setting higher standards for our leaders.

The second factor has to do with the gap between the promise of our charter documents—the Declaration of Independence, the Constitution, the Bill of Rights—and the reality of daily life. I believe that we are an idealistic people who take concepts like justice, equality, and nondiscrimination seriously and that we are troubled by our failure to achieve those goals. Americans made measurable progress in creating a more just and humane society during the first seven decades of this century. I remember believing, as I graduated from Yale, that segregation and discrimination were about to be eliminated and that the war on poverty was going to be won. Now those hopes seem naive, and any realist has to admit that progress on the social agenda has slowed in most areas, and even slipped back in some.

So there are reasons to be skeptical about whether this society ever plans to fulfill its promises of equality, compassion, and justice for all who live here. Yet I believe the majority of Americans are still committed to those ideals and will respond to leadership that calls upon our best instincts rather than feeds our worst fears. Reform over the last 100 years has come in cycles. The prerequisites for a new burst of social improvement are gathering now and could be unleashed before the century's end. The neglect of the past decade should not be taken as a sign of things to come. Perhaps the tragedy of the Los Angeles riots will shock us out of our paralysis and back to the task of turning ideals into action.

While those ideals are clear, and in some ways straightforward, achieving them is always more complicated. We need to be more open to and patient with complexity. Even highly educated people, ordinarily stimulated by difficult problems, demand simple, quick solutions from their political leaders today. Single-issue litmus tests have cost us more than a few very able politicians who told us the truth while others dissembled.

If reform is to occur and succeed, Americans must be willing to accept the complexity of American pluralism and confront issues of race, class, gender, maldistribution of income, and urban poverty. Only by addressing the full spectrum of interrelated social and economic issues can a fair and rational public policy emerge. Quick fixes and grandiose promises are both meaningless. We should not want to read any candidate's lips. A mature appreciation of our complex reality must recognize that all things are not possible, trade-offs are required, sacrifices must be made, and social improvement comes in incremental steps over time.

For most of our history, intellectuals have played an important role in helping the general public understand complexity. But there is a growing alienation of intellectuals and the academy from the political process. Perhaps isolation would be more descriptive. There was a time when university professors of divergent views were called upon to advise at all levels of government, and when a steady stream of government leaders came to campus to test their mettle with challenging students and faculty. But no more. Academic advisors, when they exist at all, come from a narrow ideological band to reinforce the predispositions of those in power; and government leaders, from the President on down, rarely risk putting their ideas and policies to the test with the younger generation.

But this is only part of the story. In a provocative piece in *Dissent* entitled "Intellectuals in Politics," the philosopher Richard Rorty warns that many professors

> ...have given up on the idea of democratic politics, of mobilizing moral outrage in the defense of the weak, of drawing upon a moral vocabulary common to the well-educated and the badly educated.... Because these theorists no longer think of themselves as citizens of a functioning democracy, they are producing a generation of radical students who think of the system as irredeemable....

I would not go so far as Rorty in laying the blame for students' disaffection entirely at the doorstep of disenchanted professors. But to the extent that they are being led to believe the situation is hopeless, and, therefore, opt out of the political process, they and our society are being done a disservice.

In fact, I would say the outlook is far from bleak. Our country has demonstrated, time after time, an extraordinary resilience. That resilience rests, in part, on the very skepticism about leadership that is at the heart of our democratic form of government. The right to be openly skeptical, to express criticism freely, gives our system its self-correcting quality and is its greatest virtue. In searching for ways to reinvigorate participation in the process, we should not attempt to reduce skepticism. Rather, we should make it constructive, give people a sense of its efficacy, and prevent it from hardening into a cynicism which begets a sense of futility.

I put my greatest faith for the future in individuals like you who have come to the New School—intelligent and informed, but always seeking more information, committed to equality and justice, but not discouraged by the fact that our democratic experiment is a work in progress.

The founders of the New School believed that education, the process of dialogue and critique, was the surest route to social amelioration. They sought to create an active and informed public that would have the knowledge and the inclination to question authority and to choose good leaders. Their message remains compelling. As graduates of the New School, you carry their legacy of a progressive approach to social problems, a basic optimism, and a commitment to making democracy work.

The disappointments of the present period, I am certain, are temporary rather than conclusive evidence that the American experiment is failing. I urge you not to abstain from the political process—indeed, to accept the responsibility for reforming it. You can help end the drought of leadership, reaffirm our country's ideals, help others tolerate complexity, and encourage real, if incremental, change. To do so takes intellectual engagement with the issues, active participation in political life, a firm fix on the restorative power of the principles of American democracy, and a basic confidence and trust borne of a sense of history.

We remain the oldest continuous democracy in the world, encompassing a very large geographic area and the most diverse population ever to have made democracy work. If it does not quite work the way we want it to, then by all means let us be skeptical of it. But let us use our skepticism not as a reason to secede from the process, but as a motivation to make it work better. And let us, above all, avoid the deadly sin of cynicism.

# Text and Context

(SELECTED FROM WELCOMING REMARKS,
SEPTEMBER 1986)

The university is a context—one of ideas, disciplines, people, activities. These elements exist and occur independent of one another, or in relation or even in opposition to one another. They support, challenge, and often act as catalysts for one another. The university is a world of intellectual and artistic ferment—a context into which each of you enters. And your task is to make sense of that context. You must draw meaning from it by selecting those elements which respond most directly to your needs and weaving them together into a text—the text which will represent your pursuits while a part of this university community.

That text is an original document. It is shaped from the ideas and programs and resources which now surround you, from the many possibilities this university has to offer. The philosopher Paul Ricoeur has spoken of these possibilities implicit in the text. He said that "like a text, human action is an open work...[which] 'opens up' new references and receives fresh relevance from them....The text speaks of a possible world and of a possible way of orientating oneself within it." That possible world of which Ricoeur speaks is unique for each of you because each of your texts has one element which is a part of no other. And that element is you. You are the determining factor in the course of study you will follow and in the benefits you will derive. You must bring your own experience, views, and aspirations and insert them into this context which now opens before you.

Your text—be it written or visual—will include a foundation of the courses you choose to take at Eugene Lang College, Parsons, the Graduate Faculty, the Graduate School of Management, Media Studies, or the Senior College. Your text will be formed by the discipline in which you choose to concentrate—major, if you will. Yet that specialized knowledge will be most relevant in the context of the broader view you achieve through courses outside your chosen discipline. Your text will be the sum of your formal education in the 2 or 4 or 6 or more years you will be with us. But its context will have a profound effect. What you learn outside of your classrooms and studios—from your teachers and fellow students, from the great international center of ideas, culture, and commerce of which you are now a part—will be of fundamental importance. The text, in short, is you. And you will merge your text with this university's and New York City's context to create an education of your own.

I have been talking a great deal about this university and what it has to offer. But the emphasis really must be on you. In creating your own original text, you will exercise an unusual degree of freedom. In fact, freedom is the essential precondition for the adventure on which you now embark. And freedom is the point on which text and context must converge.

The university should provide you with the opportunity to make choices and to define a program that addresses your individual educational needs and objectives. That we do. The university also must adhere unswervingly to the responsibility to provide an environment in which all views can be expressed and heard freely. That is a collective responsibility which we all share and which we generally fulfill admirably. You should approach your work with a sense of freedom as well—in other words, with an open mind. You should seek out views which oppose your own settled notions. You should allow the diverse influences and interests which are alive at this institution to impinge upon you and perhaps shape new perspectives for you. Regardless of whether you are pursuing undergraduate or graduate studies, professional training, or the liberal arts, you should strive for a liberal education in the true sense of that term: an education for freedom.

I hope that as a person seeking to be liberally educated, you will pursue specialization and general learning, mastery and perspective, knowledge and wisdom—always sensitive to text and context. Both elements of each paradigm are essential.

# Freedom Carries Responsibilities

(COMMENCEMENT, PARSONS, MAY 1990)

It is a paradox of our time that as our population becomes more diverse, dangerous pressures arise for conformity in the way we think and how we conceive of the good society. Perhaps those forces reflect a fear of difference, whether ethnic, racial, or religious. Maybe they represent a futile opposition to change, a desire to maintain the status quo or even push back the clock to a simpler era of greater homogeneity. Or possibly they reveal a fear of verbal or visual expression, of concepts and ideas, that question conventional wisdom.

One unwelcome manifestation of this fear is the intrusion of Congress into the work of the National Endowment for the Arts. Most of you are familiar with the controversy at the Corcoran Gallery over an exhibit of the photographs of Robert Mapplethorpe. Stimulated by that episode, Congress now requires that the NEA apply a sort of values test to the *content* of the work it supports. And the NEA in turn is warning the recipients of its grants that this values test exists and requiring that they sign an acknowledgment of this limitation on what they may produce. It has implied that there will be consequences if the test is violated.

Listen to the words which Congress adopted and which the NEA elected to include in the conditions it attaches to all its grants:

> None of the funds authorized for the National Endowment for the Arts ... may be used to promote, disseminate or produce materials which in the judgment of the National Endowment for the Arts ... may be considered obscene, including, but not limited to, depictions of sadomasochism, homo-eroticism, the sexual exploitation of children or individuals engaged in sex acts and which, when taken as a whole, do not have serious literary, artistic, political or scientific value.

This is a clear instruction to judge visual expression on grounds other than artistic merit. It is an open invitation to government bureaucrats—really an injunction to them—to exercise censorship. The criteria on which work is to be censored are so broad that they are likely to be used for political ends and cannot help but make every artist and designer feel under suspicion. What constitutes obscenity? What does "including, but not limited to" mean? Who will be the judge? What are the penalties? Should the government even be making decisions about the "literary, artistic, political or scientific value" of the products of our culture?

This condition cannot help but chill the environment for free expression, as it was meant to do. It creates a climate in which local government agencies are emboldened to exercise their own forms of censorship. The controversy in Cincinnati over the Mapplethorpe exhibit is a direct result, in my view, of the encouragement Congress has now given for limiting freedom of expression. And we are now treated to the sorry spectacle of the director of one of the country's oldest contemporary art museums being indicted for pandering obscenity.

All of us who are concerned about the visual arts and about freedom of expression have a duty to resist these threats to that cherished right. It is up to all—but particularly those of us who are older, who are in education, who have some influence—to protest the stifling intentions of Senator Helms in Washington and Sheriff Leiss in Cincinnati. We must oppose local cultural vigilantes who want to rip down images that offend. We need to say with one voice that it is wrong for the National Endowment for the Arts to place an antiobscenity condition on the support it gives to individuals and institutions. And if we cannot persuade the NEA to remove this condition, then it may be necessary to refuse its grants.

You who are the new generation of artists and designers must also play a role in defending and promoting free expression. The best way you can do this is by using that freedom with great energy. Do not be intimidated by those who would impose their tastes and narrow views on works whose artistic merit eludes them, whose message they cannot grasp. Let your creativity play fully in your work, unconstrained by perceptions of popular fashion or forbidden visual forms. Be willing to challenge conventions and settled assumptions, to take risks, even to make sacrifices in defense of freedom.

I am optimistic that the new censors will not prevail, because they strike at a set of values deeply rooted in America, values which evoke broad support when leadership rallies to their defense. So stay the course. Do not compromise.

Complete freedom of expression, however, carries with it some sense of responsibility. Having the right to say or paint something does not end the ethical reflection. For example, those of you working in commercial settings should ask yourselves whether the images you create or are asked to include, say, in an ad campaign perpetuate negative stereotypes based on race, gender, ethnicity, or other individual differences.

Last fall, there was a controversy at Parsons over an image in the Shin Matsunaga exhibition which employed a racial stereotype in an advertisement for a soft drink company. We were asked to take the offending print down, and when we refused to do so, it was defaced. There can be no doubt that defacing the print was wrong, constituting as it did a form of censorship. And I think it would have been wrong to remove the offending piece from the exhibition. However, I believe it is also wrong for a designer or artist to employ images that gratuitously insult groups in our society on the basis of race, ethnicity, sexual orientation, or any other personal characteristic.

Even though you are entitled to free expression, the practice of art and design should not be thought of as value-free. Artists and designers must be guided by sets of values. There may be no single set of values that is appropriate for all, but an "anything goes" approach is insufficient. It is not enough to say, "I am an artist; what I do is art; therefore I do not have to observe any limits." And it is not enough to say, "I am a designer; I work for a client; whatever a client asks me to do is acceptable; anything I do that promotes a client's product successfully is all right."

These laissez-faire attitudes detach the practice of art and design from any larger context of ethical values, and in this sense they are irresponsible. Of course, it is important to judge art and design by their own internal criteria, to make aesthetic judgments about what is good art, what is beautiful, what works. But it is also necessary to think about the effect of visual expression on its audience. Even though we categorically reject the right of government to dictate or proscribe the content of art and design, it is perfectly appropriate for you to ask yourselves questions such as whether you are using racist, sexist, or homophobic imagery; whether you are engaging in obscenity, pornography, or exploitation; whether you are promoting corporations whose products or practices are objectionable—for instance, products that cause injury to health or practices that befoul the environment.

These kinds of issues and choices face artists and designers every day. They are complex, and there are no pat answers. Choice—the freedom to choose—is one of the most powerful tools that an artist or designer can use. Responsibility is the lens through which choice must be viewed. You should have the freedom to express yourselves in any way you wish. But you should use this freedom wisely.

The last year has witnessed genuine progress around the world in ending political oppression by totalitarian regimes. And the last generation has recorded significant progress in making the world more tolerant of diversity and in reducing discrimination. But prejudice and fear of difference run deep in human history. Progress in attacking the most blatant examples of intolerance should not allow us to ignore more subtle manifestations of prejudice in verbal and visual communication. There is work to do, and you will be well placed to do it. I hope you will be sensitive to images which exploit women, or mock people of African, Latino, or Asian heritage—images that employ negative stereotypes of any kind. I hope you will raise questions about the use of such images in a commercial setting and understand their meaning in your own individual work. As artists and designers, you have a sense of your potential and a responsibility to help create a more just and humane world.

# Establishing a Network for Collective Influence

(COMMENCEMENT, PARSONS, MAY 1992)

In 4 years, Parsons will be 100 years old. We are planning a great celebration, and we want all of you to be part of it. There is reason to be proud of Parsons: it is the largest art and design school in the world, and one of the best; an estimated 71,000 people have studied at Parsons, not even counting the 146,000 who have enrolled in the evening division; it was a pioneer in adapting art to industrial settings, in training those applied artists who came to be known as designers, and in using practicing professionals as its principal design faculty; it positioned itself early as an institution which knew no national boundaries. Not bad for starters.

But what does it mean to be a Parsons graduate? What rights and responsibilities are granted to the 571 of you who earn degrees today? And, by the way, when anyone talks to you about rights and responsibilities, be prepared to hear more about the latter—I am no exception.

You and the other Parsons graduates are—or should be—a network. Networks are important. We may think of them first as a way of making professional contacts to further one's own career or to obtain business assignments. "Networking" was one of the catchwords of the 1980s. But networks did not just begin in the last decade, and they are not just for individual advancement. Networks based on collegiate affiliations have exercised persuasive influence over entire societies. Think of Oxford or Cambridge, Harvard or Yale. The networks engendered by these institutions do not just offer job opportunities; they shape entire fields of endeavor: law, government and public policy, diplomacy, business, and many more.

If we were to ask what institutions rise to this level of influence across the fields of art and design, I do not think we could find any. Surely Parsons, in fashion design, comes closer to a network than any other; but in terms of comprehensive influence, I would submit there are none fully developed. Parsons, by virtue of its age, size, location, and distinction, certainly has the potential to be the most powerful network in the visual world. We have alumni living in all fifty states of the union, and in eighty different countries on six continents. That the vast numbers of Parsons graduates do not yet form a coherent alumni body is a failing we at the university must correct by keeping in touch with our alumni and by helping them interact with one another. If we do not, then Parsons defaults on an important responsibility, yields influence to the less talented, and deprives the world of a potent force for visual progress.

As we prepare for Parsons' hundreth anniversary, I cannot think of a better goal than establishing and invigorating a Parsons network to rival, in the field of art and design, those other heady collegiate networks. And since we are just at the beginning, we can take a fresh approach. By all means, the Parsons network should be effective in helping its members rise in their careers. But we can also invest our network with higher purposes that transcend self-interest and benefit a wider community. Let me reflect for a moment on some characteristics of the Parsons network I envision.

To begin, Parsons prides itself on encouraging every student to find his or her own visual voice. Your senior exhibitions offer persuasive evidence for that proposition: there is no standard Parsons style, but rather a stunning array of work whose common threads are conceptual and technical excellence. But we know life as an artist or designer can be tough. Recognition and tangible rewards can be years off. Temptations to compromise one's art can be immediate and compelling. Parsons alumni need to support one another in resisting those temptations and remaining faithful to the high ideals and aspirations that animate each of you on this day.

Being true *to* yourself does not mean being absorbed *in* yourself. Art is a medium of communication. In producing art, you are not engaged in a monologue; you are having a visual impact on a world inhabited by others. The buildings that give character to an urban landscape, the interior spaces in which we live and work, the furniture and tools which fill those spaces, the art on the walls and the sculpture in the courtyards, the clothes we wear, the imagery that advertises products we buy, the design of electronic and print media together with the photographs that connect us to our environment, the signs that show us the way in both a practical and spiritual sense—all depend on what you who graduate today invent and create. You help determine the shape, texture, and color of what we see and touch. If each member of our extended community holds fast to the standards of excellence imbued at Parsons, our network can literally improve the visual world and make the environment a better place in which to live.

The pleasures and insights that come from observing art or using design can be deepened and enriched for laypeople by the experience of making art or design. Parsons' parent university, the New School, was founded on the belief that learning is lifelong and that average citizens, enlightened amateurs if you will, can enrich their lives through education. When Parsons joined the New School in 1970, it started a continuing education program that quickly became the largest source of art and design education for adults in New York.

Think of the collective influence Parsons could have if all its graduates worldwide shared their talents, insights, values, and standards in the classroom. We should affirm the importance of adult education in art and design and encourage nonprofessionals to develop their own talents for personal enrichment. The elevated taste, sensitivity, and appreciation for good design that will flow from this investment will build an audience and an appetite among the general public that will advance the quest for visual progress.

Events of the past 2 years should make it evident to all of us that the phenomenon of art does not exist solely between art's maker and its viewer. Political considerations all too often intervene. Thus the Parsons network should advocate public policies that respect and encourage individual free expression, that support artistic excellence, and that develop young talent. We should resist infringement on individual artists and museums, whether at the hands of Sheriff Leiss in Cincinnati, the City Council in Chicago, or the NEA, and Senator Helms in Washington. The Parsons network should also counter those more subtle philistines, whether they be in Albany or our national capital, who censor by cutting funds for the arts. And more affirmatively, the Parsons network should encourage private foundations and corporations, as well as government agencies, to give the arts the support they need to be free and to nurture young talent.

Finally, there is an overarching purpose of equal importance, whether your place in the Parsons network is in the United States or in one of the eighty other countries where our alumni live. Art and design have the capacity to transcend divisions of national boundaries and of racial, religious, ethnic, or class distinctions. Parsons' determined pluralism—indeed, the very composition of this graduating class coming from fifty-one different countries and representing most major racial, religious, and ethnic groups in the world—means that your outlook is a good deal more cosmopolitan than most. The Parsons network thus can be a bridge across dangerous ravines created by those less well educated and more provincial than you. Each of you has the responsibility, as artists, designers, and citizens, to pursue the most just and humane social arrangements possible. Let the Parsons network be a force for liberation from the hatred and prejudices which afflict every society. Members of the Parsons community should be a source of reform, not an engine of repression which reinforces the old order of gender, racial, and sexual discrimination or other harmful stereotypes.

I warned you that the responsibilities would seem more vivid than the rights. But let me affirm one central right all of you have as alumni of Parsons: you have the right to ask one another and Parsons for help and support over a lifetime. We care deeply about both your professional and personal well-being. We pledge to keep Parsons strong so that you will always be proud to exercise that right. And we promise not to lose touch. You are lifelong members of this community, and we want you to be active participants in the Parsons network. Otherwise, the goals I have just discussed will be an evanescent dream. With a genuine Parsons network, drawing energetically on all alumni, those goals can surely be reached.

# PART II

# Freedom and Diversity

# Academic Freedom and Freedom of Expression

# The University in Exile

(SELECTED FROM FIFTIETH ANNIVERSARY
CONVOCATION, APRIL 1984)

A half century ago, as darkness enveloped political, intellectual, and religious freedom in Europe, ten distinguished German scholars accepted the invitation of New School President Alvin Johnson to leave their native land and establish a University in Exile in New York City. They came largely from the University of Frankfurt, the Kiel Institute for World Economics, and the Berlin Hochschule. All but two were students of economics, political science, or sociology. In that first academic year, 1933-1934, eight lecture courses and seven seminars were conducted. Those ten scholars were the first of over 170 intellectuals from throughout Europe who escaped totalitarian oppression and found safety at the University in Exile. This rescue effort inspired similar action by many American institutions, resulting in the emigration of thousands of European scholars to these shores. Since that small beginning, more than 1,000 scholars have taught at the Graduate Faculty; over 50,000 students have attended; and 7,000 have earned graduate degrees.

The University in Exile forever changed the New School for the better. Because of the Graduate Faculty the New School became a university, a university which still more closely resembles a European colloquium than an American one. But the transforming effect of the University in Exile on the New School went beyond mere form to the substance of what was taught and studied and to the kind of institution this was to be—then and today.

The catalogue of that first year articulated the new institution's central values in its concluding words: "It goes without saying that every professor in the Graduate Faculty will be absolutely untrammeled, teaching freely and fearlessly and what he believes to be the truth." The irony of that phrase "it goes without saying" is inescapable. They are stirring words still. In 1933, they carried overtones which may be lost today.

Alvin Johnson and his colleagues could not possibly have imagined the monstrosities that were to follow during the next dozen years. But they perceived, however dimly, that the gates of hell were swinging open across the Atlantic. And on this side, America was at the very bottom of the Great Depression, torn by economic and social uncertainties of every kind. Yet Johnson and the New School Trustees were willing to pledge material and social resources to the cause of academic freedom, freedom of thought, and freedom of expression.

It was also the threat to intellectual freedom that moved the ten scholars to accept the invitation from the New School. Even more savage threats were foreshadowed, to be sure, but they were virtually unbelievable. It was not for sheer survival but for those freedoms that the scholars left home, family, and friends, and the comfort of their native language, to settle at this young and still untested institution.

Alvin Johnson grasped the larger significance of the rescue mission and saw it as a natural expression of our central purpose. As the first Graduate Faculty catalogue observed:

> The New School is under obligation to express by work and by act its own faith in the value of academic liberty. Without freedom of inquiry and teaching in the higher educational institutions there can be no intellectual freedom in society at large; and without intellectual freedom the democratic system under which we live cannot long endure.

That message spoke not only to conditions in Europe but to fears in America that economic depression would unravel the social and political fabric of this society. In the fall of 1933 democracy faced a double test: totalitarian repression abroad and internal despair and collapse at home. The American and European scholars gathered here placed their faith in intellectual freedom and social research as a response to both.

So the occasion today is meant to recall the special circumstances and purposes of this institution, to celebrate the contributions of its members—and a generation of émigrés—to this country and to scholarship around the world, and finally to reaffirm the New School's commitment to honor that legacy with a revitalized Graduate Faculty that includes once more the tall trees of international intellectual life. Further, through the honorary degrees we confer today, we recognize the continuing role of the New School in nourishing and protecting those who risk all in defense of intellectual freedom and human and civil rights. As Alvin Johnson wrote, "In extending its hospitality to a group of German professors who have been displaced, the New School conceives of itself as acting in the capacity of a representative of American institutions, in the first instance, and ultimately, of American democracy." Let us reaffirm today our role as a representative American institution—one that has made a difference.

Why do we make so much of the University in Exile? Why has the special tie between the New School and German scholarship remained vital for 50 years? Recall that the University in Exile started with only ten émigrés and through all its years only thirty more taught there. To be sure, through the New School many more were helped to find positions in the United States at well-established institutions like the University of Chicago, Yale, Harvard, and the University of California.

Since the founding of the Massachusetts Bay Colony in 1630, Americans have believed in the efficacy of the "city upon the hill," the symbolic power of small examples to inspire hope among the oppressed. The University in Exile was a twentieth-century equivalent, a symbol of the enduring commitment of Western society to the values of academic freedom, human rights, political liberty, equality, and justice.

The second observation relates to the first. Most of the émigrés were dispersed across the American landscape. For all their brilliance and accomplishment, they were peripheral to the institutions that took them in. Only the New School found virtue in the clustering of émigreés; only the New School appreciated the beneficial potential of their influence on American scholarship; only the New School respected and encouraged the folkways of different cultures; and only the New School placed them at the heart of the university.

Finally, the very term "University in Exile"—so monumental a name for so modest an enterprise—conveys the true ambition and meaning of that historic emigration. A *university* transcends lecture halls, laboratories, and even libraries. It is not defined by geography or confined to a particular place. A *university* is a community of thinking, study, discourse and collaboration which rises above disciplines, methods, languages, and nationalities. The University in Exile reminds us that we are all part of that greater community, of one university. It can be removed from one locale to exile in another, but it can never be exiled from our hearts and minds.

That was the message brought to the New School by Thomas Mann when he spoke at a dinner for the University in Exile in 1937. He recalled that the Nazis had removed from the wall of the University of Heidelberg a plaque bearing the inscription "to the living spirit." Of course, the "living spirit" was the tradition of free and unfettered inquiry that had thrived for so long in the German university system. Because of the University in Exile, Mann said, the removal of the plaque would have no effect. The "living spirit" would be preserved in America through the émigré scholars at the New School.

What Thomas Mann did not know was that the University in Exile would be given a permanent home at the New School. That was assured in 1934, when the New School organized the early group of University in Exile scholars into the Graduate Faculty of Political and Social Science. Composed almost entirely of German social scientists, the Graduate Faculty immediately established itself as a unique and important institution—a graduate school steeped in the scholarly standards of Germany's best universities, and populated by scholars who were the repository of European ideas then seldom exposed to American students....

# Addressing Apartheid: The Question of Official Views

(LETTER TO THE UNIVERSITY COMMUNITY, MAY 1985)

One element of the national outpouring of opposition to the South African government's system of apartheid has been the effort to put individuals and institutions on record condemning that system. Later in this personal letter I elaborate my own unequivocal abhorrence of apartheid. But first, it is worth pausing to reflect on the nature of a university and to consider whether universities should make official statements on public issues and whether it is appropriate for university presidents to state publicly their personal views on such issues.

It has been suggested that the New School for Social Research make an official statement condemning apartheid in South Africa. That may seem like an easy and sensible action for the Trustees to take. But it is not. It seems easy because the Trustees as individuals are all opposed to apartheid. And yet, it must be asked, should the University through its governing body take official positions on important public issues not directly related to it, even issues as self-evident as opposition to apartheid?

I believe that because of their special place in a democratic society, universities have a unique obligation to conduct themselves in ways which enhance and do not impede the search for truth and understanding. They are a unique forum for unfettered expression, free inquiry, and disagreement. In order to protect these freedoms for all members of a university community, a university itself should not take "official" positions on public issues. However, no one expects neutrality from the individual members of a university community; indeed, it may be argued that the privileged status of members of a university community obliges them to speak out on matters that concern them and on issues in which they possess expertise. It is through the discovery of knowledge, the exploration of ethical and philosophical principles—particularly where there is controversy—and the application of reason to complex issues and conflict that individuals within a university community have exercised leadership on social and political issues for centuries. That is as it should be.

When a university as an institution, speaking through its Board of Trustees, takes official positions on issues not immediately related to its own affairs, several dangers arise. The most fundamental is the one already mentioned, the potential for the "official view" to chill the freedom of individual members of the community to pursue their own views. In addition, the society may be less willing, through tax exemptions, direct support, and other means, to sustain a university's protected status. Still another danger derives from the inherent difficulty in arriving at an institutional view. That is difficult because universities are not political entities, and so no political mechanisms exist—and if they did, they would introduce divisions at odds with a university's fundamental mission.

Not all universities have been neutral at all times. We can think of occasions—some ancient, some in the recent past—when a university departed from its neutral position on worldly issues. But the existence of exceptions serves to remind us of the importance of the general rule.

Earlier I suggested that a university might properly take a position when the issues concern it or its members directly. For example, our university's Trustees, administrators, and friends have worked for more student aid; they have opposed hurtful modifications in the federal charitable deduction. I feel certain they would steadfastly resist any effort by external agencies to abridge the freedoms of expression and inquiry—freedoms upon which the very existence of the New School depends. And, by virtue of stock ownership in its endowment, a university cannot escape the need to weigh ethical considerations in how it votes on shareholder resolutions or what stock it will or will not own. Not to vote on a shareholder resolution—for example, a resolution calling on a company not to urge on poor mothers in undeveloped countries use of infant formula as preferable to nursing—can be said to be taking a position. When faced with the reality of an inescapable choice, obviously a reasoned vote is appropriate. So, too, with the fact of stock ownership. A university may choose for a variety of reasons, including disagreement with the nature of its conduct, not to own stock in a particular company. Decisions and the process for reaching them will often be complicated and demanding, but that a decision should be made is not in question. Our purpose, in my view, is to place a university in a morally reasoned position rather than to use it institutionally as an agent to effect social change.

If a university should not have an "official" view on public issues, are there appropriate ways nevertheless in which it can express its values? I think so. One has only to look to the heritage of the University in Exile and to its rescue mission in the 1930s, which saved a generation of distinguished European scholars. That was a powerful statement in support of intellectual freedom and human rights and a courageously appropriate institutional act. The New School for Social Research has continued to provide safe haven for exiled intellectuals denied those basic freedoms in their own societies.

If a university should not take official positions on public issues unrelated to it, must a president also refrain from expressing personal views? Does he or she have the same right of freedom of speech that a university guarantees other members of its community? I believe the president does, provided that a personal statement is clearly so identified. How a particular president chooses to exercise that freedom may vary from incumbent to incumbent. And how he or she does it may well affect the public's view of that president and possibly also of his or her institution. There are those who believe that a president's expression of personal views, no matter how clear the institutional disclaimer, will be seen by many as indistinguishable from an official view. The concern is real, but I do not find it compelling. More to the point is that taking frequent personal positions on public issues is bound to diminish a president's effectiveness in serving a university because it is a distraction and will sometimes be divisive. A president's first obligation is to the welfare of the university as a free and open institution.

To date I have chosen not to make a public statement on any issue not directly related to the New School or higher education. I have taken as my standard two criteria for selecting an issue on which I would make a personal statement: (1) the issue must be of overwhelming moral importance, clearly distinguishable from other current concerns; and (2) the issue must be of intense interest in the New School community, not just a personal cause.

I think the South African government's system of apartheid meets those criteria. Under that system, the structure of South African society is based upon race as the fundamental organizing principle. Only 14 percent of the land is set aside for ten homelands for South Africa's 20 million Africans, who constitute nearly three-quarters of the total population. The remaining 86 percent of the land is declared white country. Africans have virtually no right to live, work, obtain education, or participate in political activity in white areas. The rights of Coloreds or Asians in those areas, while greater than those of the Africans, are also severely limited. The legislative system which is apartheid would seem unreal were the consequences not so real, so tragic. The persistent effort of the white minority in that country to regulate virtually every aspect of life in order to preserve racial separation is staggering in its complexity and moral obtuseness.

The effect of apartheid is not mere segregation, not merely separate but unequal facilities and access to housing, employment, and education. It is far worse. Apartheid produces a society in which the most fundamental freedoms and essential qualities of human dignity are denied to the overwhelming majority of the population. It is a system of forced labor and dehumanization.

Free people in a free community, such as a university, respecting the individuality of all human beings, should not be silent in the face of total official denial of these values. No marginal efforts to liberalize the apartheid system (such as the recent modification of the ban on interracial marriages, or deceptive efforts to grant democratic participation on minor policy issues nationally or in geographically limited areas locally) should blunt condemnation of the present South African government.

One need not be an historian to realize that apartheid is doomed to fail in South Africa, as it has elsewhere in the world. The only questions are when and at what human cost. The internal dynamic already unleashed within South Africa will move inexorably toward a more just society. However, there are actions which the United States government can and should take to hasten the fall of apartheid.

In closing, one other comment needs to be made. It is said that there are many evils in the world—widespread human rights abuses, for example—and that even the most concerned person could not comprehend them all, or address them all. True enough. But the difficulty of making distinctions is not a defense for silence. When we think of South Africa, we are thinking of official, governmental racial discrimination of unprecedented scope. That issue, more than other evils extant in the world today, connects with the peculiar history of the United States where, in my lifetime, racial segregation was lawful. It is no longer lawful, but it still exists. When I think of South Africa, my determination to work for the complete eradication of racial discrimination in this country is made more intense. As individual citizens, we perhaps have only a limited impact on other societies; I feel certain we can and must change our own for the better.

# The Matsunaga Exhibit and Freedom of Expression

(LETTER TO THE UNIVERSITY COMMUNITY, NOVEMBER 1989)

A specific work of design on exhibit at the Parsons Gallery has caused anger and concern among many individuals at the University. The work itself and actions that have been taken in response to it represent a clear instance when the values of freedom of expression and freedom from intolerance and harassment come into conflict. We need to understand that tension and work toward resolution and reconciliation through a prompt and mutually respectful exploration of the issues involved. I write to describe the events that have occurred, to explain the reasoning for the decisions that have been made, and to suggest a process of discussion that I believe we should now pursue.

The exhibition of 350 works by the noted Japanese graphic designer Shin Matsunaga was displayed at Parsons from October 18 through November 17. Mr. Matsunaga is one of a number of graphic artists in Japan now gaining international recognition for their innovative blend of Japanese calligraphic traditions with modern typography and Western approaches to design.

Mr. Matsunaga was invited to exhibit his work here on the recommendation of the Parsons Exhibitions Committee, which includes faculty members and staff and is responsible for gallery programs and procedures. The Committee based its recommendation on Mr. Matsunaga's acknowledged distinction as a designer and on viewing a sampling of his works. As is often the case with exhibitions organized outside Parsons, the Committee did not review each individual piece selected for the show. Mr. Matsunaga and his associates, together with a group from the Parsons Gallery, installed the show in New York.

One piece in the Matsunaga show was a 1983 newspaper advertisement, in Japanese, for a soft drink manufactured by Calpis Food Industry. The advertisement incorporates a caricature of a person of African heritage that is deeply offensive to African Americans and indeed to all of us who are concerned about insensitivity and harassment on racial and ethnic grounds. (The caricature was the company's logo and was not created by Mr. Matsunaga, who incorporated it into the advertisement. The company has since discontinued the logo in the face of international protest against it.) On Tuesday November 14, the piece was defaced by a signed message written in marker across it, and a number of other individuals subsequently added their signatures to the message.

Assertions have been made that the University should have removed the particular design piece from the show or issued a disclaimer of responsibility for the piece. Deep distress has been voiced that some individuals indicated their opposition to the piece by defacing it. I understand the depth of emotion and forcefulness of opinion from all perspectives on this issue. It is indeed a very difficult and complex one.

The presence of racism in our society and beyond represents one of the greatest and most pervasive examples of injustice in our time. We all bear a share of responsibility for its persistence, and we must undertake vigorous action to reduce and eliminate it. As a community, we must focus more attention on this challenge.

The New School for Social Research is striving to be a community that values and seeks diversity among its members, that encourages respect for difference, and that is free from discrimination and intolerance in its professional and personal relations. As I said in my remarks at the opening convocation in September, we have an affirmative responsibility to one another to be sensitive to our diverse backgrounds and beliefs. It is thus painful to all of us when acts occur or ideas are expressed, verbally or visually, that are insensitive or contain insults or attacks. Such instances of intolerance are particularly offensive when they are based on difference, be it of race, ethnicity, gender, or sexual orientation. There is no question that the design work that was defaced contains such an insulting visual image. I find the image deeply offensive and racist.

The issue of whether the University should have "done something" about the piece was not, however, one that could be decided only on the basis of the work's offensiveness. It is a question that also must take account of the University's obligations regarding freedom of expression.

The New School has been deeply committed since its founding to the protection and extension of freedom of expression. It has manifested that commitment in efforts to promote and defend the rights of minorities to free expression. The University's position is embodied in two policies: one on the free exchange of ideas, adopted by the Board of Trustees on January 21, 1987, and the other on freedom of artistic expression, enacted by the Board on October 4, 1989.

The artistic freedom policy was adopted as the United States Congress was considering a measure, offered by Senator Jesse Helms, which posed a direct threat to artistic freedom. The university's policy is based on the premise that visual expression in an academic community enjoys the same protections as verbal expression. It states, in part, that "authorized display or performance, regardless of how unpopular the work might be, must be unhindered and free from coercion." It goes on to say:

> The University recognizes that the right of artists to exhibit or perform does not preclude the right of others to take exception to particular works of art. However, this latter right must be exercised in ways that do not prevent a work of art from being seen and must not involve any form of intimidation, defacement, or physical violence.

The import of this policy is that the University does not and cannot sponsor, or give approval or disapproval to, the content of speech, written expression, or works of art, design, and performance. Individuals may be invited by the University, or by students and faculty of one of its schools, to speak, publish, display art, or perform at the University; but this does not mean that the University gives "official" sanction to what those individuals say or do. It has no such sanction to give or withdraw. If an officer of the University had issued a disclaimer of responsibility for the design in question or for the offensiveness of the image it contains, that action would have implied that the University does make official judgments on the content of expression. It would also have implied that any expression for which responsibility is not disclaimed has the University's sanction.

In the instance of the Matsunaga exhibition, there were other pieces which some found offensive, especially those which employ images that are considered sexist. A disclaimer for one piece in the show would have raised questions about the University's position on other potentially offensive pieces. It quickly becomes evident that if the University begins making judgments on individual instances of expression, then it must make judgments on all acts of expression, a role that is patently inappropriate for an institution of higher education. We must avoid any suggestion that the University takes official positions on, or gives sponsorship to, the content of expression.

The University's policy on free expression does make it clear that the New School has an unambiguous responsibility to create and preserve an environment in which free expression can be exercised, no matter how offensive that expression might be. Members of the university community do have the right to take exception to particular instances of expression. There are many appropriate ways to articulate such objection, including the posters that were displayed outside Parsons and the demonstrations that occurred in the Parsons Gallery and outside my office on Friday November 17. I strongly support the vigorous protest against the racist image in the Matsunaga exhibition and indeed would have been troubled if there had been no response from students and faculty. However, members of the university community do not have the right to prevent expression from occurring or from being seen or heard. And this injunction extends to the

University itself acting as a corporate body. The University should avoid any action that has the effect of inhibiting free expression. Removing the work from the show would have had exactly that effect: preventing a specific instance of expression from occurring and chilling the environment for free expression in general.

It is also painful, particularly in view of the New School's historic defense of freedom of expression, when members of the university community choose to violate these policies, as some have done by defacing the piece in question. A community and society in which freedom of expression is cherished cannot long endure when individuals, no matter how just their cause, take it upon themselves to dictate what is or is not permissible expression.

The issues that the Matsunaga piece has so pointedly brought to our attention were already under discussion at the University before the exhibit arrived here. I said in my convocation address that I would appoint a faculty-student committee to reflect on issues of diversity, harassment, and freedom of expression in our community and to suggest the appropriate response when such conflicts arise. That committee was formed last month and is now at work. I will ask it to give particular attention to the concerns and actions attendant on the Matsunaga exhibit.

I believe that, in an academic community, we have an obligation to respond to such issues as opportunities for education, no matter how controversial and conflict-laden they have become. We all have much to learn and do about racism and other forms of intolerance in our communities and beyond. But we need to be equally vigilant in our efforts to explore and comprehend the meaning and importance of freedom of expression and the responsibilities that such freedom imposes on us.

Our search for understanding will rely on the kind of reasoned dialogue that is at the heart of the educational process. The events of the last few days make it evident that we should not depend solely on the deliberations of the committee that I have appointed but should expand these discussions to include our entire community. I have asked the deans of the academic divisions to plan with their faculties and students other ways of exploring these issues, whether they be especially organized discussions or attention devoted during regular class sessions.

Among the topics I would suggest be explored are: the persistence of racism in America and other societies; how our commitment to freedom of expression should be interpreted and applied; how our commitment to freedom from intolerance should be manifested; what we should do when two fundamental values come into conflict; and the responsibility of artists and designers in using images that offend. I would like to think these important issues will receive wider and more intense scrutiny now than if the offending piece had been censored.

The pain and discomfort inflicted on members of our community by the Matsunaga piece inevitably raise larger questions about the general climate at the University. I said in my convocation address and again in this statement that we strive to be a community free from intolerance, one which respects, even celebrates, difference. The discussions which now go forward should test our collective performance against our stated aspirations and identify specific measures that can make the university environment supportive of all its members.

There are lessons to be learned from the Matsunaga exhibition. In addition to the important philosophical questions I have just recited, there are some practical implications. We need to clarify the procedures and criteria by which judgments are made about what exhibits are accepted in our galleries and what works of art are displayed. I have asked the Dean of Parsons and the Parsons Exhibitions Committee to review and set forth the current policies and procedures. I also believe we need a general public statement which explains the relationship of the University to works displayed in its galleries.

No one should believe that, because a work of art or design which is (or is perceived to be) racist, sexist, or pornographic hangs in a university gallery, the University endorses or is insensitive to racism, sexism, or pornography. And perhaps an introduction in a catalogue, or one posted at the entrance to an exhibit, describing the context of the work would make it clear that those responsible for the exhibition are not unaware of images that might offend.

Part of the pain in the Matsunaga episode is that it was not apparent that those responsible for the exhibition recognized the racist character of the image until it was protested. Part of the frustration of those most assertive in challenging the inclusion of the piece in the exhibit derives from their feeling that the University did not take their concerns seriously or respond promptly enough with a forum for discussion. And part of my concern is that so many people who were distressed by the piece chose to remain silent until it was defaced and did not use many available means to learn about why the piece remained in the exhibit without a disclaimer. Only one person wrote me, and I met with him in a conversation which covered the issues discussed here.

I took the objections to the Matsunaga piece seriously from the start, but I now realize that I should have made my views known to the community sooner and should have acted more promptly in creating a forum for discussion. But I stand by the decision to leave the offensive piece in the exhibition, and I do not think it was proper to deface it.

I conclude with a request to all members of the university community. Let us not frame the issue as if freedom of expression and freedom from intolerance are incompatible or are enemies. They are both cherished values, and we should not have to choose which one we hold more dear. The question, I think, is how to use freedom of expression more vigorously in pursuit of a society free of prejudice and intolerance of all kinds.

There are few people in this community who are not deeply torn over the issues raised by the Matsunaga exhibit. They are, on the one hand, deeply committed to freedom of expression and, on the other, passionate about the elimination of racism. The conflict that has occurred is not between opposing groups who have no sympathy for each other's point of view. It is a conflict within ourselves over two equally compelling values. I do not doubt that those who are most outspoken on the University's inaction regarding the design piece are also enormously concerned about freedom of expression. The struggle to rid this society of racism has depended and will continue to depend on constitutional protections of free expression, especially in a time when forces in our society with less noble motives seek opportunities to curtail those protections. I am equally convinced that those who argue that the University would not have acted, on freedom of expression grounds, are devoted adherents to the goal of a nonracist, nondiscriminatory society. Expression cannot be truly free in a society in which all citizens do not share a sense of inclusion and in which individuality and difference can be reasons for exclusion.

It would be a sorry outcome if we let this episode divide us to the benefit of those who do not share our commitment to freedom of expression and to the search for a more just and humane society.

# A Sanctuary of Nonrepression

(SELECTED FROM AIMS OF EDUCATION CONVOCATION, SEPTEMBER 1990)

Our founders, and those who initiated the University in Exile, forcefully rejected the idea that any member of an academic community might be subjected to persecution or harassment on the basis of race, ethnicity, religion, or ideology. Mindful of our history, this university today must be firmly dedicated to being a community in which intolerance, be it overt or subtle, is repudiated. It is not enough to list in our catalogues the characteristics on which we do not discriminate. The issue is far greater than discrimination in employment or admissions. It is a question of how we treat one another. We stipulate that those characteristics on which we do not discriminate—and the list is much longer than it was in our founders' time—will also not be factors that impinge upon our personal and professional relationships. No one in this community should have to endure coercion, torment, ridicule, intimidation, or exclusion or be subject to acts of enmity or insensitivity. Our university must be, in the words of political theorist Amy Gutmann, a "sanctuary of nonrepression."

All of us share the responsibility for achieving that objective. The university trustees, faculty, and administration can articulate fundamental policies, but the quality of our community depends even more on the everyday attitudes and practices of its members. For the most part, this university has been spared ugly episodes of harassment on the basis of individual differences; and I believe the vast majority of our community, virtually everyone, shares the values of which I have just spoken. But it takes only a few isolated instances of harassment to engender fear and mistrust among people who have felt the lash of discrimination in their lives, and to undermine the confidence we all have in the special capacity of a university community to transcend the divisions that plague the society around us.

Shortly there will be in place a formal policy on discriminatory harassment. A draft is being discussed throughout the university, and I will recommend final language to the Trustees soon. It is worth taking a moment here to recite the core of that policy and to invite comments from you while it is still a draft.

Discriminatory harassment refers to intimidation by threats and acts of violence, and personal vilification of university members on the basis of their race, color, religion, gender, sexual orientation, ethnic origin, or handicap. Speech or other expression can constitute discriminatory harassment by personal vilification if it (1) deliberately insults, stigmatizes, threatens, or intimidates an individual or a small number of individuals on the basis of the characteristics just mentioned; (2) is addressed directly to the individual or individuals whom it insults or stigmatizes; and (3) makes use of "fighting" words or nonverbal symbols.

In the context of discriminatory harassment, fighting words or nonverbal symbols are words, pictures, or other signs that, by virtue of their form, are commonly understood to convey direct hatred or contempt for human beings on the basis of one or more of the categories of personal attributes contained in the policy on nondiscrimination.

The implementation of this policy will take great wisdom and care. There is no pat formula for words or phrases or visual images that are proscribed, or for contexts or settings that make such forms of expression objectionable. Each case—and we all hope and expect there will be very few—will have its own dimensions and unique characteristics and must be evaluated by a special faculty-student committee constituted for this purpose.

Let me be clear that a policy on discriminatory harassment does not and must not compromise the University's commitment to freedom of expression. All new students have received the policy on free expression, and I urge you to read it.

At the very heart of the New School's identity is the certainty that all ideas and artistic forms, no matter how objectionable, can find expression here. The university's policy on the free exchange of ideas is explicit when it says:

> A university in any meaningful sense of the term is compromised without unhindered exchanges of ideas, however unpopular, and without the assurance that both the presentation and confrontation of ideas takes place freely and without coercion.... Faculty members, administrators, staff members, students and guests are obligated to reflect in their actions a respect for the right of all individuals to speak their views freely and be heard.

Our policy appreciates the legitimate right of dissent, even protests against a speaker, but not actions that involve intimidation or that cause an event to be canceled. And the policy does not apply only to speech or written language. It extends to visual expression and performance as well.

Some may see a conflict between the New School's firm commitment to freedom of expression and its equally strong determination to prohibit discriminatory harassment. But I do not. General statements of opinion and artistic images—no matter how offensive—must be protected. But acts that discriminate against or defame or degrade specific individuals cannot be seen to rise to the level of protected speech under the university's freedom of expression policy. Freedom of expression should not be a shield for acts intended to harm by discriminating or by singling out in order to defame.

Every member of this community should feel confident that the university will take action against verified acts of discriminatory harassment. But I would also ask that such acts be kept in perspective and that the university community as a whole not be tarred with the brush of institutional racism or sexism or any other "ism" or phobia because of the acts of an irresponsible few. Such a response displays the very kind of group characterization that we seek to avoid as we try to treat each person on his or her individual merits.

I have spoken of two values that are at the heart of any university: freedom from intolerance and harassment and also freedom of expression. We do not have to choose between the two. Both are essential to the existence of a community that is based on reason and respect for individuals. Both are deeply held by the vast majority of our friends and colleagues. Both values are so intertwined and interdependent that without one, the other's meaning is sharply diminished.

As the New School pursues its commitment to reflect, better than it now does, the diversity of this city and country, it will play a role in the most urgent domestic issue of our time: how to make American democratic pluralism work. Discourse on this issue will no doubt be intense, perhaps even uncomfortable. But rather than shrink from those conversations—or see them, as the media does, as a rise of tension on campus—let us embrace the dialogue as a sign of progress, a necessary step in fulfilling the promise of America so eloquently articulated in the Declaration of Independence.

Whether you have just arrived at the New School or whether you can look back on years of membership in this community, may your time here help you become a more sensitive, open, tolerant, and understanding person, capable of appreciating and respecting a broad range of traditions and points of view. We are here to help make that possible, but you have to take responsibility for allowing the forces around you—at this university and in this city—to stretch you and help you grow.

# Reaffirming the Commitment to Freedom of Expression

(REMARKS TO THE INDEPENDENT COMMITTEE
ON ARTS POLICY, MARCH 1991)

In the 1960s and 1970s I worked for Kingman Brewster, president of Yale. I well recall struggling to make it possible for controversial speakers, those who would generally be thought of as "right wing" or "conservative," to be heard: General William Westmoreland during the Vietnam War, William Shockley and Arthur Jensen in racially tense New Haven, for example. And there were the pitched battles over the Marine recruiters and representatives from Dow Chemical. In 1978, when I moved to the University of Chicago with President Hanna Gray, our first test was to make it possible for former Defense Secretary Robert McNamara to speak at an occasion honoring him with the Pick Peace Prize.

The challenge deepened as I moved to the New School. In 1985 representatives of the Army War College, invited to speak by a class at Lang College, were driven out, literally, by egg-throwing protesters. I heard about this days later, and then only as an interschool squabble in which undergraduates were complaining that graduate students had horned in on their event. I was appalled that no one saw in the episode an issue of free speech—so appalled, in fact, that I asked the Board of Trustees to enact a policy reaffirming the university's commitment to free expression. I also appointed a faculty committee to give some careful thought to the issue, and its report led to a strengthening of the policy on the free exchange of ideas and, later on, to the addition of the statement on artistic freedom.

It may seem odd that a value so fundamental to a university needs to be the subject of a specific policy. One might think that membership in a university community brings with it an affirmation of the principles of academic and artistic freedom. Sadly, this is not true today—either for students or for many faculty. As a consequence, a good deal of our time has been spent discussing these issues in our community.

In one academic year I have been attacked for being both too rigidly attached to the principle of free expression and too willing to abandon that principle in favor of censorship. And I have been praised for defending free expression. It is instructive that a set of actions and policies which I see as entirely consistent and interdependent can evoke such disparate reactions.

My overweaning devotion to free expression was criticized when I decided to leave in place a print in an exhibition in the Parsons Gallery which contained an unflattering racial stereotype. That decision brought a protest in which a member of the faculty defaced the print and encouraged other faculty and students to follow suit. Spinning out of the episode were charges of institutional racism and Eurocentrism in the curriculum, among others.

Then, in the spring of the same school year, my reputation as an advocate of free expression grew when the New School sued the National Endowment for the Arts because we thought the antiobscenity certification attached to a small grant to redesign a courtyard was unconstitutional. With the help of good amicus briefs from the Rockefeller Foundation and the ACLU, we and the Bella Lewitsky Dance Foundation, which brought a parallel suit using our legal briefs, managed to force the NEA to drop the condition from its 1990 grants. The Lewitsky case elicited some good language from the federal judge.

In California, Judge John Davies ruled against the NEA on constitutional grounds. The court held not only that the language of the condition was unconstitutionally vague, producing a chilling effect on speech, but also that the oath would cause grant recipients to "steer far wider of the unlawful zone than if the boundaries of the forbidden were clearly marked."

The court found that this vagueness was not cured by the NEA's policy adopting the *Miller* standard on obscenity because, among other things, the NEA could change its policy anytime. The decision also stated that while the government may be able to put restrictions on whom and how it subsidizes, once the government does subsidize, it cannot do so in a manner that carries with it a level of vagueness that violates the First and Fifth Amendments.

Our case, on the other hand, was settled short of a decision on the constitutional question. Judge Louis Stanton applied heavy pressure on the NEA to remove the antiobscenity certification from the form we are required to sign. He made his view clear that the NEA's frequent flip-flopping had essentially proved our point: that a grant recipient could not hope to know what was required of it under the antiobscenity certification. The NEA finally did rescind the certification and replaced it with language similar to the NEA's own internal guidelines—something to the effect that the grantee recognizes that if it is convicted of creating obscenity with NEA funds, the NEA will move to recover the money. At our insistence, this resolution is available to all other grantees.

Our settlement goes beyond the California case, which applies only to grantees in the Central District of California. The settlement also weakens the government's chances of a successful appeal in California, making that decision more likely to stand. Taken together, the two cases represent a complete victory for our position.

We hope and believe that our case—which some in the New York arts establishment sought to dissuade us from filing—had a beneficial influence on the congressional debate which led to better language in the 1991 reauthorization of the NEA. The decision about obscenity is now left to the courts, where the sensible standard articulated in the *Miller* case will apply.

So much for Mr. Free Speech. Now enter Mr. Censorship. All in the same year.

College campuses nationwide have been grappling with so-called hate speech and discriminatory harassment. While the New School has been relatively free of overt conflict among students of different backgrounds, we nevertheless thought it necessary to have a policy in place—both to act as a deterrent and to provide a fair and just way of handling ugly episodes if they did arise.

Our policy on discriminatory harassment follows the model policy proposed by Stanford law professor Thomas Gray. We believe the policy, which quite narrowly defines the line between protected expression and discriminatory harassment, would withstand a constitutional test. I should point out that all three tests must be met for an utterance to constitute discriminatory harassment: it has to be *deliberately* insulting or intimidating; it has to be addressed *directly* to an individual or small group of individuals; and it has to make use of *fighting words*. So the print in the Parsons Gallery would not constitute discriminatory harassment, nor would a lecture by Professor Michael Levin contending that African-Americans are genetically inferior to whites intellectually—no matter how offensive either of these instances of expression might be.

Despite the narrowness and specificity of the policy, it has drawn some opposition from within our faculty, particularly from the art and design faculty. These opponents do not want to concede that there should be any constraints on the use of words and symbols, notwithstanding limits recognized by the Supreme Court ("fire" in a crowded theater) and widespread support for a sexual harassment policy. They see this policy as having a chilling effect on free expression and being tantamount to censorship. Other opponents see the policy as too narrow and, once again, too respectful of free expression. Some of these people think that Professor Levin, or let's say David Duke, should not be permitted to speak because their very presence would be insulting or intimidating. And many would say that general racial insults, not directed at any particular individual or individuals, should be prohibited and punishable.

Now, as a practical matter, it was a good thing that our stand on the racist print and the NEA suit preceded the discriminatory harassment policy, because we had built up enough trust in our defense of artistic freedom to open people's minds to the case for the discriminatory harassment policy. While there is some opposition to the discriminatory harassment policy, we have been able to bring many people —who probably had doubts—around to supporting it. We see the freedom of expression and the discriminatory harassment policies as being of a piece, consistent with each other, reinforcing each other. I resist the pleas to set these values in some hierarchy that pits good people against each other, especially when they should be making common cause against the real merchants of repression in our society.

Those of us in the majority must recognize the existence of harassment—sometimes using words and symbols—on the basis of race, religion, gender, sexual orientation, and other personal characteristics. And it is a healthy development that young people on college campuses won't stand for discriminatory harassment and expect the institution to reject it as well. But it is also true that those who see the elimination of discrimination as the highest goal must also see the difference between discriminatory harassment and expression that merely offends, the difference between hateful speech intended to harm a specific individual and a print in the Parsons Gallery which contains a racially offensive stereotype.

Hair-trigger readiness to abridge free expression in pursuit of a favored political position seems to be prevalent across the ideological spectrum. To be sure, there are examples aplenty: from Jesse Helms on obscenity to George Bush on the flag to the black alderman in Chicago who ripped down the portrait of Mayor Harold Washington at the Art Institute. And the media have made much of politically correct thought on campus. Political correctness strikes me as a superficial symptom of a deeper ailment in our colleges: the absence of the confrontation of opposing views in civilized discussion and the acceptance of censorship by demonstrations as a fact of life. Both concern me deeply. Both have eroded genuine intellectual freedom on campus. Both cut at the heart of what a university is all about.

Have you noticed that government officials don't speak on major college campuses as much as they used to? Indeed, controversial speakers of all kinds are less welcome these days.

And it isn't just the left who might be expected to go after, say, Defense Secretary Richard Cheney or FBI Director William Webster. It's the Palestinians who tried to prevent Yitzhak Rabin from speaking at the New School last December; or the gay activists who tried to disrupt a *New York Times* event at the New School in protest against an editorial; or the students at Trinity College who opposed Minister Farrakhan. Stopping speech to make your point is thought to be fair game—so much so that faculty and student groups now quietly indulge in self-censorship to avoid the inconvenience or embarrassment that attends a controversial speaker. When we do have a controversial speaker our whole top administration drops everything to become a council of war for a day or two so that we are prepared to do our part to thwart the censors when they arrive. And if we didn't, the few events that did feature controversial speakers would be disrupted almost every time.

This general tendency to the bland also reveals itself in the makeup of courses and panels. Balance now means you have one event reaching to the confirmed radical, another to the progressive center and, when we are lucky, one to the right of center. It is all too rare that well-informed experts who disagree occupy the same space so students can learn from the interplay of their views.

It seems to me that we have a great deal of work to do to encourage faculty and students to help in promoting a diversity of viewpoints on every issue. And trustees can help— first by making it clear that a university itself doesn't take official positions on issues that do not directly affect higher education. The trustees themselves have contributed to the erosion of free speech on campus by compromising their fundamental responsibility to be sure that all views are not just heard, but are welcome. When a university itself takes an official position—whether it be boycotting nonunion lettuce or using the endowment portfolio to advance certain public policies, like the end of apartheid, or opposing a particular war—they make it harder for contrary views to surface on campus. So I think we start with the trustees and get it straight that the board should not take official positions on matters not directly related to higher education.

Next we work on the faculty and, with their help, the students. Faculty-student committees to rearticulate the university's policy on free expression are a start, but real progress is made, I think, incrementally. We must encourage the presence of speakers from widely divergent viewpoints and work hard to be sure they are heard. We need courses, panels, and symposia which put people of different views together. We need to support students and faculty who have the courage to challenge the "politically correct" notions of the day. I hesitate to call them the "silent majority," but I am convinced that an overwhelming majority of our students and faculty are committed to the values of intellectual and artistic freedom. But they need help in understanding that those values are not slogans, but complicated concepts. I offer no heroic, magic solutions—just a return to some essential notions of what a university is all about, and an old-fashioned belief that leadership matters and has a big role to play here.

If we cannot sustain the conditions of vigorous and civilized debate on university campuses, then I despair about the larger society's capacity to bridge the widening ravines that divide us. In the end, our society may not be able to survive the diversity it embraced in a more optimistic and self-confident era.

I think the jury is still out.

# THE MULTIPLE MEANINGS OF POLITICAL CORRECTNESS

(SELECTED FROM AIMS OF EDUCATION ADDRESS, SEPTEMBER 1991)

If I am at least partially correct in divining who you are and what brought you here, then the topic of "political correctness" must have crossed your minds. The term "political correctness," I confess, is not one of my favorites. It is invoked rather loosely these days but it is most commonly used by those who allege that free thought, inquiry, and expression are under duress on college campuses.

I think we should face up to the fact that from time to time our campuses *are* less hospitable to different points of view than they should be. These moments come in cycles—recall the age of conformity in the 1950s or the fervent prowar sentiment during World Wars I and II. I do not believe the pressure today toward common attitudes about multiculturalism, feminism, and other issues approaches the intensity of these past episodes.

But the intellectual atmosphere at some universities today does seem less tolerant than it should be. Conservative ideas and speakers are not always welcome on many campuses, and there are some students who at least perceive pressure to adopt a correct position on certain issues. So it is timely for us to examine our own practices to be sure we are a community in which all points of view can be held and heard.

That should be relatively easy for the New School, since it owes its existence to an earlier effort to enforce politically correct thought on campus. In 1919, when Columbia President Nicholas Murray Butler tried to suppress opposition to World War I among his faculty, historian Charles Beard and several colleagues quit in protest. Beard, John Dewey, Thorstein Veblen, and others joined together to found the New School, at which respect for freedom of speech, thought, and inquiry would be core values. Over the years, the New School has been dedicated to providing a forum for both conventional and unconventional wisdom—even ideas that some found irresponsible and highly offensive. That tradition continues today.

Nothing could be further from the central purpose of this institution than pressure on faculty and students by their peers to agree to a politically correct party line or to be silent. If you encounter such pressure from any source at the University, resist it. You should talk with your deans and faculties—or with me. Every member of this community enjoys a guaranteed right to hold and express his or her own views no matter how outrageous.

This guarantee is set forth in the University's policy on freedom of expression and artistic freedom. But a policy is only as good as its implementation. All of us—students, faculty, administration—bear joint responsibility for sustaining free expression on this campus. And we bear equal responsibility for making sure that free expression guarantees are not abused to license acts of discriminatory harassment. These acts include aiming words or deeds at a particular individual on the basis of a personal characteristic, with the intention to hurt, and using fighting words as defined in the University's policy on discriminatory harassment.

When university communities falter in their obligation to ensure an atmosphere which encourages free expression, they become vulnerable to forces in our society which have little respect for artists and intellectuals. The phenomenon of "political correctness" has been a gold mine for those who believe educational institutions are fomenting social changes which undermine an older view of a homogeneous American society free of class, race, ethnic, gender, and other divisions. These defenders of the old order have expanded the term to cover virtually every effort to redefine this antiquated conception of our nation.

Here are some examples of other issues which have become intertwined with political correctness:

- In New York State a plan to revise the public school history and social studies curriculum has been denounced as political correctness run wild. Proposals to give attention to the experience and contribution of different groups are said to emphasize the "pluribus" over the "unum"—our cultural differences over our common heritage.
- It has been suggested that slaves be described as "enslaved persons" and that Thanksgiving be seen, not as a celebration, but as an occasion for sober reflection about the atrocities committed against Native Americans.
- The movement to replace terms like "Far East" with "East Asia" arouses concern that history is being rewritten under political pressure.

On college campuses a similar controversy is sparked by efforts, for example, to modify the standard Western civilization courses to reflect contributions by African-American or women writers—at the expense of Plato or Proust, Hegel or Heidegger, Foucault or Freud.

Efforts by universities to offer protection against discriminatory harassment are attacked as impinging on free speech with the intent of enforcing politically correct modes of expression. Listen to President Bush at the University of Michigan commencement last spring. He said that politically correct thinking "has invited people to look for an insult in every word, gesture, and action... in their own Orwellian way, crusades that demand correct behavior crush diversity in the name of diversity."

It is a short, if not logical, leap from that rhetorical excess to the conclusion that affirmative action is political correctness in another guise. Thus efforts to make our colleges more representative of the larger society are under assault. Recall that just last year the U.S. Department of Education sought to prohibit special scholarships designed to make it possible for African-Americans and Latinos to have the choice to attend high-quality private colleges.

I could go on, but you get the point. Political correctness

has a double meaning these days. It is used both to characterize pressures for a kind of conformist thinking on race, gender, and class and *also* as a weapon to resist genuine and legitimate reforms in the way our society deals with its diversity. To be sure, there are examples of overzealousness on both sides. There is plenty of room for legitimate concern with efforts to suppress unpopular views on campus, with discriminatory harassment policies that blatantly transgress the First Amendment, with curricular changes that are intellectually sloppy, or with affirmative action programs that are poorly implemented.

But there should be an equal concern about using the concept of political correctness to distort a genuine and needed debate occurring in our society. "Political correctness" has become one more code phrase in a century-old battle between those comfortable with American pluralism and those threatened by it. This battle has flared at times when change was most needed—the 1890s, the 1920s, the 1950s, and the present—every 30 or so years, it seems. The symbols in the 1920s included the Scopes trial, prohibition, and Sacco and Vanzetti. And McCarthyism in the 1950s stood for a lot more than a single senator from Wisconsin. In our own time we have the controversy over the National Endowment for the Arts and the canon.

We should resist the temptation to enter the war of escalating rhetoric. Rather, we should do what members of intellectual communities do best: identify and understand the issues that underlie the conflict. Let me offer a few ideas to start the conversation.

First, the curriculum. Sometime after the midpoint of this century, the effort to offer a curriculum that introduced college students to what they needed to know broke under the weight of an exponential growth in knowledge. Four years is simply not enough time to introduce students to science, the arts, and Western literary and philosophical traditions—let alone to the rest of the world.

Faculties are still struggling with the problem, some preferring a retreat to a core curriculum, others a structured distributional sampling, still others little or no structure at all. This puzzle would exist even without advocates of a multicultural curriculum.

In fact, the explosion of knowledge, together with the practical imperatives flowing from an interdependent world, would pose much the same challenge for the curriculum even if we were a homogeneous society. The process of curricular reform has always been, as it should be, continuous. Many of the changes now attacked as politically correct began *before* the present controversy, simply as a recognition that we need to know more about other traditions, other parts of the world.

I think it is just plain irresponsible to dismiss genuine efforts to make the curriculum more pluralistic as pandering to political correctness. Those who advocate returning to a more structured core curriculum for pedagogical reasons make a mistake in linking their quest with those who really do want to resist the inclusion of different traditions simply because they do not respect them.

My second consideration has to do with the implications of the charter documents of this country—the Declaration of Independence, the Constitution and Bill of Rights, the *Federalist Papers*. They contain some very radical notions about individual rights and the organization of societies. We know it is taking time to bring our practice into compliance with those theories—and we have a way to go yet—but the pace of change has accelerated very sharply. Suddenly, words like "equality," "justice," and "nondiscrimination" are not sources of self-righteous cant, but are seen as holding promise for tangible rearrangements in material resources and relations among people.

It should not surprise us, then, that the prospect of genuine social change engenders fear among people who believe they have something to lose as the redistribution of power and wealth occurs. Their fear produces opposition to measures designed to open opportunity to those who have been traditionally bypassed—measures like faculty affirmative action programs and scholarships targeted to underrepresented groups.

Those who would resist change face a daunting challenge. It is hard to make the pejorative interpretation of "political correctness" stick to ideas that draw their strength from the Constitution while at the same time lamenting the deterioration of a common heritage. The real problem is an unwillingness to share the essential elements of our common heritage with all who live in this country.

Paradoxically, it is this resistance to the full implementation of the American experiment which poses the greatest threat to the cohesion of our nation. And this is my third point. The defenders of the old order really know that social problems in America are getting worse and they fear a social explosion. They recognize that neither New Deal types of programs nor the Republican alternatives have worked to avert the rise of poverty, urban decay and despair.

In the absence of any plan to address the real social problems that are dividing our society, these defenders shift the field of battle to an intellectual plane where they think the old order has the advantage. Thus, one should see the exploitation of political correctness for what it is: a diversionary tactic.

But it won't work. Can anyone really believe that relatively small changes in the way American history is presented in grade school matter that much compared with the pervasive problems of poverty, adult illiteracy, unemployment, drugs, and all the rest?

Does anyone believe there is a curriculum which can celebrate some common view of our culture powerfully enough to offset the real conditions that poor children return to each night in urban slums?

The controversy over "political correctness" is a lot more than concern over a multicultural curriculum that gives short shrift to the classics or over a campus atmosphere that discourages young people from expressing their ideas for fear of offending a code of correct attitudes. In the hands of its exploiters, "political correctness" is also a sophisticated attempt to divert our attention from real social problems, a brazen effort to appropriate the intellectual high ground, a determined campaign to retard social progress and, in the end, the desperate last gasp of a 100-year losing battle to preserve the United States as a society which tolerates only as much diversity as can be fully absorbed—that is, melted in.

There are indeed mistakes being made on campuses. But they do not add up to a threat to the integrity of colleges; nor do they signify an era of intolerance and oppression in academia. The institutional protections for free inquiry at universities are very strong, and the grip of traditional views of knowledge and how it should be conveyed remains powerful. That some excesses occur in the process of reform is to be expected. Better those mistakes, however, than an entrenched refusal to make our universities more diverse and comfortable for diversity. We should be proud of the fact that the rising generation of Americans is confronting the real issues on which the future of the American experiment hinges—how the most heterogenous democratic society in the world deals with ethnic, gender, racial, class, religious, and other distinctions which have been the ruin of countries throughout history. Universities can be the model for what is possible for the larger society—indeed, can represent the best hope for the future of this nation.

So rather than join the muddled national debate over political correctness, I suggest that we at the New School focus on the principles of what a university is supposed to be and make sure that our university is a healthy intellectual community.

There are two broad areas we must continue to address. The first is the process of change that so worries the defenders of the old order: making our faculty, staff, and students more reflective of the composition of this city and country than they are, maintaining an atmosphere on campus that respects individual difference, and revising our curriculum to be sure that it is sufficiently pluralistic. I have spoken to these issues in the University's diversity initiative and they remain a high priority for all of us.

Second, we need always be alert to the condition of genuine free expression on our campus. The New School's first president, Alvin Johnson, spoke to a fundamental quality of the New School when he said:

> The New School is dedicated to freedom. It looks neither to right nor left, but like the Israelites under Moses passing through Edom, means to tread through no man's grain, to break no man's fence, to muddy no man's well, but to march straight toward the promised land of a more intelligent, a more peaceful, a more understanding, and, therefore, a more liberal humanity.

That commitment to freedom remains strong today. It is the nature of this place that it attracts a faculty with a progressive outlook. And while there may not be as much intellectual tension within the faculty as I would like, there surely is no accepted school of thought or party line here. Within our community, all points of view on just about every issue find expression. And whatever perspectives may not find ample exposure in the formal curriculum usually surface in the panels and guest speakers of the Adult Division courses, which are open to all full-time degree students free of charge.

Most important of all are the obligations and responsibilities each of us assumes in becoming a member of a university community: a respect for individuals, a willingness to tolerate the expression of deeply offensive views, and a commitment to air disagreements openly in rational discourse. Faculty members carry the additional obligation of designing a curriculum that is multidimensional, discloses no bias, adheres to the highest standards of intellectual rigor, and encourages each student to develop and express ideas even if at odds with their own.

Let us work together to build an intellectual community with these characteristics and leave to others the struggle over the symbolic meaning of "political correctness."

# Are Freedom of Expression and Freedom from Intolerance Mutually Exclusive?

(LETTER TO THE EDITOR, NEW YORK TIMES, DECEMBER 13, 1989)

The article "Debating Art: Censorship or Protest?" was a balanced and largely accurate report on the display at the New School's Parsons School of Design Gallery of a graphic design containing a racist caricature of a person of African heritage. While the article addressed the complexity of the issues and diversity of views on the decision that the piece should remain in the exhibition, there is more to say about the reasoning behind that decision.

The presence of racism in our society and beyond represents one of the greatest and most pervasive injustices of our time. We all bear a share of responsibility for its persistence. The New School is striving to be a community that values and seeks diversity among its members, that encourages respect for difference, and that is free from discrimination and intolerance of all kinds. It is disturbing to all of us when acts occur or ideas are expressed that are insensitive or insulting, particularly on racial grounds.

However, the question of how the university should have acted in response to the controversial piece is not one that could be decided only on the basis of the work's offensiveness. The New School's policy on freedom of expression asserts that visual and verbal expression enjoy the same protections in an academic community. The university has the responsibility to preserve an environment in which free expression can be exercised, no matter how offensive that expression might be. Individuals may be invited by students or faculty to speak, publish, display art, or perform; but this does not mean that the university sponsors or gives "official" sanction to the *content* of what those individuals say or do. It has no such sanction to give or withdraw.

Issuing a disclaimer or removing the graphic design from the exhibition would have implied that the university does make official judgments on the content of expression and that expression for which responsibility is not disclaimed has the institution's approval. Any suggestion that the university, acting as a corporate body, makes such judgments can only chill the environment for free expression. Yet no one should believe that, because a work of art or design which is (or is perceived to be be) racist or sexist hangs in a university gallery, the New School endorses or is insensitive to racism or sexism.

It is an unfortunate but inescapable corollary to the New School's position on free expression that protected acts of expression may occur which are insensitive, intolerant, or intended to offend. They may cause very deep pain and anger, as occurred at the New School. Vigorous protest against such acts—in this case, a graphic image—is entirely appropriate and called for. In fact, the university's policy recognizes the right to take exception to specific instances of expression and to dissent openly and emphatically. What the policy proscribes is dissent that prevents expression from occurring, including the defacement of art. Offensive as the image was, and justified as was the protest against it, defacing it was wrong.

I believe the article may have given the misimpression that the New School is divided between those who are deeply committed to freedom of expression and those who are passionate about the elimination of racism. There are few people here who are not torn over the issues the exhibit has raised. The conflict that has occurred is not between opposing groups who have no sympathy for each other's point of view. It is a conflict within ourselves over two compelling values.

The issue should not be framed as if freedom of expression and freedom from intolerance are incompatible. They are both cherished rights, and we should not have to choose which one we hold more dear. The question, I think, is how to use freedom of expression more assiduously in pursuit of a society free of prejudice and intolerance of all kinds.

The struggle to rid this society of racism will continue to depend on constitutional protections of free expression, especially in a time when forces in our country with less noble motives seek to curtail those protections. However, expression cannot truly be free in a society in which all citizens do not share a sense of inclusion and in which individuality and difference can be reasons for exclusion.

# Democracy, Pluralism, and the University

# Representation for the Un(der)represented

(ANNUAL REPORT, 1990)

With those optimistic observations as background, I want to talk with you about a challenge that suggests our progress is not as strong as we would like, a challenge that must be met if our other accomplishments are to have enduring value and meaning. The challenge is how to help the New School live up to its very high aspirations to be a genuinely multicultural community free of prejudice, intolerance, and harassment. Below I suggest a series of concrete actions which will build a more diverse and healthy university community, actions which call for an investment of funds donated for this purpose. But first let me make some general observations.

In the past year, hardly a week has gone by without a fresh report of tensions on college campuses on the basis of race, ethnicity, gender, or sexual orientation. The news media report a "rise of racism" on college campuses, leading all of us to wonder if the progress toward a healthy society that we thought had been made in the last quarter century was illusory.

These reports are indeed deeply troubling, and they remind us of just how tenacious and insidious the impulses of intolerance can be. But the widespread condemnation that manifestations of prejudice and discriminatory harassment have received is a positive sign, an indication of what may be a far more potent trend on campus than rising racism. The surfacing of long-standing tensions in ways that demand resolution can have a positive outcome if those tensions are properly understood and confronted.

The present generation of college students has a higher standard for human relationships than generations of the past and a greater disposition to upholding that standard. Our students accept as a given the progress made since World War II in ending legal barriers to equality, establishing codes on nondiscrimination, and pursuing affirmative action programs. They see their challenge as the building of a society free of prejudice, harassment, and discrimination in even the most subtle forms. Those experiencing discrimination or harassment feel empowered to oppose transgressions against their rights and to demand that the university community respect their rights. While the condition of national leadership in the last decade has not encouraged our students' vigorous participation in the political process, they are nonetheless idealistic in their aspirations for their personal relationships and in their expectations of the institutions of which they are a part.

This empowerment derives both from the society's more explicit commitment to equal opportunity and protection against discrimination and from the growth in the numbers of people in underrepresented groups on college campuses. As further progress is achieved in making university boards, faculties, staffs, and student bodies more representative, the surface manifestation of turmoil and tension is likely to intensify, thus increasing the challenge to fragile institutions but also the potential for genuine reform.

There are lessons to be learned from what is happening on college campuses. Universities have often been the seedbed for reforms urgently required by the larger society. We should see something of the future for American society in the open rejection of prejudice and discriminatory harassment on our college campuses and the quest for a higher standard of relations between people of different backgrounds. The results of the last three decades of struggle for equal rights are mixed and, in a way, dangerous. Genuine progress has been made in ending legal segregation and discrimination and in expanding opportunities for groups historically excluded from full participation in American society. Yet the disadvantages suffered by large numbers of people in these groups have actually worsened, and the plight of those who are especially vulnerable is now more entrenched.

It is the gap between the promises of the New Deal and subsequent reform movements, on the one hand, and this stubborn reality on the other which breeds disappointment and disillusionment. The hope and trust generated by the initial progress of those reform movements have been largely dissipated by a calculated, if largely unsuccessful, effort to roll back their accomplishments. The counterreform effort of the past decade has proceeded from very different assumptions about human nature, individual rights, and the good society. Yet history tells us that once unleashed, powerful ideas like equality, human rights, and freedom from discrimination cannot be resisted for long. Those ideas, embedded in our founding principles, have gathered moral force in the twentieth century and will soon again dominate public discourse on campuses and beyond, even if the philosophical differences elevated in the last decade make progress more difficult.

It seems to me that the central issue of our time is how to create a political economy which gives a fair chance to every citizen, guarantees a threshold of economic and personal security to all, and eradicates discrimination on the basis of individual differences. Closely linked to this central issue is the imperative to create a culture that has common elements reflective of the rich mosaic of traditions available to us, and that also respects the integrity of those traditions. Racial prejudice in American society is a special problem which has been particularly resistant to amelioration. Many believe, as I do, that race is the most serious domestic issue of our time. However, our aspirations rightly include treating all people alike. The impulse that animates the younger generation is all-inclusive in demanding a higher standard of respect for individual differences and an end to discrimination and harassment of all kinds. Our concern for all people who suffer discrimination must be evident, as we seek to make the most pluralistic democracy in history work.

Universities have a vital role to play. It should be easier for communities drawn together by a commitment to reasoned discourse to bridge individual and group differences. Very few universities—despite good intentions—have achieved a diverse faculty and student body or secured an environment sufficiently free of prejudice and intolerance, or built a curriculum adequately reflective of non-Western, nonmainstream traditions. It is fair to say, I think, after three decades of conscious effort, that good intentions are not enough anymore: tangible, measurable results are what matter.

What are the implications of all this for the New School for Social Research? We have often spoken of the special character of the New School, its commitment to New York, its mission to address unmet educational needs and underserved populations, its capacity to innovate and change. Those traditions should be a source of strength in stepping up to the challenges I have described. I believe we should agree on three central goals for the immediate future:

- A determined and prompt diversification of our governing boards, faculty, staff, and student body so that we much better reflect the composition of our home cities
- A review and revision of the curriculum of each of our schools to be sure that non-Western traditions are appropriately included
- A concerted effort to rid our community of discriminatory harassment as well as more subtle manifestations of prejudice and intolerance

I have in mind, not a set of cosmetic changes, but a steady evolution of the New School for Social Research. I am convinced that the kind of university we seek cannot be achieved through separation and avoidance or timid gestures to diversity. The steps we must take constitute a seamless web; what we seek to achieve is unattainable unless all elements of our plan proceed together. I believe the key point of intervention is the composition of the community itself. Much of the rest will follow once the reality of a more representative community begins to influence the practical aspects of institutional life. Stimulated by a very thoughtful set of recommendations contained in the report of the faculty and student committee chaired by Professor Richard Bernstein, I propose these specific actions:

- The Board of Trustees and the visiting committees for each of the University's seven schools should sharply increase membership from underrepresented groups.
- Each school should set specific numerical targets for entering students from underrepresented groups, targets which should increase annually until each school reaches an acceptable level of diversity. Because the cost of high-quality private education presents a formidable barrier to such students, we need to raise outside funds for a new "University Scholars" program which provides 50 (growing to 200) special scholarships annually to African-American and Latino students (above and beyond all other forms of financial aid). Particular attention should be focused on Ph.D. programs in which progress has been painfully slow. It will be impossible to achieve more diverse faculties until universities train more African-American and Latino Ph.D. students.
- Funds should be gathered to create special dissertation fellowships for African-American and Latino graduate students in the final year of their Ph.D. studies. The fellows would teach part time at the University, most likely in Lang College, while completing their dissertations.
- Each school should set specific numerical targets and timetables for increasing underrepresented groups in full- and part-time faculty and staff positions. The University will seek to raise extra resources to advance this effort so that normal budgetary constraints can be eased.
- A plan should be devised to increase the presence of African-Americans and Latinos in all the administrative offices, especially at the senior management level. Particular attention should be given to career development opportunities for talented staff already at the university.
- Each school should engage in a comprehensive review of its curriculum and make revisions as necessary to ensure that non-Western traditions are properly reflected. Special funds will be needed for the development of new courses and programs as well as the revision of existing courses. A particular commitment should be made to broaden the

curriculum of the Adult Division in order to provide programming of interest to more diverse audiences.

- When necessary, special support programs, such as the highly successful Higher Education Opportunity Program (HEOP) at Parsons, should be created or expanded. HEOP offers scholarships, counseling, and tutorial assistance to economically and academically disadvantaged students with strong potential.
- A very specific policy against discriminatory harassment should be put in place together with a process for making case by case judgments when allegations arise. A network of counselors should be created to work with students, faculty, and staff who feel they have experienced discriminatory harassment.
- The mandate of the University Committee on Equal Opportunity should be strengthened so it can take leadership in monitoring progress on every aspect of this initiative. A new position should be created to staff the work of the committee.

I believe these measures can be implemented without compromising academic standards and indeed will enhance the quality of the university's intellectual life.

Let me caution against expectations that the changes we seek will come in a year or two. While it should be possible to record tangible, measurable progress quickly, the larger goals will take longer to achieve. Scholarship monies will be essential to opening opportunity to underrepresented groups, and it will take time to raise the funds. The current pool of African-American and Latino scholars is much smaller than we would like and is actively sought after by many institutions. This reality will hamper our efforts to achieve a more diverse faculty. Curriculum review and revision are rightly the province of the faculties at the departmental level, and decentralized processes move at an uneven pace. Individual attitudes, reflecting deep-seated prejudices in the larger society, will not change overnight.

All this we know, and that knowledge should protect us against unrealistic expectations and the cynicism that incvitably follows when such hopes are not immediately realized. Yet we must not accept these genuine obstacles to progress as excuses for inaction or lay the responsibility for poor performance on the larger society. Implicit in what I have proposed is the belief that this university community can control its own destiny if the commitment for change is widely shared and deeply held by the governing boards, faculty, staff, and students.

# The Democratic Experiment: Have We Succeeded?

(SELECTED FROM COMMENCEMENT, MAY 1990)

The American Revolution and the early years of the Republic gave rise to some radical notions about how people should live together, the inalienable rights to which all are entitled, and the protections that should be afforded to minorities. Our national rhetoric has more often than not embraced both freedom and pluralism—the "melting pot," a "nation of immigrants," a "gorgeous mosaic." Yet rhetoric and practice have often been inconsistent. Whether slavery, immigration quotas on ethnic groups, the internment of Japanese Americans during World War II, the internal security acts that led to the McCarthy era, or the legal segregation that persisted into our own times, examples abound of official government acts at odds with our founding principles.

It is ironic that at the very time when aspirations for freedom and equality are manifest around the world, we seem to waver in our quest to complete the American Revolution. Old-fashioned anti-Semitism, homophobia, gender discrimination, and deep-seated racial prejudice are increasingly apparent. Intolerance in the guise of moral decency is beginning to impinge on free expression. Ugly instances of harassment on the basis of individual differences are occurring all too frequently around the country, in this city, and on college campuses where we, perhaps complacently, expect a higher standard of sensitivity. The "kinder, gentler" nation that our President seeks is revealed as a rapidly fading mirage. And our confidence has been shaken in just how civil a society we really are.

We are reminded this year that free expression is a fragile gift in constant need of being defended. There are always those ready to narrow the range of expression that is allowable in order to meet their own ideological ends or simply protect themselves from ideas and images they find discomforting. The National Endowment for the Arts (NEA) was created to promote artistic expression. But now, in order to receive funds, grant recipients must sign a pledge not to violate certain standards of offensiveness that are poorly explained and open to wide interpretation and abuse. The NEA is expected, in effect, to make judgments on the content of art and possibly the ideas inherent in art. One of the very purposes of the NEA—to create a more open society—has been undermined.

As we applaud courageous people abroad for seizing freedom from the hands of dictators and despots, are we seeing the erosion of our own freedoms through a more subtle, American form of censorship? All of us concerned about the arts and about free expression have a duty to oppose such threats to this cherished right so fundamental to our national identity. Yet even as we struggle to shield expression from those who would limit it, we must be aware of the many ways freedom continues to be denied to large segments of our society, even in places where we think freedom is in full flower.

Although the legal framework for segregation and discrimination has been dismantled in the last generation, the more difficult challenge of rooting out individual acts of intolerance and harassment still remains. The all too frequent appearances recently of racial hatred cut at the very heart of our civic values just as do attacks on free expression. Our response should not be laws that curtail expression, lest we fall into the same trap that now holds the NEA. Rather, we must strike at the conditions within our society that trigger such animosity—conditions like poverty, inequality, fear of difference, and prejudice of all kinds.

Our best hopes for America will not be realized if we are a collection of separate cultural homelands joined together only in commerce, war, and government. There is a new urgency in coming to grips with the full implications of American pluralism. We sorely need political leadership on the national level which elevates our best instincts rather than exacerbates our worst.

This process is difficult, requiring as it does a transformation of attitudes, even of human nature. It is conducted not only on the grand scale of changes in government policy but also on the smaller, more intimate scale of changes in the way we conduct our everyday lives. It is a process that occurs most effectively in the institutions that play important roles for each of us: places of work, houses of worship, cultural organizations, schools and—significantly for those of us here—universities.

The last time our nation addressed issues of social injustice with genuine resolve was in the 1960s. The New School for Social Research made an important educational contribution during that period.

But some have said this University has not done enough lately to address issues of diversity and bigotry, and I agree with them. I want to see the faculty and students of the New School once again take leadership—in challenging the status quo, in shaping the agenda for a new burst of domestic reform, and in mounting a fresh assault on discrimination on the basis of gender, race, or sexual orientation. This aspiration has implications for the formal curriculum of each of our schools, for the topics and people featured in special lectures and colloquia, and in the faculty's research programs. It also has implications for the composition of our community of trustees, faculty, staff, and students.

We must dedicate ourselves to seeking greater diversity at this university and, more important, to creating an environment which respects and honors differences. University communities can and should hold themselves to a higher standard of human relations than does the broader society; they can and should serve as examples of how people with individual and philosophical differences can live and work together in an environment of mutual respect. This should be our goal for the New School.

The American social experiment is now at a critical juncture. It is up to the best in our society—institutions like the New School, individuals like you who are graduating today—to provide the impetus for the reforms that are essential.

Much is at stake: the quality of our own lives and personal relationships, the well-being of the institutions we value and their ability to diminish discord, and the internal harmony of our nation and its stature as a beacon of hope for oppressed peoples. The reflection we see in the mirror of world events is less complimentary than we would like. But those events also teach us the possibilities inherent in commitment, courage, determination, and perseverance. Let us join these qualities to the promise of our own democratic revolution as we pursue together a more just and humane society.

# AGE OF FRAGMENTATION... OR PLURALISM?

(COMMENCEMENT, MAY 1993)

The Eastern and Central European revolutions put seven countries on the path to democracy and free market economies; the disintegration of the Soviet Union formalized the end of the Cold War and contributed fifteen new countries to the world; apartheid in South Africa is on the road to extinction; a coalition of four prodemocracy parties won elections in Thailand, completing the return of power to civilian hands; voters in Burundi and Togo approved new constitutions that establish multiparty elections; the Latin American country of Surinam voted out a military puppet regime, replacing it with a civilian president committed to the full restoration of democratic rule. In the past 4 years, sixty-one countries have moved decisively toward democracy. And during that same period, forty-five countries (including our own) found new leaders. A profound transformation occurred in the American political landscape with the advent of a new generation of leadership with a mandate for change in domestic priorities. But this has not been a period of unalloyed progress: we should remember that twenty-two countries regressed toward more authoritarian regimes; the powerful coalition that contained Saddam Hussein failed to stop ethnic cleansing and other horrors in the former Yugoslavia; and six armed conflicts now underway in the former Soviet Union, in places like Nagorno Karabakh and South Ossetia, alert us to the potential for disorder and disintegration that could sweep from Moldova to Tajikistan.

Few students in recent times have had the world change so fundamentally while they studied. How do we make sense of all that is happening? What implications might these transformations have for leaders and for those who choose and influence them? How should you think about your own place in this new world?

As an historian, I always seek a pattern in historical events, no matter how random or chaotic they may appear. I asked myself the other day: How might future historians characterize these years? As the age of democratic revolutions? The age of fragmentation? The age of global interdependence? My own first thought—not so simply phrased—was the age of contention between local and cosmopolitan values. But my more optimistic hope is the age of pluralism.

Our time seems to be awash in paradoxes. There are many signs that internationalism will triumph and that democracy and freedom will overcome authoritarian repression: European integration, the globalization of finance and communication, the Rio Conference on the Environment, more widely accepted international standards for human rights, and a reinvigorated United Nations with peacekeeping forces in thirteen locations. And yet, paradoxically, the lifting of repression and the movement toward democracy appear to unleash fierce attachments to narrow group identities, some based on geography, others on religion and ethnicity. With these newly liberated identities, the uglier side of human nature seems to emerge as well: the rise of nationalism, the reemergence of anti-Semitism, the flowering of neo-Nazi groups, the increased violence against foreigners in even the most prosperous countries, and, of course, the awful spectacle in the former Yugoslavia and the dreadful potential in the former Soviet Union.

How can it be that in 1992, the year of European integration, Yugoslavia fell into genocide and the Czechs and Slovaks divorced? How do we make sense of these apparently contradictory trends?

We are seeing, I think, graphic depictions of two tendencies that characterize individuals and political groupings alike. One of these tendencies is to focus on one's own self-interest. The other is to focus on interests that transcend the self and are shared by others—what might be called communal interests. At the level of political discourse, self-interest may be manifested as a preoccupation with local concerns, while communal interest is reflected in a cosmopolitan outlook.

These two tendencies, the self-centered and the communal, the local and the cosmopolitan, reside together in most of us and in the larger groups of which we are a part: towns, cities, states, nations, ethnic and religious groups. Each is a fundamental and necessary part of our being. They coexist in varying degrees of balance and harmony. Sometimes they compete with one another, and the balance has to be adjusted. Sometimes they are in direct conflict. And sometimes they can harden into more dangerous tendencies.

The local outlook can easily degenerate into parochialism, in which interests are confined to a very narrow sphere, with indifference or even hostility to larger concerns. A parochial view heightens our sense of sameness and difference. Parochial communities define themselves by the similarities they share and by how they are different from others. However, when similarities take on the aura of good and differences become bad, parochialism degenerates further into bias, prejudice, hatred, and even violence.

We tend to think of the cosmopolitan outlook as inherently good, with its connotation of belonging to the whole world, transcending national prejudices, and subscribing to universal values like democracy, human rights, and economic growth. But cosmopolitanism too has dangerous possibilities. Leaders with a cosmopolitan outlook can become transfixed on their associations with other leaders. They risk seeing themselves as citizens of the world and becoming detached from the needs of ordinary people. Cosmopolitan tendencies can soar to a level of generality that makes them irrelevant to everyday reality. Another danger occurs when a nation begins to see its values as universal, and thus good for everyone, and so tries to impose those values on others. A cosmopolitan outlook can become elitist, and it can quickly degenerate into dogmatism.

It seems to me, as we have watched democracy advance and retreat in recent years, as we have witnessed revolution and civil conflict, that it has been easy to indulge in stereotypes about these two spheres of interest. The guilt of stereotyping lies with the media, some international organizations, and even some scholars. All local concerns are parochial and thus bad, goes the conventional wisdom; all cosmopolitan outlooks are unifying and peaceful and thus good. This, I think, is a fruitless way of understanding the world's current opportunities and predicaments. We must acknowledge the legitimacy of both the local and the cosmopolitan, understand that they represent two dimensions of human character and striving, look for the constructive aspects of each, and try to meld them together.

I would posit a third human tendency, perhaps not so prevalent, something I would call the tendency toward pluralism. A pluralistic outlook values diverse ethnic, racial, religious, and cultural identities and advocates tolerance and mutual respect for difference. Yet it assumes those separate and autonomous identities can operate within a common society or civilization. I believe that the creation of healthy societies, based on pluralistic tendencies, is the central challenge of our time.

Some are discouraged about the prospects for pluralism but I am not. We must be patient. Social progress is not a steady, straight, uncomplicated march to a better world. Transitions take time; developing pluralistic, democratic cultures, nurtured by the institutions of civil society, may take generations. When people are free to choose, especially after years of forced harmony which suppressed differences, the early exercise of democratic rights may not fully reflect liberal democratic values.

The troubling signs I spoke of earlier occur against the backdrop of the simple fact that millions of people are freer today than 4 years ago. Our own recent election was a clear statement for pluralism and a decisive rejection of the divisive rhetoric of Pat Buchanan at the Houston convention—a rhetoric that appalled and frightened ordinary people, including many who had been part of the Reagan revolution. Or consider the peaceful demonstrations throughout Germany last December in which more than 1.5 million citizens protested right-wing violence that led to the burning deaths of three Turkish women in the city of Molln. Or, on our own continent, reflect on the election results in Canada, where the supporters of an expansive and pluralistic society triumphed over those who would divide their country.

It is, of course, not certain that the quest for pluralism will prevail. As always, leadership matters. Think of the alternative if Boris Yeltsin had lost the April referendum. Look at the carnage that Milosevic and Tudjman have wrought in Bosnia. Feel the difference of spirit in this country with a new generation of leaders.

We need leaders the world over who understand that the goal is pluralism, who resist the temptation to play on local fears for political gain, but who also respect the legitimate concerns of ordinary people, frightened by change, and who are prepared to educate them. Those leaders must be of a special character and background, comfortable with other cultures, able to communicate with other world leaders, but also connected to their own people and their own local roots.

American history offers an example of the kind of leader I am talking about: Harry Truman. Here was a man anchored in local issues and concerns, a product of the Kansas City Prendergast machine, a county supervisor until age 50, when the machine anointed him to run for the Senate, a man who reflected the attitudes of his time about racial and religious minorities, a man elevated to the vice presidency through a smoke-filled room at the Chicago convention and then made President by fate. Not a textbook preparation for world leadership. Yet this remarkable man was a key player in the end of World War II, the establishment of the United Nations, the rebuilding of Europe and creation of NATO, and the relatively smooth transition to a peacetime economy at home—not to mention the desegregation of the military and the civil service. Indeed, at considerable political risk and with the consequence of splitting his party in 1948, Truman advocated a strong civil rights program which included an antilynching law, the end of the poll tax, and the establishment of a Fair Employment Practices Commission.

A reading of Truman's most recent biography reveals that the provincial stereotype of the man from Missouri was not the whole story. As a child, as a local Kansas City haberdasher, and as a courthouse politician, he read voraciously: Plutarch's

*Lives*, the Bible, Ben Franklin's autobiography, Mark Twain, Sir Walter Scott, *Don Quixote*, and biographies of his favorite leaders, especially Andrew Jackson.

Truman was an amalgam of practical local experience, deeply steeped in local perspectives, and a cosmopolitan outlook shaped by his reading, his curious mind, his service abroad in World War I, and the rush of events that greeted his sudden assumption of the presidency. His was a story of continuous growth, a curve that accelerated sharply after age 50. It was, I think, this blend—roots in and respect for the concerns of ordinary citizens, an optimism about the capacity of people to learn and widen their horizons (as he had), and an appreciation of other cultures and universal values—that made Truman such an effective leader. It was precisely his ability to synthesize the local and the cosmopolitan that made him a great educator able to persuade his natural, local constituencies to embrace fair and just social arrangements at home and America's potential to foster democracy abroad. People trusted him, and through that trust they grew to accept a broader view of the world less riven with prejudice and strife.

Leadership, of course, is not the responsibility of only a few. All of us, especially those of us privileged with a good education, must help our democracy choose political leaders appropriate to our domestic needs and our global obligations. You have attended the New School for Social Research, an institution with a special character: deeply local in its reflection of American and especially New York culture and at the same time cosmopolitan and diverse, enrolling as it does students from 101 countries with a faculty known for its attention to the historical and comparative dimensions of social science research. You have studied at a place which encouraged you to deepen your understanding of your own cultural heritage and yet celebrated a vision of the world in which respect for difference and commitment to human rights are the norm. Thus you are well prepared for a leadership role in this new era in which the challenge will be to reassure millions of people that local perspectives and interests need not be in opposition to the free flow of ideas, people, and markets. That reassurance will come most credibly from people at peace with their own local backgrounds, not from the self-proclaimed elite citizens of the globe who dismiss local concerns as anticosmopolitan and regressive.

I hope—and believe—that you are ready to embrace this opportunity and responsibility. I wish you all the best.

# PART III

# Art and Society

## For Vera List

It would be difficult for any president of the New School to discuss the role of the visual arts within the university or the larger community without special reference to Vera List. Although Alvin Johnson early on recognized that art could communicate ideas as powerfully as any other medium, a belief reflected in the New School's early adult education programs, it was Vera List, a longtime member of the Board of Trustees and now Life Trustee, who provided the inspiration and wherewithal that enabled the university to expand and build upon that conviction.

An ardent supporter of human rights and artistic freedom, she and her husband Albert List in 1960 made possible the establishment of the New School Art Center, an exhibition program that for more than a decade illuminated the role of art in the political process. It was succeeded by the New Museum of Contemporary Art, which resided at the New School during its formative years, and is today one of the nation's most important and provocative smaller museums. During the 1960's, she also founded the List Poster Program, which commissioned distinguished fine artists to create posters for the benefit of non-profit institutions and causes, including an edition of three posters depicting Martin Luther King, which were sold to support a New School scholarship fund honoring the late civil rights leader. One of New York's most prominent art collectors, Vera List also launched the New School Art Collection, which today includes hundreds of outstanding works that occupy the halls and walls of New School buildings for the enjoyment and edification of students, faculty, staff and visitors. By 1970, when Parsons School of Design was merged into the New School, this university, thanks to her leadership, was indeed well prepared to assume the stewardship of a great school of art and design.

With her name now appropriately gracing the Adult Division's Vera List Center of Art and Politics, her many contributions to the New School have been permanently acknowledged. Nevertheless, I could not resist opening this section on Art and Society by calling your attention to her remarkable example of enlightened trusteeship.

J.F.F.

# The New School and the NEA Challenge

# SAYING NO TO THE OBSCENITY CONDITION

(STATEMENT ON NEW SCHOOL NEA LITIGATION, MAY 1990)

The New School for Social Research has decided to seek injunctive relief in federal court from a condition concerning obscenity attached to a recent grant from the National Endowment for the Arts. We believe the condition is at odds with the Constitution in a fashion which poses a disturbing threat to freedom of expression. What follows is a summary of the facts of the case and our reasons for pursuing this course of action.

The New School for Social Research submitted an application to the National Endowment for the Arts in May 1989 requesting a challenge grant of $45,000 to support the redesign of its courtyard at 66 West 12th Street. The funds requested would pay fees for the sculptor Martin Puryear and an architect, not selected at the time of the application, to collaborate on the design and planning of the courtyard and adjacent areas as a "site-specific environment." The landscape architect Michael Van Valkenburgh has since been chosen to work with Mr. Puryear.

On March 26, 1990, the New School was informed by letter that the NEA had approved its grant application. Enclosed with the letter was a summary of terms and conditions applicable to the grant. Among those terms and conditions was the following:

*Restriction on the use of FY 1990 Appropriated Funds.*
Public Law 101-121 requires that:
"None of the funds authorized to be appropriated for the National Endowment for the Arts... may be used to promote, disseminate or produce materials which in the judgment of the National Endowment for the Arts ... may be considered obscene, including, but not limited to, depic-

tions of sadomasochism, homoeroticism, the sexual exploitation of children, or individuals engaged in sex acts and which, when taken as a whole, do not have serious literary, artistic, political or scientific value."

The terms and conditions also state that:

"Grant recipients assume legal responsibility for administering these awards in accordance with these General Terms and Conditions and for complying with any provisions included in the grant agreement. Failure to comply with these requirements may result in suspension or termination of the award and Endowment recovery of funds."

The terms and conditions further provide that:

"Submission for a request for funds under the grant (either through a Request for Advance or Reimbursement or Letter of Credit, as applicable) constitutes agreement to comply with all terms and conditions of this grant...."

In a letter to John Frohnmayer, chairman of the NEA, on April 27, 1990, I expressed concern about the NEA's requirement that grant recipients certify their compliance with the statutory language (the "obscenity condition") set forth in the NEA's award letter. I noted that the obscenity condition was not in effect when the grant application was made, questioned its constitutionality and wisdom as public policy, and discussed the chilling effect on free expression it was likely to have. I also posed a number of questions to Mr. Frohnmayer regarding how the NEA's practices will be guided by the obscenity condition. I pointed out that Public Law 101-121, which included the original statutory language, did not compel the NEA to communicate the obscenity condition to its grant recipients or to require them to certify their awareness, understanding, or compliance with it. The NEA, at its own discretion, chose to impose this requirement on grant recipients. Stating that the NEA also had discretion to withdraw the certification requirement, I requested that Mr. Frohnmayer do so.

In Mr. Frohnmayer's response, dated May 2, 1990, he expressed concern about the "obscenity provisions" but asserted his obligation to uphold the law despite his own reservations about its constitutionality. He suggested that the certification procedure was an effort to make grantees "aware" of the law. He did not respond to my questions or to my request that he withdraw the certification procedure. In a follow-up letter of May 11, 1990, I reiterated our disagreement with the way the NEA has implemented Public Law 101-121 and noted that the National Endowment for the Humanities, which is also subject to Public Law 101-121, has chosen not to place the obscenity condition on its grants. I again asked that Mr. Frohnmayer withdraw the requirement that grant recipients verify their acknowledgment of the obscenity condition. To date, Mr. Frohnmayer has not responded.

The New School for Social Research has concluded that it cannot accept a grant that carries with it a limitation upon free expression. What is at issue here has nothing to do with obscenity. Obscenity is not a constitutionally protected form of expression, and the New School believes that the existing laws on obscenity, like all other laws, should be observed.

However, we believe that the NEA's certification procedure, which incorporates verbatim the language of Public Law 101-121, goes well beyond a limitation on obscenity and is unconstitutional on a number of grounds. Among these are the following:

1. The procedure, and the obscenity condition it contains, restricts far more speech than the Supreme Court's obscenity standard would possibly permit. It requires the NEA to deny funds for work it "may consider obscene" and requires, in turn, the New School not to use NEA-provided funds for works that the NEA "may consider obscene." At the same time, it defines obscenity in a manner inconsistent with binding Supreme Court rulings.
2. The NEA procedure is a form of prior restraint on expression, which offers no prompt and fair way of determining whether material at issue is obscene.
3. The New School cannot know in advance what the NEA in its sole judgment may consider to be obscene at some point in the future and could fall afoul of NEA criteria despite a sincere belief that we were in conformity

with them. We could then be subjected to whatever "legal responsibility" the NEA imposed upon us which we, by signing the certification, agree to accept.
4. The certification procedure is akin to a loyalty oath which is so vague that we cannot possibly know what it is to which we are swearing.

Given our view of the unconstitutionality of the certification procedure, we have concluded that we cannot accept a grant to which such a condition is attached. As we considered how to respond to the grant award, three options were apparent: simply rejecting the grant, accepting the grant with a protest against the obscenity condition, or pursuing litigation to challenge the procedure's constitutionality and seek injunctive relief from the condition. We have decided on this last approach.

We have a number of reasons for the decision to seek a judicial remedy. The New School for Social Research has had a deep commitment to freedom of expression since the institution's founding in 1919. That commitment was reaffirmed when the New School organized the University in Exile, an effort to rescue scholars, artists, and intellectuals endangered by Nazism. We recognize a responsibility to defend the right of free expression when it is threatened and when we are in a position to act effectively and meaningfully in response to such a threat.

The controversy surrounding the National Endowment for the Arts does indeed involve a threat to free expression. In its 25-year history, the NEA has had a profound and beneficial effect on the cultural life of our nation. It has compiled an admirable record of encouragement of the arts and artists. The effort by Congress to restrict the NEA's grant-making ability, and the NEA's own response to that effort, have damaged the NEA's ability to fulfill its mission, undermined confidence in the NEA, and had a corrosive effect on free expression.

We do not believe that it is sound public policy or that it is consistent with the Constitution to attach to grants conditions that infringe upon free expression, visual or verbal. We recognize that obscenity as defined by the Supreme Court is not a form of protected expression and that it is appropriate for government agencies to assure themselves that grantees will abide by the law. But Congress is obliged to write constitutional laws, and the section of Public Law 101-121 purportedly dealing with obscenity can hardly be deemed constitutional. Our challenge is directed at that law only by implication since we are seeking to remove a condition which the NEA, not the Congress, attached to our grant of its own volition. The condition uses the exact statutory language in Public Law 101-121. We believe the NEA's transformation of an already unconstitutional instruction given to it by the Congress into an oath required of all grant recipients greatly amplifies the chilling effect of the underlying law. Means were surely available to the NEA to fulfill its obligation to Congress without requiring its grant recipients to pledge to engage in so sweeping a form of self-censorship.

In the absence of a substantive response to any of the inquiries we have posed to the NEA, we feel the necessity of taking more concerted action. Rejecting the grant would absolve us of the need to challenge the certification procedure, and we applaud the courage of those institutions and individuals who have chosen this course. However, such a course would leave the certification procedure in place, forcing the many individual artists who rely on NEA funds to choose between their livelihoods and their principles. It is appropriate that an institution assume the burden of challenging this infringement on free expression. As a university whose academic divisions include the largest college of art and design in the country, Parsons School of Design, we perceive a special responsibility to assume that role.

We continue to hope that the National Endowment for the Arts will withdraw the certification procedure on obscenity. It is clearly within Chairman Frohnmayer's discretion to take this action. We would welcome the opportunity to withdraw our legal action, to accept the grant, and to proceed with our courtyard project. We believe that the issues involved in this legal action are of extraordinary importance to our society and that the principles at stake must be defended vigorously.

# A Conditional Victory

(STATEMENT ON THE REAUTHORIZATION
OF THE NEA, NOVEMBER 1990)

Congress' action to reauthorize the National Endowment for the Arts without an antiobscenity restriction is a welcome event. The reauthorization recognizes the enormous value of the NEA's work over the past quarter century in enriching our nation's cultural life. It rightfully acknowledges that determining what is obscenity is not the NEA's responsibility. That is the province of the courts.

However, the legislation raises a number of serious concerns. By inserting a "decency" provision into the legislation, Congress has sent a troubling signal that future NEA funding decisions may be based on criteria other than artistic quality. The reorganization of the peer review panels reinforces this signal. The allocation of a greater portion of NEA funds to state arts councils will undoubtedly weaken the NEA's ability to support a broad spectrum of the arts.

Despite these reservations, the reauthorization legislation does make one thing clear. There can no longer be any question about the inappropriateness of the "obscenity condition" that the NEA attached to grants awarded in the 1990 fiscal year. Congress' elimination of that condition from the new law indicates its own awareness that the condition had a chilling effect on artistic expression. A substantial number of legal scholars have contended that the condition is unconstitutional. The New School for Social Research, which received an NEA grant for the 1990 fiscal year, has challenged the constitutionality of the condition in federal court on the grounds that it violates the First and Fifth Amendments. We now await a decision in the litigation.

The obscenity condition is entirely antithetical to the purposes of the NEA. Given Chairman John Frohnmayer's own stated doubts about the condition's constitutionality, it now seems only right that he rescind the condition from all 1990 grants to which it was previously appended. Nothing can be gained by holding on to an unworkable and inappropriate condition that Congress itself has now rejected. Much can be gained by disposing of the condition and beginning to repair the distrust that the NEA's actions engendered in the arts community.

Though flawed, the NEA reauthorization legislation has succeeded in deterring a misguided attempt to undermine free expression and curtail the vitality of the arts in the United States. The members of the arts community must now be vigilant in observing how the NEA interprets and administers its new congressional mandate to ensure that political considerations do not intrude upon NEA decisions in the future.

# A TRUCE WITH THE NEA

(MEMORANDUM TO THE UNIVERSITY COMMUNITY, FEBRUARY 1991)

I am very pleased to tell you that the New School for Social Research has reached an extremely favorable agreement with the National Endowment for the Arts in its lawsuit challenging the constitutionality of the "obscenity condition" that the NEA placed on 1990 grants. The agreement achieves the fundamental objectives of the New School's suit. It removes the obscenity condition from 1990 grants and makes clear that obscenity determinations must be made by the courts, not by the NEA. Recipients of 1990 grants will not have to attest to a condition of dubious constitutionality in order to receive their funds.

Under the agreement, that provision has been deleted in its entirety and a paragraph substituted, stating:

> The National Endowment for the Arts intends to enforce Section 304(a) of the Department of the Interior and Related Agencies Appropriation Act of 1990 after a grantee has been convicted of violating a criminal obscenity or child pornography statute and all appeal rights have been exhausted.

This provision means that only after a grant recipient has been convicted of obscenity in the courts and has exhausted all appeals will the NEA try to recover its funds. It also means that the definition of what constitutes obscenity will adhere to the standard established in *Miller v. California* and not the broader definition that the obscenity condition contained. The New School has always acknowledged that obscenity is illegal, and the new provision merely reiterates that understanding.

As a result of the agreement, the New School terminated its lawsuit against the NEA and will now receive its grant monies. Since the agreement was reached out of court, Judge Louis Stanton, before whom the case was argued, will not issue a decision regarding the obscenity condition's constitutionality. However, parallel cases were brought against the NEA by the Bella Lewitzky Dance Foundation and the Newport Harbor Art Museum in U.S. District Court for the Central District of California. These lawsuits made essentially the same arguments as did the New School's litigation and, in fact, relied heavily upon the New School's legal brief. In a consolidated decision in the California cases, Judge John Davies did declare the obscenity condition unconstitutional, stating that "the NEA certification requirement is unconstitutionally vague because it leaves the determination of obscenity in the hands of the NEA"—a Fifth Amendment violation—and that "because the certification requirement includes unconstitutionally vague provisions, it also violates grantees' First Amendment rights by causing a chilling effect on their artistic expression." He concluded his opinion by saying: "This is the type of obstacle in the path of the exercise of fundamental speech rights that the Constitution will not tolerate."

The New School agreement, combined with the California decision, confirms that the obscenity condition and the congressional action that led to its imposition were misguided from the start. The outcome negates an action by the NEA that contradicted the NEA's own responsibility to promote, and not inhibit, artistic expression. The case demonstrates the constitutional dangers involved when government grants contain conditions meant to suppress unpopular speech. We believe our litigation had a constructive influence on the congressional debate that led to the reauthorization of the NEA without the language contained in the obscenity condition and on the subsequent deletion of the oath from its 1991 grants.

Now that the case is closed, I hope that the arts and education communities can turn their efforts to healing the rift that has occurred between the National Endowment for the Arts and the artists and institutions it is meant to support. It is in the interest of all those dedicated to the arts to help restore the NEA to its place as a defender and nurturer of art and of the free expression that is at the heart of our country's democratic values.

# Support for the Arts: Where Does It Come From?

# Is Public Funding Compatible with Artistic Freedom?

(COMMENCEMENT, PARSONS, MAY 1991)

Most of you know that the New School was the only institution of higher education to challenge in the courts an antiobscenity oath which the National Endowment for the Arts placed on all its 1990 grantees.

Our challenge had a happy outcome three months ago when the NEA was forced by a federal court to retract the oath. In addition, we and many others successfully prevented such unconstitutional language from being written into the 1991 reauthorization of the NEA.

The antiobscenity oath was but a short battle in a larger cultural war. The issue, as defined by Senator Jesse Helms, the Reverend Donald Wildmon, and others, is whether federal tax money should fund offensive art. That's what they say, but I think what they really want is the suppression of art that offends them, no matter who pays for it.

The not-so-hidden agenda here is an attack on free expression and the First Amendment. A fairly small but well organized group of people are bent on restoring what they think of as "traditional values" in American society. The most far-reaching effects of Senator Helms' campaign are not that it has caused a few artists to be denied NEA grants, or that the NEA's activities are now constantly under a magnifying glass, serious as these may be. It is not even the debate about whether government funds should be used to support controversial art. The most profound question is whether the federal government should subsidize the arts at all. Even those of us who have vigorously supported the NEA over the years must now reflect on whether federal funding is compatible with artistic freedom.

The first thing we have to concede is that for most of our 215 years as a nation, the federal government did little to support the arts directly—no strong European-style Ministry of Culture here. Indeed, it was something of a revolution in thinking when Franklin Roosevelt and Harry Hopkins used the New Deal's Works Progress Administration to help artists, musicians, and writers during the Great Depression. But like so many New Deal initiatives that established future precedents, at the time the measure was seen as a temporary response to an emergency.

It was not until the creation of the NEA during Lyndon Johnson's administration in 1965 that the federal government provided monies for the arts in a big way as a matter of formal policy. The models of the already successful National Science Foundation and National Institutes of Health, especially their reliance on peer review, were appropriated.

At its high point (in fiscal year 1988), the NEA spent $167 million to promote the arts annually; as much as 93 percent of that went to general support of established institutions. In that same year, corporations contributed $184 million, private foundations nearly $30 million, and private individuals $56 million. These figures don't include small individual gifts or grants from state and local arts councils, which exceed another $100 million. Thus the federal government is only a minority partner in arts funding. Much more important for the arts is federal tax policy, which offers incentives for foundations, corporations, and individuals to make their own choices about where to invest in the arts. Not even Senator Helms has yet suggested that a private gift to fund offensive art should not be tax-exempt.

There is, I think, an important clue in these statistics. What makes America unique is that large parts of our society are not controlled or supported by government. Private resources and not-for-profit institutions play a more powerful role here in shaping culture than in any other major country in the world. All of you, after all, decided to come to Parsons, a private college, rather than to a lower-cost public alternative.

Our traditional skepticism about central or public control of cultural life, combined with a plethora of sources of funding for the arts, has led to an important fact: the United States does not have and has never had a national policy for the arts. There is no agency of government that says what is morally good or bad art, what art is consistent with the values of this country and what is not, what art is worthy of subvention and what is not. For example, at least until recently, the NEA has been guided by a peer review process in which people knowledgeable in the arts make judgments on the basis of aesthetic quality alone. It was the express intent of the framers of the NEA that political judgments not intrude on the endowment's work.

Our approach to the arts in this country is based on the principle of pluralism—a pluralism in the kind of art that is made and in the makers of art, and a pluralism in the sources of funding and encouragement for the arts. The NEA was meant to strengthen that pluralism, to make it more dynamic, to spread the funds ever more broadly, to enhance our country's democratic commitment to freedom. It has, in fact, been diversifying art, encouraging experimentation, and bringing the arts to neglected segments of our society.

I believe the sharp cleavage over the NEA now is a proxy for a much bigger conflict: a battle over American pluralism itself. Arrayed against each other are, on the one side, those who embrace modern America and celebrate its diversity, and, on the other side, those who yearn for a mythical time of greater simplicity when Americans were homogeneous in their beliefs and in their ethnic makeup. This is not a new conflict; it comes in cycles: the 1920s with the Scopes monkey trial, Prohibition, and Sacco and Vanzetti; the McCarthy period in the 1950s, and the Moral Majority and creationism in the 1980s.

One may get the impression that Senator Helms' real purpose is to put the NEA out of existence, to get government out of the business of funding art. But that may not be so. It is possible that he and his allies would be all too happy to have an NEA that reflected a real national arts policy, a policy that would dictate what is good art and what is not, one that reflects their own beliefs.

The NEA fight has raised some troubling questions. We now

see that it is much harder to insulate funding for a Robert Mapplethorpe exhibit from the political process than a grant to promote, say, research in cell biology. Government support for the arts will always be buffeted by those who wish to exploit it for political ends. And government support for the arts is an awfully inviting instrument for manipulating the way people think and act. We need to ask ourselves whether federal funding for the arts must inevitably lead to control of expression. If it results in an arts policy that says what is acceptable art, then perhaps no central government support for the arts would be better.

The issue before us, I think, is this: Just how should we nourish creative talent? How do we create a culture which at once respects our different traditions and also provides some common unifying elements? How do we carry this country's democratic experiment to the next plateau, a place which is genuinely open to many cultures and their implications for our society?

The arts have a crucial role to play in achieving these goals. Certainly, we should do all we can to increase the variety of ways in which the arts get encouraged and supported, particularly from nongovernment sources. For example, recent changes in the tax laws which make charitable giving less attractive, should be reexamined. And private foundations, individuals, and corporations need to step up their contributions to the arts as a way of ensuring the continuation of our pluralistic traditions.

If the arts are critical, that means that artists are central, and that means you. It is easy enough to use Senator Helms and Reverend Wildmon as a heuristic for what not to think—just see where they are on an issue and go to the other side. But thoughtful people, educated people, should not have their ideas determined by reflex.

As artists and designers, you have an obligation to think these questions through, to act and not just react. Otherwise, the determination of public policy that affects you directly will go by default to those who lack your sensitivity and appreciation for the artistic process.

# Looking at the European Model

(SELECTED FROM COMMENCEMENT,
PARSONS/PARIS, MAY 1993)

Parsons has never been a parochial institution; from its earliest days it embraced an international vision of the arts. I was reminded of our cosmopolitan tradition at our New York commencement, when I spoke with Stanley Barrows, who received an honorary degree on that occasion. He was a legendary teacher of interior design at Parsons at the time when Parsons virtually defined the interiors field. And in the 1930s, he had been a student at the Parsons Paris program when it was ensconced on the Place des Vosges. He regaled me with stories of the creative excitement at Parsons in those years, when the circle of artists and designers drawn to Parsons included people like fashion designer Schiaparelli; painter Betty Carter; Grace Fakes, the leading expert on French paneling; interior designers William Odom and Van Day Truex, both of whom became president of Parsons; and Jean-Michel Frank, the furniture designer who created the Parsons table.

Stanley Barrows illuminated for me Parsons' historic relationship to this magnificent city and its deep ties to European art and design. The cross-fertilization of American and European approaches to art is central to Parsons' mission. Parsons has always drawn upon the best from both sides of the Atlantic. The education you have received is richer for its exposure to the principles and techniques of two continents.

There is a particular dimension of art and culture in which I believe a comparison between the United States and Europe is quite useful—and in which the United States, I am afraid, comes out looking very inadequate. That is the area of public support for the arts.

The world's leading patron of the arts is the French government. The budget of its Ministry of Culture is $2.3 billion in 1993, compared with a mere $175 million for the NEA. That calculates to per capita annual spending on the arts of about

$41 in France and less than $1 in the United States. The French arts budget expanded 6.5 percent last year, though the country's overall budget grew at only half that rate. Mr. Clinton's first budget, by contrast, proposes no additional funding for the arts.

The numbers tell only part of the story in France. President Mitterand and Minister of Culture Jack Lang have pursued a program of investment in the arts that has touched virtually every aspect of French cultural life. They have built grand, new buildings; started museums, libraries, and theaters around the country; restored pipe organs and formal gardens; and sponsored events to stimulate reading, concertgoing, and film attendance.

That is the record of just one country. But just to assure you that France is not an isolated case, let us look briefly at one other place, a single city: Berlin. Berlin's annual budget for the arts and culture is $600 million, which computes to an incredible $175 per citizen. For a city of 3 million inhabitants, it has three opera houses and eight orchestras.

The significance of these examples goes far beyond the dollar expenditures, as impressive as they are. The size of the budgets bespeaks the place of respect that artists hold in France and Germany and throughout Europe. As *New York Times* critic John Rockwell has written, in Europe

> artists and intellectuals are not perceived as kooks or weirdos or subverters of family values. They are honored citizens whom others look up to....American artists are more likely to be pilloried for controversial values than prized as defenders of government policy. Even in those barely remembered days when the Democrats last held the White House, artists served more as ornaments than as valued members of the team. America has never had a minister of culture.

In that quote, Rockwell was referring in part to the fact that, when the Maastricht Treaty was in trouble, President Mitterand turned to Minister Lang to orchestrate a campaign through which artists and intellectuals helped convince the electorate to approve the treaty. It is inconceivable that any U.S. President would dare to marshal the artistic and intellectual community to generate support for, say, an economic stimulus package or new health care program.

But that defensive attitude about artists must change, and President Clinton must take the lead in challenging the American public to value the contributions that art makes to the health and humaneness of civilizations everywhere. A good start would be for Mr. Clinton to articulate a national arts policy, and he should look to the European experience for some lessons. First, of course, an arts policy should encourage artistic expression and strengthen a country's commitment to the principle of free expression. Second, it should nurture young talent in all the arts. Third, it should provide wide accessibility to the arts for people of all ages, races, ethnic groups, and economic classes, in all parts of a country. Finally, an arts policy should connect art and design to the economic vitality of a country. The Europeans already know, and the United States is slowly learning, that national industrial competitiveness lies in the ability to combine good engineering with effective visual design.

The United States is a lot younger than the European nations. It does not have the tradition of monarchies acting as patrons of artists. So government support for the arts is not as deeply ingrained in the national psyche. But we are working on it. I think it is important that American policy makers become more familiar with European attitudes toward support for the arts. I particularly hope that President Clinton, who has a cosmopolitan outlook and obtained part of his education in Europe, will take heed of the role that the arts play in European life and be motivated to do better himself in defending and supporting the arts. I have called on him to double the federal government's support for the arts over the next 3 years.

I think there is a message in all of this for you who graduate today. You are now part of the Parsons network of alumni and faculty who are among the most distinguished artists and designers in the world. Some of you will pursue your careers in the United States, some here in Europe, and some in other parts of the world. It is natural that your own work and career aspirations will absorb your energies at first. But save some space for attention to public issues, especially those concerning the arts. For those of you who settle in the United States, do what you can to influence American arts policy to emulate the European model. And for those of you who settle in other countries, if you are lucky enough to live in a place that has as enlightened an arts policy as France or Germany, value it and work to keep it strong. Wherever you are, you should use the power of art to bridge cultural divides and achieve greater human understanding.

Working together, the Parsons network can make a difference, can influence arts policy for the better in all nations. And think about this: If we do not care about the arts, who will?

# On Establishing a National Arts Policy

(COMMENCEMENT, MANNES, MAY 1993)

The start of a new presidential administration, and the impending debate this summer over the reauthorization of the National Endowment for the Arts, gives us an opportunity to reflect on what a national arts policy might look like.

Above all, a national arts policy must reaffirm one central principle: artistic freedom should be protected and encouraged. We must resist vigorously any effort to use government power to censor controversial ideas and images, including music, which may offend. In this last election our citizens firmly rejected the mean spirit of the Houston convention, of Senator Helms, Patrick Buchanan, and the Reverend Donald Wildmon. Let us put behind us—once and for all—the shameful behavior of the last 12 years which cast a chill over creative talent in this country.

There is, however, at least one troubling sign that the battle over art started by Jesse Helms is not over. The Clinton administration has appealed a federal judge's decision in a case known as *Finley v. National Endowment for the Arts*. That decision declared unconstitutional a provision in a law passed by Congress which required the NEA to take "general standards of decency" into account when awarding grants.

By appealing the *Finley* case, the Clinton administration, I fear, has decided to put political calculation above the right of free expression. The decency standard is nothing less than an attempt by the religious right to suppress speech and artistic expression which it finds offensive. The *Finley* appeal is an apparent attempt to placate the antiart forces.

Any new President is faced with many demands on his time at the start of his administration. But we should ask for a clear articulation of Mr. Clinton's policy toward the arts very soon. A good start would be a declaration that a democracy must support artistic expression even when, or especially when, such expression is offensive or goes against the grain of public opinion. Next, he should withdraw the appeal in *Finley v. NEA*, and I call upon him to do so promptly. Third, he should appoint a chairperson for the NEA whose stature and integrity will signal instantly that the NEA is not susceptible to political manipulation. Fourth, he should advocate the reauthorization of the NEA at higher levels of funding and without unconstitutional speech-inhibiting strings attached.

Let us proceed on the assumption that there is an opening for a good, constructive arts policy to emerge from the Clinton administration. What might the specific elements be? Because we are a school of the musical arts, I will focus on music, but surely an arts policy would also address art, design, drama, dance, film, video, television, and radio.

In addition to protecting and encouraging artistic expression, a national arts policy should serve two other fundamental purposes:

- To nurture young talent in all the arts, talent that should not be bound by gender, race, religion, ethnicity or economic circumstance;
- To provide wide accessibility to the arts for the general public of all ages, in all parts of our country. The health of the arts is one important measure of a civilization's strength and vigor and a means to bridge conflict and misunderstanding

With those purposes in mind, let me offer seven suggestions for core elements of a national arts policy.

*1.* In 1990 President Bush and the National Governors Conference set forth six goals for education to be achieved by the year 2000—but the arts were never mentioned. To his credit, President Clinton has suggested that arts education be established as a seventh goal. Every student should be exposed to arts instruction beginning in the elementary grades. We should restore art and music to the curriculum, no longer considering the arts as a frill—the first to be sacrificed to budget cuts.

*2.* The federal government should increase support for the National Endowment for the Arts. The NEA budget has lost 15 percent of its purchasing power in the last 10 years, but President Clinton has proposed no additional resources in his first budget. The federal government spends only 68 cents per person to support the arts. In France and in Canada, for example, that figure is $41 and $32. It is a national disgrace that the federal government spends more tax dollars on military bands than it does on the NEA. The President should raise the NEA budget to $300 million over the next 3 years, an increase which would provide adequate support to its existing programs and allow for new initiatives.

*3.* My first thought goes to the composition of the classical music profession, in which African-Americans, Latinos, and other groups are woefully underrepresented. Special programs funded by the federal government are needed to expose inner-city young people to classical music and give them the opportunity to train for the profession. To accomplish those goals, music must be available not only through the public schools but also through community organizations like the Harlem Boys Choir and the Harlem School for the Arts, which need and deserve significant federal support.

*4.* Offering opportunities for young people is not enough. They need encouragement to take advantage of those opportunities and family support to stay the course of musical training from the earliest years all the way to entrance to a musical conservatory like Mannes. That support will come if families themselves have an appreciation of classical music, which in turn means it must be easily available in the inner cities.

One way to build new audiences for music would be for the NEA to expand the number of tours it sponsors by ensembles of young musicians. These ensembles, which provide job opportunities for young musicians, can also reach into inner-city neighborhoods with their performances. And we need to give attention to the plight of orchestras and opera houses in big cities like Detroit where their future is in peril. The NEA should step up its support of these organizations.

5. Of course, the challenge of building new audiences reaches beyond the inner cities. I call on the NEA to create a special music task force to give systematic attention to building new audiences in every part of America, across all racial, ethnic, and class boundaries. The ensemble of young musicians tours and support for orchestras and operas of which I just spoke hold promise for audiences in smaller cities and rural jurisdictions as well.

6. In this age of many new technologies, we should not restrict our thinking to live and in-person performances. In recent years the capacity of radio and especially television has expanded, yet the amount of classical music programming as a percentage of total programming has declined. The NEA should provide support to make possible either a national arts television network or a significant increase in classical music offerings on existing channels.

7. My final suggestion speaks to the encouragement of private support for the arts. One distinctive feature of the American experience is the role that private individuals, corporations, and foundations play in supporting culture and education. Americans have long favored a system of checks and balances so that the government does not have a monopoly on the intellectual and artistic life of the country. That tradition has been nurtured by our tax system, which provides incentives for private giving to educational and cultural institutions—indeed, some $8.8 billion in 1991. The President proposes to make permanent the deductibility of the full market value of gifts of art and other property to nonprofit institutions. This device, which has been championed by New York Senator Patrick Moynihan, is a proven method of increasing private support for cultural and educational organizations. The President should push for it, and Congress should pass it.

Think how exhilarating it would be if the President were to champion the arts and commit his administration to these seven specific actions.

# PART IV

# The Challenge of Maintaining Independent Institutions

# THE ERODING SUPPORT FOR PRIVATE INSTITUTIONS

(COMMENCEMENT, MAY 1991)

As Alexis de Tocqueville observed a century and a half ago, "In no country in the world has the principle of association been more successfully used or more unsparingly applied to a multitude of different objects than in America." That principle holds true today. Indeed, by last count, there were 460,000 not-for-profit organizations in this country, together constituting what is called the independent sector. They employ 7.5 million people, are supported by 5 million volunteers, and touch the lives of countless numbers of our citizens.

But all is not well in the not-for-profit world.

Despite recent presidential rhetoric about encouraging private initiative, our society is turning more and more to government for just about everything. Government at all levels grows inexorably, while government policy seems bent on making not-for-profit institutions struggle to survive. The time has come to refocus attention on the importance of independent institutions. We must awaken the general public to their perilous condition and to the implications for our society of their deterioration.

America's commitment to nurturing independent institutions goes back to the founding of the Republic, when virtually every state granted tax exemptions without which most not-for-profit institutions could not exist. Then, when our income tax system took root in the early years of this century, it was acknowledged that charitable organizations served the public interest and hence the tax structure should foster their growth. More recently, independent institutions have received direct government subsidies. Indeed, for much of our history independent institutions played the dominant role in providing higher education, health, and welfare services to our citizens as well as enriching our cultural life.

It is worth taking a moment to illustrate some of their contributions:

- In higher education, private institutions have set the quality standards for the nation. Despite huge infusions of public funds into state systems, private colleges and universities command the top positions by almost any measure of quality you choose.
- Independent institutions have often taken the lead in defense of intellectual and artistic freedom. It was, after all, a government agency, the National Endowment for the Arts, which sought to impose content restrictions on artistic work benefiting from public monies and a private institution, the New School, which beat back that effort in the courts by forcing the NEA to drop the antiobscenity oath earlier this year.
- Private universities have been the site of innumerable scientific discoveries. Much of the pioneering work in nuclear physics, infectious disease, molecular biology, and computer science has come from their laboratories. Indeed, nearly three-quarters of the Americans who have received Nobel prizes did their work or taught at private universities.
- Beyond higher education, nonprofit institutions provide imaginative models for solving social problems which later influence public policy. The HELP and Women in Need programs to provide housing for the homeless are examples near at hand. And our own Community Development Research Center has documented the dramatic accomplishments of not-for-profit organizations in low-income housing and economic development. Other examples include path-breaking work in community-based employment, day care centers, and adult literacy.
- Not-for-profit institutions have taken the lead in reversing the deterioration of our environment. It was the National Resources Defense Council which created the coalition that passed the Clean Air Act. The Environmental Defense Fund first alerted us to the dangers of global warming,

ozone depletion, and acid rain. The Audubon Society has fiercely protected endangered species. The Nature Conservancy has acquired critical land for habitat protection. The Sierra Club, the Wilderness Society, the Conservation Law Foundation—I could go on and on.

- In the field of human rights, one of the most effective forces worldwide has been a nongovernment agency, Human Rights Watch, which takes to task governments, including our own, for flagrant abuse of basic human rights. While almost all governments pay lip service to human rights, most trade off those rights against strategic political concerns. Thus millions of people on every continent turn for protection to an independent institution, an American institution: Human Rights Watch.

Those are but a few examples of the social and scientific benefits flowing from the independent sector, and I have not even mentioned symphonies, ballets, operas, museums, libraries, and all the rest. These illustrations suggest that independent institutions are at the very heart of our pluralistic society. They represent the individual initiative and capacity for innovation that have characterized our nation since its inception.

But there is mounting evidence that we take our institutions for granted—or, even worse, fail to appreciate what they mean to us and deny them adequate financial support. In the 1980s federal subvention of nonprofit organizations declined. Faced with unprecedented deficits, governments at all levels cut aid to private institutions more sharply than they were willing to contract government operations. Recent changes in the federal tax laws diminish the value of charitable deductions, thus offering less incentive for private giving to take up the slack.

These trends should alarm us. We should ask ourselves: How would America be different if independent institutions were consigned to the margin of our society? John Gardner, former president of the Carnegie Corporation, answered that question by noting what a robust independent sector means to our national life and what would be lost without it. It "enhances our communities," he wrote, "nurtures individual responsibility, stirs life at the grassroots." It also represents our best virtues—"civic pride, compassion, a philanthropic tradition, a strong problem-solving impulse...an irrepressible commitment to the great shared task of improving our life together."

The challenge before us, I believe, is to find the right balance between the public and independent sectors and to recognize that both are essential to our quest for a more just and humane society. I do not mean here to undervalue the great good done by the public sector in this country, nor do I offer a dewy-eyed paean to the "thousand points of light" that will magically solve all our social problems with minimal government intervention. But I do celebrate the unique importance of not-for-profit organizations in American life, and urge you to take an interest in promoting public policies which strengthen them. Most of all, I hope that you, as citizens, will become involved in independent institutions of all kinds, as staff leaders, volunteers, board members, and donors to independent institutions.

In closing, let me say we are glad you came to *this* independent institution and we welcome you to your new status as alumni, as permanent members of our community.

# THE IMPORTANCE OF THE TUITION ASSISTANCE PROGRAM

(REPORT TO NEW YORK STATE CIVIC AND
PROFESSIONAL LEADERS, MARCH 1986)

We often speak of New York, with good reason, as one of the most influential states in the nation. It is not only a leader in business and finance, government, the professions, science, and the arts; it is also the leading producer of ideas that inform our national life and enhance our culture. At the heart of this "industry of ideas" is New York's higher-education system, its public and independent colleges and universities. The vitality of these institutions is directly related to the preeminence of New York in economic, civic, and intellectual discourse.

From these institutions emerge the people who create the new ideas and who lead. Some of these people—scholars and teachers—are professionally engaged in the pursuit of knowledge. But the vast majority of them form the talent pool necessary to an economy that is increasingly technological and service-oriented. There is hardly a professional occupation today which does not require both the general education which undergraduates receive and more specialized graduate education. These professions include not just the obvious ones like engineering, mathematics, computer services, and medicine, but nontechnological professions such as law, media and the arts, and policy analysis, and especially professions which address human needs, such as social services and elementary and secondary school education. Because of the pervasive need for highly trained personnel, the people of New York State have a direct interest in maintaining the strength of higher education here.

One reason for this strength is the great diversity of educational opportunities available to students. This diversity has been supported by state policies that encourage access for students at all income levels, and particularly those at lower income levels, to the full range of institutions—independent and public, large and small. The New York State Tuition Assistance Program (TAP), which provides grants-in-aid to students to defray the costs of higher education, is a primary means for improving access and ensuring an educated and skilled citizenry. An increase in the state's appropriation for TAP is needed so that the program can continue to play this role effectively.

TAP's creators, in 1974, wisely acknowledged the interdependence of undergraduate and graduate education by making grants available to students at both levels. As knowledge becomes more interdisciplinary and as the economy demands more extensive training, this interdependence is ever more apparent. So is the need to help students at both levels fund their studies.

Strong undergraduate and graduate programs are necessary to develop the next generation of scholars, teachers, and researchers—those who will staff our colleges, high schools, and elementary schools. We must be able to replenish the teaching resources throughout our state's educational system.

New York State has shown its awareness of the importance of science and technology to its economic future through the creation of the Centers for Advanced Technology. It is equally important to appreciate that the retention of research faculty at the highest level of quality throughout the state—those whose work channels directly into the state's economy—depends on a talented student population. Advanced undergraduates and graduate students are the junior partners of faculty in research, and they help create the environments in which the most productive work is performed.

It has been suggested that the state should target financial aid to technological fields. In fact, the best research is done where interaction among scientists, social scientists, and humanists is encouraged. A broad higher-education system, with depth in both scientific-technical areas and the liberal arts, is the surest guarantee of a strong scientific community, one which unites the scientific process with the study of the underlying values of science, its social use, and the study of society in general.

While the needs for technically trained personnel seem predominant in New York State's economy today, the needs actually are much broader. And the economy's needs a decade or two from now are not so easy to predict or to plan. Student support limited to only a few highly visible fields may cause other fields to decline in such a way that they may not be able to meet the unforeseen needs of future generations.

A statewide environment of active research goes hand in hand with a robust teaching enterprise. A vital higher-education system requires strong colleges devoted to teaching and the liberal arts and large universities devoted to basic and applied research. TAP for both undergraduate and graduate students promotes a system in which the various parts promote the excellence of the whole. That is why the independent institutions are recommending an increase of $500 in the maximum undergraduate TAP award and of $1,000 in the maximum graduate award, which has not been increased since the program's inception.

These increases will also help provide greater access to higher education for minorities and disadvantaged groups, increasing economic opportunity for them. Improved TAP will encourage state residents to remain in New York for their education. The better aid we can offer to students, the more likely we are to keep the best students and faculty in New York.

New York State has an enormous fixed investment in its educational system—facilities, equipment, and, above all human capital—its faculty and students. If this system is permitted to deteriorate, New York's competitive edge in the industry of ideas will be weakened, perhaps irreparably. Other states are only too eager to take our place at the creative forefront by hiring our best minds away. While improvement in TAP is not alone sufficient to protect New York's comparative advantage, it will certainly strengthen higher education so that it can better serve the state's economic needs and help maintain its position of national leadership.

# HIGHER EDUCATION'S FALL FROM GRACE

(JUNE 1987)

For nearly three centuries private colleges and universities in the United States struggled to secure their independence from church, from state, and from those who furnished financial support. In gaining that independence, higher education developed a special relationship with American society, which has been in the nature of an unwritten compact. Benefits—from tax exemption to respect for academic freedom to generous financial support—have been conferred in recognition of the central role that universities play in a democratic society through training, the discovery and dissemination of new knowledge, and the transmission and preservation of core values. In recent years, that relationship seems to be eroding.

When I entered Yale College in the fall of 1961, my fellow students and I learned we had joined a community open to all points of view no matter how unpopular. Academic freedom, with the McCarthy era still freshly remembered, was paramount. The wonders of scientific research flowed from university laboratories, fueled by government underwriting in the wake of Sputnik. The public had an intuitive belief that the application of social science could produce a better world, and that scholars and intellectuals could guide national leaders in practical and moral choices.

In the 20 years I have spent as a university administrator and history teacher, the perception of private universities and their status in our society has changed sharply. The Secretary of Education now characterizes them as "greedy." The flow of advice from scholars to policy makers is at a low ebb. Universities are no longer perceived as neutral territory where conflicting ideas and ideologies can be aired and tested. Quite a change in one generation. While the reasons for this change are complex, private universities must bear some of the responsibility. Their compact with the American public has been weakened.

The compact assumes that universities are common ground, officially neutral with respect to specific policy issues. However, once the public perceives that universities are not officially neutral on matters of public policy unconnected to education, and that universities act in ways barely distinguishable from special interest lobbies, the compact is in trouble.

The disenchantment began in the Vietnam era. Invited government officials—Robert McNamara at Harvard, for example—or those advocating unpopular views—such as William Shockley at Yale—were not allowed to speak. Episodes of censorship or disruption since have chilled the atmosphere for free speech. Invitations to controversial speakers, especially government officials, are increasingly rare at major universities these days.

Erosion of the free exchange of ideas on campus was largely a consequence of political activism by students and faculty which placed a higher priority on immediate political issues than on the traditional responsibilities of the university. As the Vietnam war dragged on, activist students and faculty pressured university presidents and trustees—because of the perceived moral influence of universities—to condemn the war and work for its end. A few boards actually passed resolutions to that effect, but most understood that trustees in their official capacity should not take stands on policy—that boards were based on an intricate rationale which sought to protect the university's neutral role yet recognize that universities are involved in society. But through the 1970s, university investment policies gradually strayed beyond that rationale.

Under the intense national concern about apartheid, many university boards in effect developed an official policy toward South Africa and used their investment power to advance that policy. While universities claim that South Africa is a special case, no university president has yet offered a set of principles to distinguish apartheid from other examples of gross human rights abuse. In that light, South Africa appears as the most visible, but not the only, issue upon which university trustees may be taking official positions—in essence, developing their own foreign policies—in the future.

At the same time that educational institutions have stepped further into the realm of official stands, they have also wandered into smoke-filled rooms and taken a stab at the game of power politics. Consider the high-powered lobbying evident in the skirmish over tax reform last year. Or, worse, the special deals benefiting single institutions which bypassed the peer review process. A recent article in the *Chronicle of Higher Education* details how dozens of universities received special federal appropriations worth millions of dollars. Such deals cast higher education in the light of a collection of separate, selfish, special interests.

Resisting harmful legislation and assaults on student aid is essential. So is maintaining university research in the natural sciences upon which the future of this country depends. Both goals may not be achieved by high-minded pleas from university presidents. But the present pressure tactics of the higher-education lobby are offensive and jeopardize the special status of higher education in our society. Universities have been lobbying strenuously to ensure that government maintains its part of the compact, without asking themselves, just as critically, whether they are doing the same.

I obviously lament the fall from grace of higher education. It is too easy, and intellectually dishonest, to say that universities are merely one more victim of a great rightward shift in American politics. The irresponsible assault on colleges and universities by the Secretary of Education invites such a convenient conclusion and distorts the discussion. While universities correct the false impressions being created by policy makers, they should also reflect on the condition of their compact with the American people. It is time to restore that compact and renew higher education's faith with its heritage.

# Making the Case for Funding

(REMARKS TO THE NEW YORK STATE DIVISION OF THE
BUDGET AS CHAIR, COMMISSION ON INDEPENDENT
COLLEGES AND UNIVERSITIES, NOVEMBER 1989)

The Commission on Independent Colleges and Universities (CICU) appreciates the opportunity to meet with you to discuss the concerns and needs of the 113 independent colleges and universities in New York State that the Commission represents. These institutions enroll 274,000 undergraduate students,[1] including 31 percent of the minority students attending college in the state,[2] and 118,000 graduate students, or about 65 percent of all graduate and professional students.[3] We collectively administer budgets totaling $6.9 billion[4] and employ 107,000 people.[5] New York State possesses the largest and most diverse system of independent higher education in the world.

Let me offer a few observations on the nature of these needs and how they have intensified.

## Graduate Education and Research

I start with graduate education and research. We are proposing a comprehensive approach to improving aid for graduate students, both full time and part time. New York State faces critical requirements for individuals trained at the graduate level, in science and technology and in education, to name just two key areas. And the importance of attracting members of minority groups to these and other fields is increasingly urgent. As our economy becomes more complex, as competition among states and nations grows more pronounced, as job skills become more specialized and thus require more advanced training, and as we seek to extend economic opportunity to ever broader segments of our society, graduate education becomes central to the aspirations of the people of this state.

The case we made to you a year ago was greatly fortified by the report of Governor Cuomo's Advisory Task Force on State Support for High Technology Research, chaired by Lt. Governor Stan Lundine (the Lundine Report). It is a careful and thoughtful study which concludes that colleges and universities need more investment from both the state and federal governments. In summing up his findings, the Lt. Governor cited a 1986 report of the White House Science Council Panel on the Health of U.S. Colleges and Universities, which said:

> Our universities today simply cannot respond to society's expectations for them or discharge their national responsibilities in research and education without substantially increased support.... The strength of the nation in trade, defense and health has been directly related to past investments in science and technology. Our future position in global markets will similarly depend on our willingness to respond to opportunity and to mobilize our strengths today.[6]

New York State has played a disproportionately significant role in much of the nation's past achievement in scientific research. Of the 140 U.S. citizens who have received the Nobel Prize in physics, chemistry, physiology and medicine since 1944, over half of them—73 recipients—have worked and/or taken degrees in New York State. In the same period, 5 other Nobel recipients who are not U.S. citizens spent significant portions of their professional lives in New York institutions.

Scientific discoveries by Nobel laureates in New York State have yielded profound benefits to society. In the health field, advances include the development by Andre Cournaud and Dickinson Richards at Columbia of catheters to chart the interior of the heart. Early work at Rockefeller University included advances in the treatment of wounds and the discovery of blood groups. In more recent years, advances in molecular and cellular biology have included Peyton Rous' demonstration that cancer can be caused by a virus, Gerald Edelman's work in deciphering the chemical structure of gamma globulin, and Bruce Merrifield's rapid assembly line method for making proteins.

Advances in physics in New York institutions have increased our understanding of fundamental properties of matter and have led to important new technologies. I. I. Rabi of Columbia first refined measurements of the magnetic properties of atomic nuclei. Charles Townes' early work at Columbia included the development of masers and later lasers. Hans Bethe of Cornell has been honored for his contribution to the theory of nuclear reactions.[7]

In contrast to this extraordinary record of past distinction, the Lundine Report was forced to conclude that support from New York State at present is "not sufficient to ameliorate the natural adversarial forces" that have converged to weaken the research universities in the state.

The report cited the following evidence of deterioration in New York State's scientific leadership position:[8]

- Ten years ago, New York scientists received more research grants from the National Institutes of Health (NIH) than any other state. Today, New York trails far behind California and Massachusetts.
- From 1982 to 1984, New York attracted only 7 percent of the 1,500 National Science Fellows (most accomplished researchers in the nation), while Massachusetts captured 23 percent and California 27 percent.
- In the last 5 years, NIH research grants to teaching hospitals and universities grew 77 percent in California and 68 percent in Massachusetts, but only 47 percent in New York.
- Further examining the impact of scientists by tracking the average number of citations per paper (number of times other researchers used one's research) shows New York in the middle of the range of the top ten states comprising the largest contributors to journal literature. New York lags appreciably behind Massachusetts and California and shows a zero growth slope, while the other two states are on a decided increase.

- California and Massachusetts have far outpaced New York in the growth in number of members in the National Academy of Sciences (NAS), the most prestigious science organization in the nation.

| | **NAS Membership** | | | |
|---|---|---|---|---|
| | *1965* | *1970* | *1986* | *% Change 1965-1986* |
| California | 116 | 203 | 402 | +247% |
| Massachusetts | 114 | 147 | 233 | +104% |
| New York | 111 | 140 | 184 | +66% |

The Lundine Report recognized that an intensive effort by the state of New York is required to reverse these trends and to restore New York to preeminent position as a source of advanced research. We believe that increased graduate aid is essential to accomplishing that goal.

It is essential because talented graduate students are indispensable to the conduct of sophisticated research in all disciplines, but especially in the sciences. Existence of an adequate supply of high-quality graduate students is just as important as state-of-the-art facilities in attracting and keeping the best scholars in New York State.

The central role played by graduate students in research is widely acknowledged by senior scientists. Joshua Lederberg, president of Rockefeller University, who received the Nobel Prize in 1954 for the work of his doctoral dissertation, said that graduate students at Rockefeller "come at an age when they are still untrammeled by too many of the received wisdoms of a prior generation. They ask new kinds of questions. So, often the most creative and most revolutionary findings are going to be made by very young people."

Professor Ronald Breslow, S. L. Mitchell Professor of Chemistry at Columbia, has said, "The differences in quality from one institution to another are reflected in the quality of the graduate students. 'How good are the graduate students?' This one of the first questions a prospective faculty member asks."

While first-rate graduate students in the sciences are a must, it is also vital to our scientific and technological enterprise that we have strength across a wide range of disciplines. We believe that the best research is done in an environment in which interaction among scientists, social scientists, and humanists is encouraged. A richly textured higher education system, with depth in all the intellectual disciplines is the surest guarantee of a strong scientific community, one which unites the scientific process with the study of the underlying values of science, its social use, and the study of society in general.

While New York State's strength in science has eroded somewhat quietly and without adequate recognition, a burgeoning set of problems in the supply of teachers looms ahead. At the elementary and secondary levels in New York City, 40 percent of the teaching force will retire in the next 5 years: one in six teachers today lack teaching licenses; some schools have as many as 70 percent "temporary per diem" teachers.[9] At the college level, William Bowen and Julie Ann Sosa, in their recent book *Prospects for Faculty in the Arts and Sciences*, have projected that in the period 1997-2002, there will be a nationwide shortage of about 5,500 faculty in the social sciences and humanities and about 1,800 in mathematics and the physical sciences.[10]

The situation regarding teachers from minority groups is particularly severe. We all acknowledge that we must have more minority teachers at every level of the educational enterprise. Yet only 12.3 percent of the elementary and secondary school teachers in New York State are minorities, while minorities make up 38.3 percent of the school population.[11] In higher education, only 10.8 percent of full-time faculty members are minorities,[12] while 24.3 percent of the undergraduate population is minority.[13] The absence of an adequate number of minority students at the graduate level suggests that minorities will continue to be underrepresented in the teaching force at every level for some time to come. Only 12.8 percent of graduate students in New York State are minority,[14] reflecting a nationwide problem. As President

Frank Rhodes of Cornell, who chaired the American Council on Education's Commission on Minority Participation in Higher Education and American Life, has pointed out, in 1986 only one black candidate received a doctorate in computer science out of 335 awarded. In mathematics, the numbers were 6 out of 730.[15] More minorities simply must be attracted to college teaching if we are to meet the educational needs of an increasingly minority state population, projected to be 33 percent minority by the year 2000.[16]

The need for skilled teachers and the strength and availability of graduate training in the state are closely connected. Graduate study, particularly in academic disciplines as opposed to teaching methods, is desirable for all elementary and secondary teachers and is, of course, essential for college-level teaching. And let us not forget that it is successive generations of college and university faculty, trained at the graduate level, who in turn train the successive generations of teachers for our elementary and secondary schools and our colleges. The different parts of our educational system are interdependent. Each part must have a steady supply of highly qualified, well-trained teachers. And so it is disturbing that the proportion of New York State undergraduates going on to graduate study in the State has declined 20 percent since 1974–75,[17] and the number of American students earning Ph.D.'s has declined 9 percent during this time period.[18]

In my view, the sad story of the erosion of New York's research standing and the decline in its graduate student population is directly connected to the state's failure to provide adequate financial aid to graduate students. When New York's graduate TAP was initiated in 1974, 35 percent of the graduate students in the state received awards. Today, only 15 percent get TAP aid.[19] Of the nineteen states that award need-based scholarship aid to graduate students, New York ranks sixteenth on the average size of award behind such states as California, Texas, and Massachusetts.[20]

An increase in graduate TAP will be useful to students at both public and independent institutions. But independent institutions have taken the lead in advocating graduate financial aid because they enroll 65 percent of the graduate and professional students in this state[21] and produce 74 percent of the advanced degrees.[22] Let me give you an idea of how strong is the view that graduate education needs our attention. While only 61 of the 113 CICU member institutions offer graduate training, we are united in advocating increased graduate aid because we recognize the critical importance of graduate education to our future ability to deliver the educational services essential to New York State's citizens.

We believe it is an urgent requirement for the state of New York to restore its financial aid to graduate students to a competitive level. In 1986, Governor Cuomo took the lead in recommending a doubling of the maximum graduate TAP award, the only time since graduate TAP's inception in 1974 that the award levels were adjusted. Unfortunately, since eligibility requirements were not raised, the increase assisted a very small and declining number of students. We hope Governor Cuomo will continue his leadership, as he did with the enhancement of undergraduate TAP in 1988, and the preservation of those enhancements in 1989. We recommend bringing graduate TAP to parity with undergraduate TAP at a cost of $14.61 million for independent-sector students when the program is fully phased in over 2 years; the cost of the first phase for next year's budget would be $12.11 million for independent-sector students.

We also believe it is time to acknowledge the difficulties of the many students pursuing graduate education on a part-time basis. There are 103,000 part-time graduate students in New York State—58 percent of the entire graduate student population. There is a heavy concentration of women (58 percent) and minorities (13 percent) in this group.[23] Many tend to be at lower income levels, often supporting families and pursuing graduate study as a means of upward mobility. Many are studying in job areas of critical need to New York State—for instance, teaching, nursing and other health professions, and science and mathematics. A new aid program for part-time graduate study would relieve some of the financial burdens faced by these students, who are often our most industrious and conscientious, encourage more prospective students to enter graduate study, and address looming shortages in a number of fields. We recommend an appropriation of $5 million that would be allocated to campuses, both public and independent, and then distributed to eligible students.

An increase in graduate TAP for full-time students and the creation of a program of support for part-time graduate study, totaling $15.26 million to independent-sector students in 1990-1991, together with the facilities program proposed by Lt. Governor Lundine, promise to strengthen the state's graduate education enterprise and its research capacity. The return on this investment will be tangible progress in economic development as well as in meeting the state's human resources requirements.

It makes no sense, in my view, to invest heavily in state-of-the-art buildings and equipment and at the same time neglect the "people side" of the research equation. The average cost of eleven "high-tech" facilities constructed with special state grants and loans over the past 10 years was $19 million. Think of it: the enhancement we ask in graduate aid for students at all institutions is just about equal to the cost of one building.

## THE HIGHER EDUCATION OPPORTUNITY PROGRAM

I have already mentioned the critical need for more minorities in graduate schools and particularly in the teaching professions. Increasing access for minorities to undergraduate education is equally important. Frank Rhodes has also reported on a study indicating that fewer than 59 percent of blacks and 41 percent of Hispanics in New York State over age 25 had completed 4 years of high school. At the college level, only 9 percent of New York's black adults and 7 percent of it Hispanic adults had completed 4 years of college, while more than four times that percentage of Asian adults and more than twice that percentage of white adults had college degrees.[24]

Governor Cuomo's Liberty Scholarship and Liberty Partnership programs are a bold and imaginative response to this urgent problem. Since we last spoke, thirty-two independent institutions have initiated Liberty Partnerships with eighty secondary schools.[25] These efforts supplement the existing ten Stay-in-School Partnership programs. Additional Liberty programs will be created next fall. This massive intervention, coupled with the incentives of Liberty Scholarships, is sure to cut the high school dropout rate and increase the flow of at-risk students to college. The colleges and universities of the state have demonstrated their desire to accept and work with minority and other at-risk students. Independent institutions already enroll about a third of the state's minority college students.[26] But we need help in serving the increased number of students that will flow to us from the Liberty programs.

Fortunately, in 1969 the state of New York pioneered the Higher Education Opportunity Program (HEOP), which may be the most successful program in the nation serving educationally and economically disadvantaged students. Today 6,550 students receive supplemental aid and special counseling and tutorial services.[27] The rate of graduation for HEOP participants (54.8 percent)[28] outpaces the national rate of 53 percent for all students.[29] But the program is woefully inadequate in numbers served. It has turned away twelve proposals for new HEOP programs, and eight other colleges that wanted programs were discouraged from applying because of inadequate state funding.[30] The independent-sector colleges seek to expand HEOP by 15,000 students by enlarging the seventy-nine existing programs and creating twenty-eight new programs by 1993. When students reach the end of the Liberty program "pipeline," starting in 1991, there will be an increase in the number of students requiring the kinds of tutoring and counseling services that HEOP offers. The state now spends $20.1 million on HEOP,[31] an amount matched with approximately $30 million of expenditures by independent institutions.[32] We are ready to respond with effort and additional funds if the state increases its investment in this critical endeavor.

With the programs at full strength, the state will be spending $132 million a year on the Liberty and Stay-in-School

Partnerships.[33] This huge investment in increasing the college-going rate of disadvantaged students will not realize its full potential if HEOP is not expanded. In more human terms, the promise of a college education made possible by the Liberty program will end in disappointment and despair for many unless HEOP is extended. We recommend a total of $75.2 million in new funds to be phased in over 4 years. The cost to the state in 1990-1991 would be $17.32 million. Let us work in partnership with the state to finish the job begun by the Liberty program. In an age when we have severe doubts about the effectiveness of government programs, let us not fail to support one that has a measurable record of success.

## INSTITUTIONAL AID

We have spoken of the role of independent institutions in strengthening the state's research capacity, meeting its need for skilled human resources in the face of severe shortages, and fulfilling its commitment to an integrated society with equal opportunity for all. These achievements assume institutions of high quality—strong faculties, vital curricula, and modern facilities—all of which depend on a healthy financial base.

The state of New York recognized over 20 years ago that independent institutions serve the public purpose and that an investment by the state in general institutional aid was an investment in a healthy and diverse system of higher education, balanced between public and private institutions. The Select Committee on the Future of Private and Independent Higher Education in New York State, chaired by McGeorge Bundy, stated the following premise for its report's conclusions:

> ...The value to society of strong private institutions of higher learning is clear and great. As an extension of this proposition, we have taken it as axiomatic that any deterioration in the established quality of these private institutions—whether in terms of faculty, curriculum, academic standards or physical plant—would be harmful not only to the institutions themselves but also to the public good.[34]

The Committee's principal recommendation followed directly from this point. It called for "direct assistance from New York State to private colleges and universities," saying:

> We think it is clear that the value of these institutions to New York is so great that such assistance is justified. And we believe that without it there is likely to be serious deterioration in one of the State's great assets—her remarkable array of strong and diversified private colleges and universities.[35]

Governor Cuomo and the Legislature accepted this recommendation, and the so-called Bundy aid program began in 1969. Though it has become an integral part of higher-education financing, Bundy aid has been increased only four times since its inception, an average of once every 5 years. These increases have not kept pace with inflation. Since the last adjustment in 1985, the real value of Bundy aid has declined by 20 percent. We are proposing an inflation adjustment going back to 1986, an increase of $22.3 million (20 percent) applied evenly to all degree levels.

We have taken care not to promote the needs of independent institutions as if they were in opposition to the needs of the public institutions in this state. We believe a mixed system of public and independent institutions is healthy and that strong public institutions invigorate the environment for all of higher education. But we cannot help noting an inequity between the state's treatment of public institutions and its investment in the independent colleges and universities. Since 1986, we have received no additional general state aid, while the public colleges and universities have enjoyed increases of 26.1 percent or $500 million. Evenhanded support of public and independent institutions in New York has produced a varied and superior system of higher education prepared to meet whatever challenges are set before it by the citizens of the state. The failure to nourish one element now threatens that balance and represents neither good public policy nor the efficient use of limited state resources. Independent institutions continue to offer the state its best bargain, costing the taxpayer only 12.7 percent as much per student as the public system,[36] and producing the largest number of graduates each year: 59 percent of all undergraduate degrees and 74 percent of all advanced degrees granted in the state.[37]

The public debate last spring over Governor Cuomo's proposal to reduce Bundy aid made clear the importance with which the program is viewed and its centrality to the well-being of independent higher education. Bundy aid, HEOP, undergraduate and graduate TAP, and the creation and expansion of the state and city university systems are examples of the vision that has characterized New York State's higher education public policy in the middle years of this century. We hope you will agree that the Bundy program should be restored to the purchasing power it possessed 4 years ago, so that it will continue to be as effective as it has been in the past.

We recognize that New York State's resources are limited and that choices must be made. We have deliberately kept our requests modest and focused on the programs that we think are most crucial and that have the broadest impact and the greatest return on taxpayer investment. And we have proposed a phasing plan which eases the burden on next year's state budget. Our request of $54.88 million of additional investment for graduate financial aid, HEOP, and Bundy aid is about half of what we believe is required to strengthen independent higher-education in New York. But it represents a critical threshold of response to both current conditions and future challenges.

## NOTES

1. New York State Education Department, Office of Postsecondary Policy Analysis, "College and University Opening Fall Enrollment, New York State, Fall 1989," June 1989.
2. New York State Education Department, Information Center of Education, "College and University Racial/Ethnic Distribution of Enrollment, New York State, Fall 1986," August 1987.
3. New York State Education Department, Office of Postsecondary Policy Analysis, "College and University Opening Fall Enrollment, New York State, Fall 1988," June 1989.

## MAKING THE CASE FOR FUNDING 207

4. New York State Education Department, Office of Postsecondary Policy Analysis, "College and University Revenues and Expenditures New York State Fiscal Year Ending 1988," July 1989. A 7 percent increase in cost was applied by CICU for 1988-1989 data.
5. New York State Education Department, Information Center of Education, "College and University Employees, New York State, Fall 1987-1988," October 1988.
6. Lundine Report, pp. 24-25.
7. Information on Nobel Prize recipients derived from the following sources: *Who's Who in America*; *American Men and Women of Science: Physical and Biological Sciences*," 15th and 16th eds.; *Nobel Prize Winners*, Tyler Wasson (ed.), H. W. Wilson Co., 1987.
8. Lundine Report, pp. 22-23.
9. New York City Board of Education, "From Hiring to Firing: Report of the Task Force on Professionalism," 1988.
10. William Bowen and Julie Ann Sosa, *Prospects for Faculty in the Arts and Sciences*, Princeton University Press, 1989, p. 136.
11. New York State Education Department, Information Center of Education, "Racial/Ethnic Distribution of Public School Students and Staff, New York State, 1987-1988," September 1988.
12. New York State Education Department, Office of Postsecondary Policy Analysis, "College and University Distribution of Employees by Racial/Ethnic Category and Gender," September 1989.
13. New York State Education Department, Information Center of Education, "College and University Racial/Ethnic Distribution of Enrollment, New York State, Fall 1986," August 1987.
14. *Ibid.*
15. Frank H. T. Rhodes, "One-Third of a Nation." Address to the Annual Meeting of CICU, March 7, 1989.
16. New York State Project 2000, "Report on Population; The People of New York: Population Dynamics of a Changing State," April 1986.
17. CICU calculation from New York State Education Department enrollment and state residency data.
18. New York State Education Department, Information Center of Education, "College and University Racial/Ethnic Distribution of Degrees Conferred, New York State, Fall 1986-1987," December 1988.
19. New York State Education Department and Higher Education Services Corporation, Annual Reports 1987-1988 and 1974-1975.
20. *The Chronicle of Higher Education*, March 16, 1988, p. A30.
21. New York State Education Department, Office of Postsecondary Policy Analysis, "College and University Opening Fall Enrollment, New York State, Fall 1988," June 1989.
22. New York State Education Department, Information Center of Education, "College and University Degrees Conferred, New York State, Fall 1986-1987," October 1988.

23. New York State Education Department, Information Center of Education, "College and University Racial/Ethnic Distribution of Enrollment, New York State, Fall 1986," August 1987.
24. Rhodes, *op. cit.*
25. New York State Education Department, Postsecondary Equity and Access Programs Office.
26. New York State Education Department, Information Center of Education, "College and University Racial/Ethnic Distribution of Enrollment, New York State, Fall 1986," August 1987.
27. New York State Education Department, Bureau of Higher Education Opportunity Programs, Annual Report 1987-1988, March 1989.
28. *Ibid.*
29. National Association of Independent Colleges and Universities summary of "College Persistence and Degree Attainment for 1980 High School Graduates: Hazards for Transfers, Stopouts, and Part-Timers," National Center for Education Statistics Survey Report, U.S. Department of Education, January 1989.
30. New York State Education Department, Bureau of Higher Education Opportunity Programs, October 1989.
31. New York State Education Department, Bureau of Higher Education Opportunity Programs, Annual Report 1987-1988, March 1989.
32. CICU projection.
33. Higher Education Services Corporation projections.
34. "New York State and Private Higher Education: Report of the Select Committee on the Future of Private and Independent Higher Education in New York State," January 1968, p. 13.
35. *Ibid.*, p. 4.
36. CICU calculation from New York State Education Department summary, "New York State Funds for Support of Higher Education 1988-1989." Available funds divided by full-time-equivalent students in each sector.
37. New York State Higher Education Department, Information Center of Education, "College and University Degrees Conferred, New York State, Fall 1986-1987," October 1988.

# Peer Review and Maintaining Excellence

(ANNUAL REPORT, NOVEMBER 1991)

During the 1990-1991 academic year, the Middle States Association of Colleges and Schools conducted its 10-year accreditation review of the University. At about the same time, the Middle States Association became embroiled in controversy when the U.S. Department of Education delayed renewing Middle States' own accreditation. The reason given for the delay was a concern that the Association had exceeded its authority in establishing standards of diversity for the Board of Trustees, faculty, student body, and curricula of its member institutions.

The coincidence of these two events invites a comment on the accreditation process and our own experience with it, as well as on the state of the University and goals we have set for its future.

The organization of higher education in America is unique because of the importance placed on private institutions. Also unique is a reliance on the peer review process to evaluate the effectiveness of colleges and universities. Both these factors have contributed to the quality of American higher education, helping to make it the envy of the world.

The peer review process is coordinated by six regional accrediting associations, which colleges and universities voluntarily join. The New School is one of 505 members of the Commission on Higher Education of the Middle States Association. Middle States is over a century old, while its Higher Education Commission was established in 1920 to accredit colleges and universities. The regional associations derive their authority from their members, but they themselves have been accredited since the early 1950s by the U.S. Department of Education and its predecessor agencies. Since

1972, the federal government has made its scholarship and loan funds available only to students who study at an institution accredited by one of the recognized regional associations.

A college's accreditation is reviewed every ten years. When a review occurs, the college prepares a lengthy self-study report that discusses its own strengths and weaknesses, its mission and goals, and its success or failure in reaching them. The campus is then visited by a team of examiners, organized by the regional association and composed of individuals from other colleges and universities who have expertise in the fields offered by the institution under review. Members of the "site visit team" meet with faculty, students, Trustees, and administrators; they examine facilities; they look at financial statements and planning documents. The team then writes an evaluation of the institution, assessing its qualities, noting where it needs improvement, and deciding whether it is adhering to the goals it has set for itself. The team makes a recommendation on whether to renew the college's accreditation, and the association's board then acts upon this recommendation.

The accreditation process is both revealing and useful to the institution under scrutiny. The self-study exercise brings many issues and concerns into the open and clarifies the institution's priorities and needs. Peer review accreditation has served higher education well. It is an established system that provides accountability to students seeking to enroll in colleges and universities by offering some assurance of the basic quality of the education they will receive. The process of accreditation, however, has been confronted by controversy this past year.

In November 1990, the U.S. Department of Education's National Advisory Committee on Accreditation and Institutional Eligibility voted to delay continued recognition for the Middle States Association because of concern over the application of "diversity standards." This action was taken in response to findings by Middle States that Baruch College of the City University of New York and Westminster Theological Seminary in Philadelphia failed to maintain a sufficiently diverse membership in faculty or governing board, respectively. As a result, the Middle States Association is now under active review by Secretary of Education Lamar Alexander who will bring the case back to his department's Advisory Committee in the fall of 1991.

There is considerable irony in the Secretary's explanation of the scrutiny of Middle States. He has expressed concern that the association "may undermine institutional autonomy and academic freedom...." Yet the attention given to the issue of diversity was authorized, after intense discussion, by the institutions that make up the association. Indeed, the concern for diversity is not new. For example, since 1957, when it issued a policy statement on the subject, the association, has taken a vigorous interest in the status of women in higher education. Its concern with racial and ethnic diversity was sharpened in a 1978 policy statement on diversity and nondiscrimination. So the question before us is: Why has the Department of Education chosen this moment to intrude upon the work of the peer review process? It may be that the timing reflects not so much a change in the work of the association as it does a change in the attitude of a national administration that has an ambiguous commitment to American pluralism and no coherent policy for advancing racial justice and nondiscrimination.

While the Secretary of Education's concern for academic freedom may have a hollow ring, it is worth acknowledging that there are legitimate questions to be asked about accreditation practices. A process whose purpose is review and evaluation should continually be reviewed itself. A self-regulated accreditation mechanism should have frequent examinations by the colleges and universities that comprise the associations. Accreditation is a powerful tool that should be used carefully, judiciously, and, above all, fairly.

Virtually all the institutions in the Middle States Association support the fundamental goals of its emphasis on diversity. That concern not only reflects the highest aspirations of educators, but also mirrors the long-held values of this democratic society. How such goals and standards are implemented within the context of accreditation should be a subject of ongoing consideration.

Accrediting associations have been known to overstep their bounds, though very infrequently. I suspect that Middle States could have handled the Baruch and Westminster cases differently, with greater sensitivity in methods and public statements. But I reject the suggestion of the Secretary of Education that Middle States' actions undermined academic freedom. Those actions were, in fact, intended to expand access to educational opportunity to groups that have traditionally been underrepresented in universities. I hope the government's delay in reauthorizing the Middle States Association will not intimidate its members into showing less concern for the obligation of colleges and universities to play a constructive role in making American pluralism work.

The New School's experience with the Middle States Association is testimony to the professionalism with which the association approaches its work. In our last accreditation (in 1980), the association chronicled serious problems at the University, particularly with the Graduate Faculty. While that report did not make pleasant reading to me as I made my decision to come to the New School, I considered it to be a fair critique. The 1980 report and its recommendations were useful guides to me and my colleagues as we worked to strengthen the University in this past decade.

We were, of course, gratified in 1990 when the eleven-member 1990 site visit team noted that "the New School has made impressive progress" since the team's last visit, and that it had articulated "a powerful and compelling vision" for its future. At the same time, the 1990 report noted areas in which the University was not as strong as it would like to be and offered concrete recommendations for improvements. On the issue of diversity that so concerns the Department of Education, we found the site visit team's questions entirely appropriate and not at all intrusive. And we were gratified by the team's conclusion that

> the institution is justly proud of a diversity initiative codified and intensified in September 1989 to increase the numbers of faculty, students, and staff from underrepresented groups, to develop a more inclusive and pluralistic curriculum, and to establish policies and procedures for dealing with discriminatory harassment.... Within the limits of available resources, the University has mounted a determined and largely successful effort.

My only comment on this conclusion is that it is too generous—we have much more to do.

It is easy enough to be pessimistic these days, to dismiss our ambitions for the New School as worthy but poorly timed. It is certainly true that our environment is difficult: state aid has diminished sharply, the region is in a prolonged recession, the city is facing one of its periodic fiscal crises, and private institutions everywhere are cutting back. And it is also true that our programs require investment across the board—in all six schools, in people, in buildings, in current funds, and in endowment. While we have made tough, clear, and difficult choices, I am the first to concede that our plan for the University presses the outer edge of what is realistic. But isn't that what we should expect from the New School? I think there is reason for optimism about the New School's future.

We have a tradition of going against the grain, astonishing conventional wisdom, and challenging inherited orthodoxies. And as individuals—whether lay leaders, faculty, students, or administrators—we are drawn to this place by some characteristics we have in common. Each of us in our own way derives excitement from the iconoclastic nature of the New School; we are stimulated, not discouraged, by the improbable and long odds; we resonate to the gritty determination to defend intellectual and artistic freedom; we are buoyed by the chance to stretch individual potential and accomplishment; and, for the purpose of this discussion, most importantly we like to win. The New School has always attracted people with an affirmative outlook, an indomitable spirit, and a determination to prevail.

I am now completing my second 5-year term as president of the New School for Social Research. The Board of Trustees has asked me to serve a third term, and I have accepted its mandate with enthusiasm. I anticipate this new term with the same sense of excitement that I felt 10 years ago. To be sure, we start now from a higher plateau and a much stronger base. But the incline of the challenge seems just as steep as does the precipice into which we might fall if our energy flags. I invite you to continue with me in our stewardship of one of the most unusual educational enterprises in the world.

# SUSTAINING THE SENSITIVE ECOLOGY OF THE UNIVERSITY

(ANNUAL REPORT, NOVEMBER 1992)

Last year was a difficult one for private colleges and universities: record deficits, government investigations, faculty unrest, and more presidential retirements than usual. While the warning signs that all was not well in higher education had been visible for several years, 1992 will be remembered as the year when the public finally took notice. While distress grips public universities as well, the problems appear deeper —and the stakes higher—among private institutions.

This past year also presented difficulties for the New School for Social Research. I think we are weathering them well. The New School is unlike any other higher education institution. So the ways these problems confront us, and the ways we deal with them, necessarily differ from the experiences of other institutions. Yet our experience does provide useful insight into some of the larger issues confronting higher education. As I begin my third 5-year term as president, I would like to reflect on those issues as I discuss goals for the New School in the years immediately ahead.

First, let me briefly review the year just past. This annual report tells a story of a robust artistic and intellectual life at the University: first-rate new appointments, vigorous engagement in the issues of our time through a rich spectrum of guest speakers, new program initiatives, and continued growth in fund-raising. The University also achieved its twelfth consecutive balanced budget and saw its endowment increase by 24 percent through a combination of new gifts and appreciation.

Yet not all the news was good. The double impact of a decline in the pool of 18-year olds and the recession caused enrollment shortfalls in each of the past 2 years. This contrasts with the expectations in the university's multi-year plan for a 3 percent annual growth in enrollment to finance our ambitious program of academic improvement. Since 73 percent of the University's income derives from tuition and fees, there was no choice but to reduce the base of the budget by about 6 percent, a move that led to a 9 percent reduction in full-time faculty and staff. The strategy for reductions assigned a dollar target to each dean and administrative officer, so the process was highly decentralized. To guide their work, I articulated three principles:

1. High quality programs should be favored over those needing significant investment.
2. Programs central to the University's core mission should be favored over those which are peripheral.
3. Programs which cover full costs should be favored over those requiring a large subsidy.

The base reduction program, while painful, went smoothly. In reviewing the total picture of cuts, I estimate that 80 percent or so will be permanent—that is, cuts that should have been made anyway through a normal process of pruning. The remaining 20 percent will be built back within a few years as our financial circumstances improve. All in all, I believe the process was a healthy one which has left the university in a strong position for the future.

## Overarching Goals

I have written in these pages in years past about the mission of the University (1983–1984) and the specific areas for immediate attention (1990–1991). From those earlier statements can be drawn a few objectives:

- We intend to continue fashioning a genuine university out of disparate parts of this unusual institution.
- We strive to maintain its distinctive character: fresh, quick

to innovate, prepared to challenge inherited wisdom and accepted orthodoxy.
- We seek a niche for each academic program and have the ambition that each be among the best at what it does.
- We aim to attract outstanding people to the university—students, faculty, staff, Trustees, and advisory committee members—bright, fresh intellectual and artistic talent.
- We are committed to making American pluralism work by building a genuinely diverse community and making our environment comfortable for diversity.
- We see the New School as a paradigm for New York City, serving at once as a great international beacon and as an institution concerned with local problems of race, class, gender, ethnicity, and urban poverty.

Within these overarching goals are five specific issues which deserve fuller elaboration. While I discuss them in relation to the New School for Social Research, several of them also address concerns which confront many private universities.

## The Special Financial Burden on This Generation

Most private higher education institutions are facing serious structural deficits which demand corrective action. Trustees, administration, and faculty must weigh a series of trade-offs—for example, between immediate needs and future possibilities, between investment in facilities and investment in people, between preserving endowments and reserves and maintaining the momentum for academic quality, between a commitment to open doors through massive increases in financial aid and a policy of affordable tuition rates for those who pay fully. A sensible strategy for achieving financial equilibrium will seek appropriate balances and timetables, and not stark either/or choices.

In the decade of the 1980s, the New School was fortunate to be able to make significant investment in strengthening existing programs and initiating new academic ventures, and at the same time pursue a prudent, perhaps even conservative, fiscal strategy. The rebuilding of the Graduate Faculty was our most visible achievement, but the Graduate School of Management and Parsons also improved dramatically with high-quality faculty appointments and significant expansion of academic space (about 20 percent) at Parsons. Mergers were effected with the Mannes College of Music and the World Policy Institute, and Eugene Lang College and an undergraduate Jazz Program were created. A modern, well-staffed administrative infrastructure was put in place. At the same time, budgets were balanced; the endowment spending rate was cut in half, to about 5 percent; the endowment grew from $7.6 million to $37.6 million; and university reserves grew from zero to about $3.3 million. As a result, our financial health is stronger than at any point in the New School's 73-year history. We have sought and achieved a balance between fiscal prudence and our quest for academic excellence.

However, the New School is not immune to the underlying forces that have weakened the financial health of private universities. While there are many adverse factors, two stand out.

1. Many universities have underspent on maintenance and now face massive demands for funds to modernize buildings and equipment. At the New School, debt for facilities has grown from $8.3 million to $18 million since 1982, and the amount allocated for deferred maintenance in 1992–1993 is 3 percent of the budget, compared with 1 percent a decade earlier.
2. In the face of state and federal aid programs which have not kept pace with tuition increases, almost all universities have dramatically increased financial aid. In seeking to open their doors to a genuine cross section of talented students, they strive to build a healthy and diverse American society. At the New School, for example, financial aid has increased 250 percent since 1983–1984 in real terms (adjusting for enrollment variations and tuition increases).

In weighing future investment in these two major areas against the trade-off questions I posed earlier, I come to somewhat different conclusions for each.

Some universities with very generous financial aid policies have been forced to cut back on student scholarships. That will not happen at this university, because we view financial aid as critical to our goal of being an academic community open to all on the basis of individual merit, not family circumstance. Our ambition remains to increase the percentage of tuition returned to students as gift aid by at least half a point a year (adjusted for tuition increases and enrollment variations), perhaps more, for the next 5 years. The deans of the University's six schools have rated financial aid as their highest priority.

With respect to facilities, the University will not take on significant new debt, which burdens the operating budget. Future expansion will have to be supported by fund-raising and by converting existing rental payments into debt service. We should continue a stepped-up deferred maintenance program, but stretch out the schedule to avoid imposing a significant burden on the operating budget. To help finance this more ambitious maintenance program without forcing unacceptable trade-offs on the people side of the budget, the Trustees have increased the spending rate from the endowment by 1 percent for 3 years. It is sensible to think of the endowment and the buildings together as the University's capital assets and reasonable to invest one form of capital in preserving the other.

Clarity on these two major engines of expenditure allows for judgments about other parts of the University's budget. Most other areas have seen little growth, and some significant retrenchment, in the past 2 years. Deans, faculty, administrative officers, and their staffs have felt a shift from the expansion and enhancement mode of the 1980s to a period of severely limited expectations in the last 2 years.

The large question before us is whether to continue with a "no growth," "limited improvement" approach or to resume a carefully calculated program of investment in academic quality. The Trustees and I firmly believe the New School for Social Research should distance itself from the prevailing mood of gloom in higher education and recommit itself to investments designed to make its core programs better.

But some may ask: Should we not wait for a year or two of solid enrollment performance and increased fund-raising? Would it not be wise to take advantage of the general environment of retrenchment? The answer to these questions requires a comment about the rhythm of institutions of higher education.

Academic enterprises are sensitive ecologies built on real achievement, hope, and expectations. They rarely stand still: progress or decline are their natural inclinations, and the space between the two is brief and fragile. The New School has been on an upward track for 10 years and is now widely recognized as one of the most improved institutions in the country. But in the past 2 years the rate of ascent has slowed to a near standstill. It will be difficult to secure the gains we have achieved if a sense of static or even impending decline develops. And the fact or perception of slippage feeds on itself psychologically, picking up speed and requiring very expensive countermeasures to arrest the downward spiral.

We are able to consider a new period of improvement precisely because we have managed our affairs conservatively in the past decade. We have made hard choices on the expense side by eliminating weak, costly and peripheral programs; we have increased our fund-raising by 1200 percent; we have accumulated reserves to cushion the University against future economic hardships. But we have taken some calculated risks as well.

Last year, amid the sharp retrenchment program, the University also pursued a countercyclical strategy through a series of investments designed to stimulate enrollment growth.

The Trustees, inspired by a suggestion from their colleague Robert Milano, created the Fund for New Initiatives to provide seed money to strengthen existing programs which yielded net income, and to create new programs which would operate at a surplus. Awards to ten programs will generate an estimated $500,000 in new net tuition income this year and the prospect for significantly more in subsequent years. The Trustees have donated $1 million for additional investments through the Fund for New Initiatives in 1992-1993.

This strategy for innovation, together with wider recognition of the enhanced quality of the University's major academic programs, appears to have reversed the enrollment decline. A strong performance by virtually all the University's principal programs in the spring, summer and fall of 1992 suggests a return to stability—probably even modest growth—which will provide the income stream for a fresh round of academic advancement.

## THE NEED FOR A STRONGER FACULTY ROLE IN GOVERNANCE

All universities became much more complicated over the past 20 years, a trend that led to the growth of a professional administrative cadre to manage the financial and other nonacademic aspects of higher-education institutions. The managerial side of universities, facing unrelenting financial constraints, has come to dominate academic decision making; and as a consequence, a chasm between faculty and administration has grown at many institutions. This unhealthy situation was brought on, not by a design to subordinate academic priorities and prerogatives, but by inadequate attention to how governance patterns should adjust to the changing nature of universities. It has been compounded by an instinctive distrust of institutions that arose in the 1960s, a distrust exhibited by some faculty currently rising to senior status who see institutions as the "other." The situation is exacerbated by administrative decisions that seem to emphasize "good business practices" and appear insensitive to the textured relationships upon which academic quality depends. Much work needs to be done to restore a sense of "ownership" and responsibility on the part of faculty members and to elicit a renewed commitment of time and emotional energy devoted to strengthening their home institutions. These changes must come through closer ties between administration and faculty, greater involvement by faculty in decision making, and a good faith effort to rebuild the bonds of trust and consensus upon which universities depend.

The New School's experience differs from this general pattern. Evolving as it did from a school for adults taught almost exclusively by part-time faculty, it has had practically no tradition of faculty governance on a university-wide basis. In the past 10 years we have worked to enlarge faculty participation in governance, especially at Parsons, and have created University-wide, faculty-staff committees for the libraries, computer services, honorary degrees, diversity, financial aid, and student life. Where faculty elsewhere have often experienced a sense of loss of authority and responsibility, the trend here has been toward more faculty involvement, albeit from a very low base.

But we are far short of where we should be, since no faculty group exists which can advise the officers and Trustees on large policy and budgetary issues. In this next period I would like to strengthen faculty governance in each of our schools and at the university level. To that end, I will invite each of the University's six faculties to elect two representatives to a University-wide faculty advisory committee which will work with the President and Provost on a variety of policy matters.

Among the issues needing attention at every institution of higher education is the amount of effort devoted to teaching as opposed to professional activities and outside consulting. This university has maintained its teaching expectations while other institutions have reduced theirs below a level that is economically sustainable. That erosion has led to public criticism of the academy and is harmful in raising both public and private support. Talk has begun elsewhere of reversing the trend that earlier reduced teaching requirements to three and four courses a year, and I fervently hope our faculty will maintain its present teaching load and increase its presence on campus. There is no way a formula of higher salaries, more financial aid, lower teaching loads, less faculty counseling, and higher tuition will work at private universities. Rather, we must find a way to blend higher salaries and financial aid with higher-quality education through first-rate teaching and more individual attention—practices that justify tuition levels so much higher than at public institutions. And that will require more, not less, effort from members of the faculty.

## THE LIBERAL ARTS: CORE OF THE UNIVERSITY

The past 20 years have seen a shift in the balance of power, prestige, and financial well-being within universities between the liberal arts and the professions. This is due in part to the fact that professional schools have commanded greater and more reliable sources of income. Furthermore, professional schools have been able to articulate a clear sense of mission, while liberal arts faculties have struggled to accommodate an expanding realm of knowledge, debating what should be taught and how.

The "identity crisis" of the liberal arts has caused some apprehension about the future course of the great traditional universities. Concerns have risen about whether there will be enough new young scholars to replace the current cohort of senior scholars now approaching retirement. Will there be enough people, and of high enough quality, to carry on the fundamental university mission of the discovery and transmission of knowledge? Will the liberal arts remain strong enough to exercise their central role in defining and sharpening universities' intellectual values and sense of purpose?

Our university's greatest expansion has come in the professional schools, starting with the acquisition of Parsons School of Design (1970), followed by the creation of the Graduate School of Management and Urban Policy (1975) and the Jazz Program (1986), and the merger with the Mannes College of Music (1990). These mergers and acquisitions provided the driving energy in transforming this institution into a university—but, paradoxically, made that evolution difficult to consummate fully. Thus the New School for Social Research faces a variant on the question of balance between professional education and the liberal arts.

The strengthening of the liberal arts—by which I mean Eugene Lang College, the Graduate Faculty, and the Adult Division—will be a primary goal for the period ahead. And improving the liberal arts components of the Parsons, Mannes, Jazz, and Graduate School of Management programs will provide the richest potential pathway for even greater interaction among the divisions and a greater sense of coherence throughout the University.

*1.* Eugene Lang College is our most explicitly "liberal arts" school. I remain committed to building Lang as a distinctive, high-quality, liberal arts college for students who want somewhat less structure than that of traditional colleges, who are alive to the benefits of studying in a great urban center, and who like the combination of small classes and access to the larger university.

*2.* The growth of Lang College, sharing, as it does, faculty and strength in the social sciences with the Graduate Faculty, should help complete rebuilding of the Graduate Faculty. The restoration of Ph.D. programs in sociology, political science, and philosophy, and the creation of a Committee on Historical Studies, which now compete with the best graduate schools for the most talented students, was the most important accomplishment of the past 10 years. Our next task is to build a new Committee on Political Economy and to strengthen the Economics Department. Following hard on these will be the refurbishment of the Liberal Studies program, the creation of a new Committee on Gender Studies and Feminist Theory, and fresh attention to anthropology. Of critical importance will be strengthening the Department of Psychology, especially its clinical studies program.

Our past success will test the Graduate Faculty in two ways: larger and wealthier universities will attempt to attract our faculty, and competition with those institutions for the best graduate students will require more financial aid. We must move vigorously in the next 2 years to meet these challenges. To be sure, we will lose some faculty to other institutions—that is to be expected and is a normal occurrence. The real test is whether we can replace them at an equal or higher level of quality.

The complete rebuilding of the Graduate Faculty and the raising of funds to secure its future remain central to the agenda of the Trustees.

3. The third element in building the liberal arts is the original New School, the Adult Division. That adult education in the liberal arts is at the center of our institution is one of its distinguishing characteristics. We have never focused heavily on the typical fare of adult education, such as career development; and we should concede that the training we offer in such fields will be more limited than that offered by other institutions. We must reaffirm the New School's commitment to the liberal arts, visual, and performing arts and public policy for adult New Yorkers who wish to study for personal enrichment.

In addition, the New School should place renewed emphasis on its liberal arts baccalaureate program for adults. Originally begun in 1944 for returning veterans, the New School's B.A. program now enrolls nearly 300 students. It is a program that provides the advantages of great breadth and flexibility to its students, and we should encourage its growth to 1,000 students by extending it to new populations.

4. The University's professionally oriented schools—Parsons, Mannes, and the Graduate School of Management—also face questions about the liberal arts that need attention. The ongoing challenge is to define the role that the liberal arts should play in a professional curriculum and what portion of such a curriculum should be devoted to so-called liberal studies. The obvious answer to that question is "more," and I think most members of our professional faculties would agree.

The obstacle to increasing the proportion of liberal studies in these curricula is that the development of professional skills takes a great deal of curricular time. While faculties want to increase the time devoted to the liberal arts, they are loathe to give up any part of the professional curriculum. This is a problem that demands our most creative thinking. Our professional students' success in their chosen fields can only be enhanced through greater exposure to the liberal arts. Their ability to think through problems, to articulate issues, to be aware of current dilemmas in the world, and to be leaders who shape the future of their professions rests on the quality of their liberal arts education, as much as on the quality of their professional training.

A final point regarding the liberal arts. The University as a whole has less science and math in its curriculum than it should. A critical priority for the next period will be deepening math and science instruction at the New School in ways appropriate to our traditions and resources. I will shortly appoint a University-wide task force to formulate a plan of action.

## Expanding Our Technological Capabilities

Related to the absence of science, math, and engineering, is the University's sluggish pace in exploiting new technology. The challenge has at least three dimensions.

*1.* We must ensure that all students enrolled in our degree programs are computer-literate when they graduate. This will require significant enhancement of the University's computer facilities. The cohorts of future college students who are now in elementary school will arrive at college already computer-literate. They will have high expectations for the kinds of computer facilities available to them and for the ways that computers are integrated into the curriculum. They will have little interest in institutions that do not meet these expectations. It is both a matter of educational quality and a competitive imperative that all the University's schools strengthen computer instruction.

*2.* That admonition applies most urgently to professional programs in Parsons and the Graduate School of Management, which must train students to the "state of the art" in their fields. The design disciplines in particular are being revolutionized by the role technology plays. Parsons must train its students to be participants in the revolution and to lead it. So Parsons must strive to be in the forefront of change rather than a follower. This ambition has significant implications for curriculum reform and investment in computer facilities.

3. New technologies allow education to occur at a distance. In light of its tradition of responsiveness to mature students, the New School Adult Division should take the lead in delivering educational material to new audiences: people confined at home, working parents unable to come to our 12th Street classrooms, citizens yearning for access to a cosmopolitan culture from an isolated geographical area, and workers in the city's many businesses who seek to upgrade their skills. The New School has obtained a 3-year grant from the Fund for the Improvement of Post Secondary Education to develop three core undergraduate courses for adult "distance learners." This initiative, which clearly lends itself to making education more flexible and responsive, will be followed by other efforts to use the technologies for educational purposes.

## Broadening the Pluralistic Character of the University

Our slowness on the new technologies illuminates a paradox which has characterized the New School for some time now. Even though the word "new" is in our name, we have come to see ourselves as the defender of noble intellectual traditions. In the period ahead, innovation must reach beyond new programs to fresh ways of seeing the world and America's place in it.

No issue poses a greater intellectual challenge than America's commitment to pluralism. The United States is struggling with the gap between the promises of its charter documents and present-day reality. Racial conflict, urban poverty, discrimination in many forms, skepticism about our democratic form of government—all suggest a nation in doubt. Among the many ways of comprehending the fault lines in America, I find the division between those embracing a self-confident vision of American pluralism and those yearning for a now-extinct, homogeneous past the most compelling. I say division, but I do not mean hard-and-fast lines. Mainly I see confusion among ordinary people made worse by a season of weak political leadership. There is a significant opportunity for America's intellectuals to help sort out this confusion.

Our universities can lead in bridging these divides by offering an example to the larger society. To do so, universities must become more diverse than they are now at every level, and they must work to make their environments comfortable for diversity. For some 20 years a revision of the University's curriculum has been quietly progressing toward a greater pluralism. This trend is now taking on speed. The sharp debate about the "canon" is a response to those changes which are already well-advanced, as faculty and students become aware of a world beyond North America and Europe and see in perspective contributions to our own culture made by different traditions. The battles over the curriculum will continue to be a natural part of the process, but in the end there is enough room in a lifetime of learning to master the Western classics as well as achieve a familiarity with other traditions and confront issues of race, class, ethnicity, and gender. The New School, after all, has always stood for the idea that education must be lifelong; a 4-year undergraduate education is insufficient to produce a truly educated person.

I have spoken in other venues of the New School's diversity initiative, which focuses on increasing the numbers of faculty, staff, students, Trustees, and visiting committee members from underrepresented groups. Progress has been uneven and slower than we would have liked, which only means that more attention and resources should be devoted to the challenge. Our most impressive accomplishment has been the Graduate School's Urban Policy program, which enrolls 50.6 percent of its students from underrepresented groups. To help other parts of the University follow the Graduate School's example, I announced a significant enhancement of the diversity initiative in September which reflects my hope that the New School will be a leader in the quest to make American pluralism work.

Part of the glory of America's pluralism is the wide variety of types of colleges and universities available to students. The New School is sui generis—there is nothing quite like it. In its originality and eccentricity, it is something of a skeptic and a critic of traditional higher education. Almost totally independent of government aid (except for financial aid to students), it has had to make fewer compromises than most institutions and thus, I think, has preserved its capacity to conduct a critical interaction with the mainstream assumptions and institutions of the larger society. Preserving and expanding that freedom of action is our central ambition for the future.

I close this essay by inviting all members of the New School community and its extended family to join with me in what promises to be an eventful next 5 years. As an historian, I am perhaps too prone to invoke the imagery of a "watershed" moment in the University's history. But let me do it anyway: the period immediately ahead will either see the fulfillment and securing of our dreams for our university or offer fairly definitive evidence that our ambitions outstripped our resources. The outcome is not inevitable—either way. What we do really matters. And that is at the heart of the thrill of our work together.

# PART V

# Helsinki Watch and the Struggle for Human Rights and Democracy

# Notes from Wenceslas Square

(PRAGUE, OCTOBER 1989)

It is 10:00 P.M. and I have just returned to the Hotel Esplanade after a quiet walk down Wenceslas Square. A cold front, ending an unusually warm October, has caused fog, which brings an eerie tranquility to a place which was alive with protest a few hours earlier.

The occasion was Czechoslovakia's independence celebration, Saturday October 28, which was marked by an official ceremony in the morning and the largest protest rally in recent times in the afternoon. The main dissident groups—Charter 77, the Movement for Civic Freedom, Obroda, the Democratic Initiative, and the Independent Peace Movement—had endorsed the idea of a demonstration in Wenceslas Square. The playwright Vaclav Havel signaled the time, 3:00 P.M., in an interview on Radio Free Europe. However, he was not there because he had been arrested Thursday evening. Nor were many other dissidents present, because they had been warned by the police to leave town or face arrest.

At a few minutes before 3:00 I walked the two blocks from the Esplanade to the top of the square. I was accompanied by Ivan Gabal, a sociologist who is an organizer of the Circle of Independent Intellectuals, and his wife, Zdenka, who is leading a Prague–Los Angeles art exhibition. We arrived precisely at 3:00 P.M.; already the upper square was full. In a matter of minutes people poured in from every direction to swell the crowd to over 15,000. There were no leaders, no speeches, only a few banners and Czechoslovakian flags. It just happened, and quickly. All ages, men and women, a good cross section of the population was represented. The singing of the national anthem gave way to chants: "Masaryk," "The Truth Will Prevail," "We Will Not Let the Republic Be Disrupted," "Charter 77," "Havel," "Democracy," "We Don't Want Violence," "Dubcek," and "We Want Freedom." A brief skirmish broke out when the local police tried to arrest a demonstrator who mounted the statue of Wenceslas. The crowd surrounded the police and chanted "Shame on You" until the man was released.

Shortly, a loudspeaker declared the gathering illegal and ordered the crowd to disperse. The demonstration had been entirely peaceful, even quiet, by the standards of such occasions elsewhere. Then the riot troops arrived at either end of the square to seal it off. We moved to the side. The troops wore brown uniforms with white hats; they carried shields and nightsticks. And they were very young, recent recruits in their late teens or early twenties.

The crowd, not wishing a confrontation, gradually moved down the hill. About 10 minutes later massive numbers of riot police came up behind us and from the side streets. They cut the crowd into sections. We estimated there were 2,000 to 3,000 troops fortified with tanklike personnel carriers (and water cannons held in reserve). By 3:45 P.M. the crowd had been partially dispersed. We saw occasional scuffles and pushing but no real violence.

Following the patterns set by previous demonstrations in August and January, the crowd headed for the square in the Old Town, as did we. Our first route was blocked by the police at the entrance to the Old Town, but we found an open street by the Bohemia shop through which we entered the square. Several thousand people came into the square and many more were held just outside by roadblocks. A larger part of the original gathering at Wenceslas Square regrouped at the Charles Bridge in front of the concert hall.

Those gathered in the Old Town Square simply milled around, taking some pleasure at a group of Russian tourists who fled as tensions built. Then a dozen unarmed members of the workers' militia marched double-file through this crowd. Their presence elicited "catcalls" but they were allowed to pass. Next, a familiar sequence: the announcement over the loudspeaker that the demonstration was illegal. Moments later buses rolled into the square carrying 100 or so of the workers' militia equipped as riot troops. I am told they are less well trained than the riot police and notoriously short on patience.

The crowd moved on its own to the river side of the square. The troops formed a line and moved toward the crowd. We were between the line and the crowd and were pushed toward the crowd. We found temporary refuge alongside the Old Town Hall. But the workers' militia followed us and pushed us into a group of German tourists led by a Czechoslovakian guide who was in the middle of her lecture on the architecture of the Old Town Square. She squarely confronted the leader of the militia, supported by two men who said they had paid for their tour and didn't want it interrupted. To our surprise, the militia yielded and allowed the tour to stay in the square; we blended in and also stayed. But the militia eventually prevailed and the square was cleared.

We followed the crowd to the Charles Bridge, where it joined with the other main part of the original demonstration. The national anthem was sung again, flags waved, the chants took new life. By now it was 4:45 P.M. and getting dark. We walked over to the bridge. But soon after we arrived the crowd, which had been heading for the castle, came back as police vans and a line of riot troops came across the bridge. Then a massive number of troops in the tanklike personnel carriers came from the other direction. As darkness approached, the troops, by now weary, became more aggressive. We retreated to the steps of the Art Academy and watched the troops head the demonstrators into a confined area between the river and the concert hall. Those carrying flags were arrested and brought to the personnel carriers near us. We saw one man thrown to the ground and beaten by the troops. From a distance I snapped a picture—as it happened, the last one on a roll which had captured every stage of the protest.

The next thing I knew two riot police charged the crowd shouting "camera." When I did not give them my camera they grabbed my tie, jerked my neck, and then dragged me half a city block to the personnel carrier where the arrested man had just been beaten. There I was surrounded by six to eight troops and my camera was taken from me, the film removed, and the camera returned. While this occurred, I was able to make visual contact with the prisoners inside the carrier; they seemed in some pain but were not bloody. Once the troops had my film they lost interest in me, since others who had been arrested were coming. I returned to my friends and the crowd, a few of whom clapped in support of my release. Ivan Gabal had followed me and had shouted to the troops that I was an American and a member of the Helsinki Watch. Perhaps that was helpful in restraining them.

We next moved back to the Old Town Square, which was still sealed off. We tried to get to the hotel through Wenceslas Square but that too remained off limits. By now it was 5:15 P.M. and fully dark. The main part of the crowd was scattered, and the city seemed chaotic as people roamed around in small groups and the air was filled with police sirens from all sides. We returned to Ivan Gabal's institute to pick up his car. Our circuitous route to the hotel brought us by several hundred young men walking on both sides of the street chanting "Gestapo." This was one of several splinter groups of young people marching back toward Wenceslas Square from different directions.

Moments after we passed, the riot troops reappeared and went after the young people, who quickly dispersed up a side street. It is well understood that the troops show little restraint against the young at night.

We finally returned to the hotel about 6:00 P.M., 3 hours after it all began. The turmoil around the city continued for another hour or so.

The Leipzig experience casts a shadow over Prague. The government is frightened and thus resolved to commit however much force is needed to contain public demonstrators. The people, on the other hand, are stimulated by the East German success and also somewhat apologetic for being so passive. Today may be seen as a dress rehearsal for the "catastrophe" to follow. The troops were restrained and the crowd did not provoke them. This was not to be (in the words of the philosopher Hejdanek) the confrontation that would overturn the old order. But it was an important step in building confidence.

The violent clash in Prague in January did not intimidate the people. Just the reverse: this was the largest demonstration in most people's memory. And while the crowd avoided a violent challenge, the atmosphere was charged, the Czech passivity beginning to yield. I sensed a strong will, a feeling of movement, if not optimism, a determination not likely to be deflected. This irreversible movement faces a tough adversary in a regime which is among the most repressive in the region and which shows little evidence of liberalization. The exquisitely efficient riot troops—the sheer size of the force—will prevail until the size of the crowd grows and until the struggle turns violent.

# A Fragile Hold on the Future: Prague and Sofia, 1989

(MEMORANDUM TO THE BOARD OF TRUSTEES, NOVEMBER 1989)

I write to report on my recent trip to Sofia and Prague on October 20–29. In Sofia I was part of a nine-person delegation from the International Helsinki Federation, led by Karl Schwarzenberg, which reviewed the status of human rights in Bulgaria. My mission in Prague was to keep in touch with dissidents I met on two previous trips and to identify future visitors to the New School.

This was my fourth visit to Eastern and Central Europe and my first since December 1988. The events in the Soviet Union, Poland, Hungary, and especially East Germany, have given the people of the region fresh hope and a sense that fundamental change is inevitable. The passage of refugees from East Germany through Prague has had a powerful effect on both the authorities and the dissidents and has offered a challenge to both.

## The Outlook in Czechoslovakia

Since I am composing this in Prague, let me start with the situation in Czechoslovakia. I arrived from Sofia Thursday at noon, to a Prague basking in an unusually warm October. On the surface the city seemed peaceful and prosperous, beautiful as ever. But I knew the reality was different, since my Helsinki Watch colleagues, who had been here the week before, had seen their meeting with the local Helsinki Committee broken up by the police. Jeri Laber, executive director of the American Committee, had been briefly detained. The chair of the Prague Committee, Jiri Hajek (the former foreign minister to whom we have offered an honorary degree), was also detained. To his surprise, at the close of his interrogation, he was told by the police that his exit visa for a trip to Vienna was ready. Thus, I had the pleasure of spending time with him in Vienna last Saturday and Sunday. As always, he offered a perceptive insight into conditions in Czechoslovakia which, on the whole, seemed hopeful despite sharp instances of repression. He indicated his willingness to try again to accept an honorary degree which we will extend in January.

Jiri Hajek and Jeri Laber had warned me that my desire to see our friends in Prague might be frustrated, since the police were warning dissidents to leave town for the weekend of October 28. On that day, which marked the seventy-first anniversary of Czechoslovakian independence, a demonstration was talked about and the authorities wanted to banish the dissident leadership from town. Sure enough, journalist Jan Urban, historian Petr Pithart, our seminar leader and others were in the countryside. Still I managed to track Urban down in Marienbad (2-1/2 hours west of Prague on the German border), where I visited him on Friday. Here are my summary impressions.

SIGNS OF OPTIMISM

Significant progress has been made in reclaiming space for civil discourse and opposition. This despite specific examples of sharper repression. People within the official structures now show more courage in opposing the government.

The newly formed Circle of Independent Intellectuals has brought together 300 of the leading scientists and social scientists in the official structure (only the names of the six organizers are published). The Circle seeks to act as a bridge between the dissidents and the government and to offer a series of "white papers" on critical problems, starting with a reform of the educational system. Other issues are likely to be the environment, public health, the sociological risks of reform, the downside of free market reforms, and more.

The creation of the Circle, whose members are largely in their thirties, is seen as a critical moment, since it draws on the leading scholars in the official institutions. So far no pressure has been brought to bear on them.

The "hottest" petition in town, called "A Few Sentences," has attracted 35,000 signatures since June. It offers seven demands: release of political prisoners, freedom of assembly, freedom of expression, open discussion of the events of 1968, an end to the monopoly of the Communist Party, the legalization of independent groups, and discussion of environmental problems. The petition has been signed by members of the party and other leading intellectuals and cultural figures. The party ordered a boycott by state media of twenty-seven leading actors who signed the petition, but the boycott was never implemented.

Other examples of civil discourse and widening opposition may be noted briefly:

- Two editors of the leading samizdat *Lidove-Noviny* were arrested (Jiri Ruml and Rudolf Zeman), causing 110 journalists from the official papers to sign a petition calling for their release.
- Rita Klimova reports a growing number of informal "living room" discussions, organized by ordinary citizens throughout the city to examine the impending "crisis": the very use of words like "crisis" and "catastrophe" and "economic problems" is spreading.
- Slovac actor Milan Kovazko refused the honor of "artist of the state."
- The chief conductor of the Prague Philharmonic, Vaclav Neumann, made a statement that if the state retaliated against artists who signed "A Few Sentences," he could not cooperate with state radio and television. Ninety-three members (virtually all) of the Philharmonic voted to support him.

There are stirrings among the workers, although no formal independent union has emerged. Examples of independence are found at the factory level, where some workers are inviting dissidents to speak. For example, a machine tool factory group was asked by the state to write a petition against dissidents, but instead wrote a petition against police brutality to one of their fellow workers (Jaroslav Krbusek). When the police arrested the originators of the petition, the factory went on strike.

While there are no formal student dissident organizations, there are activists, mainly concentrated in the Faculty of Philosophy and the Faculty of Art. They are holding discussion groups, and the philosophy students are now publishing a journal with content that once would have been censored. The students at the Academy of Art held a large meeting at which Jan Urban spoke, prompting the party to order the dismissal of the Rector. However, the Minister of Education did not implement the party's order.

The membership in dissident groups is growing. There are five main groups:

- Charter 77 is still the most important. It remains unstructured, is devoted to human rights, and reflects a broad spectrum, from communist to militant catholics. Over 1,300 people have joined, 300 recently.
- The Movement for Civic Freedom (or Civil Liberties), known as HOS, was founded a year ago with a platform of political pluralism, free market economics, and the right to private property. It numbers 2,000–3,000 signers and is building chapters outside of Prague around the country. It probably has the best chance of becoming the base for an organized political opposition.
- Obroda (Renewal) is also a year old and composed of former Communists who have retained their socialist or communist convictions. They number 600–800 (of the nearly 500,000 expelled from the party) and they believe the present government is controlled by cynical opportunists. The regime is made very nervous by this group, which is chaired by Milos Hyak, who had been sentenced to death during the Nazi occupation.
- The Democratic Initiative is 3 or 4 years old and is fairly small (fewer than 200 members). It is viewed by some as a vehicle for the ego of its leader (Mandler), but it does have good contact with the Democratic Forum in

Hungary. It has a broadly democratic platform which is otherwise vague.
- The Independent Peace Movement, about two years old, has a young membership (200 plus), and a main objective of demilitarizing society. The group seeks the existence of a conscientious objector status.

These five groups together signed the call for the October 28 demonstration. In addition, there are less serious (and less organized) groups which might be termed "counterculture." They are against the establishment and (at best) deeply skeptical of the older dissidents. They are the John Lennon Peace Club, The Children of Bohemia (200 members and the best organized of this group), and the Revolver Review (in English), which publishes a journal three times a year. The total counterculture movement could turn out 5,000 young people, but they have no political agenda except possibly for the environment.

Within the past 18 months more political action and protest have been evident outside of Prague. For example, a petition in the steel mill town of Chomutov called for alerting the citizens about high smog days, a demand that has been met. In Bratislava, a group of scientists in the official structure issued a proclamation calling for environmental measures and were subject to party disciplines.

Finally, there are the events of October 28 which offered a stark contrast of strength. The official ceremony, held in Wenceslas Square in the morning, drew only 1,500 people whose entrance was restricted by ticket. The reason for tickets did not have to do with crowd control. Just the reverse: the party wanted to avoid a contest of numbers with the unofficial demonstration planned for the afternoon. As I looked on from a nearby hotel, the crowd showed little enthusiasm for the proceedings, which lacked spirit and seemed hollow—almost a parody of the intended show of popular support.

By contrast, the unofficial demonstration, beginning at 3:00 P.M. at the other end of Wensceslas Square, drew an estimated

15,000 spirited demonstrators. Gathering for the first time since the violent conflict in January, the growth of the crowd was significant in indicating that repressive measures had not frightened the people. The peaceful demonstration, featuring not speeches but songs and political chants—"Masaryk," "The Truth Will Prevail," "We Will Not Let the Republic Be Disrupted," "Charter 77," "Havel," "Democracy," "We Don't Want Violence," "Dubcek," and "We Want Freedom"—was quickly declared illegal and broken up with riot troops.

## ACTS OF REPRESSION

These signs of optimism are balanced by specific and harsh acts of repression—I have already mentioned the imprisonment of two editors of *Lidove-Noviny*. Other examples:

- It is estimated that there are two dozen known political prisoners (this number represents only a fraction of the cases because information is not readily available).
- The use of 48-hour "preventive detention" has been stepped up. Virtually all members of the dissident movement have experienced frequent detentions and other kinds of harassment aimed at them and their families.
- Charter 77 and other groups are denied permission to use open or closed spaces for meetings. Groups of five or more people meeting in homes are likely to be broken up.
- A proposed new press law would raise the fine on publishing without being registered from 500 crowns an issue to 10,000 crowns. It would also provide for confiscation of property.
- There is great concern that the constitution now being formulated will be more repressive.

## FUTURE OF THE DISSIDENT MOVEMENT

What general conclusions can be drawn from these events? There is no question that the society is in flux with the authority of the regime clearly eroding and the number of those challenging its legitimacy growing. The last year has seen more progress than the previous 20.

But the dissident movement so far seems incapable of evolving into a political opposition. It is divided broadly between the older generation—deeply influenced by the events of 1968, who have doubts about street demonstrations and a fear of violence—and younger group which is open to the possibility of political opposition and who believe they will prevail. As Jan Urban put it, "I now feel for the first time, I am on the winning side."

People of various views, backgrounds, and ages in the dissident movement spoke almost apologetically of the Czech national character, which they said is passive and eschews violence. Both those in their sixties and those a generation younger are made cautious by the experience of 1968. My guess is that the younger group will surmount that block, while the older group will not play a central role in the events to come. Several people suggested that Gorbachev needs to say (as he did in Afghanistan) that the Soviet invasion was a mistake. Such a pronouncement would rob the current Czech regime of its last remaining shred of legitimacy and might, people say, elicit a Leipzig reaction. There is talk of the "Leipzig norm": 50,000 people in the street shake the government; 100,000 change it.

A wild card in the picture is the younger generation, those in their late teens and early twenties, who do not bear the invisible scar of 1968 and show little fear of authority. They are described as unorganized, lacking a positive program, bitter, restless, angry, and willing to risk violence. Jan Urban feels the need to build bridges to this group but is not optimistic. There is a sense that the younger generation will push the regime at some point into a violent crackdown, which will provoke the fundamental change people expect.

In the meantime, the circle of dissidents will grow, the regime's failures in the economy will be criticized by official scholars, the number of people in official structures who defend dissidents and independent journalists will multiply, and the regime will intensify its crackdown against individuals. I do not know enough to assess the state of the economy, but stories abound about the heavy borrowing by the government to maintain ample consumer goods in order to head off general dissatisfaction among the people. I am told the debt has increased 20 percent in one year and approaches the "legal" debt limit.

Intellectuals ponder why Czechoslovakia has not followed Poland, Hungary, or even East Germany. Already mentioned are the shadow of 1968 and the deep psychological crisis of those in middle age who would normally provide the leadership but who are conditioned by 20 years of passivity. Other factors are the sellout to Hitler in 1938 and the failure to preserve a democratic government in 1948.

Some suggest a flaw in the Czech national character, which is described as passive, too rational. Others see an historical explanation in the Czech democratic tradition, inherited from the Austrians, which required harsher repression in order for the Communists to secure control. Part of that effort resulted in systematic purges of liberal elements within the party (500,000 people expelled) and carefully controlled access to power, including higher education. Intelligence became a handicap in gaining university admission; loyalty combined with a dull intellect, an advantage. Thus the nation lacks competent experts in any field, as this story is repeated in every walk of life.

The absence of leadership talent now takes its toll, as the country gropes for the means to deal with its economic and social problems. Thus the compact with the people—a trade of a decent standard of living for political freedom—is in danger.

## Concluding Thoughts

Czechoslovakia in some ways is the most painful case to observe within the region. While it ranks ahead of Romania and Bulgaria in the pursuit of democratic freedoms, it is clearly way behind Poland and Hungary. It has the superficial look of a prosperous Western society, yet it suffers deep suppression of political and human rights. It is a society on the brink and, as Havel puts it, change could come in 2 months, 2 years, or ...

In my judgment, the West should concentrate on Czechoslovakia by monitoring human rights abuses, by tying investment (both government and private) to progress in human and political rights, and by expanding contacts with the younger generation of artists and intellectuals from whom the new leadership must come.

The New School has a role to play, much as we did in Poland and Hungary at a later stage in the process. Our help in Czechoslovakia is more urgently needed and has greater potential for long-term benefit. We have a better set of contacts there than does any other American university, and thus a greater opportunity and a greater responsibility.

## The Outlook in Bulgaria

Let me now turn to Bulgaria, which I visited in my capacity as vice chair of the American Helsinki Watch Committee—a nine-person delegation under the auspices of the International Helsinki Federation. The "semiofficial" Human Rights Committee of Bulgaria organized a full program of meetings with government officials, including the Attorney General of Bulgaria, the First Deputy Minister of Justice, the Deputy Minister of Interior (in charge of the militia), a member of the State Council (executive branch), the Vice Minister of Foreign Affairs, the Chairman of the Committee on the Bulgarian Orthodox Church and Religious Cults, the Parliamentary Commission for the Defense of Public Interests and Rights of Citizens, the Chairman of the Bulgarian Academy of Sciences, and the Chief Mufti of Bulgaria.

In the evenings we were free to meet with the chief dissidents and managed to talk with the leadership of the major dissident groups. Our efforts were aided by Ambassador Polanski, who invited the "who's who" of the dissident movement to his home for dinner Wednesday evening. In all, we must have talked to forty dissidents in some depth. In addition we attended a meeting of some fifty members of the largest dissident group, Eco-Glasnost, in an apartment of one of its members.

## BACKGROUND

At the most superficial level, Sofia is a pleasant city with wide boulevards and extensive parks. It seems prosperous by comparison with Warsaw, for example. Sofia boasts two of the best hotels I have seen in Eastern and Central Europe (the Sheraton and the New Otani). Taxis are plentiful, the food decent. A heavy and persistent smog conceals the beauty of the surrounding mountains.

It is clear that Bulgaria wishes more contact with the West. Guest status at the Council of Europe, for example, is the lure which led Bulgaria to sign the concluding document at Vienna and undertake measures, at least on a cosmetic level, to comply with its provisions. The establishment of the Human Rights Commission, the liberalization of passport laws and travel restrictions, and the September 1989 decision of the Commission for the Protection of Public Interests and Citizens Rights concerning religious minorities are all hopeful signs induced by the Vienna agreement. Our visit itself was a sign of Bulgaria's desire to be accepted in the "European house."

It seems to me that Bulgaria suffers from a small-nation complex, feeling overlooked by the West and taken for granted by the Soviet Union. Its relative isolation has led to a naivete about what it means to be visible in the West, and I doubt Bulgarian leaders are prepared for the scrutiny of internal affairs which will flow from greater economic contacts.

That lack of sophistication was evident in the approach to our trip: assurances of officials about support for human rights, liberalization under way, and greater democracy in the future were bound to contrast with our direct observation. Indeed, our detailed knowledge of the Bulgarian penal code and of specific political cases took them by surprise.

A review of the transcript of our conversations would leave the impression that Bulgaria was liberalizing quickly. Our mission was to test those claims in two areas:

- The condition of free association and freedom of speech and the available recourse to constitutional protections administered by an independent and fair judiciary

- The treatment of minorities, chiefly the 10 percent of the population which is of "Turkish consciousness" and Pomaks.

We indicated our intention to find the facts and write our objective report. Our work follows two previous reports by the Council of Europe that were critical of Bulgaria on both counts but that noted some progress.

## The Turkish Question

The Turkish issue is perhaps the most sensitive one in Bulgaria. Despite a relatively good record on religious tolerance (Jews were protected during World War II), there is widespread antipathy to the Turks that traces back to 500 years "under the Turkish yoke." The antagonism has resulted in reports, confirmed by the Council of Europe, of forced Bulgarianization of Turkish names, prohibitions against speaking Turkish in public, and limits on religious rites such as circumcision. It is said that this poor treatment, which has accelerated since 1984, is a principal factor in the migration of 310,000 Bulgarian Turks to Turkey (about 10 percent have since returned). The sting of world criticism is keenly felt by the government, which claims to be misunderstood on the issue. Officials were surprised to learn that Helsinki Watch has done a report chronicling human rights abuses in Turkey.

I suspect that the Bulgarian regime too narrowly understood our mission as concerned principally with the Turkish question and thus underestimated our interest in dissidents and political trials.

Since I did not tour the Turkish region, I can offer only secondary testimony about the merits of the charges of mistreatment. But it is my strong impression that Turks have been poorly treated and that the conclusions of the Council of Europe mission are correct. However, I would surmise that the worst abuses are in the past. This is not to suggest significant affirmative action to improve conditions for the Turks. For example, when I asked the Chairman of the Academy of Sciences (and former Rector of Sofia University) how many of the 120,000 students in higher education were Turks, I received an evasive answer leading me to believe practically none were.

## Political Dissidents

With respect to the treatment of dissidents, I judge that harsh repression is still a common occurrence, with free association and freedom of expression severely limited under several provisions of the criminal code (especially Articles 273 and 321b). We inquired about five specific cases presently under investigation and received no satisfaction. We asked to visit several people already in prison but were denied.

But there are hopeful signs, most of which have occurred in the past 12 to 18 months. As in Czechoslovakia, the experiences of Poland, Hungary, and especially East Germany have emboldened the dissidents. There are six principal groups of dissidents (again not yet matured into a political opposition).

*1.* The Discussion Club consists mainly of older intellectuals (about 250 members) with interest in democratic theory, not unlike the older group in Prague who kept the resistance alive with underground seminars. The Discussion Club is a circle, not a formal organization. Its members hold a wide diversity of views on the economy, the environment, and human rights. They are brought together by a common agenda of open communication. The Discussion Club plans a meeting on November 2 with these issues on the agenda: tapping of phones; cutting off phone service to dissidents; restrictions on contacts with Western journalists; Decree 56, which limits access to Xerox and computer technology; and the vagueness of Article 273.

*2.* Eco-Glasnost is where the action is. It has 100 members (200 people on a waiting list) and a "nonpolitical" agenda focused on the environment. The presence of a 3-week international forum on the environment created considerable space for its petition campaign which had attracted 11,545 signatures. Its members are younger and more activist than those of The Discussion Club (although there is considerable overlap in membership). Because of its agenda, it draws heavily on younger academics, especially scientists.

3. The Committee on 273, led by a sailor from Ruse (Liubomir Sobadgiev), was organized last July around six people put in jail for "inspiring the Turks" under Section 273 of the penal code. These six leaders sent letters to the chief prosecutor associating themselves with those accused. To date, 120 people have come forward as cosigners.

The committee estimates that there are 300 to 400 political prisoners in the country (two-thirds of whom are Turks). The Helsinki Watch has started the systematic building of a list of political prisoners. The nucleus of this group is about ten people, and it is considering starting chapters in other parts of the country to monitor cases brought under Article 273.

4. The Citizens Initiative (with a nucleus of eight people) is organizing a series of local committees around the country. It is concerned with providing a constructive critique of local governments and with a broadly democratic program. It is made up of "people hungry for practical ideas for restructuring."

5. The Independent Society for the Protection of Human Rights was an early dissident group which has been persecuted; some of its members were forced into exile abroad.

6. The Committee for the Defense of Religious Rights, Freedom of Conscience, and Spiritual Values was founded in March 1989. The committee plans to campaign for citizens' rights to religious education and religious broadcasts on the state media, and for an end to state interference in religious matters. The government has thus far refused to recognize the committee and seems intent on preventing founding members from engaging in human rights activities.

On November 1 a new group was formed which intends to apply for recognition as an Helsinki Watch Committee. Organized by Anton Zapryanov, the new group seeks to include representatives of the other dissident groups. Another burgeoning force is Podkrepa, Bulgaria's first independent labor union, which was founded in February 1989 to defend the interests of writers, academicians, scientists, and artists.

While these groups are small, some with ill-defined programs, they fall into a pattern of emerging dissidents seen in Eastern and Central European countries that are further along in the march to democratic freedoms. Indeed, one member of the Parliament Committee described the liberalization process as "irreversible." An interesting feature of the membership of the Discussion Club and Eco-Glasnost is the presence of so many members of the Communist Party (20 percent by one estimate). Party members are more heavily represented among dissidents in Bulgaria than in other Eastern bloc countries.

Eco-Glasnost has been allowed to hold some meetings in the cinema (800 attended) and managed on Wednesday to push back a police line and gain entry to a central park to pursue its petition campaign. The event was seen as a significant victory, even though it was recognized that the presence of the international environmental forum and Western journalists restrained the regime. However, on the next day, several members were expelled from Sofia and at least one member was detained for several days.

This, I expect, will be the cycle of small gains punctuated by frequent setbacks and harsh treatment of dissident leaders. And yet, as Jan Urban has observed, the gains are never fully wiped out by the government's repression.

## Political Prisoners

We gained a valuable insight into prison conditions through a young man (24 years old) who had spent 4 years in Stara Zagora Prison under Articles 102 and 108 of the penal code. There the political prisoners were in three separate cell blocks (3, 6, and 10). He told of difficult conditions, hunger strikes, work stoppages, and individual stories of harassment. (In his case the authorities tried to persuade his girlfriend to end their relationship.) He estimated there were 200 political prisoners in this one place, about half of whom had committed some acts of violence (usually sabotage). Thirty were Bulgarians; the rest Turks. If his testimony is correct, then estimates of the total population of political prisoners may be understated.

This young man, who is very bright and speaks fluent English, is now enrolled in Sofia University for an undergraduate degree in English. He hopes to go on to graduate study in sociology and psychology. He is planning the first organization of students at the university and claims to have 20 to 30 people who will sign a petition. He reasons that as a dissident leader he will be safer—at least will not disappear without notice.

He believes it is necessary for him to leave the country before he is 25-1/2 years old, since at that time he will be obligated to finish his tour in the army. He tells stories of dissidents who encounter "accidents" in the army and never return.

### Concluding Thoughts

So where do we come out? I did take some solace from our meeting with the Parliament Committee, which appeared more flexible and candid than the members of the executive branch with whom we met. There was evident a range of views—from the "hard line" to what I took to be a genuine desire for reform. The two most liberal members, for example, characterized the hated sections of Article 273 as "doomed." And they conceded that there were local abuses of the rights of the Turkish minority which they sought to remedy. I do not overestimate the forces for liberalism, but at least some range of views can be discerned.

In the unofficial community, as with the Czechs, the language of "crisis" frequents dissident conversations as the sense of an impending confrontation grows. The government is seen as isolated, frightened, unable to cope with a deteriorating economy. "A political corpse" was the description of one member of the Discussion Club. "Not a false start" was the characterization of the situation by the chair of the Committee on 273. No doubt these comments are on the optimistic side, a reflection of the first glimpse of a more liberal society. But if Bulgaria were a company, Wall Street would describe it as "in play."

# Living with Uncertainty: Moscow 1990

(MEMORANDUM TO THE BOARD OF TRUSTEES, JUNE 1990)

### Introduction

I write to report on my week in Moscow at the Annual Meeting of the International Helsinki Federation for Human Rights and to give some personal observations about present conditions in the Soviet Union. Let me caution at the outset that my account flows from conversations and thus reflects individual views which I have not always been able to verify.

Our meeting was one of the first ever held in the Soviet Union without an official sponsor. It brought together representatives of Human Rights Watch committees from eighteen countries, including most of Eastern Europe, with their counterparts in the Soviet Union. The conference heard the testimony of human rights activists from throughout the Soviet Union. In addition, we met with members of both the All-Union Parliament and the Parliament of the Russian Soviet Federated Socialist Republic (RSFSR) and also with leading political figures, including Boris Yeltsin and the Deputy Mayor of Moscow, Sergei Stankevich. Our meetings yielded interesting insights on the present state and future prospects of the Soviet Union. It is fair to say that Soviet citizens are consumed with the transitions under way at home. We heard almost no discussion of international affairs, despite the fact that our conference coincided with the Washington summit.

Perhaps we should take as our text for this exercise Alexis de Tocqueville's comments on the origins of the French Revolution, in which he attempted to explain why the revolution occurred when the situation was improving. In his *The Old Regime and the French Revolution*, he wrote:

The general public became more and more hostile to every ancient institution, more and more discontented; indeed, it was increasingly obvious that the nation was heading for a revolution.... In 1780 there could no longer be any talk of France's being on the downgrade; on the contrary, it seemed that no limit could be set to her advance. And it was now that theories of the perfectibility of man and continuous progress came into fashion. Twenty years earlier there had been no hope for the future; in 1780 no anxiety was felt about it. Dazzled by the prospect of a felicity undreamed of hitherto and now within their grasp, people were blind to the very real improvement that had taken place and eager to precipitate events.*

Before trying to place present developments in the U.S.S.R. in historical perspective, let me begin with the conference itself.

## THE CONFERENCE

The International Helsinki Federation (IHF) Conference was held at Dom Turista, a large hotel for internal Soviet tourists located about 40 minutes from Red Square. Just under seventy-five delegates attended, including Federation Chairman Karl Johannes von Schwarzenberg, Honorary Chairman Yuri Orlov, and former First Lady Rosalynn Carter. Fifty people were scheduled to testify before the conference, and as many as seventy-five actually did.

Traditional human rights topics were addressed, including political prisoners, prison conditions, political laws and rehabilitation, psychiatric abuse, the status of refugees, religious freedom, freedom of the press, freedom of association, freedom of movement and choice of residence, and judicial and administrative practices.

A whole day was spent on the nationalities issue, which is perhaps the most explosive problem in the Soviet Union

---

*There are differences, of course, between pre-revolutionary France and the present day Soviet Union in that the economic situation was improving in France.

today. The U.S.S.R. contains 128 different ethnic groups by official count (but there are many more) which, as a matter of policy beginning with Stalin, have been scattered and intermixed. It is estimated that as many as 60 million people do not live in the "right" place. Recent outbreaks of ethnic violence have produced 1 million internal refugees, 40,000 in the Moscow area alone.

I comment below in detail on specific human rights issues. But in summary, there have clearly been improvements. Even compared with my last trip a year ago, the atmosphere for open discussion and dissent is freer. The very presence of the IHF Conference sends a powerful message about the improvement environment—at least in Moscow and the major cities. However, we were told that conditions in the vast provinces have been slower to change and that, even in the cities, entrenched bureaucrats of the old regime can inflict abuse on individuals with impunity. For all the improvement of conditions for prominent dissidents, what we are learning about the conditions for ordinary citizens caught in the system confirms our worst fears about how difficult it will be to build a society of laws which ensures wide and uniform protection of human rights.

While there is no question about the progress that has been made in human rights, there continue to be serious concerns. Before I discuss the specific issues, two general comments are in order. First, the bureaucratic inertia of the Soviet Union and the relatively loose control by the central government on practices in the remote provinces means that individual violations of human rights continue even in areas where official policy is now acceptable. Second, the entire Soviet system is still based on a concept of rights granted solely by the government, a concept which is in itself a violation of the fundamental rights of individuals.

With that said, the principal areas of concern are detailed as follows:

*1.* We heard a day of vivid testimony about the discrimination and violence among ethnic minorities throughout the Soviet Union. I conclude that the central government has not been energetic enough in protecting the rights of ethnic minorities.

2. There are 1 million internal refugees who are displaced people with no rights and no way to reenter the mainstream. None of the democratic reforms will benefit the refugees, who do not have voting rights, residency or work permits, or even decent housing and nourishment. There is an inadequate recognition of the problem and no apparent plan to address it. As the zone of ethnic strife continues to widen, the number of displaced persons will grow significantly.

3. The system of internal passport controls and residency permits severely restricts freedom of movement and association. Even liberals like Stankevich, who term the system "unconstitutional and unnatural," are not optimistic about quick reform.

4. The right of emigration (and return) is still not secure, and there are examples of people accepted for immigration to the United States who have not been given exit visas because they are not joining first-degree relatives.

5. Between 50 and 180 political prisoners still exist, although they are harder to track since "troublemakers" are now arrested for alleged criminal activity.

6. Prisons remain overcrowded and we are told of instances of persisting torturous conditions and inhumane treatment. Forced labor is a common practice for all prisons.

7. Former political prisoners jailed for expressions of dissent that are now permitted have not been rehabilitated. Thus they are unable to obtain decent jobs and rebuild their lives.

8. While reforms of the judicial system are in preparation, the practice of "telephone justice" continues. Those accused are not always permitted to see their lawyers at an early stage in the process. The judicial system

itself is not ready to administer the rights which the new laws propose because of the low quality and the scarcity of judges. A recent poll of ordinary citizens ranked the judicial system at the bottom of the scale of public confidence.
9. Although Gorbachev has rejected the internment of dissidents for alleged psychological reasons, the practice, we are told, continues in some provincial areas.
10. The press is far from free, since individuals are not allowed to publish newspapers or journals and unofficial papers do not have easy access to paper and printing presses. The new press law is now being drafted in the Supreme Soviet, although it remains unclear whether individuals will have the right to own publications.
11. We are told that political dissidents and nonconformists drafted into the army experience "accidents" or commit "suicide" by the hundreds.

The sheer magnitude of the Soviet Union, coupled with difficult transportation and near-impossible communication, makes human rights monitoring a formidable challenge. However, with the easing of conditions in Central Europe and the gradual opening up of the Soviet Union, there is now the possibility of useful work. The amount of time, energy, and resources that will be needed in the Soviet Union for the foreseeable future will dwarf past investments in Eastern and Central Europe. Too many of our contacts and too much of our information are Moscow-centered. One important and immediate task is to build a network of contacts throughout the Soviet Union, perhaps on a republic-by-republic basis.

In addition to the logistical challenge, a problem arises from lack of agreement about what is meant by human rights. There is a tendency among human rights activists in the Soviet Union to classify all the society's ills as human rights abuses, from the independence movement in the Baltics to the fate of Raoul Wallenberg to the desperate plight of children in the Central Asian republics. If human rights become an umbrella movement for an eclectic group of reforms, it will not achieve the focused energy necessary to register improvements in the traditional human rights areas listed above.

## The Overall Situation

On Sunday afternoon we walked down the Arbat, the central shopping area for tourists. The sunny and mild day brought out thousands of tourists and Soviet citizens in a scene duplicated in major capitals around the world. The well-dressed, cosmopolitan crowd spoke many languages in a cheerful and spirited atmosphere. The most popular tourist attraction was the Gorbachev doll, which inside contained successively smaller figures of Brezhnev, Khrushchev, Stalin, and Lenin. But the famous lacquer boxes and pins together with the work of young Soviet artists also were in demand. In the center of the Arbat young Soviet children could be seen being photographed with Mickey Mouse, an antique Soviet car, and an array of friendly animals. As we came to the end of the Arbat, we encountered two dozen artists eager to sketch our portraits, as well as an all-purpose jazz band playing scores ranging from "String of Pearls" to "Rock Around the Clock." Tourists and natives alike danced in a carefree way.

What a contrast to the real Moscow marked by a scarcity of food and other basic necessities, besieged by internal refugees, and frightened by the rise of crime. People with a comparative perspective describe a sharp decline in morale over the past 9 to 12 months characterized by a palpable rise in tension and a mood of deep crisis. Indeed, the word "crisis," so familiar from the last days of the totalitarian regimes in Central Europe, finds its way into almost every conversation.

What accounts for this air of crisis when a year or so earlier the mood was optimistic as *glasnost* and *perestroika* promised a better life for all? For ordinary people, the manifestation of crisis comes at the local food store, where the necessities of life are scarce, and much less available than even a year ago. Beyond that newly won access to information brings an unending chain of bad news, from more of the truth about Chernobyl to the state of emergency in Azerbaijan and clashes between ethnic groups. In addition, the exercise of freer expression results in unsettling attacks on established order and revelations about abuses from the Stalin era forward to the very recent past (revelations often shocking to even the most hardened critics). The one island of stability in this sea of change, Mikhail Gorbachev, once invincible, now seems vulnerable, perhaps not able to cope with the mounting problems.

The prevailing mood is uncertainty bordering on fear of the unknown. As Deputy Mayor Stankevich said, "No classical models can be applied to our situation." Even the most seasoned observers and journalists are loath to predict events. Gorbachev's great genius has come from his ability to be comfortable with uncertainty and to use events not of his making to his advantage. The question is whether that mode will work in the future, or whether Gorbachev has reached the limits of his own flexibility and ingenuity.

When he began, Gorbachev had a plan to rid the country of the curse of Stalinism and the decadence of Brezhnev, and thereby strengthen the Communist Party, improving the lives of ordinary citizens through both political and economic reforms. He attempted a process of limited and gradual reform but the movement set in motion spun beyond his control about a year ago. The central question today is whether Gorbachev will regain the initiative or lose control and power. Many informed people with different points of view predict the answer will be known in a year or so.

Let us now examine the course of economic and political reform. Common to both is the theme that limited reform appears to be impossible, since in each case Gorbachev now represents a center-right position while intellectuals, a significant number of new political leaders, and ordinary citizens have moved ahead of him.

Part of the reason Gorbachev has fallen behind popular opinion no doubt derives from the magnitude and complexity of his restructuring. Building the philosophical framework for securing individual rights, creating democratic political structures, and overhauling a listless economy all at once will likely prove too ambitious, and yet public expectations are high for all three.

In the economic arena Gorbachev has yet to articulate a plan for a "limited market system" which is clear and inspires confidence. The continued deterioration of the economy has eroded his credibility badly, and the recent miscalculation on price rises is a serious setback. After 5 years of Gorbachev in power the claim that socialism can work, that it has just been misapplied, does not evoke support. The public is suspicious that a "limited market system" is just another version of socialism. Virtually everyone with whom we spoke, including Boris Yeltsin and Sergei Stankevich, believes that Gorbachev is making a critical, perhaps fatal, mistake by resisting a rapid conversion to the free market.

Stankevich is an example of a new generation of younger leaders not bound by old shibboleths and knowledgeable about free markets. (I was pleased to learn he had been in a seminar at the New School through Charles Tilly's Center for the Study of Social Change.) Age 36, very stylish in dress, speaking fluent English, an expert on the American political system—which was the subject of his Ph.D. dissertation—Stankevich sees his political career in a more democratic and free market Soviet Union.

"The economy must be emancipated from ideological preconceptions," he said, and "the Moscow Council is ready for free enterprise, ready to make Moscow the showcase of the free market." But he noted that Gorbachev's resistance creates an unstable situation which causes Western investors to hesitate and thus deprives the country of necessary capital. "Socialism," he said wistfully, "was easy to get into but hard to get out of." He expects Yeltsin to stretch the boundaries of the possible, but he doubts economic recovery will come until Gorbachev embraces the free market, because the central government has such pervasive control of the economy.

Even so, Stankevich pointed with pride to three developments which he said anticipated economic reform:
- The first commodities exchange in Moscow since the 1920s was scheduled to open the next day.
- A Moscow shareholders corporation for reconstruction and development had been created.
- Moscow had opened an employment office to help its citizens adjust to the transition to a free market.

Yeltsin told us that the main point of his program was "decentralization of the economy" and a transition "to a free market system." Both Stankevich and Yeltsin believe there is danger in granting even limited political freedom without simultaneous economic reform and growth. "Mass poverty is not the best foundation for democracy," Stankevich opined. And Yeltsin lamented that "we have always been late—now with fast political developments and a lag in the solution to our economic problems we have reached the frontier of crisis." Both argue that land reform—private ownership of farms—is an essential prerequisite for economic recovery and for improving the lives of ordinary citizens sufficiently to lower popular discontent below the danger threshold.

At present, the old economic system is coming apart, but no replacement system is yet in view and thus the steady decline in the consumer economy. The black market and an illegal—or "second"—economy are growing. It is almost impossible for a tourist to spend rubles—no one wants them. There is a well-developed barter system using Marlboro cigarettes — a taxi ride from the Dom Turista to Red Square is two packs, from the National Hotel to the American Embassy a single pack, and for late-night rides add a pack to the normal price. But dollars are increasingly the way to go for an American to do business, since people are more willing than a year ago to break the law by accepting hard currency. Take the case of our taxi driver, a civil engineer, 26 years old with a wife and one child. His formal pay is 200 rubles a month (or about $35 at the official exchange rate). Driving a taxi, he makes 200 to 300 rubles on a good day—and from us $35 in one day, or a month's pay.

Gorbachev's failure to reform the economy, together with the formidable problems of how to proceed even if he were inclined to a free market solution, lead many to believe that economic recovery must begin on the local level. Yuri Afanasyev, director of the Moscow State Historical Archive Institute, states flatly that the economy cannot be reformed at the national level, rather only through the introduction of the free market mechanism in the republics. This economic imperative together with the desire for separation or at least a radically different relationship between the republics and the center, leads many to believe that the Soviet Union as it is currently structured will not survive. That much said, views differ widely about likely scenarios.

Gorbachev's failure to keep pace with advanced thinking in economic matters finds a parallel in the political arena. Gradually the republics and the major cities are falling under the influence of political leaders who are committed to the free market and to a more advanced conception of democracy. The Leningrad, Moscow, and Russian Republic legislative bodies, for example, all have escaped the control of Gorbachev's allies. Yeltsin is the most visible, but hardly the only source of challenge to Gorbachev, as both republics and cities pass laws that are more advanced than what is expected from the new constitution. Yeltsin has already asserted that he believes that the Russian Republic's laws will prevail when they are at odds with the central government's laws. And Stankevich says the constitution-making process is too slow and the city government of Moscow cannot wait. Thus by the end of June, Moscow will be putting in place a series of "temporary rules" likely to be more liberal. For example, he says Moscow will abolish all censorship and accord wide freedoms for the establishment of new journals and papers which can be owned by individuals. It is also likely to liberalize the laws of association.

Thus Gorbachev is confronted by both republics and cities going their own way in the absence of an accepted federal constitution. It seems unlikely that a federal constitution which pulls back from freedoms granted at the state and local level will be viable. Indeed, in the eyes of some, the central government is increasingly irrelevant. We are told that the better people are forsaking the All-Union Parliament for republic and city legislative councils because that is where the action is, given that Gorbachev's center-right coalition controls the Central Parliament.

As if all this were not enough, Gorbachev may face a split within the Communist Party at its congress in July. There is the possibility of a three-way split, with the likelihood that the most progressive wing, the Democratic Platform, will leave the party. This will further associate Gorbachev with the more conservative faction of the party, just as his battle with Yeltsin over the leadership of the Russian Republic did.

At the rank-and-file level, we are told there are significant defections from the Communist Party, often following local leaders who are quitting. There is speculation that Yeltsin will bolt the party at the July congress. Gorbachev seems to be losing the struggle to separate the party from the past abuses of Stalinism and the stagnation of the Brezhnev period. The Party is associated with all that is wrong in the society, from human rights abuses to economic ruin and corruption. Taxi drivers delight—just as they did, for example, in Czechoslovakia near the end—in pointing out special hospitals and stores for party officials, and in transgressing the boundaries of Moscow to drive by the dachas of the party powerful.

The leading group in exposing past abuses is called Memorial; it has 210 chapters throughout the Soviet Union with membership numbering in the thousands. Founded in 1987, Memorial is concerned with human rights and research about past abuses. It is busily documenting the horrors of labor camps and excavating mass graves from the Stalin period, thus bringing to light in vivid detail those horrors. Mass graves have been uncovered in practically every Soviet city. "The Soviet Union," one member said, "is built on bones." *Glasnost* has unleashed an orgy of exposures of past abuses which, while perhaps vaguely known, now gain monstrous proportions as specific examples are pulled together and discussed all at once. Labor camps, mass executions, dissidents committed to psychiatric hospitals, political prisoners, torture, and all the rest create a mosaic of horror, beginning with Stalin but continuing to the cusp of the Gorbachev era. The revulsion that these revelations evoke is laid at the doorstep of the Communist Party and the evils of centralized government.

In light of all this, one wonders why a political leader as skillful as Gorbachev insists on tying his future to the Communist Party, socialism, and a strong centralized state. Younger political leaders like Stankevich, who supported Gorbachev in the past but who are now disappointed, hope that Yeltsin's victory will force Gorbachev to be more open and to compromise with the democratic opposition. They say in the past Gorbachev has demonstrated that he "can be educated to reality" which makes him different from earlier leaders. Even skeptics, like Sergei Kovalev, believe that a Gorbachev ready to move left is preferable to any foreseeable alternative. "If I were God," he said, "I would act through Gorbachev" to solve the present crisis. That said, the democratic opposition is not likely to back down if Gorbachev remains intransigent. Both Yeltsin and Yuri Afanasyev stipulate that a peaceful solution depends on Gorbachev's capacity to regain the initiative. Both held out the specter of revolution Romanian style if he did not.

So much attention is focused on the man who increasingly seems an enigma. Does he have a grand conception, a plan for the future? Will he forsake communism, embrace the free market, shrink the empire? What does he really believe these days? Is he, as the banner on the cover of a recent issue of the *Economist* proclaimed, "Yesterday's Man"?

## Gorbachev and Yeltsin

A rapprochement between Mikhail Gorbachev and Boris Yeltsin has become a metaphor for the future of the Soviet Union. In his hour meeting with us, Yeltsin did not mention the name Gorbachev for 53 minutes, and then only once in response to a direct question about their relationship. Yeltsin freely acknowledged real tension and personal animosity between them. He summoned a recent front page of *The New York Times* and took enormous pleasure in pointing out that a larger picture of Yeltsin was on top of a smaller picture of Gorbachev. And when asked, in a different setting, whether he had in mind a role for Gorbachev something akin to that of the Queen of England he smiled in silent assent.

It is said that Yeltsin can enrage Gorbachev faster than anyone alive. Apparently Gorbachev's vicious personal attack on Yeltsin as a drunk before undecided members of the Russian Parliament backfired and actually helped Yeltsin win the leadership of the Russian Republic. An old-time member of the party, acknowledging the personal animosity, predicted the feud could be "lethal" to Gorbachev because it will demean his position, and Gorbachev is bound to lose.

Despite misgivings about Yeltsin's personal stability and lack of a specific program, Yeltsin is a more popular figure in Moscow than Mikhail Gorbachev. A taxi driver told us he admired Yeltsin's straight talk and mistrusted Gorbachev's dissembling. A deputy in the Supreme Soviet suggested that Gorbachev no longer had the confidence of the people, in part because he never submitted his political future to a democratic process. A legislative aide to a leading deputy opined that while Gorbachev had been a good leader, events had passed him by. Virtually all the intellectuals and independent journalists with whom we spoke concurred. It appears that Gorbachev's popularity is at an all-time low.

And yet there remains, even among his sharpest critics, a residual respect for what he has accomplished, as well as a fear of the unknown. While they would not admit it, I suspect Gorbachev's most persistent critics are hoping that he will move toward a market economy, accelerate the process of democratization, and find a way to redefine the relationship with republics which want full independence or more autonomy. The fear is not so much that there will be a conservative coup—most discount any threat from the army or old-line Communists—but rather that the present course will render

Gorbachev ineffective in dealing with, as the historian Afanasyev put it, "chaos, disintegration, and disorder."

Even as they heap criticism on him, opponents are sending a signal that they are prepared to work with him if he will only open himself to more radical change.

Certainly he feels the pressure. Directing a savage personal attack at Yeltsin, instituting a new law to limit insulting criticism of the President, removing authority to grant permission for demonstrations in downtown Moscow from the city government, walking out on the May Day parade—these are not acts which display confidence. Turning his back on his people—fleeing, as it were, Ceausescu style—was a particularly damaging symbol. To maintain his capacity to lead, Gorbachev needs to display infinite patience, confidence, and restraint, since the appearance of control is essential in a situation where control is in fact passing from the center to the periphery, from the center to many new sources of power. Even his critics are ready with advice: seek alliances with younger, more progressive politicians new to the scene, purge the staff of the Central Committee, resign from the General Secretaryship of the party (or even from the party itself), embrace the free market, decentralize, and so on. He need not meet the most radical or utopian standards to win back the initiative, but some real and symbolic measures are essential, and soon.

It will not be easy, because there is little doubt that Mikhail Gorbachev is a committed Socialist and Communist. Czech President Havel reportedly emerged from a meeting with him recently in disbelief that Gorbachev really believed in socialism and communism as strongly as he does. People wonder how a man who has spent his career in the party, and owes everything to the party, can break with it, can embrace doctrines he has fought against all his life. But people also acknowledge that Gorbachev "can be educated to reality," is a proud man who wants to lead, and is a skillful politician. So the struggle for Gorbachev's soul continues, with the future of the country hanging in the balance.

Perhaps a rapprochement with Yeltsin will be the key to the required shift. For his part, Yeltsin professes to be ready to work with Gorbachev. "My relations," he said, "with the President should be businesslike: dialogue, negotiations, principled, peaceful—but never detrimental to the sovereignty or interests of the Russian Federation. I am ready to meet the President more than halfway ... but he also must come halfway." Yeltsin says he supports Gorbachev's "strategic objectives," but that is hard to measure, for Yeltsin's program seems like a radical departure. Yeltsin believes that central power should be broken up and given to people in the city (village) councils. He would allow them to decide which powers to delegate to the districts (counties), and allow the districts to decide which powers should be delegated to the republics and which residual powers should in turn go to the federal government. Gorbachev tried through *perestroika* to break up central monopoly, but 5 years later it is still strong, not even dealt "a serious blow." As for economic reform, Yeltsin favors private ownership, commenting that he admired Germany, Japan, and the United States. He plans to make Russia a model for the Soviet Union, which he sees evolving as a rather loose confederation of sovereign states.

When asked for details about how he would proceed, Yeltsin was short on specifics and tended to repeat his general themes. He seemed uninterested in the ethnic troubles in the Soviet Union except in those in Russia, although he did say that the ethnic tension represented another Gorbachev mistake.

I was more favorably impressed with Yeltsin in person than I expected to be. He was street smart, articulate, self-confident, strong, wry, and charismatic. Yet he did not strike me as a deep thinker or quite up to the challenge of turning his general themes into a workable program. And there appears to me to be more than a little opportunism in his present stance. But he is a force to be reckoned with—with potential for good or bad results depending on how skillfully Gorbachev plays their relationship.

## The Future

We often asked the "bottom line" question of people with whom we met: Are you optimistic or pessimistic? Yuri Afanasyev quickly replied that he was optimistic but then he offered some definitions: "A pessimist says it can't get any worse but an optimist believes it can." It is the tragedy of Gorbachev that he believes the empire can be maintained and that he is wedded to old ideas of internal reform. Afanasyev believes *perestroika* will be seen only as the prologue to the real restructuring that is bound to happen. Afanasyev indicated that the situation has reached a crisis over the past month and that the country now faces a "naked choice": it must work as a whole or it must allow the republics to go their separate ways. Afanasyev thinks the latter course is "inevitable" and that the "country will split into pieces" led by the Baltics, Western Ukraine, Moldavia, and the Caucases, perhaps with other republics to follow. And the Russian Republic itself may fragment with autonomous republics like Bashkiria, Yakutia, and Tataria (for instance) splitting off. The only question is whether the process will be civilized and directed or chaotic and violent. In response to my question about the fate of the ethnic minorities without the protection of the central government, Afanasyev suggested the possibility of another Middle East. "We thought Marxism-Leninism would be a vaccine against the Middle East virus," he said, "but it didn't work and we are just beginning to experience the illness."

Afanasyev certainly represents the pessimistic end of the spectrum of views of the future, although many people with whom we spoke believe the next stage of *perestroika* will be fraught with danger of violence and deeper economic hardship. There is a fair consensus that the West is badly misreading the situation by trying to support Gorbachev's present course rather than pressuring him toward faster and more fundamental reforms. It appears to many, and I agree, that the West is several years too late in lending the kind of massive economic aid Gorbachev needed to "jump start" the Soviet economy, stimulate (even cosmetic) improvements in the consumer economy, buy time for his political reforms to take hold, and thereby share the responsibility for economic policy. And having withheld that aid, it is thought that the West now compounds the error by reinforcing Gorbachev's cautious instincts. Yeltsin tells a story with a wry smile. "When I visited President Bush," he said, "I was told to be patient with *perestroika*. I replied that the people have no patience left. When I next saw Mrs. Thatcher she tried to persuade me to be patient and so did Mr. Genscher. But there is little time left and if the people don't see change soon they will rebel." Yeltsin places the moment of truth 2 or 3 years out ahead.

My own conclusion is not so apocalyptic as Afanasyev's nor as simple as Yeltsin's prescription for more democracy and transition to a free market without unemployment and other social pains of adjustment. Gorbachev seems to have a firm grip on the Supreme Soviet and the apparatus of party and government, including the military. And for all their talk there is little that the mayor of Moscow and the head of the Russian Republic can do to introduce a free market economy unless the central government makes it possible. The ethnic clashes, troubling as they are, probably can be contained or at least isolated from Gorbachev's other problems. And it is certainly possible that Gorbachev will find a face-saving way for gradual emancipation of the Baltic states. The critical question, then, is whether he can transcend his own ideological limitations within the next year or so while, I judge, he still has the opportunity to regain the initiative.

As Sergei Kovalev put it, Gorbachev cannot maintain the status quo: he will either move right or become progressive. I place my bet on a carefully calibrated leftward move—far short of what people of advanced thinking want but enough to maintain center ground in a country which is moving inexorably toward the free market and much more genuine democracy. In the end I see Gorbachev in power for another few years, perhaps presiding over a process in which he does not truly believe but which he comes to realize is the only alternative to chaos. There will be no quick fix for the economy, perhaps little or no improvement at all. But the hope of a conversion to something like a free market and room for individual initiative on the local level will buy time. So will advances in democratization which I believe are inexorable, especially if Gorbachev can reposition himself in the vanguard of change.

It strikes me as a delicious irony that the tactics used by totalitarian regimes to keep the dissidents off balance—an unpredictable cycle of repression, easing, more repression—are now being used on Gorbachev. The opposition—in many forms—can press hard, win a little and ease off for a while, and then press hard again. So I end up with cautious optimism but not without full awareness of plausible scenarios which would be truly catastrophic.

# A New History for Romania?

(MEMORANDUM TO THE BOARD OF TRUSTEES,
JANUARY 1990)

### Introductory Note

I write to report on my trip to Bucharest, Romania (January 3-8) undertaken as a mission of the Helsinki Watch Committee and of the New School's Eastern and Central Europe project. I traveled with Jeri Laber, executive director of the U.S. Helsinki Watch Committee, and Karl Schwarzenberg, chair of the International Helsinki Federation in Vienna. Our purpose was to assess the status of human rights under the new government, indicate our concerns directly to the new leaders, and form a local Helsinki Watch Committee in Romania. On behalf of the New School, I sought to identify a nucleus of scholars through whom to work in helping to rebuild formal academic life.

We decided to undertake our mission only 3 days after Nicolae and Elena Ceausescu were executed and while fighting between the army and the elite Securitate loyal to Ceausescu continued. Planning was difficult, since normal communications and transportation lines to Bucharest were disrupted. Our initial plan was to gather in Budapest and fly to Bucharest on Tuesday, January 2, but that approach was blocked because the Hungarian airline canceled its flight. Tarom, the Romanian airline, had suspended all service. We speculated that its pilots and crew must have been members of the Securitate and might well be under investigation. We searched for any air link (the train link from Budapest was 17 hours and we had no entrance visas), finally settling on Austrian Air leaving Vienna on the afternoon of January 3. As it happened, we were on the first scheduled flight to Bucharest since the revolution. The tense silence in the cabin of the nearly full plane testified to the foreboding and uncertainty we all felt.

The Bucharest airport resembled a military installation with soldiers and army vehicles scattered among the grounded Tarom fleet. The Austrian Ambassador met us and with her help we cut through some of the entrance formalities on which the revolution had had little impact. Our 30-minute trip to central Bucharest was made more difficult by the icy and rutted roads, preserved by near zero temperatures, and was punctuated by four roadblocks. The reality of the revolution began to grow as we passed the Foreign Ministry, the seat of the provisional government, which was guarded by four tanks.

Our first glimpse of destruction came at the Palace Square, bounded by the historic palace, the university library, and the Party Central Committee headquarters. It was here that, on December 21, Ceausescu had assembled the crowd which stunned him with calls for resignation. The evidence of battle was everywhere: a completely destroyed university library, a burned-out palace, burned office and apartment buildings, a bullet-ridden party headquarters. Soldiers and tanks were plentiful, yet the square was full of people going about their everyday chores, carrying shopping bags and briefcases. The single candles burning at the spots where people had died offered a poignant reminder of the recent battles. At virtually every intersection between the main square and the Inter-Continental Hotel were small groups of people huddled together for warmth in the cold, snowy, dark afternoon. Some prayed, some wept. All stood quietly with heads bowed over the candles, remembering their friends and relatives who had given their lives in the past week to rid Romania of the hated dictator.

The 22-story Inter-Continental Hotel stood in sharp contrast the old city and the somber people outside. We estimated that 250 journalists and camera crews populated the hotel, which served as the second center of activity in Bucharest. How the news is gathered, the easy flow of rumors around the dining room where most of us ate, the creation of confirmation of reality and leadership through a news story is a tale for another time. Suffice it to say we were well placed.

Our work brought us in contact with the leaders of the provisional government, the American Ambassador, intellectuals who had been dissidents, students, and those forming political parties. By Thursday, January 4, the fighting had completely subsided so we felt no anxiety about moving around during the daylight hours. Each subsequent day the situation seemed more stable and gradually we had no fear about evening travel as well. The sniping had stopped and the feared acts of terrorism did not materialize. It quickly became apparent that the initial estimates of 60,000 people killed during the revolution were grossly exaggerated. While the provisional government steadfastly refused to release a corrected esimate, one of its members privately suggested that the number will be under 10,000. Our own estimates are under 5,000 people killed.

Within a day we had heard enough specific details of Ceausescu's 24-year mad rule to realize that the worst stories emerging over the years understated the terror and hardship visited upon this society. As one intellectual described it, Romania was a "red variant' of the Nazis with a dash of mafioso."

A member of the ruling body characterized the regime as "the most effective repressive system known in history." Virtually everyone with whom we spoke related specific personal stories of surveillance and harassment. It is difficult to document how many people were killed by the regime through mysterious disappearances, "suicides," and "heart attacks," or how many had been consigned to psychiatric hospitals and subjected to drugs and possibly to radiation.

By most major accounts, Ceausescu underwent a sharp personality change after the major earthquake of 1977. The cult of personality, the megalomania, the paranoia, intensified. So did the repression and the obsession with repaying foreign debt at the expense of the necessities of daily life. Tales of starvation and deprivation of electricity and heat are not exaggerated. Even now, many homes in Bucharest are still cold, and while food supplies are momentarily more plentiful, there are concerns about expected shortages as the winter wears on.

One striking symbol of Ceausescu's decline into madness can be found in the section of the old city which he completely razed to construct a giant new development lining a 2-mile boulevard leading to his palace upon a hill. Nearly complete, the palace, office, apartment, commercial, and cultural complex must be one of the largest single building projects under way anywhere in the world. The imperial and classical style conveys pretentions to grandeur on a monumental scale. The palace and grounds alone seem to me larger than Versailles. This new "city" has never been occupied; its offices and apartments sit empty, waiting for Ceausescu (now deceased) to decide about their use. Even though this part of Bucharest was off-limits to ordinary citizens until December 22, one can imagine the tales carried home by the sizable workforce and the bitterness that this luxurious fantasy inspired among a cold and hungry population.

The December revolution appears to have been a spontaneous uprising which gave expression to the simmering discontent throughout Romania. Earlier in 1989 there were several open protests against the Ceausescu regime. Silviu Brucan, a former Ambassador to the United States and a teacher of social sciences at a medical institute (who fell out with Ceausescu 20 years ago) organized a protest letter in March cosigned by five others. Also in March, poet Mircea Dinescu gave an interview to the French paper *Liberation*, which criticized the regime for stifling intellectual life and resisting political reforms. After he was placed under house arrest and harassed, seven intellectuals (including the new Culture Minister Andrei Plesu and the new Education Minister Mihai Sora) sent a letter to the head of the Writers Union protesting Dinescu's treatment.

These and other courageous public acts, coupled with the rush of events in neighboring countries, seem to have emboldened the people. "Something was in the air," many suggested to us as people in small groups began to signal one another first through "a wink and a nod" and later through conversations. The well-known chronology need not be rehearsed here. But it should be said that rumors of a plot 6 months in the making (with or without Soviet assistance) appear unfounded. I am inclined to accept Brucan's assertion to us that the revolution was "a 100 percent spontaneous social explosion, unique, original, without precedent, and hard to integrate into any conceptual framework."

Brucan has been described as the Richelieu of the revolution. He was the most impressive of those whom we met: thoughtful, smart, tough, savvy, confident. In his late seventies, he is older than the leadership of the new government, more a man of Ceasescu's generation. Perhaps for that reason, or because his style does not resonate with the young, he elected to take no cabinet ministry. But clearly he is the most powerful moral and intellectual force behind the government. He described how the new leaders coalesced into the Front for National Salvation, as the provisional government is called.

As the demonstrators invaded the Party Central Committee headquarters and the Ceausescus fled from the roof by helicopter, a number of people who had fallen out with Ceausescu were drawn there. Along with Brucan, they included Ion Iliescu, a former publishing house worker who is now President; Petru Roman, a teacher at the Polytechnical Institute who is now Prime Minister; and Dumitru Mazilu, who is now Vice President. These men are the "big four" of the Front for National Salvation. They met on the balcony where Ceausescu had addressed the crowd, spoke to the crowd, and then had their first meeting, at which they selected the name for their movement and formulated a preliminary program. Their first act was to seize the television station (some 20 minutes away) on the evening of December 22; this would prove critical to consolidating their control.

The Romanian Army held the balance for the success of the revolution. Ceausescu had grown to mistrust his army, favoring instead the elite Securitate, which was better equipped. While it is not a popular notion, it seemed clear to us that some members of the army would side with the people. Another victim of Ceausescu's whimsical suspicion, Nicolae Militaru, who had fallen out with Ceausescu, joined civilian leaders and became head of the army. According to Brucan, the fate of the revolution was still in doubt on December 24 as the leaders of the Front for National Salvation gathered at the Ministry of Defense. The Securitate was gaining ground, widening its area of action. Ceausescu by now was under arrest but there were reports of a plan to free him. Leaders of the Front for National Salvation feared a bloodbath would result if a full-scale civil war developed. So on the evening of December 24 they decided to execute Ceausescu; by all accounts his death on Christmas Day broke the back of the resistance and the Securitate began to surrender.

Meanwhile the Front for National Salvation was expanding to include people like Doina Cornea (a courageous dissident from Cluj) and students. Gradually the council grew to 145 members, and an 11-person executive committee was formed. Ion Iliescu emerged as the leader, since he could bridge the army and Parliament, which did not meet until January 4. A subgroup had met on Christmas Day and a somewhat larger group (60 people) on December 28.

The "big four" and Defense Minister Militaru in effect are running the country and, we gather, the balance of the executive committee is not very powerful. The council appears to be an uncomfortable amalgam of three groups: (1) dissidents like Cornea, who give moral authority to the revolution; (2) people like Roman, who were there when the Party Central Committee headquarters and television station were occupied; and (3) competent people needed to run the government who are judged "morally adequate" by the Front.

The Front for National Salvation is both a provisional government and an ad hoc Parliament. Its objective is to stabilize the country, to secure the conditions for democracy, and to keep the food and fuel flowing so ordinary life does not deteriorate further. Almost obsessive about the need for unity, the Front has taken a series of steps to address individual concerns of freedom of assembly and expression, abolished the death penalty, dismantled the Securitate, relaxed travel restrictions, returned small plots to the peasants, and committed itself to drawing up a constitution which would include separation of power, checks and balances, and limits on tenure. It has abolished the leading role of the Communist Party and promised free elections in an open multiparty system by April.

Thus, considerable progress has been made and with lightning speed. Ion Iliescu, with whom we met, understandably showed the strain of events and lack of rest. He reminded us that Russia was 5 years into *perestroika* but the people are still unhappy because their expectations were too high. He commented on the other Eastern bloc countries which underwent a more gradual transition. He said that he felt caught between the old forces which are resistant to change and the new power seekers who are pushing for faster reform. He reflected that the first leaders in a revolution almost always are sacrificed and those who follow are longer-term leaders. He said that the Front for National Salvation wants only to establish the structures to build on and is quite prepared to yield power after the April elections.

It is impossible not to be impressed by the many courageous decisions made and actions taken by the Front for National Salvation, but real problems remain.

*1.* The economy is in ruins. Despite stories of secret supplies and the one-time release of reserves, Romania is likely to have food and fuel shortages this winter. And it will take years for the infrastructure of a modern industrial sector to yield results. Immediate shortages of consumer goods may provoke anger directed at the provisional government.

*2.* The Front for National Salvation's decision to place stability over reform means that the bureaucracy below the top level remains in office for the moment. Thus people see the old party members who were their bosses still in place. Quite naturally, the shift on the part of old party bosses from blind loyalty to Ceausescu to the language of democracy and support for the Front is not credible. While we may understand the magnitude of the challenge of replacing an entire government overnight, those who feel ownership of the revolution are disappointed and suspicious that the old party leaders may regain control. This is a special concern in the distant provinces, where members of the old regime not connected to the Front leaders in Bucharest have appropriated the name of the Front in an effort to retain power.

3. The fact that the leaders of the new government were not only Communists but Ceausescu loyalists at an earlier point also arouses suspicion. For the most part, they did not break with Ceausescu in acts of courage but rather were dismissed by him.

4. Brucan reports that the students demanded early elections—"March/April" was the chant—so the Front moved up its own preferred schedule, which was June. As a consequence, many doubt that there is enough time for new parties to organize and campaign. While it is easy to form a party—only 251 signatures are needed—there is no source of funds to run a campaign. In addition, it is not clear that new parties will have adequate access to the mass media. Hence, there are now three counterproposals under discussion:

- Delay the elections
- Hold a referendum in April on when and how the elections should be held
- Elect people for only 1 year in April

5. Concern over the elections intensified when the Front reversed an earlier position and announced it would field candidates. Clearly, it has a massive advantage over any other party and seems destined to dominate the elections.

It is my own guess that the elections will be postponed briefly and will be free but not, strictly speaking, fair. This view does not imply evil intent or a plot. Rather, I think a transition stage will be necessary between the present provisional government, which derives its legitimacy from a revolution, and implementation of something closer to a Western-style democracy. It is, of course, possible that the provisional government will not maintain control and will yield to a more representative interim government or to the army. Under any scenario, the transition will not be easy, because Romania—unlike, say, Czechoslovakia—has no democratic tradition to draw upon and had to endure Stalinism a generation or two longer than the other Eastern bloc countries. Much is made of the passive nature of the Romanians but I am skeptical of such notions of national character. I think the lack of experience with democracy and democratic traditions rather than a "passive" or "centralized" mentality will be the problem.

Indeed, I was struck on our short visit by the liveliness of life in Bucharest. I was surprised by the openness to the West and the sophistication of both the government leaders and the intellectuals. Party formation is proceeding quickly. While the situation remains confused, several parties have so far qualified for registration—and other groups soon may. The Front for National Salvation is the largest group. A revival is expected of the National Peasant Party, which was strong between the world wars, and this is likely to be the most effective challenge to the Front for National Salvation. At present, three groups are vying for the peasant banner. Already in place are a National Liberal Party, a National Democractic Progressive Party, and a Social Democratic Party. Other groups which are not yet formal parties include a Hungarian Group, an Ecology Group, a Free Youth of Romania Group, and an Antitotalitarian Front. So far there is no Communist Party and none is likely to emerge as a serious contender. The only party outlawed is a fascist group.

None of the parties or groupings has a very clear program. "Liberty, democracy, and individual rights" is a slogan to which most subscribe. The Front for National Salvation's program of stability, movement toward democracy, and improvement of food and fuel supplies has been echoed by other parties in these early days, but distinctions are likely to emerge. The Iliescu government has resisted indicating its views on a desired form of political economy for Romania, limiting itself to the immediate goals of stability, democracy, and short-term functioning of the economy. It takes the position that major questions, such as restructuring the economy along free market lines, should await the elected government.

Privately, Brucan expressed the hope that Romania would emerge along the lines of Sweden or Austria.

Iliescu's desire for stability will be tested in the weeks ahead. We are told that two potentially destabilizing forces are ethnic tension and student movements.

At a press conference, a leader of the Hungarian minority took pains to say that Hungarians had faith in the Front and felt they were being treated fairly. The Hungarians (2 to 3 million) are concentrated in the western (Transylvanian) part of the country and constitute the largest ethnic minority within a single country in Europe. Still, they represent a majority in only two of Romania's forty provinces and 70 percent of Transylvania is Romanian. We are told that relations between the two groups in provincial cities like Timisoara and Cluj are respectful but that there are tensions in smaller cities and villages which could prove disruptive. We believe the treatment of the Hungarian minority will bear watching.

The student movement in Bucharest represents a more immediate uncertainty. Even though students are scattered around the country for Christmas vacation, there was a rally of 2,000 to 3,000 students at the Polytechnic University (Romania's largest) on Sunday, January 7. This was the first organized protest since the revolution.

Held in a multistory atrium, the rally was orderly and inspiring. There were many eloquent speeches, and genuine emotion greeted the representatives from Timisoara. While the burden of the protest was directed at the structure of the university system and plans to share power with students, some uneasy feelings about the new government were expressed. One speaker chosen by the Front to represent students on its council received a mixed reaction. The concern centered on the belief that he could not represent students because he had not been democratically elected. I suspect that all the students on the council will have to resign and stand for election by other students.

Sunday evening we met with the leaders of the rally. When asked point blank whether they trusted Iliescu, some said they did, some expressed skepticism, and some remained silent. Our conversation made clear that the students want to feel included in the shaping of Romanian democracy and have a generalized suspicion of the older generations who had been members of the party. I rather think that if democracy takes root in Romania, a younger generation will emerge as leaders sooner than in the other Eastern bloc countries. The Romanian population, after all, has the highest percentage of party members of any country in the world. It should be noted that the students with whom we spoke have no well-formed program for the future of Romania beyond generalized notions of democracy.

It is not yet clear how much of a force the students will be or how strong an organization will take shape in late January, when the university term resumes. My own guess is that students will be a significant force—a view that Brucan and others share. The student movement is reaching out to a younger generation in the factories, and it is quite possible that an alliance will emerge which will check any tendency of the elders to backslide from democracy. It is also possible that a youth coalition would press for more rapid reforms—such as quicker replacement of holdover party functionaries—and thus destabilize the provisional government.

We got a glimpse of the more radical youth through the student leaders, who asked us to meet with some young people (not students) who were staging a hunger strike in a subway station four stops from the Inter-Continental Hotel. Karl Schwarzenberg and I accompanied the students to a room off the station where some dozen people aged 15 to 30 had been holed up for 5 days. They listed twenty "demands", most of which revealed a deep distrust of the provisional government. Among the issues raised:

- "Why did the Front for National Salvation Committee around the country take shape while the real people were fighting in the streets?"
- "We don't know Iliescu and don't trust him. Why does he keep the old bureaucratic apparatus?"

- "Why does the leadership of the Front consist of people who had earlier praised Ceausescu?"
- "Who will guarantee that the elections will be free if the Front is a party?"

We were interested to see that the student leaders thought these questions and the other demands were too suspicious and asked too much. The students had not had any contact with these working-class groups before and I judge their efforts to build an alliance will require some modification of their own essentially moderate views.

The early exercise of democratic rights has been both heady and frustrating. Without legitimate representative structures in place, most groups are practicing a rather "pure" form of democracy in which almost everything is decided by majority vote. The quick actions by the provisional government in the early days have begun to yield to seemingly endless debates and lack of action in the face of mounting practical problems. It is not surprising that this first taste of democracy carries with it some disappointments.

From what we could gather, older intellectuals are more inclined to support the Front—indeed, many of them are part of it. Our strongest connections were with writer Mircea Dinescu, who is the new head of the Writers Union, and a circle called the Group for Social Dialogue. Leaders of that group included sociologists Alin Teodorescu and Pavel Campeanu (who recently visited the New School) and philosopher Sorin Vieru. Intellectuals in both the Writers Union and the Group for Social Dialogue expressed confidence in the new Culture Minister Andrei Plesu and the new Education Minister Mihai Sora.

Dinescu wants to make the Writers Union fully independent from the government and to publish magazines and journals on a printing press that the union wishes to acquire.

The Group for Social Dialogue is of great interest to the New School, since it mirrors similar groups in other countries with which we have worked. Composed of fifteen members at the moment, it is likely to grow and could be a central force in rebuilding the conditions for scholarly life in Romania. It is a natural nucleus for a Bucharest branch of our Democracy Seminar. I have invited two of its members to visit the New School in February. The group is starting a journal called *22*, hopes to operate a radio station, and will likely provide the nucleus of the Romanian Helsinki Watch Committee.

One of the most cogent analyses of the prospects for Romania was offered by philosopher Sorin Vieru and echoed by other intellectuals. They are optimistic about the future but not necessarily about their own role in the new society. As Vieru said, he finds it hard to accommodate the activist students who want change at a rapid pace. Others also fear that the students will be too extreme. But they believe that it is impossible to return to personal dictatorship. To Vieru, it doesn't matter in the short run which party wins as long as the elections are honest. He believes a coalition government will emerge which will have very little choice of course. In his view, the major decisions are preordained: (1) good relations with both East and West; and (2) a pragmatic approach to rebuilding the economy as a first priority with a major role for the state sector. Vieru believes that Iliescu is typical of a new breed of post-Soviet leaders: former Communists who want reform and who will be required by the circumstances they face to become social democrats.

A subtext of this analysis about the future of Romania concerns the role of the United States. Soviet Foreign Minister Edvard Shevardnadze visited Bucharest on Saturday, January 6. The next morning we met with Foreign Minister Celac, who said the visit had gone satisfactorily because Shevardnadze had pledged to respect the will of the Romanian people in selecting their government. But Celac expressed puzzlement over why the United States had been so "slow" in offering help to the new government. "I badly need a visit from a high-level American official for balance," Celac said. "But I cannot make the first call." He asked us to convey this message to our government. Clearly, the popular suspicion of the provisional government as a group of committed old Communists working with the Soviet Union is damaging to its prospects for survival. Visible American suppport would be reassuring to the skeptical and provide the balance that Celac desires.

My own thoughts about the future are in accord with the basically optimistic assessment offered by Vieru, although the evolution of a democratic society is far from a certainty. As in the other Eastern bloc countries, political democracy does not guarantee the emergence of a civil society. We focused on two elements that we believe to be essential to a civil society: protection of human rights and the rebuilding of scholarly life. I turn now to these two prerequisite areas.

Our human rights concerns focused on several issues:

1. We believe that treatment of the Hungarian minority (discussed earlier) bears watching.
2. We are concerned about the conduct of the trials of both civilian leaders of the old regime and the leaders of the Securitate. The trials should be public and should include the normal procedural guarantees. We are told that the Securitate will be subjected to military tribunals. Such a step raises the potential for summary judgments, perhaps designed to limit the implication of others. There is special concern about acts of vengeance against the Securitate in provisional areas where we hear reports of occasional lynchings of Securitate leaders. We are concerned that Securitate prisoners are being kept under inhumane conditions and are troubled by the provisional government's refusal to indicate how many people have been detained.
3. We believe that it is important to document past abuses, and that focusing on this history will be important to the healthy development of the society. We are not convinced that the old regime's records are being protected, and evidence exists that important records have already been destroyed. There is a tendency to blame the abuses on Ceausescu and to implicate only his immediate circle. We believe that a government commission should be formed quickly to document past abuses.
4. We are not yet convinced that there will be adequate and fair access to the mass media before the election.

Of direct concern to the New School is how we might, together with other Western universities, reconstruct scholarly life. There is much less to build on within the formal university system in Romania than there is in countries like Poland and Hungary. The quarter century of repression has essentially cut off scholars from modern literature in their fields, and many faculty are viewed as collaborators with the regime. A tight rein has been kept on the granting of Ph.D.s for the past 15 years; as a consequence, younger faculty—those under 45—are simply in scarce supply. Most of the bright and independent thinkers are undertrained and outside formal academic life.

Fortunately, there exists a nucleus of able scholars with whom we can work. I propose we consider a five-point program requiring modest funding:

1. We need to resupply (with the help of other institutions) the University of Bucharest library with books and journals. A large part of its collection burned in the fighting. Perhaps we could ask major university presses to contribute one copy of important books. We would collect and ship the books which are donated ($5,000).
2. We should start a branch of the Democracy Seminar in Bucharest at the Group for Social Dialogue. We should invite representation to the joint meeting of the New York-Warsaw-Budapest-Prague groups to be held in Budapest in March ($1,500).
3. I have invited Alin Teodorescu and Sorin Vieru to the New School for 2 weeks in February in order to begin the process of maintaining connections to American universities. Neither has ever visited the United States. I have also invited the new head of the Writers Union, Mercea Dinescu, so that we will connect to independent intellectuals as well ($7,500).
4. I would like to send up to six members of our faculty (separately) to Bucharest to give bibliographic seminars in their fields to ten to twenty scholars in each discipline. The purpose would be to help them develop undergrad-

uate and graduate courses which draw upon current literature, by which I mean the literature of the past quarter century. Courses could be given within the university or on a less formal basis outside ($2,500 each trip or $15,000 total).

5. We want to send five copies of the books which we recommend for each course so that they may be placed "on reserve" for students to read ($5,000).

These are modest efforts, but they are concrete and would be very welcome. They represent a beginning of the reconstruction of formal scholarly life and provide a model for other institutions wishing to help. To carry forward plans, the New School needs about $30,000 this spring.

Certainly the Romanian transformation has no parallel in Eastern Europe. It is at once the most exciting and the most fragile of enterprises. The transformation in 2 weeks has been impressive but now the hard part starts. The economy is in ruins; the implication of so many in the madness of the Ceausescu regime will deprive the government of its most experienced managers; forces for instability exist in emerging ethnic and student unrest; there is no tradition of a democratic culture. These are formidable obstacles to the orderly evolution of a stable civil society. Yet the dramatic act of revolution and the thorough discrediting of a depraved ancient regime present a "tabula rasa" on which Romania may begin to write a new history. Whether Iliescu and the Front for National Salvation are equal to the possibilities remains a question but they have made a promising start. I am convinced that massive and immediate external help with self-determination must be met within Romania by a younger generation "present at the creation." I feel privileged to have stood witness to some of the events, debates, and possibilities that are at work in the creation of a new Romania.

# BUCHAREST REVISITED: REALITY SETS IN

(NOTES ON A VISIT TO BUCHAREST, JULY 1990)

### BACKGROUND

On July 4-8 I visited Romania for the second time since the December revolution as a follow-up to an International Helsinki Federation mission in January. The immediate reason for the visit was to learn firsthand about the events of mid-June, when the government issued a call to the general public to help restore order in Bucharest. In response to the government's plea, 10,000 miners came to the city and went on a violent 2-day rampage. I met with government officials (the Foreign Minister, the Interior Minister, a senior adviser to the President), representatives of the major opposition parties (the Liberal Party, the Peasant Party, the Hungarian Democratic Union), opposition journalists and independent intellectuals, the new Rector and Vice Rector of the University of Bucharest, the head of the Writers Union, and Silviu Brucan, a leader of the group which overthrew Nicolae Ceausescu.

The events of June reveal much about the state of Romanian society: the fragile hold on control exercised by the newly elected government, the deep divisions and distrust in the society between students and intellectuals and ordinary people, the disturbing strain of violence and anger just beneath the surface, the imperfect working of democracy, and, finally, some considerable resilience. Virtually everyone with whom I spoke acknowledged the difficulty of creating a democratic, civil society upon the ruins of a totalitarian state. Thus a sense of realism—but not pessimism—has replaced the joy and relief of the days immediately following the revolution.

On the surface Bucharest is calm, life normal. Opposition groups meet, publish newspapers, vigorously criticize the government. Food, electricity, and other necessities of life, while not plentiful, are more readily available than a year ago. There is some evidence that the privatization of agriculture (80 percent according to Brucan) has increased production, at least of vegetables, with only a modest rise in prices. But little progress has been made in the industrial sector. The black market is expanding as a vigorous second economy prospers and, we are told, corruption flourishes.

The new government, headed by Prime Minister Petru Roman (who was also the provisional Prime Minister) has a different hue than the provisional government: it is considerably younger (average age under 50), has fewer ties to the old regime, and is commonly referred to as "technocratic." Its new program—pledging rapid movement to a free market and further advances in the democratic process—has been well-received by the opposition. Both Liberal Party and Peasant Party representatives said Roman "stole our program."

This says something about the weakness of the opposition. The campaign did not surface substantive differences among the parties but rather turned on ethnic issues (the Hungarian minority) and on who was more vigorously against the past regime and communism. A central issue was the tie of President Ion Iliescu and the Front for National Salvation to Ceausescu.

The opposition had no experience under Ceausescu, since it lacked the underground democratic structures which flourished in Czechoslovakia, Poland, and elsewhere—no Charter 77, no Solidarity movement. The opposition offered no concrete solution to Romanian problems but rather advocated another revolution of sorts by proposing to purge former Communists from political life. The slogan "The only solution, another revolution" deeply disturbed the general public, as did the act of blocking a major intersection for weeks. By all accounts the demonstrations since April in University Square—including a mix of students, opposition parties, independent intellectuals, and some fringe elements—backfired, actually working to increase Iliescu's electoral margin in late May to 83 percent of the popular vote. The opposition was soundly rejected by a population deeply yearning for stability.

As Helsinki Watch has previously reported, the election campaign saw plenty of examples of harassment and intimidation visited upon opposition parties, especially the Peasant Party in the countryside. There is no question that the Front had better access to money, organization, and the mass media and that the advantage of incumbency weighed heavily. None of the independent candidates, including some rather well-known members of the provisional parliament, won a seat in Parliament. The Hungarian candidates secured 12 seats in the Senate (out of 119) and 29 seats in the Assembly (out of 387), while the Peasant and Liberal parties did less well. The voting process itself was immensely complicated with all candidates elected at large from a 10-page ballot covering 45 parties. Most people simply chose from among the Front candidates.

The story of the head of the Writers Union, Mircea Dinescu, is instructive. Offered a slot on the Front ticket, he decided to run as an independent in the belief that his high visibility would surely earn him a seat. Even after he lost, people came up to him on the street to congratulate him on his election and to urge him to continue his lively (televised) challenges to the government. They were shocked to learn he did not get elected; they thought he was part of the Front.

One unhappy consequence of the election is the alienation of the intellectuals (and students) from the rest of the population. Both their harsh attacks on the government, which frightened ordinary citizens, and their failure to reach out to the workers produced a situation in which they became isolated from the general population.

At the same time, the intellectuals were discouraged by the electorate's failure to make thoughtful choices, a failure that resulted in the exclusion of independent candidates from the new government. That outcome represents a sharp step back from the direct involvement of intellectuals and other independent professionals in the postrevolutionary coalition. As

Dinescu put it, the general public's conception of democracy is more food and Western movies.

He believes Ceausescu's "new man" is the legacy of the dictator, a disease that will undermine the prospect of democracy more surely than the neo-Communist taint of Iliescu. "While we have beheaded the Communist dragon," he said, "the body is still pumping—not just the remnants of the party but in the mentality of the people at every level. We have not yet had a revolution in people's minds."

While there are valid specific examples of unfair election tactics, the election as a whole was free and reasonably fair given the circumstances. Even had none of the documented infractions occurred, Iliescu still would have won an impressive victory. He is extraordinarily popular with ordinary citizens, a fact conceded by even his sharpest critics. How, then, could he lose control of Bucharest on June 13-15 and resort to a vigilante force of 10,000 miners to "restore order"? How could he go on national television and ask the people to protect his government against a Fascist coup attempt? Why would he take actions which damaged the credibility of his government in the international community and interrupt Romania's application for a relationship with and aid from the West?

The surface facts are well known. The antigovernment demonstrations which had occupied the University Square (in front of the Intercontinental Hotel and National Theater) since late April were winding down after the election. Their aim had been to call attention to the Front's ties to the old regime and perhaps to provoke the provisional government into a "Tiananmen Square" mistake which might cost it the election. But with the election settled in late May, most organized groups had withdrawn from University Square, leaving perhaps twenty-five hunger strikers and a core of seventy-five others.

On the night of June 12-13, the government acted to clear the square of the remaining protesters and, by all accounts, the police used excessive force. Rumors of the police action spread through the city, and by midday on June 13 a crowd—

perhaps 2,000 or 3,000 strong—gathered at the square to protest. As the day wore on, the mood turned ugly and the police inexplicably withdrew from the square about 4.30 P.M. Thereafter, events escalated, with Molotov cocktail attacks on the Central Police Headquarters and the Interior Ministry, as well as a march on the television station where a group of protesters, variously estimated between 50 and 200, gained access. There followed an interruption of program transmission. I have seen videotapes of the events and there is no doubt that there was serious disorder in Bucharest on the night of June 13-14.

The police were in little evidence, and the army was slow to react and ineffective. Early in the evening—and then on television after midnight—the President appealed for citizens to defend the government. His plea repeats a pattern, used at least twice before in the spring, to rally citizens in support of the government in the face of large protests.

Unlike previous occasions, the workers and citizens of Bucharest, probably frightened by the violence, did not respond. But some 10,000 miners, mostly from the Jiu Valley 7 or 8 hours away, did. Arriving around 4:00 or 5:00 A.M. in working clothes and armed with clubs and picks, they rampaged through the city and destroyed the headquarters of the Peasant and Liberal parties with savage intensity, invaded the geology and architecture faculties at the university, smashed year-end student projects and expensive laboratory experiments, threatened the headquarters of the main opposition paper *Romania Libera*, cleared the square, secured the television station, and roamed through the city making "citizen's" arrests and beating people at random. In all, some 500 people were injured, 6 killed (it is said before the miners arrived) and perhaps 1,200 arrested (of whom 177 are still being held for possible serious charges). Their job completed, the miners were thanked by President Iliescu on the 15th and asked to return home.

Opposition and government interpretations of the events naturally differ but both see plots and subplots.

Many in the opposition believe that the police deliberately

used unnecessary force to clear the square on the night of June 12–13 in order to stir up trouble. They find it hard to believe that a well-equipped police force would suddenly withdraw at 4:00 P.M. on the 13th and that the army would not respond to protect the government. They further believe that organized provocateurs attacked the Police Headquarters and Interior Ministry, and that the government set up the incident at the television station by allowing protesters in so as to give credence to the threat of a coup. The miners, so this theory goes, must have begun mobilizing the day of the 13th *before* the President's call and before the police lost control. The purpose of the plot was to use the miners to destroy the opposition and send a message that future criticism of the government would entail some real risks. The persistent attacks on opposition groups, like the Group for Social Dialogue, in the Front's paper since the election is offered as further verification of this theory. Finally, the presence of plainclothes personnel, probably former Securitate, guiding the miners to locations they otherwise would not know about is proof positive that the government was behind the rampage.

The government also saw a plot. It feared an effort would be made to disrupt the installation of the new government and thus cleared the square before fresh demonstrations could gather momentum. The crowd that responded on the 13th was not spontaneous but was organized and included a core of people bent on violence intended to provoke the government into a harsh reaction, to show the government as weak, and to tarnish the government in the eyes of the international community so as to deny it the economic aid it needs to survive. Government sources also saw the hand of the old regime—the Securitate, the fascist Legionnaires (evoking images of the Iron Guard)—in what was at worst an outright coup attempt and at best a long-term plan to weaken and bring down the government.

All the forces at the government's disposal were reluctant to act because of their experience in December when army, police, and fire officers were imprisoned for firing on the crowds. The police force was depleted, having been purged of undesirable members, the firefighters refused to engage the crowd, and the army, with Defense Minister Victor Stanculescu away at the Warsaw Pact meeting, was slow to react and ineffective. So President Iliescu had no choice but to appeal to the people (not the miners specifically) for help in maintaining order.

As Silviu Brucan put it, "They blew it." All the government officials with whom I spoke believe the events of June 13-15 had damaged the government's standing internationally and deepened the opposition at home. In retrospect, some concede that Iliescu overreacted to the disorders of the 13th and made a mistake by issuing the call which produced the miners. They admit that the government had no control over the miners and that the miners' behavior was wrong. Other officials still defend their actions as reasonable, given what they knew at the time.

Where does the truth lie? I am not inclined to either of the plot theories. Rather, I think that events spun out of control and the government fell victim to misjudgments. Here is a plausible version of events:

The government decided to clear the remnants of the demonstration at University Square, perhaps because it feared that the residual protesters would be the nucleus of an effort to disrupt the opening of the new Parliament, but more likely because it wanted to reassert some control over a public space that had been occupied for 6 weeks. The police used excessive force, but not on the instruction of the government. That action intensified the public reaction as rumors of the violence, perhaps exaggerated, spread throughout the city.

The crowd that gathered on the 13th lacked the structure (and internal controls) of the previous demonstration, which had been organized by specific opposition groups. I am not in a position to judge whether there were professional "provocateurs" in the crowd, but it would not be unreasonable to suppose that real troublemakers were present—perhaps more than one organized group with more than one agenda. Certainly some fringe elements were there. I am skeptical that either the government or the openly organized opposition employed undercover provocateurs. In any event, the situation during the 13th was unstable, and for reasons not fully explained the police withdrew from the square about 4:00 or 4:30 P.M. Thereafter the crowd faced little resistance from either civilian or military authorities. Until I have some firm evidence to the contrary, I am inclined to believe the government's explanation that the police, firefighters, and army forces were reluctant to engage in what might be a repeat of the December violent clashes with citizens.

The President's assistant, Ion Mircea Pascu, gave a plausible hour-by-hour account of events on June 13–14. By 6:00 or 7:00 P.M. stories were coming to Iliescu about the assault on the Police and Interior buildings and the march on the television station. There were exaggerated stories about the extent of the organization of the mob and its access to weapons.

The Interior Minister, General Mihai Chitac, could not be found. The call went out to the army but it was slow to respond and there were reports of soldiers refusing to confront the demonstrators.*

Events simmered down during the night. The television station was secured, and the worst fears of the government did not materialize. Then the miners arrived and presented themselves to the government about 5:00 A.M., and in much greater numbers than expected. In Pascu's words, "They were in no mood to be put back on the trains," so the government assigned them to protect the square, which by then was fairly quiet. On the way to the square, the miners attacked posters of the opposition parties, sacked the Liberal Party headquarters, and beat people. It was wrongly reported to Iliescu that they also killed the student leader Marian Munteanu.

It seems possible that on the evening of the 13th, acting on incomplete and often distorted and exaggerated information, the President thought there might really be an organized

---

*This information receives independent verification from a group of dissident enlisted men who gave me a statement, to deliver to Radio Free Europe, indicating their reservations about acting against the people.

coup attempt under way. After a vigorous debate within his inner circle, he issued the call for help and went on television in what seemed to some to be a state of panic. He did not specifically call upon the miners and, because he needed immediate help, probably had in mind workers who were close by and who had heeded his call for help in February.* By early morning Iliescu realized he had a new problem: angry miners out of control who were actually being cheered on by ordinary citizens. Eyewitness accounts from people mistaken for being antigovernment are chilling. The Vice Rector of the University of Bucharest, Lapar Vlasceanu, was beaten while crossing the square as people on the sidelines yelled, "Kill him, kill him."

There is little doubt that the miners were assisted by some security forces, who were seen (on videotapes) helping arrest people and guiding the miners to the headquarters of opposition parties and newspapers. The new Interior Minister, Doru Viorel Ursu, volunteered as much and vowed to track them down. It seems to me unlikely these plainclothes people, perhaps ex-Securitate, were acting under the orders of the President or Prime Minister.

The story of Iliescu's struggle to contain the miners on the 14th shows more than a little pathos. Now realizing that the original threat—perhaps wildly exaggerated—was over, he was the captive of the forces which had responded to his call for help and were now totally out of his control. Early on the 14th Iliescu is said to have realized how badly the whole affair would play and determined to get the miners out of town even as they vowed to stay through the weekend. The government decided to take advantage of a televised soccer match in the afternoon to break the miners' momentum and thus set up two areas where large numbers of miners could view the game. By the 15th the worst was over and Iliescu met with the miners to "thank" them as they left Bucharest. His

---

*We need to know more about how, when, and by whom the miners were organized to come to Bucharest. It does not seem plausible that such a large force could have been assembled and transported to Bucharest between the time Iliescu issued his call on the evening of June 13 and 5:00 A.M. on June 14.

people say the "thanks" was as much an effort to move them along as it was sincere appreciation for what they had done, since by then the government realized the extent of the miners' unlawful rampage and the disastrous consequences it would have for Romania's image.

In the end it seems to me that Brucan's assessment was probably right: "They blew it." I doubt that the affair was staged to clobber the opposition or that it is a precursor of antidemocratic intentions by the government. Rather, I think it reveals a weak government still unconfident of its legitimacy, a government not yet functioning as a well-knit team; a society which is frustrated, angry, and given to violent outbursts; and some well-placed people of different persuasions who see self-interest in destabilizing the society.

There is no doubt that the event has frightened opposition groups and raised the anxiety level in the population as a whole. It was a decided setback to the development of a democratic, civil society—and one for which the government must assume responsibility.

## Conclusion

One poignant exchange might be taken as a parable for the problems and prospects of Romania. Presidential assistant Ion Misceau Pascu (age 40 or so) and Radu Filipescu (age 35) of the Helsinki Committee played water polo together and were friends. But now they have traveled different roads. They spent over two hours together, with me and Holly Cartner, trying to sort out conflicting plot theories about the June events and assess where the country is headed. There were some spirited exchanges, especially over the government's attacks on the Group for Social Dialogue and the group's unrelenting criticism of the government at a time when it needs help. At one point Pascu turned to Filipescu and said, "You know, we are prisoners of our destiny," to which Filipescu responded, "I know—we are in a play, have roles, and cannot always act as we want." As our meeting broke, they agreed that they should talk more and that Iliescu should talk with the Group for Social Dialogue.

I believe the capacity for them to act as they want and escape a predestined collision course is essential to building a civil society in Romania.

The situation is fluid and there are both acceptable and tragic scenarios available—and significant forces, organized and not, tilting the scale toward the less good outcomes. If anything positive can be drawn from the events of June, it may be a realization that there are good people within the government and in the opposition—a new generation of educated people, many less compromised than their elders—who must find a way to disagree and still work together in pursuit of a vision of a democratic society. While their visions may differ, their differences are nuances compared with the undeveloped notions about the good society which hamper the movement of the majority of Romanians toward a Western-style democracy.

The dual shock of what the miners did and the support they elicited from ordinary citizens is shared by educated people in the government and in the opposition. I would be surprised if the government soon again appealed to lawless forces to restore order. It is the painful paradox of Romania that those who now rule must transcend the values of those who placed and sustain them in power if Romania is to have a democratic future.

# THE STRUGGLE CONTINUES: GERMANY 1990

(MEMORANDUM TO THE BOARD OF TRUSTEES, AUGUST 1990)

### BACKGROUND

I write to report on a recent trip to both East and West Germany on which I was accompanied by Graduate Faculty Dean Alan Wolfe and Associate Dean Robert Gates.

### EAST GERMAN PERSPECTIVES

In East Germany we met with Karl Friedrich Wessel, director of the Institute for the Philosophy of Science and Human Ontogenesis at Humboldt University; Wolfgang Krotke, professor of theology at a private, Lutheran-sponsored church university in Berlin; Mayor Herbert Wagner of Dresden; and Kurt Reinschke, professor of applied mathematics at Cottbus Technical University.

East Berlin feels dramatically different from the way it did in 1986. The border is completely open—Checkpoint Charlie dismantled and now resembling a bus station. Western movies and posters for rock concerts can be seen frequently, and the general sense of energy is palpable. The once empty streets are clogged with many more cars than they were built for, so the formerly easy movement is now impeded by such unfamiliar sights as gridlock. West and east taxis pose a choice between comfort and efficiency. The large West German Mercedes taxis are comfortable, but the small, polluting East German taxis know East Berlin. Western drivers struggle with inadequate maps to guide them over completely unfamiliar terrain—a trip from the Kempinski Hotel to the Lichtenburg Station was an adventure. Also an eye-opener. There we saw firsthand the stream of immigrants—that day Romanians and Gypsies flooding in from Eastern Europe. We are told this scene is repeated throughout East Germany and we saw it again firsthand in Dresden, where the park outside the station has become a camp for Romanians. As in most countries, taxi drivers offer insight. Our West Berlin taxi driver took a dim view of the Poles streaming into West Berlin (border: 50 miles away) to buy "cigarettes, alcohol, and sex videos." He said they came in charter buses (which parked in suburbs in which they lived) without sanitary facilities. Clearly the movement of refugees and visitors from the east is profoundly disturbing for Germans, East and West. We were told it is giving rise to ugly antiforeign outbursts.

Amid the glow of hope for a better life in East Berlin, somewhat diminished by economic hardship, there are reminders that not everyone is comfortable with the pace and method of unification. "The Struggle Continues" shouted one bright-red graffiti scrawled on a building not far from Humboldt University. Our meeting with Karl Friedrich Wessel offered an insight about the reservations felt by some, perhaps many, thoughtful people. His institute, with eleven faculty members and thirty dissertations under way, focuses on the philosophy of science and human ontogenesis. As in other countries, scientifically oriented institutes in East Germany were less politicized than the social sciences and thus were sites for what little independent thinking seems to have existed there. Wessel is typical of a group of scholars whose future is uncertain. A mild critic of the old regime, he remains also critical of the rush to unification which abandons the ideals of socialism.

"How will the winners comport themselves with the losers?" he asks. "This is a central question which can be studied in Berlin, which will be at the center of the democratic transition." He says, for the moment, the people of East Germany have neither a past nor a clear future. "The pace of change takes your breath away and is very complex for the individual."

People of different generations, he suggested, have different takes on events. People of 60 or older feel some wistfulness, perhaps bitterness, that they were in the wrong generation. Unification will have minimal impact on their careers. Those in their fifties, who in one way or another had accommodated to the regime, see their lives as "messed up" and perhaps feel they have the most to lose by the unification that lies ahead, since power will flow to a younger generation. Those in their thirties and forties represent a disappointment to Wessel because they have quickly shed all their ideals in exchange for the material benefits offered by unification. Their uncritical acceptance of merger on terms imposed by the West cuts off the potential for political discourse about what the good society should look like. Finally, the very young simply see a world of unlimited opportunity.

Wessel is eager to form alliances with Western universities outside of West Germany which can provide a balance to West Germany's domination of the rebuilding process in East Germany. He warmly embraces the prospect of a branch of our Democracy Seminar in Berlin, in part because of the connections it would provide to those in other Eastern countries who are engaged in moral reflection about the kind of society they want to have—an opportunity he believes is denied to the East Germans.

Those sentiments found confirmation from Professor Reinschke, who spoke of concerns about the importation of "value-free" social science from West Germany. He said those who had been in opposition are deeply disappointed by the absence of reflective discussions about the shape of the good society. He noted that East German scholars had been subjected to a cruel paradox unknown in the other Eastern European countries: they had free access to Western television and radio but faced especially harsh deprivation of written materials. The migration of the most independent people out of East Germany denied the possibility of an underground opposition similar to that in Poland, Hungary, and Czechoslovakia or of a lively underground press. Thus there is a "pent-up" need for moral discussions, discussions that are preempted by the lawyers and economists who dominate the unification process with its focus on practical legal and economic matters.

The social sciences (philosophy and history) are weak at all the traditionally strong East German universities: Humboldt (Berlin), Jena, Leipzig, Rostock, Halle, and Dresden (technical university). All are currently in a state of flux, since weak rectors have been elected without a mandate for or commitment to full reform. This is a sharp contrast to other Eastern countries (for example, the Charles University in Prague, with Radim Palous newly installed), where strong, reform-minded rectors are taking over. This inability for self-renewal makes it all the more likely that the West German academic system will simply be installed. Reinschke also believes that non-German Western institutions have an important role to play—in sending in visiting faculty, making pre- and post-doctoral fellowships available, and organizing formal contacts such as the New School's Democracy Seminar. Indeed, Reinschke made the point that the West misreads the impending merger of the Germanys as flowing from German nationalism. He thinks that, among the East Germans at least, a desire to be part of a multicultural Europe is a much stronger motivation than union with Germany.

Thus one sees a mix of reactions to the impending unification. All with whom we spoke favor it—and quickly. Intellectuals, however, lament the rapid invasion of an unalloyed material culture from the West and the unseemly total embrace of it by ordinary people. They console themselves with the belief that a discussion of moral purposes will ultimately take place, since the East Germans must come to grips with the past 50 or 60 years and in so doing are bound to want to preserve at least some of the ideals of socialism. A Lutheran pastor, Friedrich Zimmerman (a childhood friend of New School trustee Henry Arnhold), concurred. He said that the young must reflect on the nature of humankind in order to bridge back to reality. But, he noted, conversation is hard to have at the moment because of the strength of the Western material culture. He sees the potential for the merger of East and West Germany (Eastern and Western Europe as well) to bring about a fresh conception of the ethical foundation for

European society and hopes that this potential is not lost by the focus on immediate material gains.

The Mayor of Dresden, Herbert Wagner, is an engineer in his midthirties, a member of the CDU, and new to political life. We met with him at the *Luisenhshof* restaurant in the hilly suburb of White Stag. The restaurant offers a sweeping view of the valley of the Elbe in which Dresden is located. He is certainly focused on practical questions. He says that his big problems are the uncertainty of ownership of land and the absence of a legal basis for ownership or for assessing value. The economic and political paralysis which has overwhelmed East Germany frustrates his people, who are impatient for quick improvement in their daily lives and expect miracles of their newly elected officers.

Wagner's party holds 39 percent of the seats in the City Council, followed by the former Communist Party (PDS) with 14 percent, the Social Democrats (SPD) with 10 percent, the DSU with 8 percent, the Liberals with 6 percent, all others with 16 percent, and those with no affiliation with 6 percent. His party draws from a broad spectrum of the population and has little policy difference with the Social Democrats except on the speed of unification. The CDU favors rapid unification, in part from fear that something will happen to Gorbachev and the old regime will reassert itself. The PDS drew support from the old and young; the Mayor predicts it will fade as the SPD gains.

Mayor Wagner, who sees West Germany as a model of enlightened capitalism, still expresses the worry that merger will move Germany slightly to the right on social issues because of the wholesale rejection of the past by East German voters. He was, I think, echoing in a soft voice the concerns expressed by intellectuals about the lost opportunity implicit in the rapid unification which he favors.

## West German Perspectives

The pace of life in Bonn, Berlin, and Frankfurt seemed more

intense than in past visits. Our brief tour offered contrasting vignettes: on the surface West Germany seems more prosperous and confident than ever. Everyone is conscious of the challenges involved in absorbing East Germany, and people in government are working long hours with a kind of complaining that really expresses exhilaration. But there are discordant images too: the trailer camp set up in the shadow of the Reichstag and homeless people in the Frankfurt railroad station or along the Main River. Both sets of images tell us this is a society in transition.

Pressure for quick unification comes from both East and West as the uncertainty over questions like the location of the capital, the cost of unification and its impact on the economy, and the specter of a right wing unchecked by civil authority all take a toll. The betting now is that the capital will remain in Bonn, with certain less essential functions (the President, the Upper Chamber) moving to Berlin. Cars with "Ja zu Bonn" stickers can seen throughout the Bonn area. At issue, however, is more than the bureaucrats' desire to maintain the good life in quiet Bonn. For many, Berlin symbolizes an unpleasant past, an eastward look, pretensions to empire—while Bonn seems thoroughly integrated into Western Europe, a symbol of 40 years of peaceful and prosperous development. Some fear that placing the capital in Berlin would fuel pressures for Germany to move east (and south) to recover lost territory.

Most people with whom we spoke are basically optimistic that unification will prove successful. (We were told to drop the term "reunification" since this is not a return to the old Germany.) Andreas Helfer of the Frankfurt City Council predicted a short-term inflation rate of 10 to 15 percent and unemployment at 10 percent, but felt the economy could handle both. Politically he predicted a slight shift to the right with little danger from fringe parties, right or left. The far right has barely 5 percent of the Frankfurt City Council and is totally isolated as the other parties reject its blatant anti-immigrant and subtly anti-Semitic rhetoric. Indeed, all with whom we spoke saw no threat from extremism or anti-Semitism.

## Closing Thoughts

Let me close with three reflections which add up, not to a conclusion, but to interesting times ahead.

1. It is hard to imagine the line between Western and Eastern Europe being drawn between Dresden and Prague. The events of 1989 have implications for the 1992 process which in my view have not been thought through.
2. At the moment everyone says firmly that national borders are "permanent" (a concept not grounded in history). Yet it is hard to believe that the notions of advanced democracy do not have implications for the right of self-determination for clusters of people caught outside their own country. I do not take the present borders as sacrosanct.
3. We are proceeding in Europe as if the Soviet Union is no longer a major player, but of course we know it is. Whatever happens there is bound to have implications for Europe, probably unsettling ones.

In the end our distinctive traditions—our ties to Europe—require that we enlarge our concept of a special relationship to embrace all of Europe. As Dean Wolfe has suggested, the moral reflections under way in the East offer the opportunity to enrich our own inquiries, which sometimes tend to be overly technical. We have much to give but also much to learn.

# A Fluid Moment for Yugoslavia

(MEMORANDUM TO THE BOARD OF TRUSTEES, JUNE 1991)

### Background

I traveled to Zagreb and Belgrade, Yugoslavia, during the week of May 26 on behalf of the Helsinki Watch Committee and the New School's Eastern and Central Europe program. I joined Helsinki Watch staff member Ivana Nizich, whose present project focuses on press freedom in Yugoslavia, in meetings with leaders of the official and independent media. We also met with U.S. Ambassador Warren Zimmermann; the Croatian member of the federal presidency, Stipe Mesic, whose term as Yugoslavia's President has been blocked; the ministers of information in both Serbia and Croatia; the directors of television in Serbia and Croatia; two leading human rights lawyers, Tanja Petovar and Srdja Popovic; and members of the Helsinki Watch Committee in Yugoslavia.

We met as well with the Rector of Zagreb University, the Vice Rector of Belgrade University, and members of the Institute for European Studies in Belgrade. The institute is the base for the New School's Democracy Seminar and Curriculum Project in Yugoslavia, which is coordinated by Sonja Licht and Ivan Vejvoda. Finally, one of our most useful conversations was with a wise elder statesman and author, Milovan Djilas, to whom the New School gave an honorary degree in 1990.

This report is written at a very fluid moment in Yugoslavia. Slovenia has declared its intention to become fully independent on June 26, and Croatia will follow on June 30, if the crisis over the leadership of the federal presidency is not resolved by then. Incidents of ethnic violence, principally between Serbs and Croats in sections of Croatia with a heavy Serbian population and between Serbs and Albanians in the autonomous province of Kosovo, are on the rise. Some observers are predicting that Yugoslavia will dissolve, perhaps even lapse into a civil war. Thus what follows is a snapshot of how the situation appeared to me one week in May. By the time you read this report events may have outpaced the conclusions and predictions I hazard in the final section.

Let me begin with an overview of Yugoslavia. It has existed as a nation for only 70 years. The 24 million inhabitants, composed of twenty-four ethnic groups in six republics and two quasi-autonomous provinces, speak four principal languages, use two alphabets, and practice three main religions. 41 percent of the population is Orthodox Christian, 32 percent Roman Catholic, and 12 percent Moslem. There is also a small Jewish population of about 35,000. The Serbs constitute the largest ethnic group (36 percent), followed by the Croats (20 percent), Slovenes (8 percent), ethnic Albanians (8 percent), Macedonians (6 percent), and Montenegrins (2.5 percent). However, the ethnic groups do not neatly reside in their own provinces. Two million Serbs live outside Serbia, mainly in Croatia and Bosnia and Hercegovina, while 1 million Croats live outside Croatia, mainly in Serbia and Bosnia and Hercegovina. Albanians make up almost 90 percent of the population of the Kosovo autonomous province. The republic of Bosnia and Hercegovina is very mixed, with 1.6 million Moslems, 1.3 million Serbs, and 800,000 Croats. Of the major republics, only Slovenia has a relatively homogeneous population, with only 10 percent of the population non-Slovene (the minorities include Hungarians, Italians, and other Yugoslavian citizens).

The northern republics are predominantly Catholic and were once dominated by the Austro-Hungarian Empire. The south, on the other hand, is heavily Muslim and Eastern Orthodox and was ruled for 500 years by the Ottoman Turks. Slovenia and Croatia are the most prosperous of the republics, and one source of tension within Yugoslavia derives from the redistribution of resources from the wealthy northern republics to the much poorer south. In 1990, for instance, Slovenia—with only 8 percent of the population, produced 18 percent of Yugoslavia's GNP, generated 30 percent of its exports (two-thirds of its trade with the European Community), had the highest average income, and maintained an unemployment rate that was less than half of the national rate.

The 1974 constitution provided great autonomy to the six republics and also created the two autonomous provinces within Serbia. It put in place a collective presidency of eight people whose leadership has rotated annually since Josep Tito's death. The country is now governed by consensus, with each republic having the capacity to block major legislation and policy initiatives. As a result, the federal government is inherently weak. While Tito was in power, his authority concealed this weakness and the Communist regime kept the lid on ethnic, religious, and geographic rivalries within Yugoslavia. With his death in 1980 came the beginning of a gradual disintegration of central authority and a concomitant rise in ethnic tensions, developments which accelerated geometrically after the breakup of the federal Communist Party in 1989.

## The Current Situation

Zagreb and Belgrade are a study in contrast. Zagreb is a charming city with a Western feel and a very attractive older section. Belgrade, which endured saturation bombing during World War II, retains little of its historic character and has the look of 1950s Stalinist architecture and planning. Still, both appear very prosperous by Eastern European standards. There are more cars, more imported luxury cars, and even genuine traffic jams. The national airline flies Boeing and Douglas aircraft, the airports are modern and efficient, stores are well stocked with Western goods from Pampers to Coppertone suntan lotion, food is plentiful, and there are many good restaurants. Hotels meet modern, Western standards, so the emergency traveler's kit of soap, toilet paper, Kleenex, drain stoppers, and mineral water is unnecessary. While Yugoslavians complain of a deteriorating economy, there is no doubt that Tito's independence from Moscow, the more open society, and the self-management system made life in Yugoslavia much more bearable than in other Eastern countries. This may well explain why the level of protest in Yugoslavia did not rise to the crescendo experienced elsewhere and why the break with the Communist past has been less than complete.

The present political situation is very complex. Two of the most powerful actors in the present drama are Slobodan Milosevic, the President of Serbia, and Franjo Tudjman, the President of Croatia. Each in his own way is an old-style leader whose principal goal is to remain in power. Slobodan Milosevic is described by Milovan Djilas as smart, quick, parochial, and lacking any clear economic program. Milosevic, a man of 49, rose up through the party ranks at the end of the Tito era when liberalization was on the wane, and he is the last freely elected Communist leader in the region. Franjo Tudjman, a man of 68, is an ex-general who fell out with Tito in 1971 and was a political prisoner for some years. Djilas describes him as intelligent but rigid, obsessively nationalistic, and out of touch with modern realities. Both presidents have played the nationalist card to suppress internal political opposition, both have inflamed ethnic passion with their rhetoric, and both are bent on destroying Yugoslavia in its present form. Of the two, Milosevic appears to be more powerful, more Machiavellian, and more dangerous.

It is widely assumed that Milosevic has stimulated the Serbian unrest in Croatia and in Bosnia and Hercegovina. The more benign view holds that he is "teleguiding" the Serbs to rebel. A darker interpretation suggests that the Serbian government is arming the Serbs in Croatia, perhaps even sending in professional terrorists. Milosevic's strategy is said to have two parts: first, to destroy the central government; and second, to provoke unrest so that the army will have a reason to be deployed throughout the country. His end game is to create a "Greater Serbia," which would annex large parts of Croatia and Bosnia and Hercegovina.

Milosevic has already laid claim to the so-called Krajina region of Croatia, where a sizable percentage of the population is Serbian. He has blocked the normal rotation of the leadership of the federal presidency, which should have shifted to the Croatian representative, Mesic, on May 15, and thus has precipitated a crisis still unresolved. He has also sought to undercut Prime Minister Ante Markovic, who is widely respected and recognized as one of the few forces of reason in a leadership position.

Croatia's Tudjman, despite the recent push for full independence, is thought to want a loose confederation in which the central government has specific limited powers, such as the guarantee of human rights, administration of central banking functions, and supervision of foreign affairs. But his irresponsible, extreme nationalist rhetoric unleashed forces perhaps beyond his control, forces which are now pushing for full independence. His principal political opposition comes from the nationalist right, which opposes any compromise designed to save the Yugoslavian union. There is little doubt that his rhetoric has exacerbated the violent clashes between Croats and Serbs or that there is systematic and growing discrimination against Serbs in Croatia. We are told that Serbs, who historically have held a disproportionate share of public jobs, are being squeezed out. For example, the Croatian police force, once 70 percent Serbian, is now 70 percent Croatian. And I saw a termination notice dated May 7, 1991, issued to a Serbian employee of an electronics factory in Croatia on the grounds that he "refused to give a written statement of loyalty to the Republic of Croatia." In addition to these episodes of violence and discrimination, Tudjman has increased the tension by purchasing arms from abroad to create his own national guard, now 34,000 strong. While we were in Zagreb, he held a full-dress military ceremony, bristling with nationalist rhetoric, celebrating the one year anniversary of his rule and the end of the previous Communist regime.

Some believe that Tudjman may be playing a double game with two acceptable outcomes. They believe that Tudjman's initial preference is to remain part of a loose confederation, but for that option to be viable the independence movement in neighboring Slovenia would have to be stopped. Hence Tudjman has tied Croatia's independence to the situation in

Slovenia in an attempt to raise the stakes so that the central government, the army, and the West will resist Slovenian independence. At the same time, conscious that events are spinning out of his control, he is laying plans for an independent Croatia. It is said that he and Milosevic may even have a secret bargain to divide up Bosnia and Hercegovina between them.

While Slovenia is not as much in the news, it was the initial engine for disruptions of the Yugoslavian nation. Reform within the Communist Party began there several years ago, and space was created for the development of a rudimentary civil society, with opposition groups forming around issues such as the environment, peace, and feminism. At first, opposition leaders in the other republics looked to Slovenia for leadership in reform, but after the Mladina trial in 1988, Slovene reformers turned nationalist. That trial involved an effort by the federal army to convict four dissidents accused of stealing military secrets. Because the setting for the prosecution was a military court and therefore a federal institution, the trial served as a rallying point for anti-Yugoslavian feelings. In the middle of the trial, the popular movement called the Committee for the Defense of Four changed its name to Committee for the Defense of Slovenia.

It was the withdrawal of the Slovenian delegation to the federal Communist Party convention in January 1990 which broke the party apart in Yugoslavia. Elections quickly followed in April, and the umbrella opposition group won a 53 percent majority in the Slovenian Parliament. The creation of a Slovenian army and the emergence of a genuine majority for full independence followed in rapid succession. Slovenia has taken the lead in declaring its intention to be fully independent on June 26, a prospect which is all the more appealing because of the homogeneity of the population, its historic ties to the West, its geographical location bordering Austria, and its relatively strong economy.

In each of the republics, the new leaders are for the most part either Communists or ex-Communists who broke with Tito after 1971. They exploit the language of democracy, human rights, and other liberal concepts in conjunction with a strident nationalism that has great potential as a new form of authoritarian rule. As in other Eastern and Central European countries, there is no well-developed party system. Center stage in Serbia and Croatia is occupied by politicians with close ties to the old Communist Party. Vocal opposition comes from the extreme, nationalist right as well as from the fragmented, democratic left. Aside from different levels of nationalism, it is hard to discern positive, substantive programs that distinguish the opposing parties as they all compete for ownership of the new democratic language. And here, as elsewhere, party identity is fluid, with some active groups having no representation in the legislative chambers at either the federal or republic level. The overlay of nationalism has retarded the education of ordinary citizens in democracy and produced fears among some intellectuals of a new totalitarianism from below. Indeed, all the problems of transition found in the other Eastern and Central European countries are present in exaggerated forms in Yugoslavia.

Another major player in the current drama is the federal army: some 200,000 strong, it has an officers corps that is largely Serbian. Some believe that the army is beholden to Milosevic, but a more plausible view is that it is semi-independent and somewhat adrift, since it reports to a nonfunctioning collective presidency. As in the Soviet army, a broad ethnic mix makes it difficult for the army to use force to put down one or another republic. It is widely supposed that the army would disintegrate into a largely Serbian unit if it were used against a breakaway republic. The army appears to be committed to a united Yugoslavia, which it believes provides the best chance for the army as an institution and for the protection of the personal perks its leadership enjoys. At the moment, the army is playing a valuable peacekeeping role in hot spots, and no one gives much credence to the prospect of an army coup. However, the army is hardly reform-minded and views with considerable skepticism the non-Communist government of Prime Minister Ante Markovic and its plan for conversion to a free market economy.

Thus, as I write, the republics are increasingly acting as independent countries—following the Baltic approach, but with greater success. The federal government, without a functioning presidency, continues to lose influence and has little capacity to enforce its policies. The republics feel free to pass contradictory laws and to ignore federal statutes. Local violence continues to escalate in cycles, but the army has contained it so far. Some observers believe Milosevic has overplayed his hand in crippling the federal presidency, which, among other outcomes, has cost him support within the army. There is a sense everywhere that events are moving toward a watershed moment.

## Human Rights Abuses

Serious human rights problems persist in Yugoslavia, giving it one of the worst human rights records in Eastern and Central Europe at the moment. The central government of Prime Minister Ante Markovic has a decent human rights record itself but has little or no power to curb abuses perpetrated or allowed by the six republics. And although it was slow to condemn gross violations of human rights by the Serbian government in Kosovo, the Markovic regime has now done so. This means that the traditional means of pressuring central governments to improve human rights have little use in Yugoslavia. The present American policy, especially the Nichols Amendment, has complicated the situation. There is a division of view about how useful American sanctions can be. Many people with whom we spoke—who disagree with one another on just about everything—agreed that U.S. actions against Serbia have been counterproductive and have intensified Serbian nationalism.

## Future Prospects

Making predictions about the future of Yugoslavia has something of the perils of offering a long-term scenario about events in the Soviet Union. But let me exercise the privilege of a lay observer looking at the macro picture unencumbered by a full grasp of all the complexities of the situation.

There are three main scenarios, one with two variants. The first assumes that Yugoslavia, under pressure from and with the support of the West, will hold together. This approach calls for a strengthening of the federal government through federal elections, which would confer greater legitimacy on the central government. A prerequisite for such an outcome would likely be, at the very least, a change in the leadership in Serbia. The federal scenario is favored by Prime Minister Markovic, many intellectuals, the army, and all those—business leaders among them—who have a stake in a united Yugoslavia.

A second scenario, until quite recently favored by Slovenia and Croatia, is to replace the present federal structure with a confederation something along the lines of what Boris Yeltsin advocates for the Soviet Union. As Marijan Sibl, director of the Croatian news agency Hina, told us bluntly: "Yugoslavia was a utopian idea which is dead." Under this scenario, the republics would have greater autonomy over their internal affairs, especially economic affairs, while the federal government would be formally reduced to a coordinating body with limited, specific functions, such as conducting foreign affairs, defending the nation, administering the central banks, and guaranteeing the rights of minorities within the republics. Frustrated by the present stalemate, Slovenia and Croatia now offer rhetoric that bypasses this option in favor of full independence.

The third scenario, perhaps favored by Serbian President Milosevic all along, is for Yugoslavia to break apart. Milosevic has visions of a "Greater Serbia"—incorporating parts of Croatia and Bosnia and Hercegovina—that would emerge as a country with a population roughly the size of Bulgaria. This third option has two variants: one, a peaceful separation; the other, civil war.

One might assume that this instability is ready-made for an army coup, but almost everyone agrees that a coup is unlikely. The army has no tradition of political involvement and its leaders seem intent on protecting it as an institution. As in the Soviet Union, the army is an ethnic mosaic and is thus not well suited to intervene in interrepublic, interethnic affairs.

At present, the army is playing a complicated role. It has been useful in containing Serbian-Croatian clashes and in trying to limit the possession of deadly weapons by local citizens. Yet its methods introduce another set of human rights abuses as it searches private houses without warrants, arrests citizens to be tried in military courts for arms possession, and is perhaps overzealous in curbing demonstrations in the countryside and in small cities.

Yet, for reasons cited earlier, the army remains a powerful factor in favor of a unified Yugoslavia.

All three scenarios are possible, even civil war. But almost everyone with whom we spoke doubts that civil war is in the offing. Most believe that the single most divisive force is Milosevic, who has played on Serbian nationalism to maintain his bankrupt Communist regime. His tactics touched off nationalistic movements elsewhere in the country, particularly in Croatia, which responded by electing an old-style, ex-Communist, Franjo Tudjman, who likewise has played the nationalist card. By most accounts, Milosevic has overplayed his hand, pushing the country to the brink of dissolution. His attack on the federal presidency has alienated the army; his confrontation with Prime Minister Markovic has troubled many ordinary people; and the March 9 demonstrations have emboldened intellectual and press opposition.

There are signs that Milosevic's hold on power is crumbling. The opposition—left and right—controls about 20 percent of the Parliament. The head of the Serbian Parliament has resigned, as has a vice president of one of the republics. And just after I left, another key minister quit the Milosevic government, giving the impression that the government was far from unified. Meanwhile, observers offer a scenario through which Milosevic can be neutralized by a combination of four factors—(1) street protests; (2) a forceful, positive economic program put forward by the opposition Democratic Party; (3) defections in the Parliament to the Democrats; and (4) steady pressure from the West—all leading to new parliamentary elections. The betting is that Milosevic's party would not win a majority, thus producing a cohabitation arrangement in which Milosevic would be reduced to a figurehead for the balance of his 5-year term.

Observers report that the Croatian leadership, though lagging by about a year, will follow a similar trail. At the moment, Tudjman enjoys popularity and less opposition than Milosevic, but many predict that he too will overplay his hand. There is little doubt that Milosevic and Tudjman have exacerbated ethnic tensions beyond their ability to control them as clashes escalate into violence and conjure up the horrors of the past. Serbs in Croatia recall the dreaded fascist Ustashi extermination of Serbian opposition during World War II, just as the Croats recount with equal horror the work of the Serbian Chetniks. Elder statesmen like Djilas predict a rise in the pattern of local violence and a further weakening of the federal structure before a solution is found.

Our conversations with Stipe Mesic, the Croatian representative to the collective presidency, and Milan Djilas yielded a similar sense about the future. Both placed heavy emphasis on the need for Western assistance. "There is no internal solution," Mesic told us. "The only way out is for Europe to guarantee the internal borders of Yugoslavia and to protect minority rights within each republic." Djilas opined that the West really could not afford to allow a civil war in Yugoslavia because of its potential to spread or at least to incite minorities in other countries to challenge existing borders. And he noted that six of seven countries bordering Yugoslavia have outstanding territorial claims against it. Both men viewed the recent visit of Jacques Delores, president of The European Community, as a hopeful sign that the West was about to play a constructive role. Delores met with the six presidents of the republics separately and with three members of the collective presidency. It is supposed that a very strong message was sent that the West wants to keep Yugoslavia together, although there is tolerance of (if not a preference for) a new arrangement, which is a loose confederation. The impression given at the conclusion of the Delores mission is that common ground is still possible.

One scholar posited a plausible interpretation of the present posturing for full independence. He saw it as jockeying for an advantageous position in a new Yugoslavia. He predicted that the June 26 Slovenian deadline for independence would pass uneventfully, since it is unlikely the federal army will withdraw or that Slovenia will suddenly sever trade relations with the rest of Yugoslavia, which absorbs about 40 to 50 percent of its economic output.

Djilas spoke of the current situation as a natural evolution of Yugoslavia in the post-Communist era, a painful stage that could not be avoided. The scholars at the Institute for European Studies also pointed out that Yugoslavia never had the chance to develop as a complex, multiethnic nation because the Tito regime at once skillfully played upon ethnic rivalries to strengthen its own control while using its power to check their excesses. With the collapse of the old regime, it was inevitable that those ethnic rivalries would accelerate and threaten to destroy the concept of Yugoslavia.

The question now is one of timing. The longer that widespread violence is avoided, the greater is the chance that civil war will be averted and that Yugoslavia in some form will survive. The two most crucial factors here are the mediating role of the army and constructive Western pressure (as opposed to the misadventure of the Nichols Amendment). If the Djilas view is correct, many ordinary people do not want to see Yugoslavia divide and can be rallied to its defense. A multiple-outlet, free and independent press is essential to the survival of Yugoslavia. With the popularity of independent dailies and journals like *Zaped* and *Vreme*, there are very hopeful signs in the print media. Television and radio, as we have seen, yield a different story. But in Belgrade, at least television Studio B and Radio B-92 provide a counter to the nationalism of the government-controlled outlets. Still, vast parts of Yugoslavia do not have ready access to independent news.

Both the independent media and the independent intellectual community have suffered setbacks as a result of the surge of nationalism in the republics. As one scholar put it: "It was much easier to be a dissident against the old regime. Now being a dissident involves opposition to the nation." Still, my conversations with scholars at the Institute for European Studies were encouraging. They seemed keenly aware of the obligations of intellectuals to set an independent course—to moderate the rhetoric, to slow the rush to dissolution, and to create space for reasoned and civil discourse about future options. As another institute scholar observed:

> We must foster an open debate which escapes stark "either/or" choices, a debate which illuminates the complexity of the present situation, which places the current difficulty in the context of the past 50 years, and which allows time for a steady evolution in incremental steps to a viable future.

For the moment, the best rallying point in the political process appears to be Prime Minister Markovic, who commands the most widespread respect. The survival of his government against the Milosevic assault is critical to the "buying time" scenario. Milosevic's efforts to oust him through a vote of no confidence in the last week of May failed miserably as Markovic mustered an overwhelming majority in the federal assembly. Observers report that when the vote was announced, it was greeted with a spontaneous outburst of applause expressing genuine joy—and relief. That outcome means that deputies thought to be under the control of the republic nationalists voted to maintain the one stabilizing political force in the country. The outcome may also auger well for resolving the impasse that has immobilized the collective federal presidency. Stipe Mesic struck me as a moderate, thoughtful person who is prepared to work to keep Yugoslavia together. Married to a Serb, he appears not to have been blighted by the excessive nationalism of the Croatian government.

History teaches us that no outcome is inevitable—choices and chance play a role in every conflict right up to the moment of no return when a situation degenerates into violence. The situation in Yugoslavia is clearly unstable and dangerous. Forces have been unleashed on all sides that will answer to no rational authority. There exists the possibility, for instance, that an act of terrorism or a local clash between Serbs and Croats in Krajina could spread like a windswept brushfire.

But there are also many positive forces working both to cool the present tension and to build a stable future.

Srdja Popovic put it best when he said: "In the short term I am pessimistic, but in the medium term I am an optimist." My own instinct resonates to that position. I assume Djilas is right when he predicts even more local violence fueled by the strident nationalism of two old-style, *ancien régime* politicians, Milosevic and Tudjman. But they are likely to lose ground because their strategies will create an outcome that is unacceptable to reasonable people in leadership and, ultimately, to ordinary citizens as well. Time will work against this transitional leadership, and new elections at the republic level—which some think could be called within the next two years—will most likely produce fresh faces. The growth of an independent press, the reemergence of the intellectual community as a player, the support of the West for the Markovic government, and the commitment of the army to a unified Yugoslavia all auger well for the future.

# THE CHOICE BETWEEN REFORM AND REPRESSION IN ESTONIA, LATVIA & LITHUANIA

(MEMORANDUM TO THE BOARD OF TRUSTEES, FEBRUARY 1991)

### BACKGROUND

I write to report on my recent trip to Estonia, Latvia, and Lithuania on behalf of the Helsinki Watch Human Rights Committee and the New School for Social Research. Along with Jeri Laber, executive director of Helsinki Watch, I visited government officials (Lithuanian President Vytautas Landsbergis, for example), journalists, human rights monitors, members of Parliament from all points of the political spectrum, and, in Lithuania, victims of the violent Soviet crackdown. From those conversations emerged a portrait of three states determined to recover their independence and a Soviet regime equally intent on maintaining its empire, especially its access to the Baltic Sea.

Those of you who read my account of Soviet affairs last June will recall that I saw Mikhail Gorbachev at a crossroads where he would be forced to move more rapidly toward democratic and free market reforms or to retreat down the more traditional and repressive path of Soviet leadership. The events of January in the Baltics together with the flight of reformers from Gorbachev's inner circle have persuaded some observers that Gorbachev has made his choice. But I am not so sure. It is at least plausible to suppose that Gorbachev is still groping for the middle path, which would continue reform at a much slower pace and place it firmly within a framework of communism and empire. The middle path seems no more realistic to me now than it did last June, but it does have the virtue of "buying time." In my view, if (when) he is forced to make a choice, Gorbachev will choose repression. But the longer he avoids the choice of systematic and pervasive repression, the more difficult it will be to enforce that option, and therein lies some hope for the Baltic states—indeed, for the people of all the Soviet republics.

## Glimpses of Courage and Defiance

Let me take as my text vignettes which provide the flavor of the temper of the Baltics.

Our first stop was Tallinn, Estonia, which looked quite different in the cold, snowy, dark January days than it did during a visit there 18 months earlier in the "white nights" of June. While Estonia has so far escaped the violence visited on Latvia and Lithuania, the atmosphere is tense. Visible signals of the changed mood are evident in the large cement blocks surrounding the beautiful pink castle which houses the Parliament and in the boulders blocking all the access roads. Similar scenes can be found in Riga and Vilnius, the Latvian and Lithuanian capitals, where the Parliaments are controlled by proindependence forces and serve as the heart and brains of the independence movement. They are open 24 hours a day, guarded by young men who have refused to report to the Soviet army, and well stocked with food, water, and medical supplies in preparation for a long siege.

The Lithuanian Parliament is virtually a city within a city, where key officials now live along with several hundred volunteer guards. Each evening's entertainment program brings a cadre of volunteer guards to the lobby. One cannot help but be moved by observing their determination and courage together with their hope and innocence. The night we passed by was particularly spirited, as the "Bob Hope of Lithuania" broke the tension with an hour of good cheer that was in stark contrast to the dreadful event 2 weeks earlier in which 14 people lost their lives and more than 600 were injured.

• • •

## THE CHOICE BETWEEN REFORM AND REPRESSION    321

A walk through Bastion Hill Park in Riga evoked images from my trip to Bucharest last January, when I watched families and friends huddle in the cold around candles and flowers placed at the sites where victims of the revolution had fallen. On the night of January 19-20, the park in Riga was host to an overflow crowd that had gathered to witness the assault on the Ministry of Interior by the special forces known as black berets. Five people lost their lives and over a dozen were injured that night as Soviet forces tried to thwart Latvia's independence drive. The familiar flowers and mourners marked the sites where onlookers, including the distinguished independent documentary filmmaker Andris Slapins, were killed.

• • •

The events in Latvia pale in comparison with the violence that occurred in Vilnius on the night of January 12-13. We viewed 2 hours of videotape which documented the reckless assault on public buildings defended by thousands of unarmed citizens of all ages who chanted "Lietuva" ("Shame") and epithets very pointedly expressing disillusionment in the person of Mikhail Gorbachev. What a distance, I thought, from 15 months earlier when East German youths gathered at the Berlin Wall and chanted praise of Gorbachev as they sought to bring down the Honecker regime. In Vilnius, the 1:30 A.M. assault on the television station was deadly earnest. Hundreds of paratroopers and perhaps ten tanks and armored personnel carriers confronted the crowd, which locked arms, sang the national anthem, and said in unison to the troops: "We will see you in paradise, where you will be our friends." Knowing that violent resistance offers no hope, between 15,000 and 20,000 unarmed people participated in the non-violent effort to protect their government, giving rise to what has been called the "singing revolution."

And it does evoke memories of the "velvet revolution" in Czechoslovakia. I well recall the feeling of October 1989 in Prague, when the people knew that the regime was finished and that they would soon be free. Something of that same sense can now be felt in Vilnius. But the harsh vision of tanks crushing ordinary citizens—men and women—contained on the video jolts us back to a different reality, a more uncertain future.

• • •

The next vignette occurred in the dining room atop the Viru Hotel in Tallinn while I dined with Peet Kask, a scholar who visited the New School in 1989 and who is now an influential member of Parliament. An excited young woman broke into our conversation with the news that the Bush-Gorbachev summit had been postponed, a decision which met with overwhelming praise in all three Baltic countries. Perhaps too much is read into the postponement, but the reaction well expressed the belief that the only realistic hope for independence rests on pressure from the West and/or total disintegration of the Soviet empire. Thus George Bush and Boris Yeltsin are the "odd couple" of Baltic hopes. Yeltsin's vigorous protest against the violence in Lithuania and Latvia and his mutual defense treaty with the Baltics, signed in Tallinn on January 13, are credited with stalling further military action by Gorbachev.

• • •

Of equal importance is the strong reaction of the West. Our conversation with Lithuanian President Vytautas Landsbergis perhaps best captures the Baltics' dependence on Western support. He is an unlikely leader of a revolution. An unassuming, soft-spoken, former music teacher, he seems somewhat ill at ease with the trappings of the large presidential office which also serves as his home. As we chatted matter of factly for more than half an hour, he asked for our help in countering Gorbachev's claims that Soviet intervention was necessary to protect Russian citizens and other minorities whose human rights are being violated. A strange twist of history, I thought: the Soviet government posing as the guardian of human rights. I came away from the meeting convinced that Landsbergis and his colleagues were prepared to die defending their government and that they commanded huge popular support in their determination. As our meeting broke, Landbergis came back to us with one final instruction: "Push Bush."

## The Baltics

Estonia, Latvia, and Lithuania feel like quite separate countries. Catholic Lithuania seems more Eastern European, while Protestant Estonia more closely resembles Scandinavia. And although Latvia is Protestant and in some ways closer to Estonia, its language is similar to Lithuanian, whereas Estonian derives from the Finno-Ugric family.

Estonia is about the size of Vermont and New Hampshire combined. It has 1.6 million inhabitants, of whom 61.5 percent are Estonian and 30 percent Russian. Latvia has 2.7 million inhabitants, only 51 percent of whom are Latvian, with the balance being made up of Russians and other Slavs. Lithuania is about the size of West Virginia. It has 3.7 million inhabitants, of whom 80 percent are Lithuanian, approximately 10 percent Polish, and less than 10 percent Russian. The different ethnic mixes influence the alternative paths to independence preferred by each state.

All three states have a complicated history of domination by foreign powers and have enjoyed genuine independence only briefly, between 1920 and 1940. Lithuania first united as a state in the thirteenth century, and from the fourteenth until the middle of the seventeenth century, it was part of a union with Poland. In the 1800s, it was divided between Russia and Prussia. Latvia has been ruled variously by the Germans, Poles, Swedes, and Russian czars since the thirteenth century. And Estonia was governed by the Germans from the twelfth to the sixteenth century, by Sweden from 1561 to 1721, and thereafter by czarist Russia.

The Baltics are among the most prosperous regions of the Soviet Union; this is one reason ethnic Russians are attracted to them. All three capitals were once members of the Hanseatic League and thus have a cosmopolitan tradition which can still be felt. The Baltics are also heavily fortified, housing many Soviet troops and major naval and air bases, and their "all-union" factories provide some of the most sophisticated electronic equipment used by the Soviet military machine.

The Soviet attempt to Russianize the Baltics clearly has not succeeded in 50 years. The states still feel like Europe, not the Soviet Union. And the example of Eastern Europe, particularly Poland and East Germany, has emboldened the Baltic states to reassert their independence. With the publication of the secret 1939 Molotov–von Ribbentrop pact, the base has been laid for the credible claim that their annexation was illegitimate. Indeed, the United States and several other nations, including Germany and England, have never recognized the incorporation of the Baltics into the Soviet Union.

But the three Baltic states have approached independence at different paces and with different styles. A joke making the rounds in Vilnius suggests the distinction: "Estonia thinks of an idea, Lithuania puts the idea into practice, Latvia complains and follows suit. Estonia stays behind, but eventually comes along." So it is that Estonia, which mounted the first challenge in the All-Soviet Parliament, now finds itself in the most conservative posture while Lithuania has stolen the march by declaring full independence. Latvia has declared independence, but not full independence. Estonia had made a milder expression of its intentions and offered to negotiate a transition period. There is some sentiment in Estonia that the Lithuanian confrontational style will set back the independence movement in all three states by forcing Gorbachev's hand prematurely and placing him in an untenable position with respect to conservatives in Moscow. Indeed, it does appear that Lithuania is where Mikhail Gorbachev believes he must draw the line.

All three countries now have a democratically elected Parliament with a proindependence majority. The break with the former Soviet regime is most complete in Lithuania and the ties closest in Estonia, where both the President and Prime Minister are former Communists. Predictably, Latvia is in the middle: the President of the Parliament was a member of the Communist Party, but the Prime Minister was not.

In all three states, the Communist party has split. The reform Communists are proindependence, participate in the government, and have taken different names, such as the Democratic Labor Party. There remains in each a pro-Moscow Communist Party with dwindling memberships.

Political life, paradoxically, seems most advanced in Estonia and most formless in Lithuania, where the struggle for independence dominates all aspects of life. There are many parties in all countries—"fractions" as they are called in Lithuania—but the basic split is between the pro-Moscow Communists and proindependence umbrella organizations patterned after Civic Forum in Czechoslovakia. Each of them goes by a different name: the Popular Front in Estonia, the People's Front in Latvia, and Sajudis in Lithuania. In elections last year, these organizations endorsed a slate of proindependence candidates drawn from different parties, including the reform Communists, which produced a comfortable majority. The conservative, antiindependence forces are known as the Interfront, with the pro-Moscow Communist Party at the center.

The new governments in the Baltics work imperfectly because the Soviet system never intended for the official government to exercise real power in a public way. And the Parliaments themselves are a frustrating exercise in direct democracy, especially without the mediating influence of a well-formed party system. "Intellectuals and journalists with no experience" was one old-time dissident's critical lament in explaining the uncertain path of the Parliament in Lithuania. The executive branch, chosen by the Parliament, is nevertheless totally separate from the Parliament, since none of the ministers sit in the Parliament. This arrangement produces tensions between the President of the Parliament and the Prime Minister, tensions that were most evident in the clash over price increases in Lithuania in early January. But it is clear that all branches of the state government are under local control.

The main business of the new governments is securing independence. And the principal technique is to act as if the states really are free in as many aspects of life as possible. Gradually, the three states are passing their own laws without reference to Moscow, and the process of writing a new constitution is quite advanced in Lithuania. It must be said that the primitive nature of political life, together with the preoccupation with independence, prevents sophisticated discussions about the nature of the good society which would then be reflected in the laws being passed.

Each state has passed a law making its own language the official language. Imperfections in early legislation, which upset those speaking other languages, have by and large been addressed so that people are entitled to speak their own language and only officials must be bilingual. Laws of citizenship are either passed or in draft. The Lithuanian law is the most liberal, since it recognizes all present residents (except the army); the other two states are weighing a residency requirement, which might deny some Russians full citizenship for a period.

Draft laws concerning economic reform—private property and privatization of business—are also under discussion. All three countries plan to issue their own currency. None of the states has a clear conception of how its economy would work if independence were achieved. It is worth noting that the creation of three small, independent states cuts against the trend toward larger, regional economic and political alliances.

Since last fall, young men have refused to report to the draft for the Soviet army. The refusal rate is estimated at 75 to 95 percent, which means there are some 7,000 to 10,000 draft evaders in each state. In Estonia and Latvia, alternative service is available under local law, and in Lithuania the young men report to a local militia. The Soviet army is now making an effort to track down draft evaders, but they have been given paid holidays in Estonia and Latvia and been told to go into hiding. So far, only a handful have been caught. Why has this effort yielded such meager results? In part, I suppose, because the citizenry is united in protecting the young men and in part because the Soviet army has not been in vigorous pursuit. Perhaps the army is simply not eager to enroll reluctant recruits from the Baltics.

## The Choice Between Reform and Repression

Meanwhile, more and more Baltic citizens are deserting from the Soviet army in the face of harassment and violence (including murder) from fellow soldiers who oppose the independent stance of their states. In Latvia, mothers of draft-age students have organized a group to provide help to evaders and deserters. The group has documented twenty mysterious deaths and disappearances of Latvian soldiers in the Soviet army in 1990. In Estonia, an organization called Geneva 49 has been created for similar purposes. It takes its name from the Geneva Convention of 1949, which stipulated that an occupying country cannot draft into its army citizens of the country it occupies. Since the Baltics consider themselves occupied countries, they claim protection for their young under the Geneva Convention.

Each country has an active foreign ministry and is seeking recognition from other countries. Iceland has taken the lead in recognizing Lithuania. The Baltics have petitioned for membership in international bodies. Their foreign ministers spend most of their time abroad, in part to build support and in part to be ready to form governments-in-exile should the Soviets succeed in seizing the Parliaments. Before our trip to the Baltics we had dinner in Oslo with Algirdas Saudargas, Lithuania's foreign minister, who reported to us on recent meetings with his counterparts in England, France, and Germany.

These examples should suffice to make the point that the Baltics plan to win independence by simply asserting that they have been independent all along and now will begin to *act* like independent nations in every way possible. Lithuania will have no contact with the Soviet system, and its delegates have withdrawn from the All-Soviet Parliament. President Landsbergis took a hard line against any negotiation with Moscow, since he considers independence an accomplished fact. Estonia, by contrast, seems willing to negotiate and even seems prepared for a transition period during which the Soviets can maintain their key military bases. Latvia's course is less consistent as it vacillates between confrontation and conciliation.

In the face of this challenge, Gorbachev has sought to reaffirm the legitimacy of the Soviet Union through a Sovietwide referendum scheduled for March 17 on the question: "Do you consider it necessary to preserve the Union of Soviet Socialist Republics as a renewed federation of equal sovereign republics, in which the rights and freedoms of people of any nationality will be fully guaranteed?"

It seems unlikely that any of the Baltic states will participate in the Gorbachev referendum. Lithuania has scheduled its own public poll on February 9, with the following question: "Do you agree with the proposition stated in the Lithuanian constitution that Lithuania is an independent democratic republic?" It is expected that the vote will be 90 percent in favor, and we were told by representatives of the minority communities (Polish, Georgian, Ukranian, Azerbaijani, and Russian) that a majority of their people will vote in support.

Estonia will also conduct its own poll before March 17. While the exact wording has not been fixed, it is likely to resemble the Lithuanian formulation. Predictably, Latvia, where the ethnic mix is richest, is least certain about whether to hazard a poll and has decided to wait for the outcome in Lithuania. There are fears in Latvia that the Soviet army will sabotage the vote, which could tip the results in this state, where the Latvians comprise little more than 50 percent of the population. But I suspect Latvia will gain confidence and conduct its own poll before March 17.

The Baltics have frustrated Mikhail Gorbachev at every turn with a very public defiance of his authority. It is not surprising, then, that he should have given in to the advisers who told him that he had to show more strength. Let us now look at the events of late 1990, which culminated in violence in Latvia and Lithuania last month.

## A Pattern of Destabilization

This commentary will focus on Latvia and Lithuania, since Estonia, which has been the least confrontational, has so far been spared armed intervention.

All three states have experienced systematic efforts at destabilization, which were stepped up in November 1990. It is generally supposed that the hard-core, pro-Moscow Communist minority—in league with the Soviet army stationed in the Baltics and, occasionally, the special Interior Ministry forces known as the black berets—set about to provoke incidents which would suggest a breakdown of order. In addition, Soviet authorities spread scare stories designed to heighten tensions among the minorities in each state. Russian workers, for example, were told that the independence movement would violate their human rights, force them to speak another language, deny them educational opportunity and jobs, discriminate in the allocation of housing, and all the rest. It seems plausible that bombs were planted and false arrests of local citizens on weapons charges were made as part of the plan. The end game seems to have been to establish conditions which would justify the imposition of presidential rule, thus ending the lives of the insurgent, proindependence Parliaments. Playing upon ethnic tensions is a technique as old as the Soviet Union itself, and it has been a crucial element in Moscow's control of its empire. How closely the details of the destabilization campaign were influenced by Moscow is hard to say, but I think it is certain that the Gorbachev government knew about and encouraged the general plan, including the use of force.

### The Military Backdrop

It is well to pause for a moment to define the types of military units involved in the episodes described below.

The *black berets* are a special Interior Ministry unit formed in 1989 in each republic for three purposes: to avert mass disorder, to aid in natural disasters, and to fight organized crime. In Latvia and Estonia, the black berets remain loyal to Moscow; in Lithuania, the majority have "defected" to support the local government.

*Paratroopers* are highly trained forces. Members of the special Pskov division were used in Tbilisi and Baku before being deployed in Lithuania. Their role is to execute surgical strikes in difficult situations and, once securing an objective, to turn it over to the regular *Soviet army*, which remains on patrol in all major Soviet cities and in control of buildings seized in the January events.

Each city has a *municipal police force* and some version of a *volunteer defense force*, often made up of young men who have refused to report to the Soviet army.

THE TROUBLE IN LATVIA

The following account was constructed from conversations with independent journalists, members of Parliament, and the person in the Latvian prosecutor's office who is investigating the assault on the Latvian Ministry of Interior.

The trouble in Latvia can be traced to its May 4, 1990, declaration of sovereignty and gradual acquisition of control of all state offices in Latvia. Unexplained incidents began in the summer; for example, we were told that taxi drivers were beaten in a small northern city in July and that random assaults on ordinary citizens in Riga occurred in August. By late September, local authorities had taken control of the Interior Ministry and prosecutor's office. This shift was not recognized by the Kremlin, which then moved responsibility for the black berets to the local office of the Soviet Interior Ministry on October 2. The first incidents of violence began 8 days later, when members of the black berets (on their day off) engaged in assaults on shops and people in the street. Six people were beaten.

On November 7, the Soviet army conducted a parade in Riga against the wishes of the local government, which refused to issue a permit. Shortly thereafter, an effort to move a Communist Party office out of the Latvian Interior Ministry building resulted in a scuffle in which the black berets beat up eight people. In retaliation, the Latvian Parliament passed a law on November 14 that cut off supplies to the local Soviet military installation. Tension escalated as four bombs exploded at monuments to Latvian war dead on the nights of December 4 and 5. They were followed by bombs at the Lenin monument and at Communist and KGB headquarters on December 18. In retrospect, the events can be seen as a calculated effort to provoke both sides and to give the appearance of disorder.

On January 2, the black berets seized the Latvian press house in the name of protecting Communist Party property. Since then, all independent papers have been publishing in reduced form. A proindependence rally scheduled for January 14 by the People's Front elicited a show of force in the streets and a pro-Moscow rally on the day before. Regular army and special paratrooper forces, escorted by tanks, marched through the streets of Riga. After the assault on the Lithuanian Parliament, barricades were erected around the Parliament, the Council of Ministers building, the radio and television office building and tower, and the main telephone switching station. On the night of January 14-15, the black berets invaded the local police academy, beat up ten cadets, and seized the academy's supply of arms. The next night, the black berets attacked a volunteer unit guarding one of the five bridges leading to Riga, beat up the volunteers, and burned twenty-eight vehicles. The following day, after attacking three more volunteer guard units, the black berets took over the key bridges between their encampment north of the city and the main route downtown.

The stage was now set for the night of January 19-20, when the black berets launched an attack on the Interior Ministry at 9:00 P.M., an assault which lasted 5 hours and in which five people were killed and fourteen wounded. It is unclear whether this attack was supposed to be part of larger plan to overthrow the Latvian government—in the wake of the Lithuanian events, it seems unlikely. There may have been such a plan scheduled to follow a successful "coup" in Lithuania, a plan that was never enacted because of the strong international reaction to the violence in Lithuania. It seems plausible to me that these events were a local initiative, another step in the pattern of destabilization, or simply an element in the larger plan that went forward unchecked.

## The "Attempted Coup" in Lithuania

People in Lithuania, from Vytautas Landsbergis to ordinary citizens, refer to the events of the night of January 12-13 as an attempted coup. And there is a plausible case for their interpretation. In the days leading up to the bloody night of January 12-13, there were signs that something was afoot. People who work at the airport report that a high-ranking Soviet military commander, perhaps Marshal Yazov, came to town on the night of January 9-10. Major General Tverenikov, who commanded the forces in Tbilisi and Baku, was also said to be in town. And, most ominously, about 1,000 paratroopers from the special Pskov division arrived on January 7. The deputy head of the reform Communists—which still shared quarters with the pro-Moscow Communist Party—reported a flow of Soviet military personnel through the headquarters at about the same time. On January 10, Ivozas Jarmalavicius, the chief Communist Party ideologist, announced the creation of a National Salvation Committee, which demanded that order be reestablished. The committee membership, ostensibly for its own protection, was kept secret. Then, on Saturday January 11, Soviet troops captured the press house and a building used by the fledgling Lithuanian militia.

That same evening, a small group of workers, said to represent the views of nineteen all-union industrial enterprises, appeared at the Parliament and demanded that it yield control to the National Salvation Committee. It is alleged that the workers were turned away with force, which was the pretext for the National Salvation Committee's request for military assistance.

The timing for a move against the most brazen of the independence-minded Soviet republics seemed promising. Recent unrest over the early January price increases, later repealed, had caused a split between the popular Prime Minister Kazimiera Prunskiene and President Vytautas Landsbergis, leading to the Prime Minister's resignation. And, of course, the United Nation's January 15 deadline in the Persian Gulf loomed. Assuming Moscow had advance warnings of allied intentions, Gorbachev knew a strike in Vilnius just before the deadline would be quickly overshadowed by war in the Middle East.

Events unfolded rapidly. At about 1:30 A.M. on Sunday January 13, a dozen or so military vehicles—tanks and armored personnel carriers—mounted an assault on the television tower. The television station issued a call for help, to which thousands of citizens quickly responded by forming eight rings around the tower. Within 30 or 40 minutes, the tanks moved into the crowd and began firing loud empty shells as paratroopers shot out the tower's windows. Estimates of how many of the troops had live ammunition vary. At about the same time, an attack occurred on the television and radio office building nearby. In both locations the crowd was unarmed and peaceful, greeting the troops with chants and the singing of the national anthem. The crowd was comprised of people of all ages, including children and the elderly. When the dust settled, 13 civilians and 1 Soviet officer were dead and about 600 more were injured (many with broken eardrums from the tank blasts). One other person died later, bringing the total to 15.

I analyzed the list of injured and determined that perhaps 60 percent were over age 30, with the average age probably in the early thirties. We interviewed several of the wounded in the central Vilnius hospital, including two people who had their legs crushed by tanks and one person who had been shot. They were ordinary people, in no way radical, who simply responded alone, on the spur of the moment, to defend their government. All were surprised and shocked by the violence, but none expressed regret at having gone to the defense of the television tower.

While the assault was in progress, the National Salvation Committee announced that it had taken power—but as it turned out, that claim was premature. The unexpectedly strong resistance from the Lithuanian people bogged the army down, and the violence apparently gave the Soviet military commanders pause about the price to be paid in completing the plan to seize the Parliament. In the end, the military settled for control of the printing house, the television tower, the television and radio office building, the Interior Ministry, and the militia headquarters.

In effect, the coup was aborted. The plan failed dismally, leaving Gorbachev no choice but to put some distance between himself and the killing of civilians. Everyone with whom we spoke assumes that Gorbachev was fully knowledgeable about the plan and authorized it. It seems likely to me that he did, perhaps acting on a flawed assessment of both the determination of the people and the ease with which the military could accomplish its surgical strike. Claims that the intervention was, in part, motivated by a desire to protect threatened ethnic minorities seem groundless in the face of evidence that some Russians and Poles participated in the defense of the Lithuanian government. Leaders of the minority community also reported a marked shift *toward* independence among their members in the aftermath of the bloodshed. Violence has united all the residents of Lithuania and strengthened their resolve to pursue complete independence.

The events of January 12-13 also make it unlikely that Gorbachev's new initiative to negotiate with the Baltic states through three special commissions will work in Lithuania. The violence has fortified the political strength of the "radicals" (the most fervent of these being the Independence Now faction) and marginalized the influence of those who would be willing to negotiate a gradual transition. Gorbachev missed an opportunity to work with the reform Communists, now called the Democratic Labor Party, who might have been able to mediate between him and those advocating complete independence in the near future. They believe his course has been ill advised and his alliance with hard-core, anti-independence Communists unwise, giving rise to a feeling that their own position has been undercut. Having failed to establish a partnership with this moderate group, really his natural allies, Gorbachev is now linked to a discredited local minority and is increasingly isolated from the majority of the population. As President Landsbergis told us, "If we are not crushed completely in a short time, this process [of independence] will go on."

It is unlikely that Lithuania will be crushed in the immediate future, especially when one considers together the strong protest rally of more than 100,000 people in Moscow on January 20, Yeltsin's support, and the West's sharp rebuke of the violence. I expect that the tense stalemate in Lithuania will continue and that Lithuania will make further incremental advances by continuing to act like an independent country. I doubt Lithuania will respond to Gorbachev's present, more conciliatory, strategy. His new approach has the best chance of working in Estonia, where it is possible that the commission will actually engage in discussions which will slow, perhaps even arrest, further defiance of Moscow. I cannot predict what Latvia's response will be. I doubt that any of the three states will agree, as a precondition to discussion, to repeal the declarations of independence or sovereignty that have been endorsed by their Parliaments.

## The Aftermath

Western observers seem to me to reach conclusions too quickly about the direction of reform in the Soviet Union. I have no doubt that some have put too much faith in Gorbachev's reforms, and that they formed too positive a view of him. After all, he has steadfastly maintained his faith in the Communist Party, in socialism, and in the empire. But we may also be too quick to write an epitaph for *perestroika, glasnost,* and, indeed, Gorbachev himself.

It seems to me likely that Gorbachev will survive, tightening his control in some quarters, then easing up in others. While we know that all reformers have left his inner circle, there are still reasonable, pragmatic people left. No doubt Gorbachev is more dependent than ever on the army, but that dependence is reciprocal given the absence of any plausible alternatives to Gorbachev's leadership. The people with whom we spoke still believe that Gorbachev is in control of the central Soviet government and is likely to remain in control for some time to come.

By now we should be skeptical of notions that Gorbachev works according to a plan in micro as well as macro issues.

He and the leaders of the Baltic states are playing a game with no rules, no precedents, and no guides for future moves. Another attempt to roll back Lithuanian independence would not surprise me, although in the near term it is likely to be pursued through negotiations or, at worst, through a continuation of psychological warfare fortified by dirty tricks aimed at destabilization. Gorbachev may even pursue different strategies in each of the Baltic states, allowing the impasse to continue in Lithuania and reaching an accord with Estonia.

It will be the tragedy of Gorbachev that he missed the opportunity, over the past 2 years, to resolve the Baltic crisis in a creative way. By underestimating the states' determined pursuit of full independence and by clinging to the present boundaries of the empire on every front, Gorbachev lost the chance to find a middle ground in the Baltics, a position that would not necessarily have caused precedent problems elsewhere in the Soviet Union. A kind of "Hong Kong in reverse" seems to me to have been possible, and perhaps still is, in Estonia. But in Lithuania I doubt there is a happy scenario foreseeable. I expect some period of tension, perhaps even further bloodshed, with the ultimate outcome resting on factors extraneous to the Baltics. When, and if, the central Soviet government accepts the reality that the Soviet Union must be redefined as a looser federation of states with considerable sovereignty, then it is very possible that the Baltics will be able to opt out. Until that time, an uneasy stalemate seems likely.

## Conclusion

While Mikhail Gorbachev maintains his grip on power in Moscow, it seems clear to me that Moscow's control over the Soviet empire has diminished measurably since my visit last June. At some level, leaders in the republics, which have different traditions, ethnic mixes, political philosophies, and personal agendas, have understood that there is safety in numbers. Each individual act of defiance of Moscow invites others and, in aggregate, they erode daily the authority and legitimacy of the central government. The Baltics showed

# The Choice Between Reform and Repression

early courage, but Russia and the Ukraine are now at center stage. I suppose the very best outcome is for this process, which seems to be irreversible, to continue to evolve gradually to the point where Gorbachev is forced to orchestrate the redefinition of the Soviet Union. Every day that a systematic and pervasive crackdown is postponed builds hope for the peaceful scenario of evolution. And therein lies a puzzle: How can the process be kept moving without trapping Gorbachev with the choice he desperately wants to avoid, the choice between reform and repression?

While I do not know enough to suggest what the implication of all this might be for American policy, I do believe the situation in the Soviet Union has approached a critical juncture that requires our full attention, unencumbered by an overriding need to keep the Persian Gulf coalition together. The longer the United States remains preoccupied with Iraq, the less likely that we can play a constructive role in the most important transition now under way in the world.

# A Watershed Moment

(REPORT ON TRIP TO TURKEY, JANUARY 1992)

## Introduction

I joined Jeri Laber, executive director of Helsinki Watch, on a visit to the two major cities of Turkey, Istanbul and Ankara, during the week of January 25-31, 1992. The purpose of our visit was to release a Helsinki Watch report documenting the torture of children in Turkey and to meet with officials of the newly elected government. We held a formal press conference in Istanbul, attended by twenty-five members of the Turkish and international press, and an informal press conference in Ankara. The report and our visit to government leaders received extensive coverage by the major Turkish newspapers.

In Istanbul, we met with human rights activists, writers and other intellectuals, and the Istanbul Bar Association. In Ankara, we met with U.S. Ambassador Richard Barkley, Prime Minister Suleyman Demirel, Deputy Prime Minister Erdal Inonu, and the Ministers of Justice, Interior, Culture, and Human Rights. We also talked with the head of the Parliament's Commission on Human Rights, two Kurdish members of Parliament, and the leaders of an independent human rights association. Finally, we met with the chief of police in Ankara and toured the detention facility at central police headquarters, which is the setting in which torture has routinely occurred.

This was my first visit to Turkey, a country I had known little about. What follows are my personal impressions of the political situation in Turkey and reflections on the present status of human rights. Jeri Laber and others have commented about the contrast between the routine and widespread practice of torture in Turkey and the otherwise pleasing impression one has of the Turkish people. Despite the difficult subject that we came to discuss, I too left with a positive impression of Turkey and its people. Turkey is a vital and vibrant country which fuses a rich and varied tradition with a sophisticated understanding of the modern world.

## BACKGROUND

Turkey, a country of 57 million people, has been a republic since 1923. Its slow evolution toward democracy has been interrupted three times by military coups, but after relatively brief periods of military rule, civilian governments have resumed power. It is a relatively homogenous country in terms of religion (98 percent of the population is Muslim), but it has been a secular nation since 1928. The largest ethnic minority is the Kurds, who represent about 20 percent of the population; they are concentrated in southeastern Turkey but have sizable numbers in major cities, especially Istanbul.

Under the leadership of Prime Minister and (later) President Turgut Ozal, Turkey made significant improvements in its economy in the 1980s. But a high inflation rate (about 70 percent), fueled by large deficits, has created a drag on the economy in recent years. Income is unevenly distributed, with the top fifth of the Turkish population enjoying a relatively low tax rate compared with their counterparts in other European nations. The state has controlling ownership of ten of the fifteen largest industrial companies. As a bloc, these firms are money losers rather than earners. Their cumulative subsidies are equal to about 75 percent of the country's annual deficit.

Turkish leaders are quite conscious of how the dissolution of the Soviet Union and the continued instability of the Muslim world have heightened Turkey's strategic significance. As the only Muslim country which is a secular democracy, Turkey is acutely aware of its leadership potential. It also sees increased economic opportunity in the opening of the former Soviet republics, which will naturally look to Turkey for economic relationships. A critical question is whether Turkey will be able to capitalize on its special ties to Asia and the Muslim world, or will be drawn into relationships that might retard its modernization.

Turkey, an associate member of the European Economic Community (EEC), aspires to full membership in that organization, but there are doubts about whether acceptance will soon be forthcoming. In addition to the potential of a Greek veto inspired by continuing boundary disputes in the Aegean Sea and the Cyprus issue, there is a growing concern among other EEC members (especially Germany) about the potential massive influx of Turkish workers. Turkey also worries that NATO, of which it is a member, will diminish in significance and that it will be kept out of full participation in the expanding European Community. Such worries feed the Turkish sense of discrimination by its neighbors in Europe.

Against this background, relations with the United States are important. While one senses no animosity toward individual Americans in Turkey—indeed, I felt very welcome—there remains ambivalence about the United States, in part because of its support of the recent military regime. Some people with whom we spoke (but not Prime Minister Demirel) expressed the view that the United States did not want Turkey to emerge as a strong power in the region and that the United States was made nervous by Turkey's emerging role with the Central Asian republics. Also some intellectuals with whom we spoke were critical of the excesses of free market capitalism represented by the United States. Even those who support further moves toward privatization are aware—in a sophisticated way—of the social shortcomings of Western capitalism, shortcomings they would like to avoid in Turkey.

This set of attitudes fosters a complexity which I had not seen in my work in Eastern and Central Europe, where the American democratic capitalist system was uncritically embraced. Indeed, sensitive and courageous people in Turkey who have led the human rights movement, while warmly disposed to us as individuals for our human rights work, are very likely to be critical of American policy and culture. And although they appreciate our work in exposing human rights problems in Turkey, they also bristle at the fact that we (and Western Europe) criticize their country when our own countries also have flaws. We heard the term "double standard" used frequently. I was struck by the extent to which well-educated and widely traveled people relied on American movies and CNN for their current impressions about the United States. Imagine how repeated airings of the videotape of the police brutality in Los Angeles affects the discussion of police torture in Turkey. Think about what image of the American government was conveyed by the Oliver North hearings—watched with fascination by many educated people in Turkey—which dealt with arms for a fundamentalist state on the border of Turkey's troubled eastern provinces.

It seems to me that we are about to witness a struggle for Turkey's soul. Modern forces in Turkey want to foster many of the economic and political changes encouraged by Europe and the United States, but they feel the West is ambivalent about accepting Turkey on its own terms. I came away believing the United States needs to devote a good deal more attention to developments in Turkey and needs to regard Turkey as much more than a strategically placed military ally. The absence of the American press in Turkey—in sharp contrast to the presence of European reporters—tells us something about why Turkey is so little understood among the American public.

A recent *Economist**  survey cited *four* preconditions for Turkey's continued development in a European direction: (1) revival of its economy through the reduction of inflation and more rapid privatization of the large, state-owned firms which control 40 percent of Turkey's GNP; (2) sharp improvement in what has been a dismal human rights record; (3) resolution of the rebellion in the eastern provinces by better treatment of the Kurds; and (4) development of a modern, coherent party system. I found a remarkable consensus in support of this analysis among the people with whom I spoke.

Let us move now to the political situation and then examine the condition of human rights.

*My background knowledge of Turkey was enriched by a thoughtful article in the December 14, 1991 issue.

## POLITICAL CURRENTS: A MOMENT OF OPPORTUNITY

The military coup of 1980 came at a time when many people felt that Turkish society was disintegrating, as the daily toll of politically motivated murders rose to thirty or more. The regime used harsh measures to restore order, curtailing freedom of expression, freedom of the press, and free assembly, and disregarding other fundamental human rights. In 1983 the military brokered a return to a civilian government, but installed General Kenan Everan as President through a special referendum on the constitution. Although the leaders of the two major political parties, Bulent Ecevit and Suleyman Demirel, were banned from the election, the military's preferred party lost to Turgut Ozal's newly formed Motherland Party (ANAP), and Ozal became Prime Minister.

Ozal made use of the instruments of power accumulated by the military regime and only gradually made improvements in basic human rights such as freedom of the press, freedom of expression, and freedom of assembly. While initially credited with sharply improving the economy, his administration began to lose momentum in the late 1980s. In addition, Ozal's style of governing took on imperial airs, with members of his family apparently abusing their privileged access to economic opportunity. So when the Gulf War occurred in early 1991, Ozal, who by this time had replaced Everan as President, was already in trouble. The repressive aspects of his regime had stirred increasing resentment; inflation had reduced the real value of people's wages; and personal scandal had touched those close to him. Ozal's strong support of the Gulf War was simply the shove that hastened his party's downfall.

The October elections saw the right-of-center True Path Party, led by six-time Prime Minister Suleyman Demirel, gain the most seats in the Parliament, followed by Ozal's Motherland Party and the Social Democrats (SHP), led by Erdal Inonu. The Democratic Left Party of former Prime Minister Bulent Ecevit and the Welfare Party (Fundamentalists) also won some seats. Thus the new lineup in Parliament was:

| True Path | 27% |
| Motherland | 24% |
| Social Democrats | 21% |
| Welfare | 17% |
| Democratic Left | 11% |

Demirel and Inonu quickly formed a ruling coalition, which they headed as Prime Minister and Deputy Prime Minister. Ozal, while remaining as President, has been largely marginalized. In forging the coalition, the two parties agreed to a protocol which promises sweeping change.

In the last 3 weeks of the campaign, Demirel played upon the torture issue as his central theme. Promising police stations "with glass walls," he pledged to end the widespread practice of torture. To that pledge were added other reforms in civil liberties, education, and the Kurdish situation.

No doubt the junior partner in the coalition has had a healthy impact on the new government's agenda. Erdal Inonu, former president of Middle East Technical University and a physicist, is an appealing figure. Highly intelligent, candid, idealistic, soft spoken, and understated, he radiates integrity and decency.

Demirel is a more complicated figure with a mixed record from his previous terms as Prime Minister. He too is bright and affable but, unlike Inonu, also very charismatic—a natural politician. All segments of society—even former opponents—say he has been changed by his experience under house arrest during the military regime. Even those who are skeptical are inclined to give him a chance, to put aside past abuses of power. "We need him very much," one writer told me, "we need something to hold onto ... we can't afford to probe his past." An opposition political leader said, "He is a much different, much better man ... he is now saying what we have been saying and going to prison for." The writer concluded that it didn't matter why Demirel had changed, and conceded, "He is a pragmatic politician—it makes no difference why he changed, even if the changes are only instrumental. What is important, is that he has been brought to this point by the people of the country, by correctly reading what they want."

Another take on Demirel was provided by the two men managing the front desk of the Pera Palas hotel in Istanbul. Both members of parties further to the left (SHP and Democratic Left), they nonetheless lit up when they heard we were going to meet with Demirel—"Baba" (Father), they called him. We asked them what we should tell the Prime Minister. They replied, "Do something about the cost of living, about inflation. End torture, promote human rights. Settle the Kurdish problem." They went on to insist that we tell "Baba" how much they supported him and that he was always welcome at the Pera Palas.

I asked Demirel if he had changed. He thought for a moment, looked at the ceiling of his formal receiving room, smiled, then turned to me, looked me straight in the eye, and said, "I haven't changed. The people now understand me better. Fundamentally, I have always been a democrat. Perhaps I have moved with the times also. Everything has changed—Europe has changed—and Turkey cannot be left behind. The collapse of communism was a very significant event with implications for Turkey."

What followed was a brief but remarkable civics lesson which may explain why Demirel has won such broad popular support. He said he saw himself and Turkey at a critical crossroads, a watershed moment in history:

> We don't have much time and we must be successful with our democratic experiment. A country cannot be more democratic than its people—you can declare a republic a democracy, but it is not so unless the people take responsibility for running the country. It is the job of leadership to encourage the people to take the responsibility.

He went on to say that "of the people, by the people, and for the people" is the best phrase in the English language. "We want to move," he concluded, "from a silent Turkey, to a speaking Turkey, to a Turkey without prohibitions."

Some credit this transformation in Demirel's political philosophy to his coalition partner Erdal Inonu and the SHP. Inonu reminded us that the prevailing view of the state, inherited from the Ottoman Empire, is of a superior body to which the right of individuals could be sacrificed, since the state stood apart from, and above, the individual. The most difficult challenge, he said, was to embrace the concept of the state as deriving its powers from the people. As the SHP Justice Minister told us, "We want to base the legal system on the concept that it should protect individuals from abuse of state powers." Inonu was perhaps less sanguine than Demirel about how quickly this philosophy could take root, especially in the civil service and the security force.

## Condition of Human Rights

Inonu conceded that, despite good intentions, past practices such as torture continue, although he believed the incidences were declining. The Human Rights Foundation, a nongovernment group which documents instances of torture, estimates that during recent years, the vast majority of political prisoners and more than half of the individuals arrested for nonpolitical crimes have been tortured. Documented forms of abuse include beatings, electric shocks, being hit with highly pressurized cold water, rape, and sleep deprivation. The Human Rights Foundation confirms that torture has continued since the new government was organized in early November. However, it was our impression that the documented cases in the large cities, Ankara especially, appear to have declined since November. Most people with whom we spoke said it was too early to hold the new government to strict account, but there remains concern that many of the senior and middle-level officials who engaged in torture and repressive tactics are still holding office.

There can be no doubt that the government is at work on a legislative program that promises sweeping reforms; it will be presented to the Parliament for action in about a month. Demirel has mounted a concerted effort to end the practice of torture. "Ending torture is the business of everyone in this country," he told us. "Torture is the shame of humanity." Here are some specific steps the government intends to take to implement its prohibition of torture. Most of the changes are aimed at the detention period, when the most egregious instances of torture take place. The Minister of Justice has prepared a package of reforms which include:

- Immediate access to a lawyer when a suspect is arrested
- Access to a public defender for those who cannot afford a lawyer
- Limitation of the detention period to 1 day before being charged for individual crimes and 4 days for collective crimes
- Requirement of a "Miranda" type warning of a suspect's rights
- Higher standards of evidence before a person can be arrested
- Strict prohibition of torture, with a specific list of actions which constitute both physical and psychological torture
- Restrictions on interrogation, with a specific list of the types of questions that may and may not be asked of suspects
- Prohibition on using testimony taken by torture against a suspect
- For crimes bearing a penalty of 5 years in jail, right to a trial within 4 months and to a verdict within 2 years (if these standards are not met, the case is automatically dismissed)
- Extensive reeducation of the police force
- Creation of a new investigation unit under the prosecutor's office and the Ministry of Justice, effectively removing the police and the Interior Ministry from the interrogation process
- Creation of a new juvenile court to give special protection to children

The Minister of Justice reported that all these changes in code and practice are being done to conform to international standards. He further reported that all laws, including the Turkish constitution, are being reviewed to remove any anti-democratic provisions. A number of people with whom we spoke, including the Prime Minister, wanted us to understand that these changes were proposed because the Turkish people want them and because they are right, rather than as a response to Western pressure. I am told this represents a genuinely fresh way of approaching reform.

While the reforms aimed at ending torture are the most dramatic proposals, there are other changes also under consideration. Here is a sample:

- The Prime Minister has proposed abolishing the Higher Education Council (YOK), which was set up by the military regime and has held universities under tight control. He proposes more autonomy for individual universities.
- A new press law is in draft which would, among other things, abolish the requirement that the press reveal its sources and remove restraints on criticism of the state.
- The Minister of Culture claims to have ended censorship de facto and has proposed to abolish the specific list of books that are banned. The proposed new law will allow censorship only with reference to pornography. In similar fashion, the board which reviews the scripts of films will also be abolished.
- It is much easier (we are told) to get a permit to have a demonstration.

I should underscore that most of these changes are proposed and should be acted upon by March. Some abuses they are designed to eliminate are still occurring. And we hear there is a division of view within the Cabinet on some key reforms. The Minister of Interior apparently opposes shortening the detention period to 1 day and has argued for a host of exceptions. So we will have to see what happens and read the text of the new laws with great care.

But the bottom line is that human rights, and the conditions for democracy in Turkey, seem to be improving. Perhaps most important, the people feel free to speak their minds; one does not sense the fear present in a repressive regime.

A measure of the difficulty ahead in implementation was revealed to us in our visits to the chief of police of Ankara and his deputies in charge of combating terrorism. The chief, who has been on the job only 7 months, is learning the language of human rights and tried to say the right things. His lack of enthusiasm for some of the reforms discussed above was evident, however. And he refused to admit past instances of torture at the Ankara police station—even after we told him the Prime Minister and Deputy Prime Minister had conceded past abuses. He arranged for us to inspect the detention center, once the site of torture.

The deputy chief, who had been at the station for 12 years, also refused to concede that there were any past abuses. He led to what I call a *60 Minutes* moment, when I wished I could have been able to juxtapose his denial with the Prime Minister's acknowledgment of past torture, as well as firsthand stories from victims. I came away skeptical that the police would actually abide by the ban on torture. Many people told us that the police were a "state within a state," basically out of control, and not responsive to the government.

But for the moment, I believe the police know the spotlight is on them. Apparently the chief of police has key deputies pay unannounced visits to local police stations in Ankara. And the facility we saw had been cleaned up—so much so, that it was not credible. I wondered if some other facility was now being used for detention. This facility—in the annex behind the central police headquarters—was a cross between a movie set and a museum. There was no one in detention! The facility was absolutely vacant; artificial flowers had been placed in interrogation rooms. The facility had been scrubbed and given a fresh coat of paint, and no equipment of any kind was in sight. We were led to believe that guards had no guns, sticks, or any other means to control inmates. With all that said, the basic plant is very dark and dank. Cells are small, have no light, and lack adequate ventilation. None is furnished, although a mattress is provided at night (even though some cells are too small to lie down in). So I have to say that our on-site inspection was inconclusive, although perhaps it did some good in reminding the police that the international community is watching.

It has been said that "terrorism" poses the greatest threat to human rights in Turkey. Indeed, there are at least a half-dozen paramilitary organizations in Turkey that advocate the use of violence to achieve political ends. The most active include Revolutionary Left (Dev Sol), which claims responsibility for killing almost two dozen military and police officers between January 1990 and July 1991. Also active is the left-wing, separatist group, the Workers Party of Kurdistan (PKK). The reforms I have described above may not have much impact on the eastern provinces, where the Kurds are concentrated and which are governed under a state of emergency. Nor can we be sure new protections of civil liberties will extend, for example, to students on university campuses who may sympathize—or may be accused of sympathizing—with one or another of the terrorist groups. It seems likely that affiliation or sympathy with a banned group will be grounds for punishment, even if a person has taken no action or done nothing illegal.

I am prepared to concede that there is a real terrorism problem in Turkey, and that the threat is real and, perhaps, on the rise (not only in the southeast or arising from the Kurdish situation). To understand the origin of the problem, we must appreciate how badly the Kurdish people have been treated by successive Turkish governments over many years. The Kurds number about 10 million (one-fifth of the population), in Turkey, but they are also found in Iran, Iraq, Syria, and the former Soviet Union. It is estimated that there are upward of 25 million Kurds altogether—the largest ethnic group in the world's history which has not established a homeland.

Kurds who have migrated west in Turkey are relatively better off, and while they may face discrimination, they are not now subject to harsh government repression. The Kurds in southeastern Turkey face a different fate. There, the Kurdish minority is repressed by official Turkish policy—forced assimilation, plus bans on using their own language or practicing their own culture or being educated in their own language. Since they share the Muslim religion with the Turks, the government has heretofore refused to recognize the Kurds as a distinct ethnic minority. On top of discrimination by the government come the harsh conditions of everyday life in the poorest part of Turkey. No wonder that the mixture of despair and repression has given rise to the militant separatist group PKK. Stern measures to disband the PKK have touched off the usual spiral of action, overreaction, and radicalization. No one has offered us a reliable estimate of PKK membership or indicated how extensive its support is among ordinary people. We heard estimates as high as 99 percent, but more sober judgments put the figure much lower. Indeed, it is hard to know the true measure of support, because the PKK itself demands loyalty and is capable of punishing those who do not sympathize.

Jeri Laber, who has traveled in eastern Turkey, has the impression that the situation has deteriorated since her last visit 4-1/2 years ago, a conclusion many people reaffirm. There is a sense among liberal-minded people that this is a critical moment for the Kurdish question, perhaps the last chance to find a peaceful solution.

The new government is conscious of the moment and has taken steps—so far, largely symbolic—to build a bridge to the Kurds. The SHP has twenty-two Kurdish deputies among its parliamentary members. The head of the Parliament's Human Rights Commission is Kurdish, as is the State Minister for Human Rights. Two new Kurdish newspapers have recently appeared. Laws banning expressions of Kurdish culture—for example, cassettes of Kurdish music—are not being enforced. The government has indicated its intention to abolish the village guard system which impressed Kurds in a special police force and exposed them to PKK attacks. The Prime Minister has said, "[Turkey] must recognize the Kurdish reality," and he traveled to the southeast with Erdal Inonu, who has credibility there.

But the hair-trigger sensitivity of the Kurdish issue was ignited when two Kurdish deputies refused to take their oath of office in Turkish, preferring instead their own Kurdish tongue. This show of defiance touched off a sharp reaction—overreaction, I think—in which almost everyone we spoke to felt the young deputies had made a mistake and created a backlash. They, in turn, were keenly disappointed that the Prime Minister personally criticized them and that Inonu forced them to resign from the SHP. Still, they are genuine Kurds—not Kurds who no longer sympathize with the aspirations of their people—and they are functioning *within* the system. We were encouraged that Ahmet Turk, the Kurdish head of Parliament's Human Rights Commission, said he thought that "the solution to the Kurdish problem can be found within the framework of mutual respect and tolerance."

Still, as a practical matter, the Kurdish problem does represent the greatest threat to the governing coalition itself and to its reform program. Seeing that the government is working to win support among the Kurds, the PKK has stepped up terrorist activities, hoping to provoke a strong government reaction which will radicalize the population. And the rise of terrorism makes it hard for the SHP, which is seen as the party "soft on the Kurds." Indeed, while we were in Turkey, Inonu narrowly withstood a serious challenge to his party leadership, generated in part by dissatisfaction with his policy toward the Kurds, which has cost the SHP popularity. Had he lost the leadership battle, it is possible—perhaps even likely—that the coalition would have fallen apart and the momentum for reform stalled.

Given Demirel's overwhelming popularity, the question arises: Why doesn't he call a new election and win an outright majority? There seems to me to be at least three reasons that he favors ruling through a coalition for the moment.

1. He has apparently decided that human rights and political reforms are easier to accomplish than economic reforms. Any economic reform would involve tackling the inefficient, state-controlled industrial sector, resulting

in a rise of unemployment and at least a momentary dislocation of the economy. The SHP partnership is convenient, because Demirel can blame the coalition for restraining his plans to reform the economy.
2. At the same time, he can cite coalition pressure to advance his human rights agenda, and use it to induce support from conservatives within his own True Path Party.
3. The SHP has more credibility with the Kurds than Demirel does, and he needs them to make progress in resolving the most vexing internal problems.

Thus we are likely to see the coalition hold at least through the year, perhaps longer. And the longer it holds, the firmer will be the roots of the reform program underway.

## Conclusion

Turkey is an immensely complicated country, located at a pivotal geographical crossroads, and poised at a watershed moment in its own history. I can say with some certainty that the potential for constructive, far-reaching, perhaps irreversible change is present. The Demirel government is pursuing a radically different concept of a state—one based on the consent of the governed—and has put forth a sweeping set of reform proposals for implementation. I cannot assess the odds that the reform program will succeed. On the one hand, the historical moment is right—democracy is advancing all around—and the Turkish people have given broad support to the initiatives of the new government. On the other hand, there are deeply entrenched authoritarian traditions, a bureaucracy with a culture of repression still in place, dangerous ethnic strife, galloping inflation, and an unstable party system—a formidable set of obstacles.

Whether Europe and the United States will understand what hangs in the balance and deepen their economic and political ties with Turkey is an open question. Surely there are forces abroad which would draw Turkey into closer ties with the Asian and Muslim worlds as well, and there is no doubt Turkey will play a major role in developing the Central Asian republics of the former Soviet Union. But in doing so, Turkey may enmesh itself with forces hostile to pluralist polities and open economies. So I suppose it is a question of balance, which the United States, Europe, and the leading multilateral institutions must consider. Above all, I think it wise to recognize a newly self-confident Turkey which wants to be accepted on its own terms as a modern democratic nation capable of full partnership with the international community.

# Reflections on Bulgaria

(MEMORANDUM TO THE BOARD OF TRUSTEES, JUNE 1992)

### Background

I visited Bulgaria on May 24-28, 1992 for the purpose of attending the annual meeting of the New School's Democracy Seminars.

At the conclusion of the New School's annual conference on democracy, I spent two additional days in Sofia surveying the current status of human rights in Bulgaria. The immediate focus of my inquiry was the decommunization process, or lustration (from the Latin word for purification). But I also learned about the status of minorities, problems with the new Bulgarian constitution, citizenship issues, and proposed changes in the penal code, among other classic human rights concerns. I met with President Zheliu Zhelev, U.S. Ambassador Kenneth Hill, and political officer Douglas Smith; leaders of the three major parties in Parliament; leaders of the Democratic Center (a coalition of small parties); and groups of journalists and intellectuals. Altogether, I met with about thirty people.

This was my second visit to Bulgaria. In October 1989, I participated in a mission organized by the International Helsinki Federation and led by Karl Schwarzenberg. The visit had coincided with the International Ecological Forum, which was the occasion for the first major public demonstration against the regime of long-time Communist leader Todor Zhivkov, whose government collapsed about 6 weeks later. Our mission documented a record of human rights abuses, including forceful assimilation of the Turkish minority, imprisonment for political reasons, censorship of the press, and denial of freedom of association.

There is no doubt that Bulgaria has come a long way in improving its human rights record, although some significant problems remain and are discussed below. But first, it will be useful to recall some basic demographic facts about Bulgaria and to look at the overall political situation.

Bulgaria, located on the Black Sea and surrounded by Turkey, Greece, Yugoslavia, and Romania, is about the size of Ohio and has a population of about 9 million. About 8–10 percent of its population is of Turkish origin, and another 5–7 percent are Gypsies, Greeks, Armenians, or Russians. The predominant religion is Eastern Orthodox, followed by Islam, Roman Catholicism, Protestantism, and Judaism.

Bulgaria was ruled by the Ottoman Turks for 500 years, until 1878. It became fully independent only in 1908, but had a turbulent struggle to maintain that independence until September 1944, when Soviet-dominated Communist rule began.

## Current Political Situation

The reform Communists who toppled Todor Zhivkov in November 1989 have been losing power in each stage of political reorganization since then. At present, the successor to the Communist Party, the Bulgarian Socialist Party (BSP), is out of power, having failed to win a majority in the October 1991 parliamentary election. In that election the BSP won 106 seats, the prodemocracy/free market Union of Democratic Forces (UDF) garnered 110 seats, and the Movement for Rights and Freedom (MRF), largely a Turkish group, gained 24 seats. A coalition of the UDF and MRF controls the Parliament. The President, elected directly, is Zheliu Zhelev, a former dissident who ran on the UDF ticket.

Perhaps the most significant recent development in the Bulgarian political scene is the collapse of the center of the political spectrum. The UDF, originally the umbrella for all major opposition factions, split over the passage of the new constitution in July 1991 by a Parliament dominated by former Communists. Thirty-nine conservative members (strongly anti-Communist, strongly in favor of rapid transition to the free market), known as the Dark Blue, walked out of the debate over the constitution and refused to sign it. They objected to the domination of the process by the ex-Communists. Those UDF members who remained, the so-called Light Blue, included many of the intellectuals and other opposition forces with whom both the New School and Helsinki Watch had been working. The Light Blue favors a less radical approach to decommunization and to free market transition than the Dark Blue.

Once the constitution was adopted in July 1991, the Parliament dissolved itself and called the October election. The Dark Blue and Light Blue split the UDF, but all the parties associated with the Light Blue failed to reach the 4 percent threshold for representation in Parliament; thus all Light Blue members lost their seats. As a result of the split, the UDF moved sharply to the right (rapid free market with almost no social safety net), leaving the center of the political spectrum open.

In an attempt to fill that center, a new coalition of seven minority parties called the Democratic Center has emerged, under the leadership of Stefan Gaitandjiev. This coalition includes the Liberal Party, Eco-Glasnost, Democratic Conservative Alliance, Green Party, and Social Democrats. In the October election all these elements together won less than 10 percent of the vote and none passed the 4 percent threshold for representation in the Parliament. A recent poll indicated that 20 percent of the population has confidence in these parties, but that only 3 percent would vote for them. The Democratic Center seeks to build a center-left coalition comprised of the remnants of the Light Blue, some defectors from the left of the Dark Blue UDF, and from the right of the BSP (the so-called pink faction known as the Alliance for Social Democracy).

The political situation in Bulgaria remains fluid, and many observers predict another parliamentary election later this year or early in 1993. It is a mistake to see either of the two major parties as cohesive or to attach left-right or good-bad labels on them. The most serious mistake is to dismiss the BSP simply as the ex-Communists, the nationalists, or those wanting to restore the old order. While those terms do accurately describe a large portion of the BSP deputies, about 33 percent subscribe to the program of the Alliance for Social Democracy. Alliance leaders are less nationalistic (*read* less antiminorities) than the hard-line members of their party, accept the free market economy, and have a positive vision of the political economy which is close to that of Western social democratic parties. They are younger than the hard-line faction, are not tainted with having held leadership positions in the party or government of the old regime, and are well educated and broadly knowledgeable about the wider world. One of the leaders of this faction, Philip Bokov, suggested the Alliance might well coalesce with other groups if a new center coalition emerged.

The Union for Democratic Forces (Dark Blue) strongly favors a rigorous decommunization program and a rapid transition to the free market. It is prepared to live with the social costs of the transition. Social programs are likely to be adopted only to keep the situation short of social chaos. The UDF members I met (those from the Dark Blue proposing the lustration laws) seemed more provincial than the Alliance faction of the BSP and not sensitive to the human rights implications of the decommunization process. However, the UDF has strongly supported the rights of the Turkish minority, partially out of belief and partially to cement the coalition with the MRF.

The Light Blue would like to be the nucleus of a new center-left party but is having a hard time articulating a platform which seems realistic. Bulgarian popular opinion has not yet reached a sophisticated understanding of the pitfalls of a rapid transition to the free market or come to understand less radical alternatives. Any position which seems reminiscent of the recent past of strong government control of the economy is suspect. And, of course, the social programs advocated by the Light Blue are hard to afford, given the poor performance of the economy.

President Zhelev has split with the Dark Blue and is now somewhat above politics. He was elected with 54 percent of the vote, and recent polls show his approval rating at 70 percent. Some say his own views are closest to the Light Blue, although he has a more forceful position on the protection of minority rights. He has opposed the lustration laws. The Bulgarian constitution vests enormous power in the Parliament and consequently much less in the President. The Communist majority, which adopted the constitution, assumed the BSP would control the Parliament and the UDF, the presidency. Now the BSP has become an advocate of a strong presidency because it sees Zhelev as a more palatable alternative and a brake on the decommunization and rapid free market programs of the UDF majority in Parliament.

What does the future hold? Bulgaria, like all the former Soviet satellites, is experiencing an agonizing transition. The government has put in place the basic tools for transition: privatization, a process for restitution, encouragement of foreign investment, reorganization of the agricultural sector, and a new banking law. But, as is the case elsewhere, the reforms have not brought tangible improvements for the general population, and polls show rising dissatisfaction with the UDF government.

The slim majority of the coalition, together with the independent stance of the President, suggests a period of paralysis leading to a new general election within a year. That election is likely to yield another stage of transition far short of a settled political party system capable of providing effective government. My own guess is that a democratic center will emerge at the expense of both the BSP and the UDF, thus denying any party a majority. The question will then become: How is the new coalition to be built? Will the center align with the BSP or with the UDF? Will a new center group be large enough to offset the UDF–MRF coalition if it linked with the BSP?

There is talk—or worry—about rising alienation among the people, as they tire of the inefficiency of democracy and lose their ardor for the free market once the social costs are fully understood. Might Bulgaria resort to a neofascist alternative? I do not think so. Memories of the Communist repression are so fresh that the people are likely to endure great frustration and deprivation before turning back to other authoritarian options. To my mind, the story is not how poorly democracy and the market are working but just the reverse: how well Bulgaria is coping with transitions on every front all at once. With meager internal economic resources, paltry foreign aid, a population inexperienced with individual initiative at the workplace, few institutions of civil society, and virtually no experience with democracy, Bulgaria nonetheless is making the transition.

But the lustration process poses a significant threat to the transition. As one member of the Alliance put it, "I would like to return to 1990, when everything seemed possible and people of goodwill were working together for a better future. Now we have hard times and are bitterly divided over how to treat the past."

## Human Rights Issues

### Lustration

There are two comprehensive decommunization bills pending before the Parliament. The so-called hard bill was introduced by UDF deputy Sasho Stoyanov and cosigned by twenty-two deputies. A milder form was introduced by Virgiania Velcheva. According to Stoyanov, he and Velcheva will settle their differences and present a compromise bill. The essence of both bills is that people who occupied certain enumerated positions in the Communist Party, or were members of the secret police or its collaborators, are barred from holding public office—and in the Stoyanov bill, from engaging in other activities supported by the government—for a period of five years. The Stoyanov bill also extends this ban to members of the press and private firms. If, for example, a person's name is in a secret police file, then he or she has the burden of proving innocence before a commission appointed by the Parliament. There is ultimate recourse to the courts. The two bills differ with respect to the list of past practices which qualify a person for exclusion and the scope of excluded positions in the future.

The BSP and President Zhelev oppose the sweeping nature of the lustration process, while the UDF and the MRF support it. The MRF deputies with whom I met were supportive of the harsher bill. But the leadership of the UDF is aware of the problems posed by either bill under international standards, so passage, while likely, is not assured. Even if a bill is passed, President Zhelev has vowed to challenge it in the constitutional court.

In the meantime, the UDF is attaching lustration provisions to other bills. Already passed is a new banking bill which bars high-ranking former Communists from sitting on banking commissions (under a provision known as Article 9). President Zhelev has asked the constitutional court for a ruling on the meaning of nondiscrimination under Article 2c of the constitution. If he wins a favorable ruling, Article 9 may be moot, as would other lustration provisions. The privatization law contained a version of Article 9 of the banking bill, but the provision was deleted simply because on the day that legislation was passed a number of UDF deputies were absent.

The leader of the BSP, Jan Videnov, says that decommunization is proceeding rapidly, even though the lustration law has yet to be passed. He will send me a list of specific people discharged for political reasons without due process. He says that judges and prosecutors, TV and radio personnel, members of the Academy of Science, university faculty, and plant managers have been fired in large numbers. According to Videnov, those active in the BSP are being targeted first for dismissal.

Videnov concluded that the lustration process in Bulgaria is likely to be worse than in Czechoslovakia. Indeed, both sides look at Czechoslovakia as a reference point. In defense of his bill, Stoyanov pointed out that President Havel of Czechoslovakia signed that country's lustration law.

The lustration issue puts Helsinki Watch in the odd position of sympathizing with the former Communists against members of the former opposition, some of whom we defended when they were victims of the old regime. This irony seemed lost to the UDF deputies with whom we spoke. They dismissed our concerns as evidence that "you do not understand the conditions in this country; you are looking at the issues from a Western perspective." These deputies offered the larger context of the need to get a fresh start as the overarching rationale to excuse the occasional abuses which they conceded could result from the decommunization process.

While that rationale is understandable, it must be said that the lustration process is open to political abuse and is bound to be used against some individuals, principally because of their potential as political opponents. It has even been suggested the lustration law will be used to purge some twenty or so former Communists from the UDF, but I do not give that claim much credibility. The UDF deputies with whom I talked were so absorbed in the rightness of their moral position that they were genuinely oblivious to the potential for abuse.

TRIALS OF TOP OFFICIALS

U.S. Ambassador Hill estimates that between forty and fifty top officials of the old regime are being investigated for possible trial. There are four categories of trials.

1. Todor Zhivkov's trial is under way on what amounts to charges of corruption. The trial has been stalled because of his poor health and, perhaps, for darker reasons as well. It is expected to come to a conclusion this year.
2. At least one minister has been found guilty in the aftermath of the government's cover-up of the environmental hazards posed by the Chernobyl reactor disaster. However, he has not yet been put in jail because the court has not completed the so-called motives argument (the rationale for the decision).
3. The "assimilation" campaign, chiefly against the Turks, which was intended to suppress minority cultures, also

has given rise to investigations of individuals (including Todor Zhivkov and Andrei Lukanov). Some of these inquiries are likely to result in trials.
4. Regarding the destruction of the economy, it is known that former Prime Ministers Georgi Atanosov and Andrei Lukanov are under investigation. Lukanov recently had his passport revoked and his parliamentary immunity lifted.

While it is too early to take a position on these trials, I am concerned that the charge of destroying the economy is too vague. The assimilation campaign and other human rights issues offer a better rationale for addressing past abuses.

To members of the BSP, the pattern of these investigations suggests that they are motivated by political concerns. BSP officials are particularly troubled by the focus on many of the reform Communists who engineered Zhivkov's ouster. Why, they ask, are those active today in politics—as opposed to older people who executed Zhivkov's orders faithfully before 1989—the targets of the investigations and trials?

THE PEOPLE'S COURT

The UDF has introduced a bill, which the BSP and President Zhelev oppose, which would invalidate the convictions rendered by the People's Court of 1944–1945. That court, under Soviet guidance, convicted a range of people, some of whom had committed war crimes and some of whom were just political opponents of the Communists. The bill claims that since the court lacked a constitutional basis, all its decisions should be rendered invalid. Apart from clearing the names of those convicted, the bill would restore certain property rights to the heirs of those executed and to some of those imprisoned who are still alive.

The problem with the bill is that it would clear the names of both innocent political victims and those who actually committed atrocious crimes. The opponents of the bill favor a case-by-case process through which the innocent could be exonerated.

## THE NEW CONSTITUTION

Bulgaria's new constitution consciously follows Western European models and thus does not provide a level of protection for human rights which seems sufficient by U.S. constitutional standards. One might reasonably ask whether the new democracies need greater protection for human rights in their constitutions than do Western European countries with long democratic traditions.

Even so, there are specific provisions in the Bulgarian constitution that are troublesome and that may not be consistent with international standards. The preamble to the constitution explicitly states that where the constitution is inconsistent with international law, international standards should prevail. Given the stiff requirements for amending the constitution (a three-quarters vote of the Parliament), it seems likely that reform will come through rulings from the Bulgarian Constitutional Court, which finds specific articles of the constitution inconsistent with international law.

## THE ELECTION LAW

The Democratic Center views the election law as problematic because it gives the two major parties an advantage on the design of the ballot. The UDF is coded in solid blue and the BSP in red. Other parties are assigned stripes or dots against a white background, which apparently makes it more difficult for people who cannot read to choose among the welter of opposition parties.

## CRIME AND IMPRISONMENT

The terrible economic situation has caused a rise in crime, especially among those in the bottom economic strata—the Turks and particularly the Gypsies. There is a move afoot to toughen the penal codes and end the moratorium on the death penalty. The President's legal adviser sees likely passage of a proposed law which will lengthen the time that the police can detain someone without pressing a specific charge. Apparently the proposed law would roll back recent reforms and come close to 1950s standards.

While the practice of imprisoning people for political reasons has ended, I am told there is little improvement in general prison conditions, and some people (mainly Turks) may be in jail on questionable evidence of past terrorist acts. Prison conditions should be investigated.

Status of Minorities

By all accounts conditions have improved for the Turks but much less so for the Gypsies. And as economic hardships press heavily on both groups, there is rising tension between them. I took no direct testimony from a representative of the Gypsies. But the Turkish deputies with whom I met painted a picture of hardships flowing from past discrimination and deprivation, rather than from any active, current repression by the state. I could not assess whether my correspondents were in touch with the rank-and-file of their people in rural areas, although they did express concern about how agricultural reform put the Turks at a disadvantage. The Turkish deputies also noted that the concentration of Turks in lower-skilled jobs in the industrial sector makes them especially vulnerable to being laid off, as large enterprises contract or disappear altogether. By all accounts, the situation is worse for the Gypsies, whose unemployment rate is estimated at 50 to 60 percent.

Accounts differ on the treatment of minority cultures. Apparently, there are about forty new mosques under construction or renovation as the Muslim religion enjoys a revival. But there is a conflicting picture about whether the Turkish language gets sufficient exposure in the public schools. And on a local level, the Turkish deputies claim repression and discriminatory surveillance by the police.

Surprisingly, the sharpest criticism of the treatment of minorities came from the head of the BSP, who endorsed all the negative comments in the above account. He even reported an increase in Turkish emigration because of the unjust execution of land reform. He said his aim was to appeal to the Turks and Gypsies, who were the natural constituents of the BSP on interest grounds, notwithstanding the alienation created by the former Communist government's assimilation campaign.

Overall, the citizenship laws bear further investigation. I believe the naturalization provisions may be too onerous and discriminatory, but I lacked time to pursue these concerns.

THE PRESS

As in most Eastern and Central European countries, the press presents a mixed picture. Bulgarian television is still controlled by the state and by the UDF, and applications for licenses for competitive radio stations are processed very slowly. But the print media are essentially free. The "official" newspaper (note how the language continues) is *Demokratsia,* with a daily circulation of 150,000 to 200,000. The BSP daily is *Duma,* with a 300,000 to 350,000 circulation. A new daily, *Kontinent,* boasts a 50,000 circulation and, while independent, is close to the Light Blue faction. A neutral tabloid, *24 Hours,* reaches 300,000 daily. *Trud,* the labor daily, has a circulation of 150,000. In addition, there are weeklies of note, particularly *1,000 Days,* which has wide circulation among intellectuals, *186 Hours,* and *PIK.*

When asked whether he thought it would be useful for Helsinki Watch to mount a full-scale mission to Bulgaria, President Zhelev gave a firm yes. In particular, he wants help in fighting the harshest forms of the lustration process.

CONCLUSION

The transition to democracy and a market economy is a slow process in Bulgaria, as in all the Eastern and Central European countries. Outside observers will see significant progress, really remarkable and hopeful changes. But ordinary people, intellectuals, and political leaders on the ground are more likely to feel frustration and disappointment as unemployment rises, inflation erodes purchasing power, and social tensions deepen. I was constantly asked for my own views on the transition process and for reassurance. It is hard to give an honest answer without sounding patronizing or being untruthful. The counsel of "be patient" is not well received, and rosy predictions, in the end, are not believed.

More than once I was challenged by reporters: "You are an historian. What lessons does history provide?" Without success, I tried to parry the question by explaining that my own field is American history and that I do not know enough about European history to offer guidance. That observation almost always led to a request to draw upon the American revolutionary experience. There, too, my answers disappointed. No one wanted to hear about the Articles of Confederation—the United States' first failed attempt at a new government—or know that it took 13 years between the American Revolution and the ratification of the Constitution (15 years, including the Bill of Rights) or understand that a stable party system did not take root for 30 to 40 years after the passage of the Constitution.

My own best guess—realizing that experiences will vary sharply by country—is that, on average, it will take the better part of a generation for the countries of Eastern and Central Europe to achieve the stable political systems and reasonably strong economies they desire.

The constant questions about the American experience did recall one analogy, which may be instructive. A larger question facing Bulgaria is the regeneration of a full spectrum of political views with some density in the now vacant center. A healthy political party system needs to be oriented to the future, free of nostalgia for the past (some elements of the BSP), and free of blind fear of repetition of the past (some elements of the UDF). The present political lineup is bound to go through several more iterations before it settles into a stable party system. Again the question is: What will the new coalition look like?

American historian Cecilia Kenyon wrote an influential article in 1955 entitled "Men of Little Faith: The Anti-Federalists on the Nature of Representative Government." While others argued about whether economic or philosophical convictions shaped the Constitution, self-interest or ideas, Professor Kenyon took a different approach. She analyzed the age and experience of those who favored a strong central government, and those who favored leaving more authority with the states. She found that the Federalists were younger than the anti-Federalists, more likely to have served in the army, and more likely to be engaged in work that broadened their horizons and helped them think "continentally."

I suspect the future of Bulgaria will be determined by those younger people who think "continentally," and are oriented to Europe and the future. They will not be found exclusively in any of the major parties. I expect there will eventually be a reconfiguration of the political spectrum that will see the emergence of two new groups, closer to the center, led by those who think "continentally." A good many of them will have been junior members of the old Communist Party.

# ALBANIA: A FIRST GLIMPSE

(MEMORANDUM TO THE BOARD OF TRUSTEES, NOVEMBER 1992)

### BACKGROUND

I visited Albania on November 2-5, with Helsinki Watch Executive Director Jeri Laber, on a mission to assess the status of human rights in Albania. We met with President Sali Berisha, Prime Minister Aleksander Meksi, Justice Minister Kudret Cela, and Public Order Minister Bashkim Kopliku. We also met with Gramoz Pashko, now a leader of the principal opposition party, who had been Prime Minister of the transitional coalition government. We spoke with the wife of former dictator Enver Hoxha in the Tirana Prison and with former President Ramiz Alia, who is under house arrest. We also met with leaders of the Albanian Helsinki Watch Committee, the Association of Former Political Prisoners, and the Union for Human Rights.

Albania is situated between Serbia and Greece, and is slightly larger than Massachusetts. It has a population of about 3.3 million, 70 percent of whom are Sunni Muslim, 20 percent Eastern Orthodox, and 10 percent Roman Catholic. Occupied by the Turks since 1444, Albania gained its independence in 1912-1913 but had no real central government until 1925, when Ahmed Beg Zog, who declared himself king in 1928, became the leader. The Italians controlled Albania from 1939 to 1943, when the Germans took over. At the end of the war Enver Hoxha set up a Soviet-style republic which evolved into one of the most repressive dictatorships in Europe. Hoxha ruled until his death in 1985, when Ramiz Alia succeeded him and governed until March of this year. Student demonstrations in 1990 forced Alia to call elections in March 1991. The resulting coalition with the Democratic Party, ruled until December 1991, when the Democrats withdrew. The elections of March 1992 yielded a strong Democratic Party majority, and Alia resigned to be replaced by the head of the Democratic Party, a 47-year-old cardiologist named Sali Berisha.

Hoxha's regime was the harshest in Eastern Europe, more awful than Ceausescu's Romania. While sources vary, the Association of Former Political Prisoners, formed in December 1990, estimates that about 30,000 people were political prisoners between 1945 and the present; 2,500 to 5,000 more were "disappeared." Another 70,000 suffered Soviet gulag-style internal exile, and as many as 500,000 were "persecuted people," essentially shunned and denied good jobs and education.

The primitive state of Albania becomes apparent as soon as one lands on the bumpy runway at Tirana Airport. The airport scene, from the cattle grazing at the end of the runway to the chaotic struggle outside the terminal, is reminiscent of landing strips in Africa. But the customs operation is closer to the Soviet model: it took us an hour to clear formalities. The complete absence of maps further recalled the Soviet Union in the old days.

Albania is the least economically developed country in the region. There are few factories, little export trade, scant numbers of automobiles, shortages of just about all staples from sugar to soap. Unemployment is estimated to be 50 percent, the annual inflation rate 500 percent, the average monthly wage $10 (U.S). Thus the new government has less of an economic base to work with than any other regime in the region. We were told that 80 percent of the factories no longer operate and that Albania survives solely on foreign aid. Indeed, the road between the capital of Tirana (population 242,000) and Durres (population 84,000) on the Adriatic Sea is filled with convoys of Italian army trucks bringing in food.

Situated among mountains, the capital itself is not without some beauty. Tirana's central core was laid out with a certain grand style by the Italians in the 1930s. The principal hotel, the Hotel Dajti, was built to a high standard, although now, like all other major buildings, it is in sad disrepair, lacking even hot water.

## The Political Lineup

The March 1992 elections gave the Democratic Party 92 of the 140 seats in Parliament; the former Communists, now called Socialists, came in second (38), followed by the Social Democrats (7), the Union for Human Rights (2), and the Republicans (1). A subsequent local election in June yielded a much closer division at the municipal level. The key to Sali Berisha's power has been his alliance with former political prisoners and others who suffered under the Hoxha regime.

Since the March election, the Democratic Party has split. A new party called the Democratic Alliance, was formed by intellectuals and professionals who constituted the more progressive wing of the Democratic Party. The Democratic Party is something akin to the Dark Blue in Bulgaria—in favor of rapid movement to a free market and relatively tough on the decommunization issue—whereas the Democratic Alliance is closer to the Light Blue in advocating a more gradual transition with a social safety net. The Democratic Alliance is trying to fill the vacant center of the Albanian political spectrum, while the Socialists have staked out the left with a greater concern for social issues and greater skepticism about the virtues of a completely free market economy.

Political life in Albania is less well developed than elsewhere in the region because the suppression of dissent has been so complete and because the transition to democracy came about 2 years after the revolutions of 1989 in Eastern Europe. Personalities rather than well-etched policy differences account for the political divisions and, in particular, the split within the Democratic Party.

The Berisha government is aware of international standards on human rights and has pledged to meet them. But the opposition portrays Berisha as a potential new dictator. Despite certain disturbing issues and incidents described below, I am inclined to give the new government the benefit of the doubt. Still, it will be important to follow these critical issues over the coming months, and remind the Berisha government that its actions are being closely watched.

## Former Political Prisoners

The most compelling issue that confronted us was the plight of the former political prisoners. No one could fix with precision the number of former political prisoners still living. A conservative estimate suggests that the number of people in jail for political reasons, released since 1990, will exceed 10,000.

On October 1, 1991 Parliament passed the Law on the Innocence Amnesty and Rehabilitation of Persons Punished and Persecuted which applies to 15 to 20 percent of the former prisoners—those who were sentenced under Articles 53, 55, and 57 of the penal code for creating "agitation and propaganda," trying to cross the border illegally, or engaging in antigovernment activity. Another proposed law deals with the remaining 80 percent of the prisoners—those sentenced as war criminals or spies. The law already passed does the following for the former political prisoners:

- Clears their records and restores all their citizenship rights
- Grants pension rights
- Restores property
- Allocates money for jobs, housing, and education
- Gives their children access to scarce places in higher education without examinations
- Gives compensation for years in prison

Given the widespread poverty in Albania, it would not be surprising if many people, self-described as political prisoners, stepped forward to claim these benefits. President Berisha sees an urgent need for a definition of what constitutes a former political prisoner and then a process for judging who meets the definition. But for the moment the government is hard-pressed to implement those provisions of the Rehabilitation Act which cost money, and its promises are largely unfulfilled. President Berisha admits that his government has done little to provide adequate housing but quickly points out that housing is a problem for the general population as well. He took some pride in the fact that the many children of former political prisoners had been admitted to the university system this fall on a preferential basis.

We visited the V. I. Lenin School in Tirana, a party school under the old regime, where perhaps 1,000 former political prisoners are living. The quarters are cramped—nine people from three families living in a 12' x 18' room— and lack cooking or private bath facilities. Most of the residents are unemployed. Several women said that they sold their blood in order to support their families. We heard awful stories of families banished, for example, because a 10-year-old child scuffled with a police officer over 25 years ago.

The residents of the Lenin School knew nothing about the Association of Political Prisoners, felt they had no avenue to express their grievances, and appeared isolated, frustrated, and without much hope. They indicated deep disappointment with the Berisha government, which had been elected with strong support from the former political prisoners.

We then went to the seaport town of Durres, where conditions were worse. Here too we heard moving stories of broken lives and families, tales of imprisonment for minor offenses hard to remember in the distant past, and vivid accounts of the present hard life of unemployment, subsistence rations, and horrible accommodations. We saw families living in changing rooms in cabanas along the beach, small rooms with no natural light or heat. No cooking facilities were available, and bathroom facilities were primitive. To our astonishment, we heard that the government is trying to collect rent for these meager quarters—a move sharply resisted by the former political prisoners.

Clearly the plight of the former political prisoners, the good intentions of the government notwithstanding, is desperate and not likely to improve, given the general condition of the country. One wonders how those living in unheated changing rooms will survive the winter.

## THE CONSTITUTION

The Albanian constitution is in the process of being stitched together from parts already enacted. Like other countries in the region, Albania wants to conform to international standards in order to have access to international aid and the European Community. Already in place is a new constitutional court modeled, as are other aspects of the legal system, along Italian lines. It is midway between the Hungarian model of a very strong constitutional court and the Bulgarian weaker form. The court can review legislative action on its own initiative but may not intervene in the legislative deliberations, as the Hungarian court can. Votes and legal opinions of the nine justices are public. Five of the judges are appointed by Parliament, four by the President. The court has not yet issued enough rulings to be a clear player in the governance of Albania or part of our evolving "checks and balances" system, as is the case with the constitutional courts in Hungary and Bulgaria. Parts of the constitution dealing with criminal codes have been passed, including provisions governing access to a lawyer when arrested, standards for length of pretrial detention and detention without being charged, and the role of the prosecutor's office in conducting investigations (rather than the police). Issues not so far addressed are freedom of the press, religion, assembly, and speech.

We did not hear significant concerns raised about the constitution other than from members of the independent press who felt unconsulted about the evolution of the draft press law. However, the constitution-making process should be closely followed in the months ahead.

## THE LEGAL SYSTEM

By all accounts the legal system moves slowly. This should be no surprise, since the absence of an independent judiciary during the Hoxha regime has left an acute shortage of qualified legal personnel. The most venal members of the old system have been discharged. By his own account, the new

Deputy General Prosecutor has fired about half the staff he inherited. As a result, he must still delegate investigations to the police, with all the potential for abuse that delegation entails. The lack of basic equipment such as typewriters, copying machines, and office supplies, combined with poor telephone communication throughout the country, slows the work of the prosecutor's office, which is heavily burdened by cases resulting from the crackdown on ordinary crime. Investigations are taking many months, and there is a backlog of several hundred prisoners awaiting charges and trials. But this seems to me to be a product of circumstance and not a reflection of insensitivity to the rights of prisoners.

We took an interest in the cases of eighteen former high-ranking officials. They are known as the Blockmen, because they lived in an exclusive enclave in Tirana walled off from ordinary citizens. Five are in jail, seven under house arrest, and six free but required to report daily. They are so far accused only of economic crimes, but several are being investigated for genocide and are likely to face more serious charges.

We received entreaties from the spouses of several of the Blockmen who said their husbands were sick and held under inhumane conditions. The only prisoner we saw was the wife of former dictator Enver Hoxha. Her cell in Tirana Prison was clean, freshly painted, and unfurnished. She greeted us from a mattress on the floor as if we were guests in the presidential mansion. Her stoic presence was remarkable. She began our interview with a long discourse on American-Albanian friendship under her husband, recounted her role in moving Albania toward democracy, and expressed utter surprise that she should be in jail. She had no complaints about her treatment in prison, but was bitter about the length of her pretrial deliberations, now nearly a year. It seemed to me that she actually believed herself a victim and had reconstructed the history of her life in a way that denied all the ugly realities of which she had been an integral part. She called the trial a political trial and claimed that she had broken no laws—indeed, was not a member of the government. She recounted difficulty in securing proper legal defense and complained about isolation from and discrimination against her family.

Our encounter with former President Ramiz Alia was more revealing. It took us a half an hour to pass formalities of the guards around his daughter's flat, but once inside we saw by far the best quarters in Albania. The apartment was large and nicely furnished. Alia was energetic, even cheerful, his conversation lively. Working from prepared notes, he spun a story of Alia, the transitional Democrat who gradually freed himself from the conservative forces around Hoxha to move toward free democratic elections. He reported a spirited critique of the Berisha government: runaway inflation, high unemployment, large-scale emigration. He said that Berisha had dismantled the old system too quickly, without a plan for the future. In his view, Berisha was not a Democrat, had a monopoly of power, and was practicing the politics of revenge. He reported specific examples of mass dismissals of government officials for political reasons and the use of the Commission on State Control to harass the opposition through surprise audits. He suggested that the result of the July 26 local elections, in which the Socialists scored a comeback, was evidence of growing disaffection with the Democratic Party and predicted that it would be voted out of office.

All this, Alia claimed, set the context for his own indictment, which in his view was purely political. He is charged with stealing state property because, in 1976, he signed a document outlining the perks to which high government leaders were entitled. He claimed that he himself had not benefited personally from government service: he had no property, no bank account (domestic or abroad), no valuable assets other than the few paintings he pointed to on the wall. When he resigned voluntarily, after his party lost the March 1992 election, he was promised decent treatment, a promise he now believes to be broken.

I asked him what mistakes he thought he had made. He replied that he misjudged the temper of the times. Until 1990, he thought the Chinese model of economic reform preceding political reform would work for Albania. He believed the market economy could work in a Communist framework and that gradual reform rather than shock therapy was the way to go. In retrospect, he now realizes that political reform had to accompany economic reform.

In an effort to puncture his self-serving story, I recounted the statistics of political prisoners, internal exiles, and persecuted people and asked if they were correct. To my surprise, he conceded the abuses but corrected only the numbers which he said were much too high. He claimed that he had diminished the abuses as quickly as possible.

Mrs. Hoxha, Alia, and the Blockmen pose a problem for the new government not unlike that faced by Zhivkov in Bulgaria or Honecker in East Germany. It seems unsatisfying to try them on economic crimes, yet the basis in law for charges on the more fundamental abuses is complicated. It seems likely they will be tried for these economic crimes and will be sent to prison. Our concern was solely that they receive due process, adequate legal counsel, a fair and speedy trial, and humane treatment in prison. The investigations and trials are proceeding slowly and should be monitored carefully.

## Harassment of the Opposition

Maksim Haxhia is a 34-year-old former Vice Dean of the Law Faculty at Tirana University, specializing in criminal law. Berisha appointed him as General Prosecutor (Attorney General) in March and, by all accounts, for 4 months he tried to reform the criminal justice system. Parliament removed him from office on September 17, on the grounds that he falsified a document appointing a deputy prosecutor in the Vlore district.

Opinions differ about why he was dismissed. Most agree that the charge of falsifying a document is a technical pretext, not the real reason. The government says he was incompetent—much too slow in prosecuting the backlog of prisoners arrested in a crackdown on ordinary crimes over the summer. There is no doubt that the legal system moves slowly, but sympathetic observers say that is the price of trying to give people fair trials through a system in the process of rebuilding.

There were a few celebrated issues through which Haxhia angered the Berisha government: he opposed a parliamentary law giving the police the right to search houses without a warrant in pursuit of guns; he refused to prosecute the crew of a ship which was diverted to Italy; he declined to arrest the editor of the independent paper *Koha Jone* for printing an antigovernment piece; he opposed removing immunity from a young Socialist deputy accused of fomenting labor unrest; and he challenged police for using excessive force in the crackdown on crime. Haxhia and his allies in the Democratic Alliance see his dismissal as a sign that the Berisha government does not want an independent judiciary and is not fully committed to democratic practices.

Haxhia also claims he is being harassed: he says that he is under constant surveillance, his house is bugged, his phone is disconnected, and his child has been threatened with harm. He has been barred from returning to the university and is not allowed to travel.

Harassment of the opposition goes beyond Haxhia. Former Prime Minister Pashko says his brother and sister were fired from their jobs and his daughter was brutally raped. The Commission on State Control is being used to audit the opposition and suggest financial improprieties. For example, the commission recently investigated the distribution of relief in Pashko's district and found that 1,000 pairs of shoes from a Swedish shipment of 8,000 were missing—a discovery which has led to innuendos of corruption.

Another leader of the Democratic Alliance, and a former political prisoner, is now a lawyer in Tirana specializing in defending people harassed by the government. He detailed four current cases of harassment. Two prominent ones involved the director of the Tirana Cultural Center, who has been accused of financial irregularities, and a young Socialist member of Parliament who is charged with fomenting labor unrest. We talked to three of the four accused officials and with their defense lawyers, who seemed quite solid. Time did not permit a full investigation of these and other cases, but my instincts are with the accused. The cases echo a pattern seen elsewhere in the region: the use of legal technicalities to remove opponents of the government from the political stage.

I do not conclude from these examples that the Berisha government is heading toward a new dictatorship or that the President himself is masterminding an unethical assault on his political rivals. The political situation is so fluid, the political, judicial, and economic systems in such disarray, the danger for social disintegration so real, the democratic culture so thin, that mistakes and excesses are to be expected. It is important, I think, to spotlight such episodes as a reminder to the government that outsiders are watching. But I resist coming to a firm negative conclusion about the motivation and prospects for the new government.

## Decommunization

The decommunization process is not yet under way in Albania and will present another opportunity for abuse. The Sigurimi (secret police) files have not been sealed or properly secured. Even the Prime Minister admits they have been tampered with. Apparently an interagency task force is now sampling the files while Parliament is drafting a law which would open the files of leading political figures—members of Parliament and government ministers. The Prime Minister promised to show Helsinki Watch a draft of the proposed law. He also expressed severe doubts about the lustration process under way in Czechoslovakia and Germany. Both he and President Berisha want to avoid a "reign of terror" unleashed by the files and are searching for a formula which would balance the protection of the innocent with the public's desire to keep former high-ranking Communists and informers from sensitive positions.

## The Press

The condition of the press seems similar to that in other countries of the region: the print media are relatively free;

television and radio are controlled by the government. We heard complaints of mass firings of staff at the radio and TV stations but did not have time to investigate. With the exception of the intimidation of the editor of *Koha Jone*, we heard no concrete charges of interference with the print media. The absence of printing presses and paper, however, limits the number of independent papers. Thus the press is much less well developed in Albania than it is in other countries in the region. Aside from *Koha Jone*, which is independent, and a small private issue called *Intervista*, the major print media are all associated with political parties: *Rilindja Demokratike* (Democratic Party), *Zeri I Popullit* (Socialist Party), *Alternativa SD* (Social Democratic Party), and *Republika* (Republican Party).

## Ethnic Tensions

The ethnic tensions that afflict so many countries in the region seem not as problematic in Albania, which is, by comparison, fairly homogeneous. We heard no reports of anti-Semitism (there are only 2,000 Jews in Albania) or of violence against the Gypsies (number in Albania unknown). The largest minority is the Greeks, concentrated in the south (estimated at 50,000 by Tirana and 400,000 by Athens), but there appears to be little tension among ordinary citizens.

The Greek party, Omonia, was not allowed to compete in the 1992 election because of a ban on parties based on ethnicity. But the Greeks worked through a surrogate party, the Union for Human Rights (UHR), and won two parliamentary seats. We met with leaders of the party, who feel that the election commission, by disallowing some number of party members in several districts, cost the UHR about five seats in Parliament. The Greeks want Greek language schools in areas where there is a significant Greek population—a demand common to ethnic minorities throughout the region. They also want protection of their cultural autonomy guaranteed by the new constitution.

## The Current Regime

President Sali Berisha is an impressive, charismatic figure: charming, smart, politically skillful, impatient, very direct. Berisha, who was a member of the Communist Party, has put together a broad, but not tightly knit, ruling party. He was candid about his country's problems—a judicial system that still does not work properly, the desperate plight of political prisoners, a weak economy, the lack of a democratic culture. Yet he seemed hopeful about what he could accomplish and tough enough to hold onto power. I believe he understands that Albania must be a genuine democracy, but he is also pragmatic enough to use undemocratic means when necessary to get his way. He is a transitional figure, aware of the course of history, not unsympathetic to a market economy and democratic state, but in style something of the old school.

I was particularly taken with his analysis of the Serbian crackdown of Albanians in Kosovo. He described a conflict with Serbia as "unavoidable" unless the West intervened promptly and strongly. He expects Serbian President Slobodan Milosevic to move his ethnic cleansing campaign to Kosovo as soon as Serbia ties down Bosnia. And after Kosovo, he assumes Milosevic will engage Macedonia. Berisha believes a conflict over Kosovo and Macedonia will lead to a broader Balkan war.

## Conclusion

We are told that Albania lives on foreign aid, an assertion given graphic evidence by the caravans of Italian army trucks, laden with food, that line the road from the port of Durres to Tirana. The country is so broken and desperate that it seems impossible for it to survive without massive foreign assistance. A war with Serbia over Kosovo would result in a flood of refugees, who would sharply intensify the problem.

Yet one has to admire the resilience of the human spirit and the strength that freedom confers on even a ruined society. It is too early to offer predictions about the fate of Albania and much depends on the competence and restraint of the Berisha government. It will be a desperately hard winter, especially for those living in unheated cabanas. But Albania has some advantages which give it a chance: a relatively homogeneous population so far free of ethnic tensions, the absence of extreme political factions, a good location and natural beauty, and a willingness to learn from the mistakes of other countries in the region. The critical questions are two: Will the West help financially, soon and on a sufficient scale? Will the West contain the Serbian ethnic cleansing campaign?

# LAST TRIP TO CZECHOSLOVAKIA/UPDATE ON HUNGARY

(MEMORANDUM TO THE BOARD OF TRUSTEES, DECEMBER 1992)

### Background

My trip to Czechoslovakia in early November centered on Bratislava, the capital of Slovakia, and Prague, soon to be the capital of the Czech Republic. The two cities are a study in contrast. Bratislava, just an hour's train ride from Vienna, is still a provincial capital—touched only lightly by the opening to the West—in which the depression of totalitarian rule lingers. While an attractive "old town" remains to be renovated, the Communist central planning process moved the heart of residential life to a monolithic slab of high-rise apartments across the Danube. Unattractive Stalinist government buildings together with an occasional, ugly modern structure make the central city an all too familiar reminder of Soviet influence.

By contrast, Prague has a grandeur and energy which washes away memories of 40 years of Communist domination. Indeed, some 35 to 40 million tourists came to Prague in 1992—100,000 a day in high season—making it second only to Vienna as the most visited city in Central Europe. Wenceslas Square (actually, a grand boulevard) epitomizes Prague's post-Communist evolution. When I last was in the square (October 28, 1989), it was the site of a powerful demonstration which, although broken up by the military, ignited the "velvet revolution." Now, by night, it could be any central district in Europe: elegant restaurants, lively jazz clubs, hordes of tourists, stylish shops, and very open solicitations by practitioners of the world's oldest profession.

The contrasting impressions created by these two cities reveal something about the condition of the two parts of Czechoslovakia which are to be independent countries as of January 1, 1993. Unemployment is down to 3 percent in the Czech Republic, while it hovers at 15 to 20 percent in Slovakia. Privatization proceeds apace in the Czech Republic, while political resistance retards progress in Slovakia. Local units of government are starting ambitious public works programs in the Czech lands, while little infrastructure investment is evident in Slovakia. Human rights seem relatively secure in the Czech lands, while there are questions about them in Slovakia.

Many Western observers found it hard to believe that Czechoslovakia would really fall into two parts, but it has happened. Different histories, different economic perspectives, different patterns of labor and industrial development, and, perhaps most important, a deep sense of discrimination among ordinary citizens in Slovakia all contributed to the division which now has an air of inevitability.

It is important to note that Slovakian leaders view the characterization of contrasts I just offered as the product of Czech propaganda, reinforced by a lazy Western press unwilling to venture out of luxury hotels in Prague to confront the reality of Slovakia. Minister of Culture Dusan Slobodnik, a close protégé of Slovakian Prime Minister Vladimir Meciar, showered us with examples of alleged discrimination: Slovakia, which held one-third of the population of the Republic of Czechoslovakia, had access to only 5 percent of international loans to Czechoslovakia. "We were economically repressed," Slobodnik said. "Of the four high-speed rail lines being planned, none would serve Slovakia. The main gas line from Russia falls 72 percent in Slovakia, but Slovakia receives only 10 percent of the rent." Other examples came like a torrent of anger and deprivation.

Accounts differ about where the blame for the breakup rests. Journalist Jan Urban, once a close colleague of Vaclav Havel, former President of Czechoslovakia, concedes unfair treatment of Slovakia and sees monumental insensitivity starting with Havel himself, who traveled abroad to world acclaim months before visiting Bratislava. Some see Meciar as the culprit, playing the nationalist card to advance his personal political fortunes. Others credit Czech Prime Minister Vaclav Klaus with a Machiavellian masterstroke. In their view, Klaus all along wanted to shed Slovakia because its relative poverty placed a drag on the Czech economy and its provincial representatives in Parliament constituted a political barrier to building a modern state. While publicly opposing the split, Klaus presented Meciar with unyielding economic demands which forced Meciar to become the agent of dissolution.

No doubt the truth lies somewhere in between, is laced with personal and political miscalculations, and is a mix of economic realities and regional chauvinism. I very much doubt that what now seems preordained was inevitable. But no matter. It is going to happen and is widely accepted by ordinary people as already having occurred. Thus this report continues in two quite separate sections, followed by an update on Hungary.

## The Republic of Slovakia

I joined Jeri Laber, executive director of Helsinki Watch, for a portion of her trip to Bratislava which was designed "to get a feel" for the human rights situation in a country about to be independent. Prime Minister Meciar was out of the country, but we did meet with his Minister of Culture, Dusan Slobodnik. We also met with Jan Carnogursky, Meciar's chief rival and the former Prime Minister (defeated in the June 1992 elections); the Rector of Trnava University, whom the government is trying to fire; an author under pressure from the government; the Deputy Director of the National Radio Station; and U.S. Consul Paul Hacker.

### The Meciar Regime

The June elections, which saw an 80 percent turnout, gave Vladimir Meciar's Movement for a Democratic Slovakia 49 percent of the Parliament: 18 percent went to the Democratic Left (former Communists); 11 percent to the Christian Democratic Union (CDU), the principal democratic opposition; 11 percent to the Slovak National Party; and 6-7 percent to the Hungarian parties. The CDU lost ground for not having stood up to the Czech Republic, and Meciar was elected because he promised a tougher stand.

Meciar is described as smart, tough, complex, sensitive to criticism, and vindictive against his political opponents. Some say that virtually the whole Meciar government is made up of ex-Communists, but U.S. Consul Hacker estimates that about half the current ministers held high positions prior to 1989.

Meciar is not in an enviable position. His margin of control is slim and his coalition loose. Former Prime Minister Carnogursky predicts a split in the ruling party in 1993 and a gradual realignment of the political spectrum along Western European lines. He believes that the economic and social problems are serious and that Meciar has no positive program to deal with them. My own guess is that the difficulties facing an independent Slovakia will result in an inflammation of anti-Czech feeling, since the plight of Slovakia will be blamed on Czech "economic repression."

Economic hard times will also fuel the search for external enemies, with Hungary as the natural target. Meciar has already made provocative attacks on Hungarian members of Parliament; a recent fracas over a soccer game with Hungary has been exploited by the media in both countries; the Hungarian minority in Slovakia is fearful of repression; and there is the squabble over the Gabcikovo Dam on the Danube in Slovakia, which Hungary claims has a negative environmental impact on its land.

HUMAN RIGHTS

Dusan Slobodnik pushes all the right rhetorical buttons when he speaks about human rights, promising that Slovakia will adhere to the same or higher standards as the Czech Republic. Freedom of the press is guaranteed in the Slovak constitution, and, according to Slobodnik, even though 70 percent of the press is opposed to the government, no reprisals have been taken. There is no far-right party in the Slovak Parliament, as there is in the Czech Parliament. No race- or ethnic-related deaths have occurred in Slovakia, while eleven such deaths occurred in the Czech lands last year. Slovakia will allow dual citizenship for Czechs who continue to live in Slovakia, while Slobodnik expects that the Czech constitution will make Slovaks living in the Czech Republic foreigners. He says Slovakia will allow Gypsies to become citizens, while the Czech constitution will not. He claims that Slovakia will meet all international standards of human rights.

The test of these pronouncments is yet to come—because, as of our visit, the federal government of Czechoslovakia still guaranteed human rights in Slovakia. But warning signs are already evident. The most visible symbolic issue is the Meciar government's removal of the Television Council and its dismissal of the Director of Television News Programming. The opposition alleges that this is a naked attempt to control the television and make it responsive to the Meciar government.

Slobodnik counters that the old Television Council failed to function, and the Director of Television News was dismissed, by legal means, for incompetence. The new Television Council will be made up of nine independent intellectuals chosen by Parliament; more channels will be created; and the new TV director, already selected, is not a member of Meciar's party.

I do not find Slobodnik's version persuasive. Rather, it fits a new pattern in the region in which technical reasons and bureaucratic maneuvers are used to silence or marginalize opposition. Upon close inspection, we learned that the old Television Council failed to function because Meciar ordered his supporters on the council to resign in order to give him a pretext to declare it nonfunctional and replace it. Also suspicious is the fact that the Director of Television News Programming, who had refused to give Meciar a weekly slot on television, was fired one day before the new Slovakian constitution took effect (October 1, 1992)—an event that would have made his removal more difficult.

Our meeting with the Deputy Director of Slovak Radio,

Michael Berko, did not reveal a similar pattern of control or interference at the radio station. According to Berko, Slobodnik had made efforts to influence the news but did not resort to strong-arm tactics when his efforts were rebuffed. Apparently the radio, which the government saw as a less critical means of communication, developed its independence gradually over a 5-year period. By contrast, television attempted to achieve its independence very quickly, a move that drew Meciar's attention and intervention.

We heard no evidence of direct interference with the independent print media, but the government has created financial hardships by "legally" preventing privatization of at least one opposition newspaper and of the Danubia publishing house. Lubomir Feldek, a translator and writer of children's books, claimed that efforts to harass independent writers and journalists were creating a "chilling effect." He cited Slobodnik's plan to sue the president of the Pen Club for allegedly saying bad things about Slovakia in an article published abroad. The Pen Club membership, heavily weighted with pre-1989 dissidents, is under attack as anti-Slovakian. And the director of a theater started under the Carnogursky government has been fired because of a technical flaw in his contract.

Then there is Feldek's own curious case. He is being sued for libel for an article alleging that Slobodnik was involved with fascists during the war. Although we heard about this case from both parties and from independent observers, I find it difficult to sort out the merits of the issue. My instinct is that Feldek went overboard in his attacks on Slobodnik. But I question the wisdom of Slobodnik's vindictive pursuit of Feldek, which, intended or not, does frighten writers and intellectuals. Meciar also has personally brought several libel cases.

The most serious evidence that the government seeks to curtail independent thought is the case of Trnava University. Bevis Longstreth (representing the Charter 77 Foundation in New York), Jeri Laber, and I met with Rector Anton Hajduk, whom Slobodnik (then Education Minister) had sought to fire. The grounds were technical: under Czechoslovakian law, rectors must be elected by the University Senate and hold a professorship. Anton Hajduk, a noted astronomer, was Secretary of the Czechoslovakian Academy of Science, but was not a professor. And, since Trnava University was new, it had not organized a senate.

These technical problems could have been corrected. But the Meciar government has been deeply suspicious of Trnava University, which it sees as a haven for anti-Meciar intellectuals. No doubt Meciar also resented Hajduk's "midnight" appointment by Havel shortly before he resigned the federal presidency.

Slobodnik gave us an inaccurate, self-serving account of this episode. He claimed that Havel had acknowledged his mistake and that the current federal Prime Minister, Jan Strasky, supported the removal of Hajduk. Neither claim is accurate. We spoke to Havel, who said he had not known Hajduk was not a professor but went on to say that the problem could have been easily cured. (We are told Hajduk will be designated a professor at Charles University in Prague before January 1.) Havel said that he supported Hajduk and that Trnava, which is the only center of free thinking in Slovakia, should be protected. The University Senate, since constituted, has now endorsed Hajduk, and Prime Minister Strasky has issued a letter recognizing the legitimacy of the University Senate (and by implication, its endorsement of Hajduk).

As Education Minister, Slobodnik played rough. When Hajduk refused to be fired, Slobodnik had the locks changed on Hajduk's office doors and froze the university's accounts. But the city of Trnava, which owns the university's buildings, supports Hajduk and made it possible for him to reclaim his office. The faculty is now teaching for free, and foreign contributors defray operating expenses. I volunteered to file a protest on behalf of the Committee for International Academic Freedom, of which I am co-chair. The timing was crucial, since the Slovak Parliament was to meet on November 17 to decide whether to close the university. The letter of protest was credited with having helped persuade the Parliament to defer action, but the fate of the university still hangs in the balance. The government has apparently decided to do nothing more until it formally achieves independence on January 1, at which time I would expect another assault.

## The Czech Republic

The stories of four leaders (three of whom I met) yield an interesting collage of insights into political developments in Prague:

- Vaclav Havel, former President of Czechoslovakia
- Jiri Dienstbier, former Foreign Minister of Czechoslovakia
- Jiri Hajek, former Foreign Minister of Czechoslovakia under Alexander Dubcek
- Vaclav Klaus, Prime Minister of the Czech Republic

Klaus is clearly triumphant for the moment. His Civic Democratic Party (ODS) won 37 percent of the vote in the June 1992 election and rules with a coalition that includes the Civic Democratic Alliance (ODA) with 6-7 percent, the Christian Democratic Union with 10 percent, and the Catholic or Peoples Party. The other significant parties include the Communist Party (14 percent), the Social Democrats (12 percent), and the Liberal Social Union (8-10 percent). There is also a right-wing extremist Republican Party and a separatist Moravian Party. The old Civic Forum split three ways—ODS, ODA, and the Civic Movement (OH). The Civic Movement, which failed to meet the 5 percent threshold required for representation in Parliament, is Dienstbier's party and is made up of the former dissidents closest to Havel.

The Klaus coalition is stable but falls sixteen votes short of the two-thirds majority needed to effect constitutional reform and thus relies on the Social Democrats for help on some key issues. The opposition is not a formal coalition; but on some issues the Social Democrats, Liberal Social Union, and Communists vote together.

Klaus is clear about what he wants: rapid conversion to a free market. He believes the search for a third way is a quixotic exercise. The Dienstbier intellectuals, by contrast, still search, but their program lacks clarity and their political skills are not honed. Jiri Hajek is also searching for a third way, but his prewar notions about the good society make him an appealing anachronism, out of touch with the current economic and political realities.

We met Havel for lunch on Saturday at his favorite fish restaurant on the river, just below his private apartment.* He was dressed informally in a green sweatshirt from the University of British Columbia. Behind Havel, across the river, rose the Prague castle, seat of the federal government and Havel's former office. This poignant scene is emblematic of the curious turns of history.

Havel is the most complex and elusive of the group. He struck me as a deeply conflicted—even sad—man torn between his natural affinity for the purity of motives, evidenced by Dienstbier and his former colleagues, and a sense of unique obligation to use his influence for good by engaging the political process. "Societies generally turn away from dissidents," he told us, "because they hold a mirror to society and turn instead to people like themselves who lack courage." He recalled the experience of those released from concentration camps in Germany and Austria who were not embraced. He mused about Dienstbier's inability to convert his own popularity rating (70 percent) into votes for his party, which garnered only 2 percent. Havel recounted a recent conversation with Polish president Lech Walesa and Jacek Kuron at a party in Walesa's honor in Warsaw. Walesa lamented that the former dissidents were losing power to newcomers who were taking over the revolution.

---

*We were joined by Rita Klimova, former Czechoslovakian Ambassador to the United States, and Zdenek Urbanek, a distinguished translator. I met Urbanek several times in the late 1980s when he was under virtual house arrest. Then a man in his late seventies, he appeared sick and frail. I was pleased at the transformation brought about by freedom; on this visit he was full of energy, spoke in a firm voice, and looked 10 years younger.

It seemed to me that Havel had some ambivalence about running for President. He is being advised by former dissidents at home and abroad not to let himself be used as a human face for Klaus' economic policies. But I believe that he has already decided to seek the presidency, partially out of obligation and partially, I suspect, for personal reasons.

"All parties, except the Communists and the Republicans, want me as President," he told us, "but not purely for the love of me. I am prepared to become President. I cannot then conflict with Klaus, but I must remain faithful to my own views —that is the dilemma." When pressed for an example of an issue on which they differed, Havel offered the lustration process—favored by Klaus and opposed by him—but then dismissed it as "no longer topical." I suspect there are much more fundamental differences between the two—on the pace of privatization, for example—but Havel declined to be drawn out further on the divisions.

## THE NEW CONSTITUTION

Perhaps to avoid the sensitive issue of the presidency, Havel shifted the conversation to an analysis of the proposed constitution of the new Czech Republic.

Havel said there are four contentious issues:

1. Should there be a Senate and, if so, what should be its powers?
2. What are the right administrative subunits?
3. Should the constitution have a bill of rights?
4. Should the President be elected directly by the people or by the Parliament?

On the last issue, Havel expressed pleasure at the strong powers contemplated for the President. He said he favored direct election for the first president of the Czech Republic and parliamentary election thereafter. If the Parliament failed five times to elect a President, the election would turn to the people.

With respect to a bill of rights, Havel favored leaving the

existing federal bill of rights in force outside the constitution. He fears that an attempt to incorporate an enumeration of rights in the new constitution would touch off a debate which would delay passage of the constitution.

Havel offered no comment on the Senate, or how the administrative subunits should be constructed, but Rita Klimova explained the importance of the administrative arrangements. The key question is whether to follow the German federal model, now less appealing because of the split with Slovakia. One approach would be a system of districts based on history and geography, but such a formula does not work perfectly. Bohemia, surrounded by mountains, does form a natural geographic entity. But thereafter, there is ambiguity: What are the boundaries of Moravia? Should Silesia be put together with Moravia? Klimova predicted that the ultimate compromise would result in three states with an unequal number of subdistricts: Bohemia with six to eight, Moravia with two, and Silesia as a single state. She said the key to the compromise was the allowance of a Moravian Diet with virtually no legislative power.

## Human Rights

When asked about the state of human rights, Havel responded that it would be wrong "to act on the premise that freedom has prevailed here and everything is fine. We still need Helsinki Watch." Our own sounding suggested some issues worth watching, although they do not match the scale of troubles in places like Albania, Romania, the former Soviet Union, and the former Yugoslavia.

## Lustration

The decommunization process in Czechoslovakia has been widely studied and criticized. On paper it is very thorough. In practice it has been damaging to many, including some leading political figures. But one gets the impression it is running out of steam, no longer pursued with intensity.

Havel said lustration is no longer topical. Dienstbier observed that it "has done its dirty deed by destroying some opponents of the government," but also saw it as a past issue. "There is a difference between the formal law and reality," Dienstbier reported. He said that very little had been accomplished by lustration: the former Communists were still in power in the countryside. "Even in Prague," he added, "we are now approaching a time when revolutionary fervor is over and all will be forgiven as everyone will be treated equally."

Some of the members of the Czech Helsinki Committee took a different view. Journalist Jan Stern said, "Lustration is a moral and legal morass. A list of 150,000 compromised people has been circulated. Shortly after our visit, the Constitutional Court ruled on a challenge to the lustration law eliminating Category C people (those listed as contacts or potential accomplices) from the lustration process. The court did not take issue with the law as a whole; but if the federal law is to continue after January 1 it would have to be reenacted by each of the new states. The Slovak government has made it clear that lustration (which was never really implemented) will end in Slovakia on January 1, 1993. Some observers told us it was also unlikely that the Czech Parliament would reenact the law, although some less severe version is possible.

The Criminal Justice System

We heard familiar complaints about the criminal justice system in general: too few judges and defense lawyers, which means unacceptably long pretrial detention. We also heard about the rise of ordinary crime and the advent of armed private police forces not subject to public control. It seems to me these are problems of transition, not principle—problems which need to be monitored nonetheless.

Treatment of Minorities

Havel strongly urged Helsinki Watch to follow the plight of the Gypsies, who received rough treatment from "skinheads." The implication was that the Klaus government was not vigorous enough in protecting the rights of minorities, a view also held by a new citizens' group called Tolerance.

We attended a meeting of Tolerance, which was held at Rita

Klimova's house and attended by a dozen people. The group was formed to combat discrimination against minorities, especially the Gypsies and the Vietnamese. Some of its members had experienced "ethnic trauma" in the past. As a group, they have doubts about the division of the country, think of themselves as citizens of Czechoslovakia, and worry that Czechs and Slovaks caught in the other's country will experience discrimination. Many of the members had been part of Charter 77, now disbanded, and have channeled their concern for civic improvement to this new organization.

Tolerance was started in September 1992 and is governed by a board of seventeen, which includes Petr Pithart and other major figures from Charter 77. All through the region, not-for-profit organizations, so important to the construction of civil society, are springing up. There appears to be a conscious effort to follow the American (rather than Western European) experience, in which a lively independent sector is vital to checking the excesses of both the government and private enterprise. This should not be surprising given the deep skepticism about the role of government flowing from 40 years of totalitarian rule.

Tolerance has six specific projects:

1. It convenes dialogues among people from different groups, especially the Gypsies and Vietnamese.
2. It has created a "handbook" for third-grade students dealing with the issue of difference, especially across racial and ethnic lines. It also has created guidebooks for teachers about how to teach youngsters about human rights.
3. It sponsors sporting and cultural events which bring together young people from different backgrounds.
4. It operates a "big brother" and "big sister" program which pairs students who have felt racial or ethnic aggression with a counselor.
5. It offers counseling services to victims of aggression and discrimination.
6. It monitors the handling of racial and ethnic questions in the mass media.

Tolerance is also concerned with the refugee problem, as the number in camps grows and as a backlash is expected. The group expects an additional flood of refugees from Slovakia after the split, and is concerned that the government is not making adequate preparations for them.

I was struck by the contrast between this group and Czechoslovakia's formal Helsinki Watch Committee. It seemed to me that the Helsinki Committee was caught up in issues largely past; it was more concerned, for example, about the search for a third way for the political economy than about the problems of minorities, which was barely mentioned.

I emerged from Czechoslovakia believing that Helsinki Watch had work to do, but that the problems were not so urgent as to deflect us from our attention to the former Soviet Union; Yugoslavia, where there is violence; other countries like Albania and Romania, which are treading a more perilous course toward democracy; and Germany, where the internal violence against foreigners is serious and troubling.

## HUNGARY: A TROUBLED BUT BRIGHTER PROSPECT

I know less about Hungary than about other countries in the region because the New School's Democracy Seminar in Budapest predated my active involvement in Eastern and Central Europe. In addition, because the level of repression was relatively less there, Helsinki Watch has given less attention to Hungary. My colleague Andrew Arato has tutored me in those aspects of recent Hungarian history which have made Hungary an exceptional case in the region. It was part of the Austro-Hungarian Empire from 1867 to 1918, during which period it developed as a state with the rule of law and with a relatively modern civil, criminal, and administrative legal system. During that period, and again in the 1920s and briefly after World War II, Hungary had experience with parliamentary government, even though the franchise of the government was seriously limited.

The 1956 revolution, although suppressed, did win some space for the three democratic parties, which had ruled in coalition between 1945 and 1948 and spawned the revival of workers councils. The 1968 economic reform modified the top-down, command economy by decentralizing the state-owned sector, allowing a second economy in private services to develop and opening the economy to trade and loans from the West. Finally, perhaps as a consequence of all other factors, the government felt compelled in the 1980s to allow oppositional tendencies to develop.

Hungary is of interest to me because it has perhaps the best chance of any country in the region to make a smooth and relatively rapid transition to a free market economic system and a democratic civil society. Thus the travails it is experiencing—political instability, the rise of extremism, the reemergence of human rights concerns—are instructive about the prospects for other countries in the region, countries which face higher hurdles.

A walk down Vaci Street in the pedestrian zone of Budapest gave me the feel of any major Western European capital. The stores and shops have familiar names: Christian Dior, Estee Lauder, Marks and Spencer, the ever-present McDonalds golden arches, even the Hard Rock Café. A Reebok banner hangs across a side street, and human billboards advertising tropical topless bars are plentiful. An international trade center and the new, luxurious Kempinski Hotel have recently opened. One has a choice of London or Mercedes cabs at the stand at the end of Vaci Street. The volume of cars, the rush of pedestrian traffic, the energy of the nightlife—from the jazz clubs to the late-night casinos—stand in stark contrast to my gray images of the region just 2 years ago.

But all is not perfect. A warning in an English language paper reveals tension beneath the surface: "Foreign visitors, especially people of color, are warned to be careful on the streets because of a pattern of violence against foreigners."

According to Gabor Hamza, Professor of Roman Law at the University of Budapest and leader of the New School's Democracy Seminar, Hungarians are going through a process of scaling down their expectations about a smooth transition. In his view, the taxi driver strike in the fall of 1990 was a turning point that alerted the population to the reality that the movement to free markets and democracy would have its setbacks and disruptions. Unemployment is at 11 percent and is increasing, inflation is still at 20 to 25 percent and privatization moves at an uneven pace. The rise of extremism and political instability compound worries about the future.

THE POLITICAL SCENE

Hungary is governed by a coalition of three parties, which originally held 60 percent of the 386 seats in Parliament: the Hungarian Democratic Forum (MDF) led by Prime Minister Jozsef Antal, has 42 percent of the seats; the Small Holders Party (peasant party), 11 percent; and the Christian Democratic Peoples Party, 6 percent. The opposition groups are the Alliance for Free Democrats with 24 percent of the seats, the Alliance of Young Democrats with 6 percent, and the Hungarian Socialists with 9 percent. I gather the opposition groups do not function as a stable coalition because both the Free Democrats and the Young Democrats are skeptical of cooperating with the Socialists.

Hamza says that personalities more than deeply etched philosophical issues divide the parties, although he concedes that there is a legitimate debate over the means and timetable of privatization. The Alliance of Free Democrats favors faster privatization, with the state playing a less central role in the process. It also seeks more generous arrangements for foreign investment. The right wing of the MDF worries that Hungary is being bought up by foreigners and is quick to play the nationalist card, which contains a visible element of anti-Semitism.

Hungary, like other countries in the region that had an early, gradual, and peaceful transition in 1989-1990, has a constitution which is the product of compromise—an arrangement that makes governing difficult. The Hungarian system vests substantial executive power (Hamza estimates 95 percent) in the Prime Minister, who can appoint his Cabinet from outside the Parliament (with confirmation by the Parliament). An informal compromise between the MDF and the Free Democrats in 1990 has three components:

1. The President would be from the opposition.
2. Many important issues—for example, laws dealing with the media—would require a two-thirds margin in Parliament (recall that the ruling coalition has only 60 percent of the seats).
3. The opposition would be unable to fire the Prime Minister through a vote of no confidence unless it could replace him with a new one; Hungary has a "constructive no confidence" system.

The Hungarian constitution is brief and general, leaving important issues such as the scope of power of the President for later refinement. And, as in Bulgaria, that clarification will most likely come, not through the legislature, but through rulings by the Constitutional Court.

The President of Hungary is Arpad Goncz, a playwright who spent 7 years in prison (after narrowly escaping execution) for a leading role in the 1956 uprising. He was a member of the Free Democrats, but left the party upon his election as President by the Parliament. He is the focal point of current MDF pressure because he successfully blocked Antal's recent effort to fire the heads of state radio and television, in order to install officials more sympathetic to the government. At an anniversary commemoration of the 1956 uprising on October 23, Goncz was shouted down by skinheads and other extremists who (some say) were organized or at least not resisted by the government.

THE CONSTITUTIONAL COURT

As in other countries in the region, the Hungarian Constitutional Court is playing an immensely important role in the transition to democracy in the absence of a stable, multiparty system.

Hamza provided us with a brief history of the European-style constitutional court, which he says first appeared in Austria in the 1920s, next in Hungary and Germany after World War II, and then in France in 1958. More recent appearances in the region came with the Yugoslav constitution in 1974 and next Poland in the early 1980s. The Hungarian Constitutional Court, created in October 1989 by the new constitution, had its antecedents in a 1984 Council of Constitutional Law. The powers of the various constitutional courts vary from country to country. The Hungarian court is perhaps (with Portugal) the most powerful one in Europe, while the courts in Poland and Czechoslovakia are weak by comparison. The powers of the Bulgarian court, while new and still evolving, are likely to be in between the two extremes, and not much is known about the new court in Romania.

The members of the Hungarian court are elected by Parliament for 10 years, and its President is elected by the other members. According to Hamza, the President of the Constitutional Court is a competent jurist, as are all but three of the present members. The court presides over cases referred to it by the President or the government. In addition, ordinary citizens in Hungary have standing to bring cases to the court involving administrative acts—and there is currently a backlog of 10,000 cases. The court is a major player in the legislative process by virtue of its authority to challenge major legislative initiatives (those important issues requiring a two-thirds vote *before* they are passed by Parliament).

The Constitutional Court is probably the most important check on the party in power in Parliament. And until the powers of the presidency are clearly delineated, the court plays an important role both in building a system of checks and balances and in providing the most effective check on the power of the government.

Like Zhelev in Bulgaria, Goncz has asked the Constitutional Court to clarify his powers. For example, the court is now considering how to define the President's role as Commander in Chief: Does he have the right to impose a state of emergency? Can he appoint the leadership of the army? The court has already attempted to define the limitation within which the President can deny countersigning appointments and removals from office.

HUMAN RIGHTS ISSUES

I had not expected to find major human rights issues in Hungary and therefore did not allow sufficient time for investigation of leads given to me in a meeting with Ferenc Miszlivetz, a sociologist, one of the leaders of the New School's Democracy Seminar, and spokesman for a new group called the Democratic Charter. The Charter movement began in November 1991 as an adjunct of the opposition parties in an effort to rally popular support for them and to combat the rise of extremism. It was given real life when Prime Minister Antal fired the head of the Hungarian National Bank for being one of the original 150 signatories of the Democratic Charter. The publicity that followed brought forward 32,000 additional Charter signatories in little over 6 months. While Charter membership is presently centered in Budapest, chapters are starting in other cities. About 60 percent of the members are aligned with the three major parties (about evenly), and the balance are either independent or "party affiliation unknown."

The Charter movement is of some concern to the opposition parties, which do not want it to turn into a party itself, a goal which Miszlivetz says is not planned. However, Miszlivetz sees a role for the Charter in the 1994 elections by endorsing particular candidates. While the situation differs from the effort to launch a Democratic Center Alliance in Bulgaria, I see some similarities in the makeup of the Center and Charter memberships. And if the Bulgarian Center is kept from becoming a party, it may exercise a similar role in the next election by endorsing selected candidates. Both the Center and the Charter claim to have registered some 17 to 20 percent support in recent opinion polls.

The Democratic Charter appears to me to be a loosely organized movement of people concerned about the rise of extremism, the antidemocratic tendencies of the government, and the fragmented ineffectiveness of the opposition. It serves as a kind of conscience for the country, reminding the population of its highest aspirations for democracy. Its leaders believe the border between the center-right ruling coalition and the extreme right are permeable. That concern is best illustrated by a pamphlet circulated by Istvan Csurka in August 1992 warning that foreigners, especially Jews, were taking over Hungary and should be stopped. Csurka is Vice Chairman of the MDF and his pamphlet was not disavowed by Prime Minister Antal, even in the face of philantropist George Soros' public challenge for him to do so.

Leaders of the Charter believe that the government is harassing their effort to rally popular support. The Charter organized a silent demonstration on March 15 (a national holiday) as a show of concern about the direction of the country. The skinheads were granted a permit to hold a rally at the same center-city site, immediately before the Charter's demonstration. According to Miszlivetz, minimal security was provided and army trucks were spotted bringing in demonstrators. However, the skinhead rally attracted only a few hundred people; the Charter's demonstration was attended by more than 20,000 people and went off peacefully.

Charter leaders also allege that there was official complicity with the disruption of President Goncz's October 23 speech. Miszlivetz contends that Interior Ministry police and border guards in civilian dress helped the "skinheads" and "56ers" disrupt the President's speech.

The chilling effect on free speech and opposition carries into the media. Already discussed is the failed attempt to remove the director of Hungarian television. In addition, when an actor went on TV to read the speech which the President was prevented from giving, he was fired from his theater job. And the Prime Minister has stalled efforts to pass a new Media Act (a 1975 decree is still the law) which would guarantee a free press.

Among other signs of concern that Charter leaders asked Helsinki Watch to investigate are:

- Allegations that the police planted fascist literature in the headquarters of the Social Democratic Party to discredit it
- The existence of refugee camps for foreigners along the Romanian and Yugoslav borders, where conditions are poor and due process lacking
- Stories of beatings of black, Asian, and Arab students and diplomats in Budapest; such episodes have led to the creation of a student human rights organization called the Martin Luther King Society, which is dedicated to preventing violence against foreigners
- Mistreatment of the Gypsies

The last issue is particularly vexing. The pattern of violence against the Gypsies in Hungary resembles the situation in Bulgaria. Hamza estimates the Hungarian Gypsy population to be 300,000 to 600,000, only about one-third of whom are well integrated into Hungarian society. About one-third of all those unemployed in Hungary are Gypsies. Many of them live in the less well developed sections of eastern Hungary. I heard stories of pogroms against the Gypsies, with forces entering their villages and burning down their houses. Clashes with authority—for example, in Tova—often begin with a minor crime committed by a Gypsy which elicits a harsh police overreaction ("direct justice" by beatings). That in turn leads to mobilization of the wider Gypsy community and more serious clashes with police.

These fragments of concern do not add up to a major human rights problem in Hungary, especially given the ethnic wars happening elsewhere in the region. But I take seriously the concern of good people that antidemocratic tendencies exist and find expression in Hungary and should be watched. I was struck by the language used by Ferenc Miszlivetz and others to describe their suspicions of the government, language appropriated from the "bad old days." It is, I think, premature to suggest direct parallels between the Antal government and what went before it, or to predict a slide into a new abyss. But even relatively strong countries like Hungary need help and would benefit from external monitoring.

# TROUBLE IN THE CAUCASUS

(MEMORANDUM TO THE BOARD OF TRUSTEES, JULY 1993)

## BACKGROUND

I traveled for 17 days, June 17–July 3, in the former Soviet Union visiting Armenia, Georgia, Azerbaijan, Russia, and Ukraine. I was joined by Kurt Soderlund of the New School and Rachel Denber of Helsinki Watch. Both Soderlund and Denber assisted in preparing this report. Our mission focused on human rights abuses in the Caucasus and the prospects for the extension of the New School's Eastern and Central Europe program of educational reform.

We met with nearly 100 government officials, journalists, members of political oppositions, and scholars. Our trip coincided with some distressing events—the coup in Azerbaijan, the escalation of fighting in the Georgian province of Abkahazia, the new foreigner laws in Estonia that infuriated Russian President Boris Yeltsin and caused him to retaliate by cutting off gas supplies, and the tense negotiations between Russia and Ukraine over the future of the Black Sea fleet and control of Ukraine's nuclear arsenal.

The main focus of the trip was the chaos in the Caucasus arising from the clash between Armenia and Azerbaijan over Nagorno Karabakh along with the separatist movements in Georgia which have resulted in 15,000 deaths and over 600,000 refugees, and produced both economic ruin and political instability. Those problems provide fertile ground for human rights abuses.

## THE CAUCASUS

### ARMENIA

Armenia has a population of 3.4 million, 90 percent of whom are Armenian. It is slightly larger than the state of

Maryland and is totally landlocked by Georgia, Azerbaijan, Iran, and Turkey. Its main economic resource is agriculture. Armenians are Orthodox Christian, speak an Indo-European language, and have a unique alphabet. Armenia is an ancient civilization, having been founded in the sixth century B.C., but occupied over time by Persia, the Byzantine Empire, the Seljuk Turks and the Ottoman Empire. It was conquered by Russia in 1916, enjoyed a brief period of independence from 1920 to 1922, was incorporated into the Transcaucasian Soviet Socialist Republic in 1923, and was given the status of a union republic in 1936. It declared independence from the Soviet Union on September 23, 1990. It is a member of the Commonwealth of Independent States.

Georgia

Georgia has a population of nearly 5.5 million, is about the size of West Virginia, and borders the Black Sea, Turkey, Russia, and Azerbaijan. Its natural resources include coal and minerals, and its economic base includes wine and steel. About 66 percent of the population consists of Georgians, who are nominally Christian. The country also is home to several ethnic groups, two of which have their own autonomous regions: Abkahazia and Adzhariya. In addition, there are South Ossetians, Armenians, Azerbaijanis, and Meskhetian Turks. Georgians have lived in the Caucasus region since the Stone Age and the area was not consolidated into a formal state until the early eleventh Century. From 1220 on, the Mongols and others invaded the region and for three centuries, up to 1800, the Turks and Persians vied for control. Stability came in 1801 when Czar Alexander I brought Georgia into the Russian empire. Except for a brief period of independence (1918–1920), Georgia remained under Russian control, first as part of the Transcaucasian Soviet Socialist Republic (established in 1921) and as a union republic since 1936. It declared independence on April 9, 1991. It has not joined the Commonwealth of Independent States.

## AZERBAIJAN

Azerbaijan, about the size of the state of Maine, is the largest of the Caucasus nations with a population of just over 7 million, 83 percent of whom are Azerbaijani and 8 percent Russian.* It is economically the strongest of the Caucasus nations, principally because of its vast oil reserves and its machinery and equipment manufacturing concerns. It is also a leading producer of cotton, tobacco, grapes, and tea.

Azeris are nominally Shiite Muslims who speak a Turkish language. Over time, Azerbaijan has been under Mongol, Arab, Turkish, and Persian control until Russia and Persia split its territory in 1828. (Thus more than 10 million Azerbaijanis now live in northern Iran.) It had its own independent republic from 1918 to 1920, when the Red Army captured it and made it a Soviet republic. From 1922 to 1936 it was part of the Transcaucasian Soviet Socialist Republic and then became its own union republic. It declared independence on August 30, 1991. It is not a member of the Commonwealth of Independent States.

Stalin's penchant for mixing ethnic groups can be seen in the inclusion of the mountainous enclave of the autonomous Nagorno Karabakh region within Azerbaijan. Nagorno Karabakh had about a 75 percent Armenian population in 1988. Azerbaijan's second autonomous region, Nakhichevan, is separated from Azerbaijan by a strip of Armenian land, but it is overwhelmingly Azeri in its population.

## A TALE OF THREE CITIES

Traveling to and through the Caucasus was not easy and occasionally dangerous. Because of the Azerbaijan blockade, Armenia is virtually isolated, served only by a weekly charter flight from Paris, sporadic air service from Moscow, and a train from Tbilisi. We flew to Yerevan from Paris overnight,

---

*Before the conflict with Armenia over Nagorno Karabakh, Armenians constituted 5.4 percent of the total population

traveled to Tbilisi on an incredibly slow overnight train, and then braved the new Azerbaijan airline to get to Baku.

A trip across the three Caucasus capitals covers the distance one might travel going from Boston to Albany to Philadelphia. Yet the differences among Yerevan, Tbilisi, and Baku are striking.

YEREVAN

Yerevan, located in the shadow of Mt. Ararat, lacks physical beauty or distinctive architecture. The fleet of idle Aeroflot jets which line the runway at Yerevan Airport provides a clue to the hardship and isolation produced by the Azerbaijan blockade, which has made fuel scarce. While Armenia has converted its share of the Aeroflot fleet into its own national airline, fuel shortages have prevented the Armenian fleet from functioning independently, as is the case in Azerbaijan and Georgia. With flights down to one or two a day, the airport hardly functions at all. When our charter Aeroflot IL 86 arrived at 5:00 A.M., only one passport person was on duty. It took almost 3 hours to unload and inspect the baggage. No taxis were available and the one or two buses that came by were completely full. Fortunately, we had arranged transport to the city through the remnants of the once-proud Soviet Intourist Agency, which now barely functions.

The trip to the city revealed much about life in Yerevan. There were hardly any cars on the road at rush hour, and the lack of electricity meant no traffic lights. The absence of order stimulated a kind of free-for-all on the highway with no speed limits or rules of the road obeyed.

Life has been hard since the blockade. Automotive fuel is available only from tanker trucks which crash the blockade and set up shop at intersections. Power is limited to 2 or 3 hours a day, usually at unpredictable times. Despite its opulent pretensions, the new wing of the Hotel Armenia seems like a third-class hotel, often without running water. *Hot* running water was available only once during our stay. The city virtually shuts down at dark. From the balcony of the hotel we could watch the power move around the city by sections every 2 hours, illuminating a small part of the city each time.

The economy has virtually come to a halt because of the absence of fuel and raw materials. Fuel prices jumped seventyfold during 1992. Inflation raged at 900 percent in the final quarter of 1992, according to the most recent figures from the International Monetary Fund. Virtually the entire country has been reduced to the poverty level; since no one can buy goods, stores and cafés are closed and there is no nightlife. Paradoxically, food is widely available because Armenia has made good progress in privatizing its farm sector, which is very productive.

By all accounts, what we witnessed was mild compared with conditions in the winter, when the absence of heat, water, and electricity is paralyzing. The horror of the past winter and the dread of next winter is a depressant that hangs over the population—a recent public opinion survey revealed that 70 percent of the population would like to emigrate. We were told that death rates among newborn and the elderly are up, as are incidences of suicide and mental illness. The sense of isolation grows as international mail delivery has slowed to a trickle, travel for ordinary citizens become almost impossible, and the flow of outside visitors sharply reduced.

TBILSI

We experienced the difficulty of traveling as we tried to make our way to Tbilisi, normally a 4-hour drive from Yerevan. We could not enlist a car and driver because of the fuel shortage and because no Armenian driver wanted to risk the ride through southern Georgia, which is heavily populated by Azeris. Drivers fear robbery or even being taken hostage, a practice which has been increasing. Because there is no longer air service between Yerevan and Tbilisi, the train was the only alternative. Our train left Yerevan at 7:30 P.M. and took 12 hours to make its way to the Georgia border. This was just as well, since we had been told that the train was sometimes robbed in Georgia and thus preferred to cross through Georgian land in daylight. A 2-1/2-hour customs check to leave Armenia and the prospect of a similar ordeal at the Georgian border 5 minutes down the track impelled us to leave the train and hire an Azeri to drive us the remaining hour to Tbilisi. That trip was interrupted by six roadblocks and an occasional search. I remembered Tbilisi from a visit in 1989 as a beautiful and charming town with a Mediterranean flavor. It seemed then hardly a part of the Soviet Union: relaxed, cheerful, prosperous, open to Western visitors, with food plentiful and good. Times have changed. The civil war, the conflicts in South Ossetia and in Abkahazia, and the uncertain transition to the free market have taken a toll. Once beautiful Rustavali Avenue tells the story. From the old Lenin Square to the Opera House can be seen the ravages of civil war: a burned-out Parliament and Hotel Tbilisi, several government buildings totally leveled. And on the upper end of the avenue the Iveria Hotel, once the pride of Intourist, is now a haven for refugees, as are most other hotels that were once available to tourists. The streets are dirty, the parks unkempt, the flower beds overtaken by weeds. While all three Caucasus nations have become involved in armed conflicts since independence, only Georgia has experienced civil war and only its capital has seen fighting and bloodshed on the streets. Georgia is the most heterogenous and politically unstable of the Caucasus nations— characteristics which breed tension, uncertainty, and fear. We were told that lawlessness is rampant all through Georgia, where respect for order has all but broken down.

The gap between expectations and reality is larger in Georgia than in Azerbaijan or Armenia. That gap is best symbolized by the lavish new Western-style hotel, Metekhi Palace, a joint venture managed by an Austrian firm. Constructed in anticipation of the flood of tourists that the new era would bring, it now is virtually vacant since, instability and economic uncertainty have frightened off Western visitors.

BAKU

Travel to Baku was a good deal easier despite the fact that our arrival coincided with a bloodless coup. Oil-rich

Azerbaijan is the most prosperous of the Caucasus nations, notwithstanding the drain of the conflict in Nagorno Karabakh. Its busy airport connects to many places in the former Soviet Union and to Turkey. And its new national airline appears to be well run. Baku, located on a peninsula that juts into the Caspian Sea, reminded me of a cross between the Southern California oil fields and the refineries of the North Jersey flatlands. The air was laden with the smell of oil and the soot from oil rig fires; the climate hot and dry. The city bustled with traffic and commerce and, despite the coup under way, daily life proceeded normally. The newer parts of the city and suburbs are utterly without charm, but the old quarter, with its narrow streets and functioning mosques, has considerable character.

While the war in Nagorno Karabakh was a constant feature of daily life and conversation in Yerevan, it seemed very distant from the consciousness of ordinary citizens in Baku. There is a strong desire for peace, not so much because of the economic burden of war but because of the loss of young lives in the military. A stroll down the Walk of Martyrs, a cemetery built in a park outside the Parliament, reminded one of how deeply the human toll of the Nagorno Karabakh conflict is felt.*

## THE POLITICAL SITUATION

The political situation of the Caucasus nations is somewhat the inverse of their economic conditions. Armenia is the most stable and Azerbaijan the most volatile. Azerbaijan has endured three changes of government since its independence, but I believe the return of Haider Aliev may now auger a period of stability. Thus, in the end, Georgia may have the most uncertain future, because it is held together only by the large personality of former Soviet Foreign Minister Eduard Shevardnadze.

---

*The Walk of Martyrs was initially built to commemorate the 122 Azeris killed by Soviet troops in Baku in January 1990, but it is also a memorial to those killed in Nagorno Karabakh.

## ARMENIA

Armenia is led by Levon Ter-Petrossian, who was elected in October 1991 for a 4-year term. The 240 members of Parliament were elected in May 1990 for 5-year terms. Eight parties and movements (from about 30 total in Armenia) are represented in the Parliament, but 145 members do not belong to any party. Of the rest, the Armenian National Movement has 52 members, the Armenian Democratic Liberal Organization 14, the Armenia Revolutionary Federation (Dashnaks) 12, and the National Democratic Union 9. The opposition to Ter-Petrossian coalesced in June 1992 into a loosely knit National Pact.

The principal issue dividing Ter-Petrossian from the opposition is the conduct of the war in Nagorno Karabakh. The National Pact wants to recognize Nagorno Karabakh's independence and give its armed forces more aid, whereas Ter-Petrossian is searching for a solution to the conflict that might not result in Nagorno Karabakh's independence.

Other issues include the form of government envisaged by the new constitution: Ter-Petrossian wants a strong presidential system, while the opposition favors a parliamentary democracy. The Dashnaks favor a stronger role for the central government in the economy and are for a slower rate of privatization.

## GEORGIA

The government of Georgia is led by Eduard Shevardnadze, who was called back from Moscow to his native Georgia in March of 1992 after the popularly elected President Zviad Gamsakhurdia was ousted in a civil war. Gamsakhurdia had been elected President in May 1991 by an 87 percent vote. The 250-member legislature, elected in October 1990, ceased to function after the August 1991 putsch in Moscow. Zviad Gamsakhurdia banned the Communist Party, a move which deprived almost 60 percent of the legislature of its mandate. Without a functioning Parliament, Gamsakhurdia fell into a style of direct rule which was increasingly arbitrary and which stimulated a powerful opposition that ultimately deposed him.

After ruling for 6 months through an Emergency State Council, Eduard Shevardnadze called for parliamentary elections on October 11, 1992. He was democratically elected as Chairman of the Parliament by a 95 percent vote.

More than 20 parties won seats in the October 11 election, but many members of the 255-seat Parliament are unaffiliated. Eduard Shevardnadze depends on the Interparty Faction as his ruling coalition. It includes the Green Party, the National Democratic Party, the Liberal Democratic Party, and many of the independent members. The organized opposition to Shevardnadze entails only about 40 seats and is not able to block him. The Prime Minister, Tengiz Sigua, is said to have a slender grasp on power and may be replaced shortly.

Political life in Georgia is a confused affair. The diehard Gamsakhurdia supporters, known as Zviadistis, dispute the legitimacy of the Shevardnadze government (which they refer to as the "junta") but are given very little chance of returning to power. Parliamentary opponents focus on the conduct of the wars in South Ossetia and Abkahazia and accuses Shevardnadze of not being tough enough. They are suspicious of Shevardnadze's ties with Russia and his belief that Georgia must recognize Russia's legitimate influence in the Caucasus region. They also criticize Shevardnadze for having no economic or social program and for making little progress toward free market reforms. Only about 20 percent of the land is privatized; only 20 percent of the service industries, 5-10 percent of midsize companies, and 23 percent of large enterprises are in private hands. It is said that Shevardnadze wants to pursue a course midway between the Czech Republic and Romania, but that the rapid deterioration of the economy has made him more cautious, more inclined to the Romanian model.

The attacks of the opposition, the inability to subdue the Abkahazian revolt, and the failing economy have taken a toll on Shevardnadze's popularity, which was down to a 50 percent approval rating in a May opinion poll. But the sense of crisis is so palpable that Georgia's intellectual and political elite do not believe they can do without Shevardnadze. An *Isvestia* reporter in Tbilisi told us: "I want to be independent and radical but unfortunately Shevardnadze is our last hope —I don't want to think of the consequences if anything were to happen to him."

The growing dissatisfaction about the course of events in Georgia is likely to cost Prime Minister Sigua his position. The National Democratic Party has proposed a single-party government, arguing that the Sigua government is too much of a coalition and thus unable to act decisively. The Republican Party wants Shevardnadze to be Prime Minister, but Shevardnadze has refused. It is said that Shevardnadze wants Sigua to continue as long as possible to avoid the difficulties that will arise if he has to put together a new government.

## AZERBAIJAN

Azerbaijan has the most interesting political situation in the Caucasus, owing to the early success of the Popular Front in challenging Soviet control in 1989. The rallies on the streets of Baku in late 1989 provoked the Kremlin to use force to sustain the Communists in power, resulting in a Soviet show of force in mid-January 1990 which killed 122 people. Martial law was declared, and party functionary Ayaz Mutalibov was installed as head of state. The Azerbaijan parliamentary election, held under conditions of martial law in September 1990, resulted in only 40 members of the opposition elected to the 360-member body. Under pressure from the Popular Front, Mutalibov essentially replaced the Parliament with a 50-member National Council evenly divided between his supporters and the Popular Front. But the Mutalibov government continued to suffer from a lack of legitimacy. Continued reverses in the Nagorno Karabakh war led to popular demonstrations which forced Mutalibov's resignation on March 6, 1992.

Popular Front Chairman Abulfez Elchibey then won a special election held on June 7 and became Azerbaijan's first popularly elected President. By all accounts, Elchibey, a charismatic visionary, stood for good things but was unable to run the country. His ministerial appointments were poor, he exercised little control over them, and some of his ministers were guilty of personal corruption. With no economic plan in place, inflation ran high, and Elchibey's government was losing the war in Nagorno Karabakh. By mid-1993, the Popular Front had disintegrated as a public force, and Elchibey's popularity was greatly diminished. As opposition mounted, Elchibey imposed martial law, which included a curfew, a ban on demonstrations, and censorship of the press. Those actions caused a split in his coalition, first evidenced when Etibar Mamedov, leader of the National Independence Party, broke with Elchibey. To make matters worse, Elchibey clashed with the former Communist President of Azerbaijan, Haider Aliev, over control of the autonomous province of Nakhichevan, where Aliev headed the Parliament. Aliev also questioned Elchibey's strong tilt toward Turkey and against Russia.

Elchibey had made a young colonel, Surat Husseinov, head of the forces in the Martakert district of Nagorno Karabakh in the spring of 1992. When Husseinov engineered some early victories, Elchibey helped make him a national hero. But in early 1993, when the course of the war reversed, Elchibey sacked Husseinov. In late May, Husseinov refused to accept Elchibey's authority, and Elchibey sent troops to Husseinov's stronghold in Gianja. The resulting clash ended indecisively. This attack prompted Husseinov to march on Baku demanding Elchibey's resignation. To shore up his position, Elchibey sacrificed his Prime Minister and allowed the return of Aliev, the former Communist leader of Azerbaijan, to head the Parliament. But when Elchibey realized that the government troops would not defend him, he fled to Nakhichevan, leaving Aliev and Husseinov to carve up his power. They subsequently struck an uneasy bargain whereby Husseinov would be Prime Minister and Aliev Acting President (as leader of Parliament).

## Human Rights Considerations

All three Caucasus countries seek to become Western-style democracies with free market economies. Armenia, Georgia, and Azerbaijan have joined the Conference on Security and Cooperation in Europe (CSCE) and committed themselves to observe the Helsinki process. Both Armenia and Azerbaijan have ratified the four Geneva Conventions of 1949, and Armenia has ratified the United Nations' International Covenant on Civil and Political Rights of 1966.

But the human rights record in the region is, at best, uneven. With the exception of its participation in the Nagorno Karabakh conflict, Armenia has a good human rights record, the best of the three nations. The press is free, political opposition flourishes, there are no political prisoners, and judicial reform is under way.

Aside from the abuses linked to the armed conflicts in Nagorno Karabakh and Abkahazia, the most serious traditional human rights abuses are occurring in Georgia. Our concerns there focused on the war in Abkahazia, the treatment of prisoners, the status of the press, the formation of paramilitary groups, and the harassment of the political opposition.

## Harassment and Physical Force

A previous Helsinki Watch mission had gathered evidence of police brutality in eight specific cases in which excessive physical force was used during pretrial (and precharge) detention. A report will soon be issued. The report will treat the cases anonymously, since testimony was given with the strict promise of confidentiality. This restriction reflects a climate of fear of the police and a lack of confidence in the judicial system: people fear retaliation if they make charges of police brutality.

The forthcoming Helsinki Watch report documents cases of police brutality involving people charged with ordinary crimes as well as people in political opposition. One case involves a person accused of terrorism, but to the best of our knowledge none of the others were terrorists or could plausibly be mistaken for terrorists.

What comes through is the routine use of physical force by the police. We met with Grigol Lordkiparidze, head of the Parliament Commission on Human Rights, which is looking into the treatment of prisoners. He readily conceded that the prison conditions were poor and did not dismiss our findings of abuse in pretrial detention. However we doubted that his commission would be a source of vigorous challenge to the government.

A joint meeting with the new Chief Procurator (Attorney General) Tedo Ninidve and David Zekeidze, chief of police in Tbilisi, was revealing. The Chief Procurator had been an editor of a law journal and has a record of concern for human rights. He conceded there were instances of police brutality and promised to follow up on specific charges. His attitude contrasted sharply with that of the police chief, who gave us the standard lecture about the rise of crime and terrorism, which called for sterner police measures. He accused us of being soft on the rights of criminals and insensitive to the human rights of his police force, noting that twenty-one officers in Tbilisi had been killed in the line of duty in the previous year. The chief categorically denied the charge of police brutality and defended his practice of denying demonstration permits to the opposition.

I put to him a specific case of a raid by his men on a meeting of supporters of former President Zviad Gamsakhurdia in a private apartment on June 2. Several police officers, armed with machine guns, broke up the meeting and arrested thirty participants. To his credit, the police chief quickly intervened to secure their release. But at our meeting he stoutly defended the practice of rounding up suspicious people who refused to answer questions from the police when confronted.

As the conversation continued in a confrontational vein, the Chief Procurator became increasingly uncomfortable and moved his chair away from the police chief—a symbolic distancing from the hard-line answers to our questions. I surmised that the joint meeting had been set up by the government to expose the police chief to human rights visitors as a way of "firing a warning shot." It seemed clear to me that the government does not exercise complete control over the Tbilisi police and that the Chief Procurator, while well intentioned, was no match for the police official. In these circumstances, Helsinki Watch should push hard on specific cases with the hope that the Chief Procurator will seize on them to send a message to the police.

We encountered a significant number of other examples of harassment of the opposition. Let me mention two. The opposition press has a hard time, since it must rely on a single government printing house to get its papers printed. On occasion, often before a critical anniversary or an opposition rally, the government will refuse to print certain papers, citing shortages of newsprint or other excuses. Some publications, like *Free Georgia*, have been shut down entirely. Others, like *Iberia Spectre*, have endured harassment. We met with Irakli Gotsividze, editor of that weekly, who reported that the paper and his residence have been attacked five times since November, including an attack which destroyed the paper's computers the night before our visit. And for the past 2 weeks, the printing house had refused to publish the paper because, Gotsividze contends, it had published critical articles about Eduard Shevardnadze.

We are told Gamsakhurdia supporters face discrimination in the workplace, up to and including dismissal. We met with a group of teachers from Tbilisi State University who had lost their jobs and who were prepared to have me raise their cases with the Rector through the Committee on International Academic Freedom.

We are told that these traditional human rights concerns are "boutique" issues in light of the threat to Georgia posed by the Abkahazian conflict and the general deterioration of order. But I believe it is important to bring these issues to public view, because Georgia cannot be a healthy democracy until the press is free and political opposition is allowed to operate without harassment. The climate of fear flowing from police abuses further undercuts the evolution of a free and open society.

The situation in Azerbaijan is fluid, as a new government takes command. Under the state of emergency imposed by Elchibey, there were episodes of censorship and intimidation of the press. The most notorious incident involved the beating of five opposition journalists on the order of Interior Minister Iskandar Hamidov, who did not like what was being written about him.

There is considerable concern now that members of the Popular Front will face harassment at the hands of the new government. And while we were in Baku, demonstrations in support of President Elchibey were broken up. (The crackdown on the opposition intensified after we left, and some of Elchibey's supporters have been arrested.) We met with former Speaker of Parliament Isa Gambar of the Musavat Party, who said supporters of the Elchibey government feared for their lives. Two days earlier, his party offices in Gianja had been destroyed by soldiers, presumably loyal to Husseinov. He also reported threats to independent members of the commission looking into the confrontation between Elchibey and Husseinov forces in June.

Three-quarters of the roughly 400,000 Armenians who lived in Azerbaijan have fled; it is estimated that only about 20,000 Armenians remain (most of them in mixed marriages), although the number could be higher. There are reports that the remaining Armenians are harassed and can expect little protection from the authorities. In fact, a paper associated with Hamidov routinely publishes the addresses of Armenians, thereby inviting trouble for them.

The political situation is far from democratic. The formal Parliament, elected in the Communist years, has been bypassed by the fifty-member National Council, a subset of Parliament which has dubious legitimacy. The democratically elected President has been stripped of his power by the National Council. To gain a modicum of democratic legitimacy, the new Aliev–Husseinov government must call new parliamentary elections, and those elections will have to be free and fair.

We put these issues directly to Haider Aliev in a Saturday meeting at the Parliament, just as he was concluding his coalition agreement with Surat Husseinov. Aliev, age 70, had ruled Azerbaijan rather benignly for 13 years before being replaced in 1987. He had been a member of the Soviet Politburo in the

Brezhnev period. In a desperate effort to shore up his own position, Elchibey called Aliev back as Chair of the Parliament in early June, and when Elchibey fled Baku, the country looked to Aliev as the most powerful, stable figure at a time of crisis. Aliev was obviously enjoying this encore to power and played the circumstances to his benefit. "I have been recalled by the people," he told us. "The burden of power is on my shoulders. I shall do my best to pull the country out of crisis."

Aliev, by all accounts, is a good manager, a skillful politician, and "the only alternative," as one independent journalist told us. That Aliev agreed to see us on short notice is testimony to the importance of human rights to a government struggling to win legitimacy with the West. He hit all the right chords:

> Azerbaijan will never change its path of democratic development. I pledge to use democratic means to secure the independence of our republic based on respect for human rights, respect for principles of international law, with multiparty elections, pluralism, and protection of minorities.

As he spoke, it struck me that Western companies and instruments of international aid would be crucial to Aliev's capacity to consolidate his power and rescue the economy. Indeed, all the new countries aspire to be accepted by the West and desperately need investment from prosperous nations to make a successful transition to free market economies. A pragmatist like Aliev, who understands the linkage of human rights to economic aid, might be a more reliable protector of human rights than a well-intentioned, but ineffective Elchibey—that is, more effective if he believes economic aid really is dependent on a decent human rights record. We pointed up that connection in our meeting with Aliev and stressed it again at the informal press conference he had arranged to greet our exit from his office. But he needs to be convinced of the connection by, for example, the consortium of Western oil companies about to conclude a multibillion dollar deal with Azerbaijan. We should be skeptical of Aliev's intentions. Without constant monitoring from international groups, it is likely that Aliev will lapse into his old habits of human rights abuses.

## THE STRUGGLE FOR NAGORNO KARABAKH

Our immediate concern about the coup in Azerbaijan relates to the peace process under way to end the conflict in Nagorno Karabakh. The coup came at an unfortunate time, just as all three parties had agreed to consider a cease-fire brokered by the Minsk Group of the Conference on Security and Cooperation in Europe. Some believe Elchibey's agreement was part of the inspiration for Husseinov's rebellion, since Azerbaijan enters the cease-fire in a militarily weak position. We put that question to Aliev: "Will you take advantage of the moment to score some quick aerial victories before returning to the peace process?" He dodged this question but went on to say he pledged his support of the peace process.

A bit of background about the conflict is in order. The Armenia-Azerbaijan struggle for the Nagorno Karabakh region predates Communist rule and was the subject of an armed conflict during their brief periods of independence (1918-1920). After both were reabsorbed into the Soviet Union, Stalin created an Autonomous Oblast in 1923, which placed Nagorno Karabakh within Azerbaijan. That decision was never accepted by Armenia or by the majority of the Nagorno Karabakh population, which is Armenian. In February 1988 the Nagorno Karabakh Parliament, dominated by Armenians, asked Moscow to make Nagorno Karabakh part of Armenia. That petition touched off violence in February 1988, and Moscow intervened to restore peace and to rule Nagorno Karabakh directly for almost a year. When Nagorno Karabakh was returned to Azerbaijan control, the Armenian resistance grew until Nagorno Karabakh eventually declared independence from Azerbaijan in September 1991. Azerbaijan responded by withdrawing Nagorno Karabakh's autonomous status and attempting direct rule. In a referendum in December 1991, Nagorno Karabakh voted for independence, which was again declared in January 1992.

The fighting escalated quickly because all sides had access

to Russian equipment and munitions. The advantage moved back and forth, but at the moment the Armenians have virtual control of Nagorno Karabakh, and most Azerbaijanis have fled their homes. Armenia has also opened a corridor between its borders and Nagorno Karabakh and has taken over entire districts in Azerbaijan (such as Kelbajar, Lachin) to use as sites for shelling Armenian forces in Nagorno Karabakh.

Numerous human rights abuses have occurred on all sides, including the taking of civilian hostages and the indiscriminate bombing and shelling of civilian targets. A version of "ethnic cleansing" has occurred with the removal of more than 40,000 Azeri people from Nagorno Karabakh. It is estimated that 10,000 people have been killed, many of them civilians, and 80,000 displaced from their homes. In addition, about 300,000 Armenians have fled Azerbaijan proper and 167,000 Azeris have fled Armenia, resulting in at least 600,000 refugees.

In Armenia we met with Minister of Defense Vazgen Manukian, Deputy Foreign Minister Girard Libardian, and presidential adviser David Shakhnazarian. None denied that Armenia was supporting the war effort in Nagorno Karabakh. But all denied that Armenia controls the Nagorno Karabakh government. Indeed, just the opposite is true, according to Deputy Foreign Minister Libardian, who said the Ter-Petrossian government is concerned about the unwillingness of the Nagorno Karabakh government to negotiate, citing the need for Ter-Petrossian to journey to Nagorno Karabakh personally to secure an agreement to the recent cease-fire.

The official position of the Armenian government is that it will accept any agreement satisfactory to Nagorno Karabakh. It sees a conflict between two principles: the right of self-determination and the integrity of territorial borders. It places a higher value on self-determination but understands that the international community is likely to hold fast to territorial integrity out of concern for the implications of any shift of borders to situations all across Europe. That realization makes both Armenia and Nagorno Karabakh skeptical of the outcome of international mediation.

Nagorno Karabakh has in effect won the war and now controls its territory. Nagorno Karabakh has shown tremendous dexterity at overrunning the Azerbaijan strongholds which had been used as bases for shelling, and it has been able to defeat a larger Azerbaijan force because of the mountainous terrain conducive to a guerrilla-type force supported by the population. The Nagorno Karabakh forces are loath to give up what they have won.

By all accounts, before the coup the Elchibey government had come to the conclusion that it could not prevail in Nagorno Karabakh militarily. And thus came the willingness to work through the CSCE, presumably because of its commitment to territorial integrity. But now it is possible that the new government will try to win some military victories to strengthen its position at the bargaining table. Or so goes the thinking in Yerevan. "We are tired of teaching Azerbaijan presidents that they cannot prevail militarily," said Deputy Foreign Minister Libardian, "but I suppose it will take the new government a year to learn."

That is certainly the view of Defense Minister Manukian, who had little hope for a cease-fire or any peaceful settlement in Nagorno Karabakh short of total independence, recognized and supported by the West. Presidential adviser David Shakhnazarian was more sanguine that peace could be won, but he favored slowing the Minsk process down until stability returned to Baku. He viewed the recent cease-fire accord as the last best hope for peace, and believed that it should not be undercut because of internal politics in Azerbaijan. When asked about the ultimate outcome, Shakhnazarian ran through a myriad of options without revealing where he thought the situation would settle. The fact that his options list contained several possibilities short of full independence is instructive and suggests that he expects an international settlement to end up leaving Nagorno Karabakh within Azerbaijan with considerable autonomy but with a period as an international protectorate. An "eternal cease-fire" monitored by the CSCE would de facto bring that result even if no settlement were reached.

Neither Armenia nor Azerbaijan will agree to the extremes:

complete independence or return to the status quo ante. Yet both countries are exhausted by the conflict, and the general public would welcome a cease-fire or a settlement that did not involve complete capitulation by either side. Armenia does not want to face another winter with a full blockade. Azerbaijan realizes that the conflict stands in the way of lucrative Western investment. Aliev probably has more credibility than Elchibey to win popular support for a compromise which would give Nagorno Karabakh considerable autonomy or even place it under an international protectorate for a period. Ter-Petrossian seems committed to ending the conflict. The questions really are two: Can Ter-Petrossian persuade the Nagorno Karabakh government to trust in the peace process?* And can Aliev restrain Surat Husseinov's desire to erase the stain on his record by scoring some quick aerial victories? If not, we can expect a resumption of the conflict with full application of Soviet weapons and a much more determined and better organized Azeri force. The results could be catastrophic for civilians in the region.

THE CONFLICT IN ABKAHAZIA

The other armed conflict in the region which is spawning human rights abuses is the secessionist movement in the autonomous province of Abkahazia in western Georgia. We met for 3 hours with Prime Minister Tengiz Sigua, whose fondness for hand-drawn maps helped us understand the danger he sees in separatist movements to the very existence of Georgia. While Georgians constitute two thirds of the population, there are heavy concentrations of minorities in Abkahazia (18 percent are Abkahazians) and South Ossetia (an overwhelming majority are Ossetians); and there are Azerbaijanis in the eastern province and Armenians in the south. This concern for territorial integrity gives the Georgian government considerable sympathy with Azerbaijan in the Nagorno Karabakh conflict.

The Abkahazia problem has some similarities to other con-

*Since our visit, the CSCE delegation tried to make progress in mediating the dispute, chiefly because of the intransigence of the Nagorno Karabakh government.

flicts in the region. Abkahazia was a separate republic of the Soviet Union in the 1920s; not until 1931 did it join Georgia as an autonomous region. Agitation for restoration of a separate republic goes back to 1978 but heated up in 1989 and 1990 when the Abkahazia Supreme Soviet voted independence. In 1992 its Supreme Soviet put the 1925 constitution back in force. In August 1992, a clumsy effort to storm the Abkhaz Parliament in Sukhumi by then Defense Minister Tengiz Kitovani caused an escalation of violence. The province is now effectively split, with Abkhaz forces holding the territory to the north of the Tsau River.

The Shevardnadze government has sought help from Boris Yeltsin to end the conflict, but there is widespread suspicion that conservative forces in the Russian military and Parliament are aiding the Abkhaz rebels in the hope of splitting all or some of Abkahazia from Georgia. Prime Minister Sigua openly charged the Russian army with helping the rebels and alleged that the 345th Russian Regiment had recently been moved into Abkahazia without consultation with the Georgian government. "Where do the Abkahaz forces get the planes to bomb our installations?" the Prime Minister asked us.

Following our visit, the fighting escalated and Shevardnadze imposed martial law on Abkahazia. We were told that some 3,000 to 4,000 people died in the conflict, and that international law protecting the rights of civilians is being broken on both sides. We heard stories, to be verified by a future Helsinki Watch mission, that whole towns have been blockaded, thus denying citizens the necessities of life, and that civilian targets are being bombed and shelled.

## Russia and Ukraine—Some Vignettes

Our visit to Russia and Ukraine was of a different character than the mission to the three Caucasus nations: less focused, less intense, more interested in educational reforms and New School connections.

## Russia

In Russia our most important visit was with Sergei Stankevich, former Deputy Mayor of Moscow and now political adviser to Boris Yeltsin. Valuable insights into the current state of affairs also came from Yuri Afanasyev, Rector of the Russian Humanitarian University.

By all outward appearances, Moscow seems to be thriving despite the severe economic hardship experienced by much of the population; the energy is much more palpable than on my last visit in 1991. Some signs: everyone now complains about traffic jams in Moscow, since the number of private cars has grown exponentially. Mercedes, BMWs, Jaguars, and Volvos are to be found everywhere. Satellite dishes dot the tops of major buildings. GUM department store now sports Benetton, Christian Dior, Estée Lauder and Arrow shirts, among other Western brands, on the first floor. MacDonalds is multiplying. The Savoy is now joined by the Metropole, Kempenski, and Radisson, as first-class, Western-style hotels at New York and London prices. To my eye, the streets remain clean, the people friendly, the reports of street crime vastly overstated. It was thrilling to see and feel the unleashing of economic energy and human initiative. And while Gorbachev had been an overwhelming presence 2 years ago, he is now totally irrelevant, his name scarcely even mentioned.

This is not to suggest that all is well with the Russian economy. It is not. Inflation hit 28 percent in January and since then has been averaging about 16 percent a month; production has fallen sharply. Half of all economic activity is conducted in foreign currency as a hedge against inflation. And privatization proceeds in a chaotic way. According to Afanasyev, no reliable statistics are available about how much economic activity is now in private hands. He cautioned that people who claim ownership of land and factories have yet to secure proper legal title. *Newsweek's* Carroll Bogert was more optimistic, noting that both experts and ordinary people had come to the realization that Russia would have to solve its own economic problems—indeed, that the people would have to lead the process of reform through individual action.

Evaluations of Boris Yeltsin's performance and prospects varied widely. Bogert felt that he was doing well, having gained real momentum from the April referendum and then used it to marginalize his conservative opposition in Parliament. But Afanasyev, who proved remarkably prescient in 1990 in predicting Gorbachev's demise and the breakup of the Soviet Union, was less hopeful: "I see no bright prospects for Yeltsin—he will not survive another election." Afanasyev declared himself an optimist about Russia's long-term future but very cautious about prospects in the short run. He believes Yeltsin will ride the momentum of his April victory for a short while—maybe 12 to 18 months—during which he will register some gains in economic reform and, perhaps, win a new constitution. Most observers believe Yeltsin will compromise on a new constitution which will contain less sweeping presidential powers than the one Yeltsin put forth, but which will result in a strong presidency.

We saw Yeltsin's opposition firsthand. We met with Parliament member Vitaly Urazhtsev, head of the Russian Revival Party, which is dedicated to bringing the Russians trapped in the new nations back to Russia. Urazhtsev treated us to a half-hour diatribe about Yeltsin's shortcomings. He accused Yeltsin of everything from ruling in an authoritarian manner to personal corruption. He dismissed the April referendum by noting a low voter turnout and predicted that Yeltsin's effort to elect a new Parliament would produce a majority opposed to him. "It is insane to hold an election in an exhausted country," he told us, "and no new constitution will bring peace and order to Russia." Without firm leadership, he predicted, Russia would break apart and slide into Yugoslavian chaos.

As we would expect, Yeltsin adviser Sergei Stankevich was much more optimistic. I had met him on an earlier visit and then, as now, was impressed with his good sense. Our visit coincided with a confrontation between Russia and Estonia over a new law on foreigners which is prejudicial to Russians still in Estonia (about one-third of the Estonian population). Yeltsin had responded by declaring the law "legal apartheid" and temporarily suspended the gas supply to Estonia until Estonia agreed to defer implementation. The law treated as foreigners anyone who moved to Estonia during the period of Soviet domination.

Stankevich chronicled the abuses suffered by Russians in the former republics, including disenfranchisement in Latvia, discrimination in pensions in Latvia, prohibition from owning newspapers and property in Estonia, loss of jobs in Kazakhstan, an forced education in the Kazak language. He accused Latvia and Estonia of waging a cold war to expel Russians by creating socially unbearable conditions. (He made an exception of Lithuania, which he said treated the Russians fairly.) He warned that Yeltsin would have to react very strongly to mistreatment of Russians because of domestic political pressures that he faced from conservative opponents. Thus, this issue both destabilized domestic politics and caused serious tensions with Russia's neighbors. Stankevich chided the West for a "double standard" in criticizing human rights abuses in Russia but going very easy on the Baltics. He said this double standard reduced the credibility of the West and of nongovernment human rights organizations, making it harder for Russia and Western nations to work together on other human rights issues.

I reminded Stankevich that Helsinki Watch had criticized both Latvia and Estonia on their citizenship laws and promised a new mission to push this issue more forcefully. I returned the challenge by saying that we needed Russia to take a much more vigorous pro-human rights position in the former republics, where it is still the most influential economic and political force. Stankevich seemed taken aback by the thought but then managed some politically correct promises to work together.

I also put to him the question of Russian military involvement in the Nagorno Karabakh and Abkahazian conflicts. He denied such involvement, noting that Russia had too many internal problems to be mixing in these relatively minor internal skirmishes. The only exception, he said, was a determination to maintain a strong boundary around the territory of the former Soviet Union in the south as a wall against Muslim fundamentalism, which concerned Russia greatly. "That's why Tajikistan is so important to us," he said—an observation subsequently borne out by Russian intervention in July. He wrote off the incidents of Russian involvement in the Caucasus conflicts to mercenaries and the vast amount of equipment which was left behind as Russia retrenched.

Conspiracy theories abound about Russia's behind-the-scenes role in destabilizing the new Caucasus nations with the hope of reasserting influence, perhaps even reabsorbing them. I find no credible evidence of Russian military involvement in Nagorno Karabakh. That is not to deny the presence of Russian mercenaries or the possibility of an occasional unauthorized assist by Russian technical advisers. But the withdrawal of Russian forces from both Armenia and Azerbaijan makes it unlikely that the Russian army is playing any role in the conflict. If there is a Russian military role in the region it will be found in Abkahazia, where my instincts tell me there is some Russian military support for the separatist movement. It may well be that such involvement is not sanctioned by the Yeltsin government.

On an another matter, Stankevich conceded a serious refugee problem in Moscow. Despite the intention to be open to internal movement, limits have been placed on the influx of refugees to maintain social order. "We lack the money or the expertise to carry out our good intentions," he concluded.

Stankevich, who bears responsibility for negotiating the new constitution, was optimistic about its chances for passage and did not believe that the presidential powers proposed by Yeltsin were too great. He was also positive about the evolution of political parties, noting it would take at least two national elections before a stable system emerged. He expected the current number of forty parties to increase, and for five or six of them to be represented in the new Parliament.

UKRAINE

Kiev was our briefest stop and thus my impressions of it are the most sketchy. Ukraine is the second largest country in

Europe, after Russia, and has a population of 52 million people (70 percent ethnic Ukrainian, 2 percent Russian). It is bordered by Belarus, Russia, Moldova, Romania, Hungary, Slovakia, and Poland. In addition to rich agriculture, Ukraine has abundant reserves of iron ore, coal, and natural gas. The name "Ukraine" was not widely used until the nineteenth century, and the territory has been subject to many rulers over the years. Along with Russia, it traces its lineage from the nine-century Kiev-Rus dynasty, which had close ties to the Byzantine Empire and which accepted Orthodox Christianity in 988. The Kiev-Rus civilization reached its zenith in the tenth and eleventh centuries when Kiev was one of the largest and most important cities in Europe. In succession, the Mongols, Lithuanians, Poles, and Turks dominated Ukraine. In 1793 most of Ukraine became part of the Russian empire, though there was a brief period of independence following the Russian revolution. In 1924 the Ukrainian Soviet Socialist Republic became part of the Soviet Union. Ukraine declared independence on August 24, 1991.

Bohdan Krawchenko, director of the Institute of Public Administration and Local Government, offered interesting insights into recent developments in Ukraine. He noted that few, if any, countries the size of Ukraine had become independent in the nineteenth or twentieth century without the backing of a major power, and none with a large army and nuclear arsenal. He said Ukraine was confused about its identity and future; every part of society was in flux. Yet there existed a broad social consensus on independence and little unrest despite a poor economic situation.

At the moment, there is a power struggle between President Leonid Kravchuk (former Communist leader) and Prime Minister Leonid Kuchma. That struggle, which began with the President's attempt to curtail the power of the Prime Minister, has resulted in a realization by the two leaders that they need each other and in turn also need a better, more legitimate Parliament. The betting is that there will be a new parliamentary election soon.

Kiev seemed very Western, and the people we spoke

with had a strong Western outlook. The Ukrainian diaspora is hard at work funneling economic aid and technical assistance to Ukraine. The human rights situation seems pretty good with the exception of the status of Russians in the Crimea, which is a cause for worry. Ukraine has a liberal citizenship law, which recognizes all residents at the time of independence as citizens. The press is free, although the television station still is under government control. (It is said that more accurate information on Ukraine comes from Moscow television news.)

We heard some stories of harassment of political opposition, but they were not specific enough or numerous enough to suggest a major problem. We met with three former dissident leaders who were reassuring about the condition of human rights in Ukraine. The Ukraine Legal Foundation has received complaints of human rights abuses (which it does not handle) and promised to analyze these for our review. That foundation is making real headway in reforming Ukraine's judicial system.

On the large issues of war and peace, Krawchenko was reassuring. He said Kravchuk understood that good relations with Moscow were critical and that fair treatment of the 12 million Russian minority (the largest concentration outside of Russia) was essential to that relationship. Kravchuk appreciates that Russia laments the loss of Ukraine, of all the former republics, most keenly—for economic reasons and because Ukraine is seen as one of the sources of Russian culture. Hence he will take care to avoid provocation, knowing that at the moment Ukraine is too weak to play geopolitical games.

## A Footnote on Educational Reform

Within the past 18 months, the reform movement in higher education has picked up momentum in the former Soviet Union—as illustrated by three examples described below in Armenia, Russia, and Ukraine. The New School Democracy Seminar already has a branch in Ukraine and will likely start a branch in Armenia next year. The need for the New School's seminar, curriculum reform efforts, the Journal Project, and exchange opportunities is urgent, since the former Soviet Union has received much less attention from Western institutions than have Eastern and Central Europe. There is, as it were, a "new frontier" which can absorb infinite quantities of assistance. It is heartening to see the importance that leaders in these new nations attach to rebuilding higher education as a key to both economic revitalization and the construction of civil society.

In Armenia we met with the Minister of Higher Education, the Rector of Yerevan State University, and representatives of the American University of Armenia. We heard a familiar story: the humanities and social sciences were in direst need of rebuilding, modern textbooks in translation were in great demand, and scholarly journals were the highest priority for the faculty. In Armenia the special problem of the blockade placed a high premium on visitors from the West to help cut the isolation. And, of course, fellowships for advanced graduate students and younger faculty were emphasized as a better means to produce a modern faculty than retraining older, Communist-era professors.

Because Armenia had one of the best higher education systems in the old U.S.S.R., it had a disproportionate number of students, especially in the sciences. Thus, its higher education capacity is overbuilt and it is negotiating to send its faculty to places like India, Thailand, and Algeria, and throughout Africa, as its own system contracts. There are fourteen institutions of higher education (divided between Yerevan State and Yerevan Technical University)—twelve in Yerevan and two pedagogical institutions outside the capital. Total enrollment reached 50,000 but will now drop back to 25,000.

Yerevan State University has 20 faculty departments and 10,000 students. The new American University of Armenia has 280 students, principally enrolled in master's degree programs in business and engineering. The American University is a source of pride throughout Yerevan and has a generous attitude toward fostering reform in the state university. It should be possible for the New School to work with both.

Historian Yuri Afanasiev is Rector of the Russian Humanitarian University, which is a new institution created to reform the humanities and social sciences throughout Russia. Thus it is a perfect partner for the New School. It is also responsible for the coordination of the purchase and distribution of foreign publications to 216 other institutions in Russia (hence the perfect conduit for our Journal Project). It has a faculty of 500 for 5,000 students, starting from high school up through 150 Ph.D. candidates. It has taken on responsibility for creating curriculum materials for 300 courses, starting with history, cultural studies, philosophy, sociology, and economics. It runs in-service retraining seminars for 500 faculty from around Russia.

A critical need is library material, especial scholarly journals. The university library, inherited from the former Communist Party school, is "70 percent rubbish," according to Afanasiev. No university in Russia has been able to buy material produced abroad since 1992. Hence, our Journal Project is most welcome.

In Kiev, educational reform is centered in the quasi-private Mohyla Academy, founded originally by Cossack nobility in the seventeenth century. The academy was a principal force for introducing Western thought to Ukraine and one reason that Ukrainian culture differs from Russia's. It lasted 100 years as a university, before becoming a theological institute and later a Communist Party school and naval academy.

Last year Mohyla Academy reopened with support from private sources and the government (but not the Ministry of Higher Education). It has 238 first-year students in three faculties: humanities, social science, and natural science. The disciplines chosen for focus—economics, sociology, political science, public administration, history, and ecology—were the weakest in Ukraine. The university has adopted a Western-style 4-year B.A. program to be followed by a 2- or 3-year master's degree. Eventually, it wants 1,500 students and plans to add faculties in fine arts and law. English is a requirement for admission and all students are bilingual.

In addition to the courses, there are affiliated research centers in history, sociology, and economics. The Soros Foundation has provided funds for visiting professors from Yale, Columbia, and Berkeley who supplement the 125-person faculty (mostly part time). The University of Kiev–Mohyla Academy also is a logical partner for the New School's East and Central Europe program.

The creation of private universities and new public institutions free of the bureaucratic encumbrance of Ministries of Education is a heartening development which will accelerate the cause of educational reform. While these new institutions are natural partners for the New School's project, we should not neglect the large traditional state universities which still educate over 90 percent of the students in the former Soviet Union. In these institutions, we should pursue our tested strategy of identifying a small unit—a particular faculty or department—under good leadership and focus our energies and aid so as to produce a reform model within the larger university.

# THE SPECIAL CASE OF TRNAVA UNIVERSITY

(DEMOCRACY SEMINAR CONFERENCE, PRAGUE, JULY 1993)

## BACKGROUND

I write to report on the annual meeting of the New School's Democracy Seminar in Prague and the special case of Trnava University in Slovakia.

## DEMOCRACY SEMINAR CONFERENCE

The Democracy Seminar, which was launched by the New School in 1985, actually consists of a network of seminars that meet in cities throughout Eastern and Central Europe, as well as in New York City. These seminars share a reading list on democracy and democratization, and they exchange visitors and scholarly papers. From its beginnings as gatherings of dissidents in Warsaw and Budapest, the Democracy Seminar has grown to include fourteen cities from Tallinn in the northwest to Sofia and Bucharest in the southeast, and today it counts 300 scholars as active participants. Since 1990, representatives of each seminar have gathered annually in late May for a 3-day conference which affords them an opportunity to put their work in comparative perspectives. This May's conference was at Celakovice, a former Communist management facility about 20 kilometers northeast of Prague.

The title of the Prague conference was "Democracy on Trial: East and West After the Cold War." As the topic implies, the conference looked at issues of concern to both the new democracies of the east and the mature democracies of the west, thus beginning to realize our ambition that the seminars promote a common scholarly agenda among international colleagues. A flavor of the discussion can be gleaned from the topics of the conference papers: "American Public Culture and Liberal Intolerance," "Excesses and Shortages of Democracy," "The Difficult Birth of a Balanced Political Scene in Post-Communist Slovakia," "Local and Regional Identity as Factors of Social and Political Integration," and "Transitions at the Crossroads: Distorted Identities and Virulent Xenophobia in Eastern and Central Europe."

In addition to the papers, the conference featured a new format, "the substantive working groups," which are ongoing research projects dealing with issues that concern all the new countries. Project titles included "Political Parties and Party Systems," "Nationality and Marginality in the Contemporary World," and "The Tradition of Women's Movements in Eastern and Central Europe."

In my view, the Prague conference elicited a richer and more textured discussion than any of the previous three. This reflected in part the continuity of the group, which must be the longest-running cross-disciplinary and cross-national conversation in the region. More important, it is the product of the individual seminars, which have begun to pose, and then work on, more sophisticated questions.

But more sophisticated work can lead to other types of problems. In a moment of frustration, New School Professor Jeffrey Goldfarb confessed that he had trouble "understanding what is 'going on' in the region." He went on to say, "It is our responsibility as scholars to try to make sense of political life and to interpret it to ordinary people."

That strikes me as a good standard by which to measure the success of the Democracy Seminar network. And I do believe that significant progress has been made, even while conceding that our project is in its earliest stages. In the first years we tended to share "war stories" very specific to each country, stories that looked back, that worked out anger and frustration. Next our conversations became very general, abstractly theoretical, largely unanchored by a connection to the inchoate reality on the ground. But this year marked a watershed when we focused on intermediate-level questions like the formation of political parties and party systems, the devclopment of the institutions of civil society, the problems of ethnicity, and the status of women.

Perhaps it is this progress "in making sense" of political and cultural life which explains the greater optimism among our members than was evident in previous years. Certainly a more realistic set of expectations, helped by a more sophisticated understanding of the problems of Western democracies, brought a more balanced perspective about the disappointments of the transition period. And in the end, the fact that the "worst case" scenarios—total collapse or a Communist countercoup—had failed to occur contributed significantly to the more hopeful assessments of the future.

## Vignettes

One happy by-product of the conference was that it provided numerous opportunities to pursue two special interests of mine. First, as chair of the Helsinki Watch Committee, I found the conference to be an excellent forum to learn about the status of human rights in the countries of the region. Second, as an American political historian with a special interest in recent political developments, I learned much from the conference, especially about the way in which the various political groupings within each country are contributing to the development of a party system. My two interests come together because the status of specific human rights issues is frequently intertwined with domestic politics. To apply effective pressure for the protection of human rights, one almost always needs to know the political nerve points.

• • •

In this regard, I had two good sessions with Karl Schwarzenberg, former adviser to Czechoslovakian President Vaclav Havel and former chair of the International Helsinki Federation. He sees the health of political parties as a key indicator of the likelihood of further progress in the region, and he believes the current condition of most parties is an impediment to progress. "Party systems have broken down through all of Europe," he said. "In Eastern and Central Europe, parties do not yet correspond to social reality and the initial coalitions of dissidents have everywhere broken up. It is hard to know what political parties—even those in power—stand for."

Still, Schwarzenberg is optimistic about the future of Poland, Hungary, the Czech Republic, and Slovenia, where he believes that relative political stability and tangible, if modest, economic progress are promising. He also offered a more hopeful scenario for Slovakia, whose future, he thinks, depends more on trading relations with a resurgent Ukraine than with the Czech Republic.

In response to my questions about the most urgent human rights issues in the region (outside of the war-torn former Yugoslavia and the chaos of the former Soviet Union), he cited four:

1. The treatment of Gypsies and, more broadly, people of color is bad throughout the region.
2. The refugee problem is growing—and will explode with the closing of the German borders. The new societies are not ready to accept "strange, foreign, exotic" influences. Even the Czech society, which is relatively more prosperous and confident than most in the region, is very closed to foreign influences. The issue of access to citizenship should be one of Helsinki Watch's prime concerns.
3. The status of the media, especially television, needs constant monitoring. There remains quiet intimidation and self-censorship throughout the region, and television remains government-controlled in almost every country.
4. Attention must be focused on the judicial system, since it is an important prerequisite in building the general population's confidence in democracy. Schwartzenberg suspects that the judicial system—staffed as it is by old-style judges educated not to make independent decisions but to follow recommendations—functions poorly in most countries.

Schwarzenberg concluded with an overall observation that indigenous human rights groups needed to be restarted in the countries of the region. Many of the courageous dissidents of the 1980s are now in politics and thus not appropriate to lead Helsinki Watch committees. And their penchant for political activism, so apparent in the "bad old days," should yield to a younger generation of human rights advocates with a more judicial temperament.

• • •

Jan Urban, an independent journalist in Prague and frequent visitor to the New School, has been working on a "theory of transition," a set of observations he believes useful in understanding this period in all countries of the region. He sees six common themes:

1. Political life is still heavily influenced by ideologues. They foster the view that politics is a continuation of past conflicts.
2. Political parties do not yet work—coalitions are unstable and constantly shifting.
3. The leaders of political parties have failed to articulate a positive vision for the future of their countries.
4. There continues to be an inability to talk openly and candidly about the problems of social and political life.
5. The independent media need constant protection—there remains a tendency to self-censorship.
6. Governments do not provide adequate physical security.

• • •

Conversations with seminar colleagues Gabor Hamza (Hungary), Dimitrina Petrova and Rumyana Kolarova (Bulgaria), and Pavel Campeanu (Romania) revealed political trouble for the ruling coalitions in all of these countries.

In Hungary, the Democratic Forum has been split by the Hungarian Way faction, which believes that Prime Minister Jozsef Antal's government is not sufficiently suspicious of foreign influence and investors, not "Hungarian enough." The constitution requires a super (two-thirds) majority on certain questions, such as the budget, for which Antal may not be able to muster sufficient support. The failure to pass the budget and the loss of an effective coalition may force early elections in what has been one of the most stable of the new democracies.

Bulgaria already is in an unstable political condition with a caretaker, Prime Minister Lubin Berov, who is unable to fill important posts like Foreign Minister and Justice Minister. The government of the Union of Democratic Forces (UDF) was forced to yield power to Berov, who is not identified with any party and is supported by a shaky coalition of the former Communists, the Turkish party, and the Light Blue splinter faction of UDF. The Dark Blue faction of UDF now has only 87 seats in the Parliament; the splinter Light Blue, now called New Union for Democracy, has 17; the Movement for Rights and Freedom (Turkish party) has 24, and the Bulgarian Socialist Party (former Communists), 105. Although the former Communists have the largest delegation in Congress, they do not want to diminish the government for fear of creating a backlash. But there is no question that their power is growing, and it is thought that they stand to gain more seats if an election is held in the fall. However, the former Communists are showing signs of splitting into three groups —those close to former dictator Todor Zhivkov, the reformed Communists around Andrei Lukanov, and a younger group of former Communists.

For the moment, the former Communists are using their power to achieve legislative gains which favor their economic interests. For instance, the former Communists helped the Berov government survive a recent vote of no confidence; in exchange for their support, the former Communists extracted a trade-off: a new act for the redistribution of land centralizes the process in the Ministry of Agriculture, a stronghold of the former Communists, rather than placing responsibility with the elected regional committees. The act also provides that land within city limits cannot be returned if there is a building on it or if permission to build had already been granted, a provision which is said to favor the former Communists.

The former Communists are also trying to use their legislative power to curtail the process of lustration or exposure and removal from public employment of individuals who participated in the Communist regime. The former Communists in Parliament are trying to render inoperative the new lustration law in science and education by linking its effective date to the passage of several other laws which are unlikely to win approval. The lustration issue continues to bring together an unlikely opposition coalition of former Communists, President Zheliu Zhelev, the Light Blue faction, and human rights activists. The new law passed in the first place last December when the Turkish party reversed field and supported it in exchange for wider freedom on religious matters. Helsinki Watch has been opposed to the law because of its very broad criteria for exclusion of people from jobs, its presumption of guilt, and its failure to treat individuals on a case-by-case basis.

The political situation in neighboring Romania also reflects an unstable party alignment. About eighty parties ran in last fall's parliamentary elections. The ruling Front for National Salvation split apart before the elections, with President Ion Iliescu's faction retaining 29 percent of the Parliament's seats, and former Prime Minister Petru Roman's group winning about 10 percent. The Democratic Convention, an alliance of seventeen anti-Communist parties, claimed about 20 percent of the seats. Together, the ultranationalist Romanian National Unity and the neofascist Romania Mare captured a total of 12 percent. The party of the Hungarian minority, the Democratic Union of Hungarians in Romania, won about 9 percent. The remainder of the seats were divided among about a dozen other parties representing small ethnic minorities.

In order to govern, Iliescu has been forced into an alliance with extremist groups on both the right and the left. In the most recent presidential election, Iliescu, who won over 85 percent of the vote in his first contest, garnered only 40 percent. His slippage no doubt stems from voters' concern about the severe economic crisis in Romania, which has made only tentative steps toward a stable, free market economy. The unemployment rate is 15 percent, and when the state subsidy of certain essential goods was terminated on May 1, prices skyrocketed: for example, the price of bread now is five times what it was on May 1. According to Pavel Campeanu, as the Iliescu government slips in popularity, it plays on ethnic tensions and fears to divert attention from its failures in the economic sphere.

By contrast, the economic situation in the new Baltic nations seems better. Journalist Alex Grigorievs reports that inflation is slow in Latvia and that Riga is booming with tourism, financial services, and a sizable black market trade with Russians in smuggled fuel and copper.

A burning issue in Latvia is the absence of a citizenship law and the resulting disenfranchisement of the large Russian population, most of whom were not permitted to vote in the early June elections. (About 34 percent of the population is Russian.) Latvia has linked progress on the citizenship issue to withdrawal of Russian troops still stationed on its soil. With substantial numbers of Russians not allowed to vote, the Latvian Way, led by former Communist and current President Anatolijs Gorbunov, was the overall winner. In the face of pressure from Moscow to ensure the well-being of ethnic Russians in Latvia, Gorbunov is likely to be able to present himself as an effective mediator between the Russians and staunch Latvian nationalists.

According to Grigorievs, it will be hard for Latvia to adopt an acceptable citizenship law, in part because its fellow Baltic nation of Estonia has been accepted into the Council of Europe despite its very restrictive citizenship law. Grigorievs believes the minimum position should be that anyone born in Latvia is a citizen. He reports that the Helsinki group in Latvia is extremely nationalistic and cannot be counted upon to fight for an acceptable citizenship law; thus he hopes that U.S. Helsinki Watch will continue to follow this issue.

## Slovakia and the Special Case of Trnava University

Politics in the new country of Slovakia follow the patterns seen elsewhere in the region. Of special interest is the role that the defense of Trnava University has played in weakening the government of Prime Minster Vladimir Meciar.

The first blush of independence has been disappointing for ordinary citizens of Slovakia, as prices are increasing, salaries are flat, and the federal deficit is growing at an alarming rate. Prime Minister Meciar's approval rating has plunged from 35 percent in late 1992 to a low of 15 percent in May 1993, and he is having trouble holding together a coalition capable of governing. While the next elections are not scheduled until 1995, there is some speculation that new elections may be called within a year. Meciar's weakened position has emboldened his protégé Michal Kovac to strengthen the Slovakian presidency by striking an independent course from Meciar. Kovac has claimed vast authority over appointments, including the formal recognition of the appointment of Anton Hajduk as Rector of Trnava University—a move that observers believe Kovac will push through as a symbol of his independence. Kovac was Minister of the Economy during the Communist regime and has had broad international exposure through his work for the Czechoslovakian Central Bank as its London representative. He is described as more flexible and pragmatic than Meciar, and with a 50 percent approval rating, he is likely to be a force in Slovak politics for the near future.

Trnava University, which is located about 40 kilometers outside of Bratislava, was established by the Federal Czechoslovakians after the fall of the Communists. The new university's mission is to concentrate on the social sciences, social work, and teacher education. Federal President Vaclav Havel appointed astronomer Anton Hajduk as Rector of Trnava University. Hajduk assembled a faculty which the government of Prime Minister Meciar viewed as a hotbed of opposition. In the summer of 1992, the Meciar government tried to dismiss the Rector on technical grounds, and when

Hajduk refused to yield his office, the Meciar government tried to defer the opening of the university by freezing its accounts. International attention to the university's plight, together with donations of private funds to pay some of its costs, kept the university going until it won a reprieve when the Parliament forced the release of its funds in January 1993. Thus, Trnava University successfully finished its first year with 220 students and is recruiting another entering class of 220 students from 1,400 candidates taking the competitive entrance examination.

But problems remain. Rector Hajduk still has not been recognized by the Slovakian government, although there are signs that President Michal Kovac is prepared to process his appointment. And the government so far has frozen the university's budget at the 1993 level, even though the student body will double during the 1993-1994 academic year. Trnava University has also been denied any capital monies to build dormitories or to expand its classrooms and library. The International Committee on Academic Freedom has filed a letter of protest to President Kovac. It is my expectation that international attention will help strengthen Trnava University as the price extracted from the Meciar government for its continued harassment of the university becomes too high.

On balance, Meciar's failed attempt to close the university was a serious misjudgment which has come to symbolize skepticism about the commitment of his government to democracy. Trnava University has skillfully cast itself as the test case of Meciar's intentions.

I am eager for the New School to conclude a formal relationship with Trnava University. Such an agreement would be Trnava's first affiliation with an American university and would be helpful in its fight for survival. The affiliation would include student exchanges, access to Western academic journals through our Journal Project, and help with curriculum development through joint courses and New School visitors.

## Conclusion

I conclude this sampling of conditions in Eastern and Central Europe with a sense of cautious optimism. Each year which goes by without total economic collapse or a return to authoritarian regimes enhances the prospects for a successful transition to stable democracies and viable free market economies. Putting aside the exceptional case of Bosnia and the former Yugoslavia, it seems to me that every country in the region has made progress this past year. Further advances will be measured in small increments over many years. The moment for dramatic change has past. Whether our attention and concern will remain concentrated on the region will test our commitment to sharing in the sometimes tedious work of reconstruction, now that the excitement has past.

The task that the New School has undertaken to help rebuild conditions for scholarly life needs another 10 years of patient investment before we will be able to say that our role is finished. We will not be able to follow through on the expectations we have raised—the commitment we have made—unless those providing financial support for our efforts are willing to "stay the course" with us. I very much want history to note that the New School began its involvement in the region at the earliest sign of the dissident movement and then stayed on with a deep involvement for as long as it took to complete the transition to civil society.

# AMERICAN BUSINESS SHOULD CONSIDER HUMAN RIGHTS BEFORE INVESTING

(NEW YORK TIMES OP-ED ARTICLE, JULY 1993)

Our June Helsinki Watch mission to the new Caucasus nations of Armenia, Georgia, and Azerbaijan revealed serious human rights problems. It also illuminated a strategy for addressing human rights abuses that was unavailable in the region under the Soviet regime. These new countries are committed to economic reform and desperate for foreign aid; investors are in a position to set human rights conditions before granting such aid. Human rights improvements not only will benefit the citizens of these countries, but will provide a more stable climate for foreign investment.

The coup in Azerbaijan, which occurred during our stay in Baku, returned veteran Communist leader Heidar Aliev to power. He joins other former Communist leaders who now head the nations carved out of the Soviet Union, among them Georgia President Eduard Shevardnadze, Turkmenistan President Saparmurat Niyazov, and Kazakhstan President Nursultan Nazarbayev.

Few of these old-line Communists have an authentic commitment to human rights. Problems abound from the extremely repressive Central Asian regimes in Turkmenistan and Uzbekistan to armed conflicts resulting from separatist movements in the Abkhazia and South Ossetia regions of Georgia and between Azerbaijan and the Armenians in Nagorno Karabakh. These include the indiscriminate shelling and bombing of civilian targets, the taking of civilian hostages, and blockades that deny the necessities of life to the civilian population. The fighting has claimed an estimated 13,000 lives. Less dramatic human rights abuses exist in Azerbaijan under cover of the state of emergency and in

Georgia, where the opposition press is censored, political opponents harassed, and suspects tortured by police.

The abuses that persist in the Caucasus nations occur within the context of new states that have expressed a commitment to democracy and free market economies. All the new states have weak economies and are seeking foreign investment and aid from agencies like the International Monetary Fund, the World Bank, and the European Bank for Reconstruction and Development. And therein lies an opportunity and an obligation.

We should not write off old Communists like Heidar Aliev on the assumption that their past records render them forever insensitive to human rights. Aliev is a practical man and one with experience. Paradoxically he may be more effective in protecting human rights than deposed President Abulfaz Elchibey, who, while well-intentioned, was by all accounts unable to manage the country.

We met with Aliev on the Saturday night that he consolidated his power by striking a deal with rebel Colonel Surat Husseinov. "Azerbaijan will never waver from the path of democratic development," he told us. "Our state must be based on principles of international law, respect for human rights, pluralism and protection for ethnic minorities, and multiparty democracy." Those words were said with a conviction that belied Aliev's 13 years as President and 4 years as a member of the Politburo.

Aliev is a good politician. He understands Western concerns and knows that the path to economic development depends on Western investment. He knows that liberal rhetoric is a reassuring prerequisite for that investment. What he isn't sure of is whether he can get away with a gap between liberal rhetoric and uneven respect for human rights, whether the West will be tough-minded about linking investment to a good human rights record.

We have no doubt that Aliev will work hard to secure foreign investment. He recently met with a consortium of five oil and gas companies that originated under Elchibey's government to discuss a $30 billion investment. The consortium includes the U.S.-based companies Amoco, Unocal, and Pennzoil, and is reportedly concerned that the current turmoil in Azerbaijan will unfavorably affect the deal. Other Western businesses may soon be active there as well. We are told that 5,000 to 7,000 Western companies already have representatives stationed in various parts of the former Soviet Union. That provides a significant potential for leverage.

Businesses considering investment in the former Soviet Union should ask these questions:

1. Does the country respect freedom of the press, speech, association, and assembly?
2. Are political opponents allowed to contest for power, unharassed by the regime, under a system of free and fair elections?
3. Is the society built on a rule of law giving citizens access to a fair and impartial criminal justice system that is based on the presumption of innocence and that protects them from physical abuse?
4. Are the rights of ethnic and religious minorities respected?
5. Does the country abide by international law, particularly in the conduct of armed conflict with respect to protecting the lives and property of civilians?

Just as the Sullivan principles provided guidelines for investors in South Africa and helped hasten the end of apartheid, these questions will remind the rulers of the new nations that the international community is serious about the respect for human rights. We urge businesses to investigate the human rights record of countries where they are considering investment, both as a matter of moral obligation and as a way to ensure the economic and political stability that is a precondition for democracy and a free market.

# Advancing Reform in Higher Education in Eastern and Central Europe

(ANNUAL REPORT, 1993)

Literally hundreds of Western institutions are active in providing assistance to Eastern and Central Europe and the former Soviet Union. But few have been working in the region as long as the New School for Social Research and few if any reach into as many different countries. Our work began nearly a decade ago through the initiative of sociology professors Jeffrey Goldfarb and Andrew Arato. Professor Goldfarb, with the help of Polish dissident Adam Michnik, established "Totalitarianism and Democracy" seminars in Warsaw, New York, and Budapest. Professor Arato brought some of Hungary's leaders in the democratic opposition to the New School on teaching and research fellowships. The Democracy Seminars, initially underground in Warsaw and Budapest, attracted leading dissident intellectuals. They featured a common reading list, facilitated the exchange of scholarly papers, organized clandestine visits by New School faculty, and, when possible, sponsored visits to the New School. Since 1988, the Graduate Faculty's journal, *Social Research,* has published special issues on Central and Eastern Europe. The first issue appeared in the spring of 1988, before the collapse of Communism, and was authored by scholars resident in the region.

The Democracy Seminars resonated powerfully with the roots of the Graduate Faculty during the Nazi period, when the New School set up the University in Exile to rescue 167 endangered scholars, most of them Jewish. A core group of 10 stayed at the New School to found the Graduate Faculty; others were placed at American universities from Yale to Chicago to Berkeley. Concern for intellectual freedom, help for scholars in peril, attention to questions of democracy—all remain at the heart of the New School's mission. Our work in Eastern and Central Europe, then, was a present-day manifestation of that historical commitment.

The Democracy Seminars evolved into a more comprehensive East and Central Europe program, supported initially by the Ford Foundation and the Andrew Mellon Foundation, and given recent help by the Pew Charitable Trusts. In addition to the seminars, the program now includes a curriculum development project, a summer school and fellowship program aimed at training future faculty, and a scholarly journals project. The program has been led by an extraordinarily energetic and talented member of our faculty, Elzbieta Matynia, and is strongly supported by Graduate Faculty deans Ira Katznelson and Alan Wolfe. It now stretches from the three Baltic capitals of Tallinn, Riga, and Vilnius through the Central European cities of Warsaw, Budapest, Prague, and Bratislava to newer locations in Sofia, Bucharest, Belgrade, and Lviv. We hope to add Tirana and Yerevan during the next year.

The Democracy Seminar continues to be one of the principal features of the program. There are now 14 local branches and 250 regular members. Another 250 individuals participate occasionally, and during the past year 7 New School faculty members paid visits to one or another of the seminars.

Early participants in our seminars have emerged in key roles in political and academic life in the region, thus giving the New School an unparalleled network of friends in important places. Among them are: in Poland, Jacek Kuron, Minister of Labor, Andrzej Celinski, Senator, and Jacek Kurczewski, Deputy Marshal of the Parliament; in Czechoslovakia, Piotr Lukasiewicz, Minister of Culture, Petr Pithart, former Prime Minister, Martin Butora, one of the major advisers to President Havel before the split, Rita Klimova, Ambassador to the United States, and Jan Palous, Deputy Minister of Foreign Affairs; in Hungary, Miklos Haraszti, a member of Parliament and one of the leaders of the Free Democrats, and Gabor Demsky, Mayor of Budapest; in Latvia and Romania, members of Parliament Alex Grigorievs and Calin Anastasiu; in Bulgaria, Boyan Papazov, adviser to President Zhelev.

Seminar participants have also emerged as important journalists and commentators. They include Adam Michnik and Marcin Krol in Poland, Jan Urban in the Czech Republic, and Ferenc Koszeg in Hungary. And, as you might expect, some of our colleagues have returned to formal academic life in leadership positions: Miloslav Petrusek, Dean of the Faculty of Social Science at Charles University; Radim Palous, Rector of Charles University; Jacek Kurczewski, Dean of the Faculty of Applied Social Science at Warsaw University; Edmund Mokrzycki, co-director of the Graduate School for Social Science in Warsaw; Janos Kis, chair of the Political Science Faculty at the Central European University in Budapest; Andrei Marga, Vice Rector of the University in Cluj, Romania; and Antoni Todorov, chair of the Political Science Department at the New Bulgarian University in Sofia.

It is clear from the topics discussed and the participants that the Democracy Seminar is far more than an abstract academic exercise. The network provides settings in which the theoretical and practical dimensions of building democratic societies can be worked out and tested in real situations. The Democracy Seminar is one vehicle for the engagement of scholars in charting the directions of their new democracies.

The New School's East and Central Europe project has expanded beyond the Democracy Seminar into a broad effort to help in the renewal of academic and intellectual life in the region. The Communist regimes had a corrosive effect on higher education. Curricula were politicized, and many faculty were corrupted. The social sciences were virtually devastated: political science was banned altogether in many countries; other disciplines, like economics and philosophy, were pursued in a rigid ideological framework. Libraries lacked journals and monographs, which are essential vehicles for communication among scholars. Those academics who wanted to maintain their independence were isolated and cut off from the latest developments in their fields—and from even the most basic interaction with colleagues outside the Soviet bloc.

The task of rebuilding—really reinventing—the universities, and the social sciences in particular, is formidable. Many universities in the United States and Western Europe, together with government agencies and private foundations are involved. During the first 2 years of its East and Central Europe program, the New School concentrated on broad curriculum reform efforts, specifically through the establishment of university-based "curriculum centers" throughout the region. These centers coordinated curriculum and bibliographic workshops for local faculty and provided texts, syllabi, and other instructional materials from American universities. Currently, the New School is working with eight universities throughout the region to create new courses, sometimes taught in collaboration. A course in political sociology in Warsaw and Budapest (1992), a course in the social constitution of democracy in those cities plus Prague and Bratislava (1993), and a newly slated course in political sociology in Sofia (1994) all involve local faculty working with New School visitors.

In addition to the collaborative courses, the program has helped reconstruct basic courses in the social sciences at universities throughout the region. The New School has provided help in constructing reading lists, supplying necessary textbooks, and providing funds to edit collections of recent scholarship in translation for use in the courses. Of particular interest is the work of New School Professor William Hirst. With the support of the James McDonnell Foundation, Hirst has focused on rebuilding psychology in Romania, a discipline singled out for particular destruction by the Ceausescu regime.

Academic leaders throughout the region indicate that Western scholarly journals are *the* critical need for reconnecting scholarly life to the wider conversations from which academics in the region have been isolated for nearly half a century. Arien Mack, professor of psychology and editor of *Social Research*, had the inspiration and energy to persuade over 450 journals to donate multiple, 3-year subscriptions to libraries in the region. With the help of the Mellon Foundation and the United States Information Agency, the Journal Project has sent over 21,000 journals to more than 200 libraries in Eastern and Central Europe and the former Soviet Union.

Another aspect of the New School's initiative addresses the need for a younger generation of teachers. The retraining of senior faculty, tainted and scarred by collaboration with the old regime, is not an efficient or promising route for reform of higher education in the region. Thus the New School has focused on training very junior faculty and graduate students. With the help of the Pew Charitable Trusts, the Graduate Faculty provides a 1-year intensive fellowship in New York for beginning graduate students, who return to their home universities conversant with the style and standards of Western scholarship.

All told, some 60 scholars from the region have spent time at the University in recent years. About half of them came on visiting fellowships for stays ranging in length from 2 weeks to a full semester; the other half came for shorter working visits, which usually included one lecture open to the public. In addition, the New School operates a 3-week summer institute in Cracow, Poland which brings together 45 graduate students (12 from America, 33 from the countries of the region) to focus on issues of democracy and diversity.

We are mindful that the totality of our efforts and those of other institutions is very modest measured against the task of reforming higher education in ten countries in Eastern and Central Europe, let alone the fifteen new nations formed from the Soviet Union. While these efforts are not well-coordinated, we have learned, I think, that a certain amount of disorder and duplication is probably a good thing—certainly to be preferred to a highly centralized reform effort working only through official channels in the various countries.

It has been the New School's style to bypass official structures and pursue three independent avenues of reform. The first, which has characterized much of our efforts to date, involves working directly with talented individuals within the state universities who are well placed to lead minireform efforts within specific departments or schools—the dean of a philosophy faculty, the chair of a sociology institute, the coordinator of a history project. Work with Antoni Sulek in sociology at Warsaw University, Rumyana Kolarova in political science at Sofia University, and Miloslav Petrusek in the social sciences at Charles University are three effective examples of this model of intervention. We think it important not to "give up" on the large state universities but rather to plant seeds of reform within them which will, by example, accelerate the reform of the entire university system over time.

A second and even more promising avenue can be found in new public institutions created by governments for the purpose of bypassing the entrenched state universities and bureaucracies of higher education ministries. On my recent trip through the former Soviet Union, I opened conversations with Yuri Afanasyev, Rector of the Russian Humanitarian University, a new institution with 500 faculty members and 5,000 students. Based in Moscow, it has responsibility for curriculum reform, teacher training, and the provision of Western monographs and scholarly journals for 216 institutions throughout Russia. In Kiev, Ukraine I met with the Rector of Mohyla Academy, a new quasi-private institution, located on the site of a major seventeenth-century university. Mohyla derives 70 percent of its monies from the Ukraine government but not from the Ministry of Education. The balance comes from tuition and private grants. It is organized on the American model of a 4-year B.A. program followed by a master's degree and eventually a Ph.D., and all students must speak English. Mohyla will eventually enroll 1,500 students in the existing faculties of humanities, social science, and natural science and the planned faculties of fine arts and law.

These two institutions—and there are others—demonstrate a recognition by the new governments that reform of the entrenched state universities will be slow, painful, and difficult. Because these models represent indigenous reform, I find them the most exciting.

Perhaps the most dramatic change can be found in the third route to reform—new, independent universities started with funds from private Western sources and staffed heavily with Western faculty and administrative leadership. Examples include the American University in Bulgaria (in affiliation with the University of Maine), which enrolls about 50 students in master's degree programs in the social sciences, philosophy, history, and computer sciences; the American University of Armenia (in affiliation with the University of California), which enrolls 280 students in master's degree programs in business and engineering; the Central European University in Budapest, which enrolls 500 students in graduate-level programs in art history, economics, European studies, environmental sciences, history, legal studies, medieval studies, political science, and sociology; and the Graduate School for Social Research in Warsaw, affiliated with the Polish Academy of Science, which enrolls 50 students in sociology, political science, law, history, economics, psychology, and theory of culture.

These institutions do not need the kind of curriculum help (or even library resources) which the New School has to offer. But they do need a structured opportunity for their students to do graduate-level work at the Graduate Faculty, perhaps even through a joint Ph.D. program. Given the small size of their graduate programs, particularly in the social sciences, they are not able to offer the depth of instruction required for a first-rate Ph.D. The New School will be exploring how best to work with these new institutions in the years ahead.

It is a natural evolution that our program will more and more be working through institutions, new and old, in the region. We take pride in the fact that 80 percent of all the funds donated for our work has been spent in the region. Costs are kept low because the New School's faculty time and other services are donated; no New School faculty members receive stipends for participation in any aspect of the project, except for the Cracow summer school. Thus our work for nearly a decade—in fourteen countries, teaching hundreds of scholars and thousands of students—has cost only $900,000.

The adoption of Western academic models in the countries of Eastern and Central Europe has occurred at the initiative of local leaders who see those models as the most effective counterbalance to the entrenched, repressive methods that characterized the old regimes. The reform of higher education is not an instance of the West imposing its values and structures; nor is it a one-way street. We at the New School, our financial supporters, American higher education, and the American public more widely have a great deal to learn from our work in Eastern and Central Europe. At a very basic level, the curriculum project causes us to rethink how and what we are teaching our own students. Work in the training of faculty reminds us that we do not give enough attention to preparing our own graduate students to teach. Senior faculty members who have taught in the collaborative courses abroad report a beneficial effect on their teaching at home. And many have found their research agendas shaped and enriched by conversations with colleagues in the region. This is also true for a generation of our graduate students who discover a fertile field of dissertation topics in the transition to democracy and free markets that is under way.

We draw insight and encouragement from the importance that these societies in the process of regeneration attach to intellectual life and higher education. They feel acutely the absence of well-trained professionals—in law, economics, science, social work, teaching, medicine, management—a lack Americans do not appreciate. They have an implicit faith that knowledge can be applied to the solution of social and economic problems, a proposition in which Americans have less confidence than they once did. They believe that a healthy democracy nourished by the institutions of civil society depends upon a broadly educated population, an axiom many Americans take for granted. It is good for the soul of a university president, so accustomed to defending American higher education against critics who believe it is undercutting our society's core values, to see the central role these nations in transition assign to higher education. Americans should be reminded by their example of the critical contribution higher education makes to the economic strength and spiritual health of our own society. And we should take pride that our system of higher education is the model for the reform effort throughout Eastern and Central Europe and the former Soviet Union.

# SOUTH AFRICA: THE CASE FOR CAUTIOUS AND COMPLEX OPTIMISM

(MEMORANDUM TO THE BOARD OF TRUSTEES, MARCH 1994)

### PURPOSE

My wife Cynthia and I spent 11 days in South Africa (February 25 to March 7, 1994) learning about the political, economic, and social transformation under way and its implications for higher education. The primary purpose of the visit was to explore how the New School for Social Research might help institutions of higher education prepare for the new South Africa. South Africa is a welcome commitment because of our scholarly attention to societies in transition.

The easiest way for the New School to play a role would be to use the Time Warner funds to admit more black South African students at the graduate level. But that is an expensive course which benefits relatively few people and removes talent from South Africa at a crucial moment. Thus I sought advice from educators in South Africa about alternative approaches we might consider, some of which parallel our work in aiding the reconstruction of the social sciences in Eastern and Central Europe.

I visited three historically black institutions: the University of the North in Pietersburg, Ft. Hare near East London, and the University of the Western Cape. We also visited the University of Cape Town, the University of Witwatersrand, and the Centre for Education Policy Development, which is advising the African National Congress (ANC). Other visits included Helen Suzman, long-time leader of the Democratic Party, and Francis Wilson of the Independent Electoral Commission; Richard Steyn, publisher of the *Star*, and Gabu Tugwana, editor of the *Sunday Nation*; Frank Ferrari and John Gerhart of the African-American Institute and Ford Foundation respectively; Geoffrey Budlender, director of the Legal Resources Centre, a lawyers' human rights group; Patrick Chan of the Urban and Rural Development and Education Project; Trevor Abrahams, National Director of the South African Council of Higher Education; Morley Nkosi, a Graduate Faculty economics graduate involved in costing the ANC reconstruction program; and Gavon Mbeki, one of the heroes of the ANC struggle and the father of the likely Foreign Minister in the new government. We also met the deputy head of the ANC Department of International Affairs, Sankie Nkondo, at the ANC headquarters at Shell House.

Perhaps the symbolic highlight of the trip was attending a press conference at which Nelson Mandela announced the creation of the ANC press headquarters. While his speech was brief, the in-person glimpse confirmed my sense of Mandela as an extraordinary person.

Before discussing the educational picture, I want to offer personal reflections on what I saw and comment on the political scene.

## Overview

South Africa, which is about the size of California, Oregon, Washington, and Nevada combined, has a population of 38 million (28 million black, 5 million white, 3.5 million colored, 1.5 million Asian). Its government is divided among three cities: Pretoria (executive), Cape Town (legislative), and Bloemfontein City (judicial); Johannesburg is its financial capital. Its territory also includes four so-called black homelands which are recognized as independent nations only by South Africa. All four homelands will participate in the forthcoming elections and be reincorporated into South Africa.

It is my wont in a new situation first to gain an understanding of the overall picture at a quite simple level and then to add more details and complexity to the picture. Thus I asked perhaps 100 people, "Are you optimistic or pessimistic about South Africa's future?" Cape Town Political Science

Professor Andre Du Toit replied, "We face a deeply ambiguous situation with quite contrary forces at work. Thus it is hard to know whether to be pessimistic or optimistic." While Du Toit may well be correct, most people without hesitation expressed optimism—people from different parties, from different professions and backgrounds, and from different races. All the American observers with whom we spoke, from Paul Taylor of the *Washington Post* to Harvard Professor Richard Neustadt and Ford Foundation South Africa Representative John Gerhart, concurred.

Most everyone acknowledged that the road to reconstruction will be bumpy. The forthcoming April 27 election produces a mixture of anxiety and exhilaration. Despite the reluctance of the alliance of the conservative forces—black and white—to participate, the campaign is proceeding vigorously with the two prominent leaders, Nelson Mandela of the ANC and F. W. de Klerk of the National Party, fighting for the center, which is likely to encompass as much as 85 percent of the electorate. The broad and vital center of South African politics is captured by a mosaic of images which includes pictures of de Klerk on billboards surrounded by black children, his cheering reception while campaigning in colored areas, his capacity to apologize for apartheid, Mandela's extraordinary lack of bitterness, and the ANC's reassuring position on economic issues and courting of the white vote.

In response to a *Star* poll which asked 100 South African business leaders, "What election outcome is best for the country?" 63 replied an ANC victory and 30 a National Party victory, with the remainder scattered. Talk at the white country clubs turns easily these days to the example of neighboring Zimbabwe where the whites who stayed retain considerable economic power in a black nation.

In New York we are fond of sampling the opinion of ordinary people by asking political questions of taxi drivers. On our way in from the Cape Town airport we spoke with our driver, an Afrikaaner who had recently lost his job at the Bayer Chemical Company. I asked what the new South Africa meant for him. Completely accepting the direction of events, he criticized the National Party for resisting change: "Why didn't they begin desegregation in the 1950s? Now it will proceed too quickly with people being hurt." Make no mistake, this taxi driver was no liberal. But like many ordinary citizens, he seemed to accept change when it was accomplished in a legal framework—much as attitudes in the American South changed once Jim Crow laws were struck down.

But I am getting ahead of my story. South Africa is a deeply troubled society, unlike any other I have ever known. The new government—and the only question is whether the ANC will have a super majority of two-thirds in the Parliament—will face extraordinary expectations, limited resources to address deep poverty, and the political restraint that comes from the need to encourage foreign investment and to reassure white domestic capital. Not an enviable challenge for a liberation movement with no experience in governing and not yet disciplined as a political party.

The depth of that challenge can be seen in a short drive south of Johannesburg to Soweto or in the informal village that flanks D.F. Malan Airport in Cape Town or in Park Station in Johannesburg, source of the famous Blue Train by day and shelter for 1,500 homeless people at night. By some estimates, 7 million people are homeless in South Africa; another 4 million live in substandard housing. Unemployment runs 42 percent among all residents but as high as 75 percent for young blacks. We visited Soweto (short for South Western Townships), Protea, Orange Farm, Eldorado Park to the south and Alexander to the north of Johannesburg, and Khayelitsha and Langa outside of Cape Town.

By far the most desperate circumstances are found in shanty towns like the one bordering Kliptown, south of Johannesburg. Home to migrants from rural areas, these informal settlements are jammed with corrugated metal shacks which house up to four families without electricity, heat, or water. There may be as many as 1 million people living in such circumstances around Johannesburg, with more coming daily. The beautiful farms that border the Golden Highway to Cape Town are yielding to shanty settlements, which start as scattered shacks on a grassy hill and evolve into teeming rural ghettos.

The townships vary widely from the upscale Beverly Hills section of Soweto—near the one-time homes of Nelson Mandela and Bishop Tutu, and now occupied by wealthy black businesspeople living in ample houses with nice yards—to middle-class sections like South Protea to the more typical rows of four-room cement blocks, often with a makeshift shack in the backyard for extended family. Schools, convenience stores, community centers, grid-pattern roads, phones, and electricity mark the more developed townships.

Since 1991, when most of the apartheid barriers tumbled down, some wealthier blacks have moved into white suburbs and colored areas, while others have taken their places in the better townships, and still others have managed a transition from the informal settlements to the bottom rung of the formal townships.

But it will take years—maybe decades—for the imprint of apartheid to fade. Even though I thought I knew what that word meant, I never visualized the breathtaking and ruthless efficiency with which it was implemented. Nor had I ever thought it possible to separate a society so completely and neatly into white, colored, Asian, and black; everything was separated: schools, housing, stores, townships, and homelands.

It is literally still possible to live in South Africa and believe you are in a white world, more white than any major American city, with a modern infrastructure equal to the best in Germany. Take Sandton City to the north of Johannesburg. The suburbs are lush, with broad tree-lined boulevards, wonderful old European-style houses, many with pools, supported by modern shopping centers, and with Jaguar, Mercedes Benz, and BMW dealers readily available. Sandton Center—which sports two Hyatt Regency style hotels complete with atriums, many European restaurants, a luxury mall with a marble floor inside and palm courts reminiscent of the real Beverly Hills—could be anywhere in the richest country in the world. The stark contrast between a tour of the townships in the morning and elegant dining at a Portuguese restaurant in the evening was the greatest discordance I have ever experienced. And this situation is taken as normal—not right, but the way things are and are likely to be for a while.

South Africa's infrastructure has no parallel on the African continent. Johannesburg and Cape Town make Moscow, Prague, even Budapest, seem primitive. The highway system looks like California, complete with elaborate clover-leaf interchanges. South Africa Airlines could be Lufthansa, the trains run on time, and communication systems are more modern than in most of Europe. There can be, therefore, no excuse for tolerating "third world" conditions for most of the population while spending lavishly on the creation of a modern Western society for the 12 percent of the population that is white. The absurdity of it all is best symbolized for me by the modern pedestrian bridge being built today over the N2 (a four-lane, divided highway) so that people living in the old and new sections of Khayelitsha can commute from shanty town to rural ghetto without disrupting the orderly flow of traffic between Stellenbosch and Cape Town.

This is not to suggest that the white world is not subject to disruption. There are watchtowers along the N2 (reminiscent of the Berlin Wall) for South African Defense Forces personnel to guard motorists against rock-throwing youths. And visitors to the five-star Carlton Hotel in downtown Johannesburg are virtually forbidden to venture out of the hotel after dark without a guard. They are also severely warned about walking about during weekends when the city is virtually deserted and a white face can scarcely be found. Still, the concern for crime strikes me as vastly overstated, reflecting more the general white anxiety about transition than a crime wave any greater than we might experience in New York City.

Indeed, most of the violence is black on black, in the townships, where hostels for single men often spawn conflicts between, say, Inkatha members (followers of Zulu chief Mangosuthu G. Buthelezi) and permanent residents, most of whom are loyal to the ANC. We were exposed to potential trouble when our driver ventured unknowingly into a "no go" area (really a few square blocks) in Alexander which Inkatha had taken over from ANC supporters. Our driver's cousin—whom we were seeking out—said the only reason we were not attacked was because we were with him.

There were some 5,000 political killings in South Africa last year, but 93 percent of them occurred in three areas: East Rand, Natal-Midlands, and Natal South Coast. Many with whom we spoke felt that the Western press is presenting an inaccurate picture of South Africa as an entire nation on the edge of violence. ANC press liaison Paulo Jordan told me that this is the one serious flaw in reporting about South Africa in Western papers.

## Political Situation

Yet fears of right wing terrorism and single acts of violence by deranged individuals do not seem misplaced. Against that background the lack of security around Nelson Mandela is shocking and inexcusable.

The ANC scheduled a 5:30 press conference at the Carlton Hotel, where we were staying, to announce the creation of its press center at the Carlton. The objective, said Paulo Jordan, was to make it easier for members of the press to get information—by which he really meant to get them out of the ANC headquarters, where they were underfoot. Because ANC relations with the international and local press corps has had rough patches, Nelson Mandela was on hand to smooth any ruffled feathers. There he was sitting 15 feet from me at a table, quietly listening to Jordan's pitch, patiently hearing the party faithful introduce him as he had a thousand times, laughing at a hypothetical story about tricking Foreign Minister Pik Botha—very human, very real, very reassuring yet awesome and enigmatic. Here before me was the one person on whom it all depends, a man who can quiet angry black youths, soften the edges of black radicalism, win the trust of many white leaders. His removal from the scene would dash hopes for a peaceful transition—indeed, might touch off civil conflict that would degenerate into chaos. And yet there was no visible security:

the conference was open to all, no credentials required, when I entered the Cartlon with my New School bag. I was not even searched because I was staying at the hotel.

After about 30 minutes of ANC business, Mandela rose to make a short speech. On everyone's mind was his trip the next day to Durban to meet with Chief Buthelezi, head of Inkatha, who so far had refused to register his party for the election. Once the darling of local and international business for opposing sanctions in South Africa, Buthelezi is now odd man out—no longer, with Mandela and de Klerk, one of the big three. Polls show that his party might not even beat the ANC in its home province of Natal, and might not win enough votes to earn a place in the forthcoming government of national unity.

Buthelezi's credibility suffered greatly when he aligned himself with the white right in the so-called Freedom Alliance that includes Inkatha, the Afrikaaner Volksfront, the Conservative Party, and the homeland of Bophuthatswana. This unlikely coalition is held together by a common interest in local autonomy and a weak central government. While their individual positions differ some, they generally agree on autonomous provincial taxing powers, some exclusive provincial executive powers, and constitutional limits on the intrusive potential of Parliament.

Much of the fear of political violence stems from the Freedom Alliance's refusal to participate in the elections. Some predict that Inkatha will prevent the election from proceeding in parts of Natal and that the Afrikaaner Volksfront paramilitary wing will undertake acts of terrorism. Close to the military, these Boer hard-liners are thought to be well armed and to have sympathizers in key places within South Africa's transportation, communication, and power network.

For Mandela, the stakes are high: he needs to get Buthelezi into the election without giving much more away. Already the ANC has agreed to compromises which weaken the central government, and some observers think Mandela has made a mistake by being too patient with Buthelezi, by inflating his importance. Against that background, Mandela came to the podium. He started with a self-deprecating joke, smiled warmly and easily, then in a few sparse words delivered his message. First of conciliation: "It is my duty to persuade Buthelezi to join the campaign and I will do everything in my power to do so. But I am clear that I cannot compromise on two principles: there can be no postponement of the election and South Africa must remain united—there can be no secession." There it was, straight and simple: patience, dialogue, conciliation, compromise without sacrifice of essential principles.

It remains to be seen whether the hopeful signs coming from Mandela's 10-hour marathon conversation the next day are real. Buthelezi did agree to a provisional registration by the March 5 deadline and Mandela agreed to international mediation of the constitutional questions, presumably after the election. But later Inkatha failed to complete the registration formalities and, as of this writing, will not appear on the ballot. The party is provisionally registered but failed to provide party lists as required by law, and has indicated that it will not participate in the election.

Here I need pause to discuss the curious case of Bophuthatswana, the only one of the ten homelands which has refused to participate in the election. During our visit, protests against the dictatorial style of President Lucas Mangope escalated, leading to his capitulation on March 11 to participating in the election. In a critical misjudgment, the military wing of the Afrikaaner Volksfront sent armed forces to the capital of Mmabatho expecting to help black Bophuthatswana troops loyal to Mangope. Instead, the local army turned on the Volksfront, killing three before the South African army moved in to end the bloodshed. A total of forty people were killed before order was restored.

A surface reading of events might see here confirmation of the worst fears of spreading violence and impending chaos. But there is a more hopeful interpretation that views the Bophuthatswana episode as a positive turning point. First, the Freedom Alliance is badly weakened: Bophuthatswana has withdrawn and will now be part of the election, and the white right is split between those preferring political participation and those advocating violence. The abortive mission of the Afrikaaner Volksfront greatly strengthens the moderate faction now planning to participate in the election. This means that Buthelezi is isolated in his election boycott. Second, as many had predicted, the militant white right is less well organized and less powerful than rumors have suggested. Third, de Klerk and Mandela worked well together in a crisis, with Mandela supporting the decision to restore order through the South African army—an army once described as the agent of apartheid.*

Without Inkatha, there are twenty-eight parties registered but only four count: the ANC, de Klerk's National Party, the Democratic Party (white liberals during apartheid), and the Pan African Congress (PAC). The PAC leadership split with the ANC in 1958 and is to the left, especially on issues like land reform. It has its strongest appeal in the rural districts and among militant black youths. Ironically, it may benefit from a technical election rule, a concession by the ANC to the Freedom Alliance, which allows two separate ballots—one for the national election and one for the provincial ticket (local elections come at the end of 1994). The double ballot was meant to help Freedom Alliance at the provincial level, but opinion sampling has discovered that many people think the second ballot is for the voters' second choice in the national election, thus benefiting the PAC, which is the second choice behind the ANC for many black votes.

How will the election go? What are the issues? Polls show 20 percent of those likely to vote still undecided. The large personalities of F. W. de Klerk and Nelson Mandela dominate this election. Both the National Party and the ANC struggle to live down their past—apartheid and radicalism—and both vie for the center and are fuzzy on the issues. Mandela talks of jobs, peace, and freedom, of economic growth as the key to South Africa's future. De Klerk also roots his vision of the post-sanctions future in economic growth and says his party

---

*My take closely follows Bill Keller's insightful analysis in the *New York Times*, March 13, 1994.

is more competent to manage government efficiently and win the confidence of business.

Indicative of the campaign is the housing issue, which both major parties have been wary of: Mandela not wishing to raise unattainable expectations, de Klerk not wishing to highlight past failings. Whether by design or not, the Minister of Housing unveiled a plan in early March to build 1 million new homes, a plan developed by the National Party government without consultation with the Temporary Executive Committee, which is the precursor to the new government of national unity. The ANC reacted angrily, calling for the resignation but then followed with its own full page ads promising 1 million houses after the election.

The PAC, with its call for redistribution of land and its blatant disinterest in appealing to or reassuring whites, plays a useful role for Mandela by making him appear moderate. And the two white, right-wing parties perform the same service for de Klerk. While Mandela is the towering moral figure of the moment, de Klerk should not be dismissed as a cynic, adjusting his beliefs in pursuit of personal power. By all accounts, he has the toughest job in the election as representative of the party of apartheid. But he is a natural campaigner, a better stump speaker than Mandela, and has exhibited considerable courage in campaigning in difficult situations. His security, while better, is also inadequate and his removal from the scene would also be disastrous.

There is no question that the ANC will win a strong majority, but will it gain the two-thirds super majority needed to run the country with greater ease and to pass a permanent constitution? A lot is at stake.

The temporary constitution is the product of negotiation. It provides for a 5-year transition government of national unity that is certain to make Nelson Mandela President and F. W. de Klerk Deputy President (the runner-up automatically gets the second spot, but any party polling over 20 percent gets a Deputy President). Any party gaining more than 5 percent is entitled to a Cabinet seat; there is no 5 percent threshold for membership in the Parliament. The ANC strength is estimated at 62-70 percent, the National Party at 15-25 percent, the PAC at 5-10 percent, Inkatha 3-5 percent, followed by the Democratic Party and others.

Some sympathetic to the ANC believe it would be just as well to fall slightly short of a two-thirds majority. Such an outcome, they argue, would produce a true coalition government with the need to negotiate. It would also help keep the ANC membership in line. (The situation recalls Franklin Roosevelt's problems after his big victory in 1936, when it became harder to enforce party discipline.) Moreover, it would be reassuring to whites and perhaps foreign investors. Finally, less than a two-thirds majority might ease the burden on the ANC to meet so quickly the vast expectations it faces.

Others argue that the ANC should win the two-thirds majority because the black community needs to assume complete control—to win at the ballot box that which the quiet revolution has not yet achieved. They argue further that the central government is dangerously weak, a product of the suspicions many have about institutions and the compromise on regional autonomy already made to court the Freedom Alliance. These observers dismiss the expectations argument by noting that the ANC will have the same burden at 62 percent that it would have at 67 percent and therefore might as well have clear control. My own uneducated guess is that the ANC will end up somewhere with between 60 and 65 percent of the vote.

Will the elections be fair? I think so, but not perfect. An Independent Electoral Commission is supervising the election through a force of 180,000 trained monitors. In addition, many outside groups will be sending observers. The atmosphere leading up to the election appears fair, with the major parties having access to the media. But there will be some violence preceding and on election day; there will be episodes of intimidation, illiterate people will make mistakes in marking ballots, and disputes will arise over voter eligibility. Helen Suzman, a member of the Independent Electoral Commission, believes a 60 percent voter turnout would be good under the circumstances. I believe independent observers will judge the election to be essentially fair without evidence of systematic widespread fraud.

Most observers believe the ANC will win eight or even all nine of the new provinces. The most doubtful is the Western Cape, where the National Party is doing well with the colored vote and where both the PAC and the Democratic Party have strength. Natal, with Inkatha strength, and the Eastern Cape, with PAC strength in the Traskei, are two other provinces hotly contested but expected to go to the ANC.

On the national level, there is one worrisome provision in the interim constitution which forces members of Parliament to resign if they leave or are expelled from their party. The provision freezes party composition for 5 years and may well prevent the kinds of natural realignments that occur when liberation movements are swept to political power (such as Solidarity in Poland). Some oppose this provision as inherently undemocratic, while others believe it will retard the healthy development of modern parties, especially within the black community.

An unanswered question for me is how unified the ANC is. One of our colleagues, Neville Alexander, who spent 10 years on Robben Island with Nelson Mandela, believes that the leadership of the ANC is too moderate, too middle class, not sufficiently in tune with the feelings of young urban blacks, women, and the rural poor. He predicts growing divisions within the black community along class lines once the ANC comes to power.

## The Economy

There is no question that economic sanctions bit hard in South Africa and hastened the end of apartheid. Sanctions cost South Africa $32 billion to $40 billion between 1988 and 1989, including $11 billion in net capital outflows and $4 billion in lost export earnings. These losses increased unemployment, inflation, and interest rates. And there is little mystery about who paid the heaviest price for sanctions: the black community. It surprised me that not a single person with whom we spoke wanted to talk about sanctions, which were taken as a matter of fact, not a moral force. There were no statements like "While sanctions imposed a heavy burden on those they intended benefit, the price was worth it." or "Sanctions imposed a severe punishment on poor blacks only to accelerate changes which would have happened soon anyway." No second guessing, no reflections, no thanks to the outside world, and no recriminations; just silence, perhaps because both sides are all too aware of the human cost and find it too painful to confront.

As Cape Town economist Francis Wilson, who also chairs the Ft. Hare governing board, noted, "There is a paradox about sanctions: economic decline brought de Klerk to negotiations but the lingering effect of sanctions will make it hard for the new government to survive unless it can stimulate economic growth."

The new ANC government will face a conflict among three economic goals: the provision of immediate relief to those in need, the need to rebuild the postapartheid economy, and the desire to pursue an agenda of reform in land holding and business concentration. Mandela's dilemma is reminiscent of Franklin Roosevelt's struggle with the three R's of relief, recovery and, reform.

For the moment, fostering economic growth appears to be central, since it is believed that only sharp growth will provide the latitude to invest in housing, health, primary education, and other social programs for black South Africans. While there is talk of a wealth tax to finance these measures, the ANC has taken pains to reassure large businesses that it has no plan to socialize them and to reassure white farmers that it is state-owned land that will be redistributed and their own farms will not be confiscated.

Economists at the University of Cape Town believe consumer and government spending will lead recovery and can produce at least a 5 percent growth rate starting next year; one economist even predicts an 8 percent growth rate. Given the lack of precise ANC plans for reconstruction of society, it is hard to know what the cost will be or what growth rate will be necessary. But everyone believes that the ANC must deliver social benefits to the townships quickly to remain politically viable.

Just how fast the ANC-led government can take control is anyone's guess. I have heard estimates that the top ANC talent pool is 200 deep; that does not seem an adequate number for the executive branch, taking into account the fact that some will be active in Parliament and some in provincial governments. The ANC policy team has been augmented by a series of independent analytical groups organized to provide policy guidance in fields like education, health, land policy, local government, and macroeconomic policy. There are twenty special task forces, each of which has one or more advisory councils. In total, there are perhaps 300 people supplementing the ANC planning effort. This is not to suggest that the transition will be smooth or that the "political appointments" will soon have control over the civil service, which is protected in the interim constitution.

One area that is not expected to do well is higher education which is already 13 percent of the national budget. Other priorities like housing and health may well come first and within education, primary, secondary and basic adult literacy training are likely to be the priorities. Virtually everyone with whom we spoke believes higher education will be lucky to hold its own, even though enrollments are growing sharply. And within higher education there is bound to be pressure for redistribution between the elite, historically white universities and the historically black universities.

## Higher Education

Depending how one counts, there are about twenty-two institutions of higher education in South Africa. Cape Town, Rhodes, Witwatersrand, and the Afrikaaner institutions at Stellenbosch, Pretoria, and Potchefsteroom are strong, historically white universities* Among the historically black institutions, Ft. Hare is the oldest and most prestigious, having

---

*These institutions are rapidly being integrated, with nearly half of the present enrollment nonwhite.

graduated generations of black leaders including Nelson Mandela. But the strongest today is probably the University of the Western Cape (originally a colored university). Also worth noting are the University of Zululand, The University of Durban-Westville, and the University of the North. Another important group of institutions—white and black—is the technikons, which are something akin to our technical colleges.

Some of the historically black universities were deliberately located in very remote places; for example, the University of the North is in an isolated rural area 20 kilometers north of the small regional capital of Pietersburg. We visited the Faculty Development Council of the University of the North to explore how the New School might be a useful partner in its rebuilding program. We came at registration period (the school year begins in February) amid student strikes about overcrowding. This campus, built for 4,000, currently enrolls 13,000 students with individual lecture classes running up to 2,000 students. Because of its remote location, there is no off-campus housing and the overflow of students are living in the hallways of the dormitories. Given the budget constraints, the faculty size is frozen so that faculty are in the classroom 18 hours a week and grade all exams and papers without the help of teaching assistants.

At first glance, it seemed impossible for the New School to be of any help in such a chaotic situation. But our meeting with the Faculty Development Council produced some good ideas not unlike those learned from our Eastern and Central Europe experience. For example:

1. The University of the North (UN) would like to have an advanced Ph.D. student from the New School teach for 6 months or a year.
2. The teaching exchange could be combined with a mini-sabbatical (3–6 months) for younger UN faculty, possibly at the New School. It would be useful to find ways of helping the faculty finish advanced degrees.
3. Co-taught courses would be valuable. Our faculty members could make short, intensive visits—teaching in the

co-taught courses, giving a public lecture, or organizing a faculty seminar.
4. In the administrative area—for example, planning and budgeting—New School visitors could help or brief sabbaticals for UN faculty at the New School would be useful.

There was broad agreement that we could be most useful in faculty development; there was no support for student exchanges. The faculty at the University of the North explained that pedagogical reform is very much needed, since current teaching styles are very conservative and heavily emphasize rote memorization. The culture of dialogue and debate needs to be engendered—challenges which interaction with New School personnel would advance.

Over and over again we were told about the double isolation suffered by faculty members at historically black universities: isolation within their country from the research community and isolation from the international intellectual community because of sanctions. It is fair to say that there is a pent-up desire for contact of all kinds.

The two other institutions with which we met endorsed the models for cooperation suggested by the University of the North's Faculty Development Council. At Ft. Hare, a university of about 4,000 students situated between East London and Port Elizabeth, a talented provost, Sipho Pityana, is organizing a Research Resource Center to build research capacity in a faculty which had been devastated by the old regime. He has in mind creating a modest graduate program, principally at the master's level, with faculty brought in on special grants. The center would provide research infrastructure—for example, a computer facility linked to Internet—and training in research methodology such as statistical analysis. Pityana would like us to design and staff an intensive workshop on research methods. I could imagine becoming a partner in building this center.

The University of the Western Cape (UWC) is the most advanced of the historically black universities, partially because of its urban location and partially because of excellent leadership for nearly a decade by Vice Chancellor Jakes Gerwel. Two of UWC's faculty members have already been involved with Alice Amsden and Lance Taylor of our faculty on a project advising the ANC on macroeconomic policy. The UWC very much wants to connect its training and research programs to the immediate needs of the new South Africa in fields like education, health, and government. In fact, the university has just started a new school of government, focusing on the training of managers for not-for-profit institutions and local government. The possibilities for a partnership with the New School's Graduate School of Management and Urban Policy are obvious and would be welcome.

UWC is also pioneering new master's programs which would replace the British thesis-only system with a mix of course work and a thesis. There are diverse ways we could help in this process, especially in the field of gender studies, which is new for South Africa. The status of women is much neglected by all races in South Africa and much in need of attention.

I have appointed a steering committee of faculty to help design our South African program and will shortly appoint a part-time staff person to move it forward. This project elicits great interest among the faculty and staff of the New School, especially among those from underrepresented groups who have felt that the university's deep ties to Eastern and Central Europe are too narrow. And within the Graduate Faculty, there is growing interest in providing the new Committee for the Study of Democracy with a three-point geographical context: Eastern and Central Europe, Latin America, and South Africa. While each area poses different challenges for transitions, there are common themes through which knowledge of one region enriches understanding in the others.

## Conclusion

I said at the outset that I am cautiously optimistic and that the sense of the possible "on the ground" in South Africa is more buoyant than the removed analysts would have us think. As 84-year-old Robben Island "alum," Govan Mbeki, told us, "One *has* to be optimistic—if you lose optimism then you are pessimistic, which means you expect a civil war which would be a horrible war along color lines." That one has to be optimistic is the unspoken parentheses that precedes the reassurances we heard everywhere. But then our conversations were mainly at a leadership level or among the urban poor.

If by optimism we mean a reasonably fair election which results in a centrist government which shows a generosity of spirit and is competent, then we will not be disappointed. But if we expect a smooth transition, unmarred by random violence or even major disorder in a few locations, that is another story. And no one can really predict whether the economy will recover fast enough to allow the ANC government to meet the immediate needs of the people who put it in office and thereby hold the center of the political spectrum against more radical young blacks without resorting to measures which alienate the moderate white community and thus undercut de Klerk's hold on his party's center.

One can safely predict that the transition will take time, perhaps a generation or more, and that it will be interesting, perhaps the most dramatic transformation presently underway around the globe.

# THE "GREAT GAME" REVISITED: PROBLEMS AND POTENTIAL IN CENTRAL ASIA

(MEMORANDUM TO THE BOARD OF TRUSTEES, JULY 1994)

On June 1 to June 9 I traveled with my colleague Kurt R. Soderlund to three of the five Central Asian republics of the former Soviet Union: Kazakhstan, Kyrgyzstan, and Uzbekistan.* The purpose of the trip was to explore the possibility of extending the New School's East and Central Europe program to one or more of those new nations. The presence of Muslim fundamentalism adds a measure of complexity to their post-Soviet transition toward democracy and free markets and is of interest to our faculty. I also had an opportunity to assess the human rights situation in each country and to learn something about economic and political developments.

## CENTRAL ASIA: AN OVERVIEW

Five new countries constitute what is now known as Central Asia: Kazakhstan, Kyrgyzstan, Tajikistan, Turkmenistan, and Uzbekistan. They are bounded by China on the east, Russia on the north, Afghanistan and Iran on the south, and the Caspian Sea on the west.

### KAZAKHSTAN

Kazakhstan is by far the largest in geographic area, about four times the size of Texas, and with 17 million people, has the second largest population in Central Asia. Although it is home to 108 nationalities, 42 percent are Kazakh and 37 percent Russian, and the balance are mostly Ukrainian, German,

---

*Kurt Soderlund assisted with the preparation of this report. We are also grateful for the support of Brian Kempel and Nancy Humm of the Soros Foundation in arranging our meetings in Kazakhstan and Kyrgyzstan.

Uzbek, and Tartar. Kazakhstan is the least Islamicized of the Central Asian countries, in part because its nomadic history carried into the twentieth century. The Kazakh people began to come together in the mid-fifteenth century under Janibek, who is considered the first Kazakh khan. But Qasim Khan is credited with establishing political unity and distinguishing the Kazakh people from the Uzbeks, with whom they share ethnic stock and a similar language and culture. From the early 1500s to 1731, the Kazakh tribes struggled to maintain control of their territory, ultimately looking to Russia in 1730 for protection. Kazakhstan became an autonomous Soviet republic in 1920 and was elevated to full republic status in 1936.

It is essentially a vast flatland which contains about one-third of the agricultural land of the former Soviet Union. Kazakhstan exports grain, wool, and meat. Grain—mostly wheat—occupies more than two-thirds of the cultivated acreage. It also has a rich mineral base in iron, copper, lead, gold, and silver. It has major oil resources near the Caspian Sea. It also possesses a portion of the nuclear arsenal of the former Soviet Union.

## Kyrgyzstan

Kyrgyzstan, by contrast, is a mountainous country about the size of Nebraska. Of the more than 100 nationalities represented in Kyrgyzstan, the Turkic-speaking, Muslim Kirghiz, also nomadic herding people, make up 52 percent of the country's 4.5 million residents. Russians comprise 22 percent of the population and are largely concentrated in the capital of Bishkek, where they are the majority. Other groups are Uzbek (mainly in the south around Osh), Ukrainian, German, Tartar, and Chinese (Uygurs and Dungans). The Kyrgyz mountain range divides the country into a Muslim south and a Christian north; the only surface routes presently open between the north and south go through Uzbekistan.

The people of Kyrgyzstan have a sense of national identity that goes back at least 1,000 years—some say as many as 5,000 years. The Krygyz lived unmolested for 300 years until the Russian protectorate was established early in the twentieth century.

Today, Kyrgyzstan is the poorest of the three countries we visited. Because of its terrain, livestock rather than farming is the mainstay of the agricultural sector. It also has fewer mineral resources than its neighbors and virtually no oil, although it does have coal. While its neighbors may have contributed economic strength to the former Soviet Union, it appears that Kyrgyzstan was a net beneficiary and thus faces a difficult economic future as an independent country.

## UZBEKISTAN

Uzbekistan has the largest Central Asian population at 21.6 million, 72 percent of whom are Uzbek and only 8.3 percent Russian. The others are principally Tajik, Kazakh, Tartar, and Karakalpak. Its capital of Tashkent, with 2 million people, is the largest city in Central Asia; its two ancient cities, Bukhara and Samarkand, are predominantly Tajik.

Slightly larger than California, Uzbekistan has a flat desert landscape and was ruled locally until its absorption into the Soviet Union in 1924. It is the world's third largest producer of cotton (about one-half of its agricultural land). Rice is also an important export: it produces about one-half of the supply for the former Soviet Union. In the rich Fergana Valley tobacco, fruits, mulberry trees, wheat, and corn are also major crops. It is a mineral-rich country with deposits of copper, zinc, lead, gold, and coal as well as gas and oil reserves.

The process by which Uzbekistan was developed into the U.S.S.R.'s major cotton-producing region provides a striking example of the inefficiencies and potentially deleterious effects of central planning. Lacking sufficient natural water for growing cotton, Uzbekistan developed extensive irrigation projects to divert a considerable amount of water to the region from the Aral Sea. To meet production targets, massive amounts of pesticides and fertilizers were used to increase crop yields. Eventually, even crop rotation was abandoned.

The consequences for the region are severe. Once-fertile land, well suited for other crops, is now depleted of nutrients and contaminated by chemicals. Irrigation has significantly diminished the size of the Aral Sea to the extent that this lake —once the world's fourth largest—is in danger of drying up altogether. The impact on the surrounding ecosystem has been dramatic. Most tragic of all, the chemical contamination of the soil has caused severe health problems for the local population, including abnormally high levels of child mortality, birth defects, and a range of diseases among the adult population. The legacy of the cotton "monoculture" has one other striking dimension: about 80 percent of the Uzbek population now lives in settlements established to farm these cotton fields.

## General Orientation

We entered the region on a Lufthansa flight from Frankfurt to Almaty, capital of Kazakhstan, and drove 3 hours to Bishkek and seven hours to Tashkent. Samarkand is another 3-1/2 beyond Tashkent. Air travel within the region is largely confined to the local derivatives of Aeroflot, and is not particularly safe. Thus we exited the region via Turkish Air to Istanbul. The foreign carriers serving the region give a clue to developing economic influence: Aeroflot, of course, serves most major cities (except Bishkek, where international flights are suspended for lack of fuel), followed by Lufthansa, Turkish Air, and Korean Air.

Competition for economic penetration in the region is brisk. While Russia is still the dominant force, all the new nations are seeking to reduce their economic dependence on Russia. Turkey, China, and even South Korea are becoming increasingly important. For example, in 1990, Kazakhstan's imports from China were less than 4 percent of its total exports. By 1992 the proportion had risen to 44 percent.[1] But the growing influence of Turkey is the most interesting to watch: the Turkish media are penetrating the region, military officers are being trained in Turkey, and individual Turkish citizens are making generous contributions to the building of mosques throughout Central Asia. Turkey's direct foreign investment into the region would probably be much greater if it were not suffering a severe economic downturn.

The rise to power in Russia of ultranationalist Vladimir Zhirinovsky (born in Kazakhstan) has sent shivers through the region. Russia still has 50,000 troops in Central Asia, largely concentrated in Tajikistan and Turkmenistan to guard the borders with Iran and Afghanistan. Their activity needs to be watched carefully, lest they also play a role in domestic political life in pursuit of reestablishing Russian hegemony in the region.

All five leaders in the region have popular support, although their styles are quite different. The most democratically inclined is Askar Akaev of Kyrgyzstan, the most repressive are Islam Karimov of Uzbekistan and Saparmurat Niazov of Turkmenistan. By all accounts, the most effective is Nursultan Nazarbaev of Kazakhstan, who steers a middle course between Akaev and Karimov. Tajikistan is the most troubled of the five, riven by a civil war between rival tribes and confronting the most serious threat of rising Islamic fundamentalism. Akaev is the most committed to a rapid transition to free market, while Karimov apparently prefers the Chinese model of gradual market reform combined with tight political control. Nazarbaev searches for a middle course.

None of the three capitals we visited possesses much architectural charm or boasts historical sites. All resemble modern Soviet cities with well-laid-out boulevards and ample parks, but undistinguished "block" architecture. None has an "old town" comparable to the charm of Tblisi or even Baku. Indeed, it is hard to find an old building. Bishkek, less than 100 years old, was constructed almost entirely during the Soviet era, and destructive earthquakes in Almaty and Tashkent have conspired against a distinctive local style. Almaty and Bishkek, however, are graced with snowcapped mountains in near view the year round, and both have an abundance of trees and parks fed by the mountain runoff. Tashkent is a dreary industrial city, less attractive than the other two. Samarkand, by contrast, is blessed with many historic sites, since it was the center of the silk route and dates back at least 2,500 years. Fought over by Alexander the Great,

Genghis Kahn, and Tammerlane, it was once one of the most important cities in the world.

## KAZAKHSTAN

### POLITICAL CLIMATE

In Kazakhstan, Nursultan Nazarbaev is firmly in control, although he committed an error in manipulating the March 1994 parliamentary elections in a way which brought a negative judgment from European Community monitors who found the election "unfair." Of the 177-seat Parliament, 42 seats had to be chosen from the "President's list" of loyal supporters. Registered parties and civic organizations could nominate candidates for the balance of the seats. These included the Union of National Unity of Kazakhstan (SNEK), which is closely associated with Nazarbaev and advocates moderate privatization, foreign investment, and good relations with Russia; the Socialist Party (formerly the Communist Party) with 30,000 members, which calls for slower privatization, greater protection for pensioners, and the support of large, inefficient industries through government subsidies; and the People's Congress, which advocates interethnic harmony, favors a bicameral Parliament, and opposes shock therapy. The Federation of Trade Unions, closely allied with the government, also fielded candidates.

Many Kazakh nationalist groups (Azat, Zheltoksan, Alash) joined together in the National Democratic Party which was not registered in time for the March elections. Among Russian organizations, LAD was the most politically active, calling for Russian as an official state language and dual citizenship.

SNEK was the big winner (33 seats), followed by the Federation of Trade Unions (11), the People's Congress (9), the Socialist Party (8), the Peasant Union (4), and LAD (4). The balance were independent or represented other organizations. In ethnic terms, 105 members are Kazakh, 49 Russian, 10 Ukrainian, 3 German, and 3 Jewish.

The overwhelming majority of the members support

Nazarbaev. Disinterested observers believe Nazarbaev would have prevailed in the election even without the manipulations he employed; thus he brought criticism from the West for no real gain.

Even with a comfortable parliamentary majority, Nazarbaev faces criticism for his handling of the economy and privatization. On May 27 Parliament passed a resolution by a wide margin (including members of Nazarbaev's party) which demanded that the legislative body be given a role in the economic restructuring, that some ministers be replaced, and that Parliament be granted the authority to review presidential decrees that were issued before it was sworn in. Some see this vote as the first step in the evolution of an independent legislative branch.

We met with critic Nurbulat Masanov, who spoke of a nascent opposition movement, including the so-called progressive wing of Nazarbaev's government which favors quicker market reform. Nazarbaev has been ambiguous about the right to own land, and at the moment only leases are available. Starting April 29, 3,500 medium-sized state enterprises, which comprise around 70 percent of the country's businesses and 30 percent of its entire economy, were to be sold at auction.[2] Under Nazarbaev's privatization plan, the state retains 51 percent ownership of factories; each enterprise's workers get 29 percent ownership, and the public is allowed to purchase 20 percent through mutual funds that work on a voucher system. No single mutual fund can own more than 10 percent of any one company. However, there have been dozens of special deals through which foreign firms have been allowed to purchase 100 percent ownership of former state-owned properties. For example, Phillip Morris has bought Almaty Tobacco, Unilever has purchased a vegetable oil processing plant, and the Chevron oil deal is now beginning to move: Chevron has 10,000 employees in Kazakhstan.

Still, the economy is hurting; by unofficial estimates 500,000 people are unemployed (official estimates: 50,000), not counting those who are furloughed part of every month. Inflation is running at 50 percent a month, and the currency has been devalued eight times in the past half year. Ordinary citizens report a common tale of woe in transition: the cost of housing up fivefold since April, transit fare up tenfold since December. Meanwhile, wages have only doubled. Food, while plentiful in the bazaar, is very costly. Television is increasingly accessible (including CNN segments available in some private homes), and it provides a window on the world's more developed economies. "Every day we watch more and more television," one university staff member told us, "but every day our standard of living goes down. The contrast is disillusioning." There is widespread skepticism that the privatization scheme will provide tangible wealth to the general population; and in any event it is proceeding slowly, leading to widespread rumors that former Communist officials are reaping the early rewards.

A clinical psychologist at the Kazakhstan National University reported a dramatic rise in his caseload as people disoriented by the fall of communism struggle to adapt to the market economy and seek out help. He says that drug and alcohol abuse are up, as is the suicide rate.

Despite all the hardships, President Nazarbaev still retains broad support—indeed, there is no other large figure on the horizon should he falter, a reality that sobers even his critics. Leonid Solomin, a former colonel in the military and now president of the Trade Union Association, told us that "there is no alternative to Nursultan Nazarbaev—any other leader would risk an ethnic conflict and destabilization of social order. We must be the constructive opposition."

Because industrialization proceeded further in Kazakhstan, its trade union movement is the strongest in the region with over 500,000 members and growing. Solomin contends that the unions, despite government harassment, have delivered higher salaries, better working conditions, and grievance procedures. Solomin credits the AFL-CIO for providing important organizational support and a modest amount of funding. And through the union's political wing the movement counts eleven members of Parliament—it has won the right to strike and to bargain collectively. Ninel Fokina, chair of the Helsinki

Committee, who organized this portion of our trip, said that the union movement is the "only truly progressive force in the country because it has a broad social base, good organizational skills, and clear goals."

When Solomin spoke of ethnic conflict, he referred to the reality that Kazakhstan is the most diverse country in the region, the only one where the dominant ethnic group is in the minority, and the place where the Russian presence is most pervasive. Much of this diversity owes to Stalin's practice of using Kazakhstan as a prime destination for internal exiles in the 1930s and 1940s.

As is the case elsewhere in the former Soviet Union, the circumstances of the Russians pose a problem. They are concentrated in the main cities—are a majority in Almaty, for example—and once filled the most highly technical jobs and many government posts. Today, they are frightened by local nationalism that takes the form of discrimination in jobs and housing, by a law making Kazakh the main language by 1996, by the refusal to designate Russian as a second official language, and by the refusal to allow for dual citizenship (residents will be required to accept Kazakhstan citizenship in March 1995). As a consequence, the unofficial count has 400,000 Russians leaving last year, draining the country of its most skilled labor, a trend accelerated by the questionable March elections. It is said that 80 percent of all Russian families with small children have left or will leave soon. The official explanation is that the Russians are fortunate to be able to pursue better economic opportunities in Russia, but most people say it is fear that pushes people out, not economic opportunity that pulls (recall that economic life in Russia is not easy). Nazarbaev formally encourages the Russians to stay, but observers doubt his sincerity and see no concrete action by his government to arrest the trend.

The other major factor affecting the feel of life in Kazakhstan is the resurgence of religion. Anara Tabyshalieva, a sociologist in Bishkek, wrote an article called "Muslim Revival" which documents the growth of active mosques in Kazakhstan from 25 in 1978 to over 300 today. Muslim educational institutions have appeared in Almaty, Bishkek, and Dushanbe, and seven others are under construction. Yet we are told that the fundamentalist issue is overblown by the Western and Moscow press and that in fact people go to mosques as a ritual and are not deep believers. It is said that religion is not a public issue and that religious pluralism is likely to be the outcome as Orthodox, Catholic, and Jewish populations remain, and Western missionaries (including American Baptists) seek a following. One of our dinner partners even reported that, while Muslim, she does not practice and gets her spiritual nourishment from the evangelist Robert Schuller on Sunday television!

These reassurances about Muslim fundamentalism are widely offered in all three countries. I frankly do not know how to assess the situation, but my instinct is to be skeptical. Islam is growing in strength in many parts of the world. Poverty, dislocation, and alienation provide fertile soil for Islam's mix of religious and social teachings, and there are surely forces at work recruiting Muslims back to active practice. Mitigating that trend, among other forces, are nascent women's movements which rightly fear that Muslim fundamentalism could erode the status accorded women under the Soviet regime. We should be skeptical of bland reassurances and scare predictions alike.

HIGHER EDUCATION

We met with the Minister of Education, the First Vice Rector of the Kazakhstan National University, the Rector of Almaty State University, and the President of the National Academy of Sciences, as well as with a group of young faculty and a group of undergraduate students.

There are seventy institutions of higher education in Kazakhstan and three or four new, small private institutions. But the two most important are the public universities in Almaty.

The Kazakhstan National University is the country's most prestigious institution but for that reason may be harder to reform. It has 13 faculties, 7,500 students, 140 full professors, and 750 other faculty. In addition to meeting the First Vice Rector, we spoke with the chairs of economics, philosophy, and political science. We heard a familiar story from them: the need for help in reforming the curriculum in subjects heavily politicized in the Soviet period, the need for modern textbooks and journals, the need for retraining opportunities for faculty. The university currently has exchanges with the University of Kentucky, the University of Oklahoma, the World Bank, and universities in Italy and France, but many of these programs are limited to business and economics.

Rector Tokmohammed Sadykov of Almaty State University explained that his university is the oldest in Kazakhstan (founded in 1926) and currently enrolls 13,000 students in 13 faculties and 43 disciplines with 1,200 faculty members. Since it had been at one time a pedagogical institute, Almaty's life as a full-scale university is new and thus most of its academic departments are new. It struck me as more open than Kazakhstan National University. I was very impressed with the group of twenty English-speaking undergraduate students with whom we met: a mosaic of ethnic backgrounds, all bright and articulate, outspoken about their concern that the political process pressured them to identify by ethnic background. Most spoke only Russian fluently and resented the impending change to Kazakh as the official language. Perhaps most puzzling was their cynicism about the political process and politicians: only three of twenty had voted in the March election. Their focus seemed to be on private careers rather than public life and the development of civil society.

The Academy of Sciences was a familiar scene: the old male barons in formal conclave. We met with the heads of the relevant institutes (economics, history, and philosophy) in a useful meeting in which they struggled to impress us with their openness to change and new ways of thinking. I resisted my first impulse to dismiss them as beyond redemption, and I am glad I did. They were thinking hard about the underlying problems of transition within the special context of Kazakh history. The economist spoke of the need for an economic plan that was not a straight Western import but an approach reflective of their own present circumstance. Stories of Jeffrey Sachs' shock therapy for Russia were greeted with derision. Another noted that the mix of nationalities in Kazakhstan had resulted in a relatively greater emphasis on the individual, which should make this society more fertile ground for the free market (compared with the more authoritarian tradition of a more homogeneous Uzbekistan). The philosophy professor mentioned the issue of separation of powers and the need to build in checks and balances lest the President be too powerful. A lawyer discussed Kazakh conceptions of law which made it difficult, for example, to communicate with American lawyers working to reform Kazakhstan's judicial system following Western models.

## HUMAN RIGHTS

The Helsinki Committee for Kazakhstan did not provide a crisp and clear catalogue of human rights abuse. But we learned of growing discrimination against Russians in housing and jobs; of laws which ruled out parties founded on an ethnic basis; of harassment charges by opposition parties during the elections, improper treatment of refugees, actions by the Mayor of Almaty to bar access to apartments for returning exiles who are not Kazakh, and poor prison conditions. The composite was a not uncommon litany deserving of some attention, particularly since the government is not immune to Western pressure. Still, conditions are not terrible, and there are no political prisoners.

There are not many independent papers in Kazakhstan and some are owned by multipurpose businesses which have to keep on the good side of the government. We met with Igor Meltser, the editor of *Caravan*, the largest independent paper (circulation 350,000—read by 1 million), which has been crusading against corruption in the Almaty mayor's office. Dependent on government printing presses, *Caravan* was shut down for a month before the elections when the government printing house claimed mechanical difficulties. Its office, now under heavy security, was denied heat, light and phones. Other independent media, such as Radio MAX suffered similar shutdowns. And when *Caravan* printed in Bishkek, its trucks were harassed on the way to Almaty—drugs were planted on them by security forces.

I had the impression that Human Rights Watch/Helsinki could do useful work in Kazakhstan with a limited investment of time and resources. There are "classic" human rights problems here which can be addressed by the usual tools of exposure and public embarrassment.

## Kyrgyzstan

By contrast to Almaty and Tashkent, Bishkek is a quiet, gentle city, the most beautiful of the three capitals. Perhaps this reveals something of the Kyrgys as a people. One senses a serenity and self-confidence in Kyrgyzstan, a country which has a sense of ancient roots.

But a walk around the center of Bishkek reveals hard times: relatively few cars on the road, construction cranes hanging over stalled projects half completed, bronze statues in the central park stripped of their metal for scrap value, the main Intourist hotel boarded up waiting for Western capital to refurbish it. Lacking the mineral riches or agricultural strength of its neighbors, Kyrgyzstan is weak economically. The end of the Soviet Union has hit it hard, and it has been slow to develop an economic strategy. Kyrgyzstan may be viable in the short run only through massive infusions of foreign aid. Its tax collection system is in shambles, the constitutional provision against land ownership hampers agricultural reform, and it is cursed with large Soviet military factories hard to convert to civilian production. While President Akaev is committed to market reforms, he is constrained by the Parliament, which is a holdover from the Soviet period. The Parliament has blocked land reform and refuses to lower the tax on private production (currently 45 percent of profit), a move that has led most small and moderate-sized private firms to conduct business in cash or foreign currencies to avoid the banking system. The loss of tax revenues has badly hampered the government.

With its airport closed to international flights because of fuel shortages, Bishkek is hard to reach and is easily overlooked by foreign businesses, which prefer Almaty or Tashkent as a base of operation.

Kyrgyzstan may be more vulnerable than Kazakhstan to the rise of Muslim fundamentalism, especially in the south around Osh, the site of a bloody clash in 1990 that left as many as 500 dead. Kyrgyzstan south of the Kyrgyz mountain range (which we did not visit) is susceptible to the Muslim influences from Tajikistan. And while we heard the by now usual reassurances against fundamentalism as a destabilizing threat, it is significant that the government-funded Center for Early Warning of Conflict is following this issue closely.

In the next elections, scheduled for February 1995, Kyrgys will choose a new Parliament of 105 seats (down from the Soviet Parliament of 350). There are presently nine parties, which observers believe may boil down to four or five by the election. While President Akaev has no party, two of the center parties, Motherland and Social Democrats, are close to him. On the extremes are the Communist Party, still the best organized, and Flag, the nationalist group on the right. Other parties include the Democratic Movement of Kyrgyzstan led by Soviet-era dissidents; the Republican Party of Krygyzstan, which is made up of academics; the Party of Unity, which is primarily a business group; and the Peasant Party.

The issues, although not yet fully articulated, are likely to be the pace of privatization, the rate of inflation, land ownership, the degree of outside influence in economic reform, and the availability of a social safety net. U.S. Ambassador Hurwitz told us stories of how early deals with foreign companies were concluded on unfavorable terms, making the government acutely sensitive to protecting the country's interest in future transactions. Assessment of the government's skill in negotiating such deals is a hot political topic.

As in the other Central Asian countries, the President is all powerful. Akaev shrewdly organized a referendum in January to demonstrate his popular support. He won a 96 percent approval rating, as 90 percent of the people voted in an election in which old-style manipulation was rampant. Akaev's democratic supporters thought he paid a high price for the extra margin of support won through fraud, a tactic that evoked comparisons by his critics to the recent election in Turkmenistan.

But even opposition leaders, such as Chinara Jakzpova, former Minister of Education, believe Akaev is the best person to run the county for now, given the alternatives. She plans to support him for the moment while testing the possibility of opposing him in the 1996 presidential elections. Her Center for Strategic Research is building a shadow government as it hires ministers who fall out with Akaev and also prepares alternative approaches to economic reform.

Aron Brudney, chair of the Institute of Philosophy of the Academy of Sciences, agreed that Akaev was the best person to run the government for the present. But he is concerned about the current course of political development, which concentrates too much power in the President. "If there were a less good person as President," he told us over dinner, "we would not be sitting here having a free discussion." He believes the Communists are gradually regaining power as democratic forces suffer from a lack of organizational skills. He believes the Communists may actually win a majority in the 1995 parliamentary elections owing to three factors:

1. Older people are most likely to vote, and they vote Communist because of economic problems—central to this group is a well-organized, World War II veterans bloc.
2. The Communists are the best organized and most skillful propagandists, and they hold key positions in universities and the media.
3. There are factions within the government itself which favor a slower transition to free markets and democracy.

The key to the future is Akaev, whom Brudney called "the

President of success." If he stumbles, people will desert him quickly because he does not have a political party to hold them. That is why some of his key advisers are unhappy with his decision to remain above politics; they are urging him to form his own party. Brudney compared Akaev to Gorbachev: more popular outside his country than within, fortunate "not to have a Yeltsin challenger, yet." He said that Akaev had no clear view of policy and "like a bicycle rider, must peddle fast not to fall down.'

Akaev reminds me a bit of New York Governor Mario Cuomo: he skillfully uses the old-style Parliament and the lack of money to excuse inaction. Democratic forces, disappointed with his performance, are quick to see him as a good man struggling with a conservative Parliament and a venal bureaucracy. That rationale may weaken with a new Parliament, especially one which has a genuine constructive opposition.

We gained considerable insight into the transition from our consultation with Brudney. It was not an easy discussion, in part, because of his own sense of dislocation. Initially, he seemed bored by our talk of the current economic and political conditions in Krygyzstan as we asked questions he must have answered for other Western observers. But he came alive when I said, "Let us talk as academic colleagues, not political commentators. How are you helping your country find a usable past?" That led to a lively recital of Krygyzstan history replete with references to poets, writers, artists, and other cultural figures. When asked about his "heroes," he named literary figures, not politicians. Indeed, writers—not generals or past political heads—grace the face of the new Krygyzstan currency.

HIGHER EDUCATION

We had a short but stimulating meeting with Asher Akaev, Minister of Education, and Jusenhaev Shashev, his deputy for higher education. Akaev clearly articulated the needs for educational reform and the importance of education for building the base for a democratic society. There are twenty-six public universities (including five technical institutes) in Kyrgyzstan and seven private institutions.

During our conversations in Krygyzstan, we heard frequently about "rootless intellectuals trying to make a living." University professors and scholars at the Academies of Science occupied high status positions during the Soviet period, were paid well, and had access to privileges. But now their status is reduced, wages are flat, and the privileges are gone. We heard that professors made less money than taxi drivers, miners, and other industrial laborers. As a consequence, professors either leave the academic system to seek their fortune as interpreters or consultants for business or struggle for survival with extra part-time work, often involving unskilled jobs. Their plight has led to petty corruption, with universities charging "fees" to students for entrance into popular courses. Against this background, the New School's attention to rebuilding scholarly life was well received as encouragement to those who wish to continue in academic life as self-respecting professionals.

We found educational leaders in Kyrgyzstan the most open and responsive to the possibility of working with the New School. The First Vice Rector of Kyrgyzstan State National University, Mahmut Kuchakov, quickly grasped what the New School had to offer. His university, founded in 1933, has 18 faculties, 1,100 teaching staff, 8,500 day students and another 5,500 correspondence and evening students. It used to admit 3,000 new students annually, but lack of money has cut the intake to 1,500 for next year.

Within the state university, there is an American School headed by a lively dean, Kamila Sharshnekeeva. While this year-old unit currently focuses on business, it has the ambition to be a full-scale independent university. The curriculum focuses on free market economics, English, and business law and will shortly add teacher training and journalism. At present, it admits 40 business students and 15 teacher training students each year. Its students pay $700 (U.S.) annual tuition. The American School aggressively seeks exchange programs and has placed nine students in the United States, mainly at its affiliate, the University of Nebraska at Lincoln.

An equally new and refreshing university on a more ambitious scale is the Kyrgyzstan–Russian University, supported by Bishkek and Moscow. Located in the former Russian Army Officers Club, it has handsome and well-equipped facilities and is led by a dynamic rector, Vladimir Nifadyev (a physicist). The university is trying to pattern itself on the Western model, in which faculty are expected to do both teaching and research. Created in 1993, it has five faculties: engineering, economics/law, humanities, international relations, and medicine. Its research strengths are in physics, plasma physics, and explosives. It offers a 2-year associate's degree, a 4-year bachelor's degree and a 1-1/2-year master's degree. This new institution has 32 faculty, mostly Russian, and eventually hopes to reach 2,000 students in the steady state from its current enrollment of 250. Admission is on the merit system (at least 25 percent are Kyrgyz), and it has 10 applicants for every place (25 to a place in economics). Fluent English or German is required to graduate and, indeed, we visited three classes in which I addressed a comprehending student group in English.

The Russian University is eager to work with the New School, to receive faculty visits and help with curriculum development, and to participate in our Journal Project.

We visited one other new (and independent) institution, the Bishkek International School of Management and Business. It is 2 years old and enrolls 50 students in a 2-year M.B.A. program. In addition, the school offers midcareer retraining to 300 people a year. It seems to have good access to visitors from England, the United States, Netherlands, Germany, and Japan, and nearly half its students went abroad this year for study tours. While I would not rule out working with this institution, it is sharply focused on practical business training and thus is not our best potential partner.

## Human Rights

Kyrgyzstan has the best human rights situation of the three countries we visited. It is blessed with the most competent local human rights group, the Kyrgyz-American Bureau on Human Rights and Rule of Law, which is led by the very able Natalya Abhava. Because this group is so competent, and the environment so open, we gathered the most complete sense of human rights problems here. One must be careful to place the overall picture in context lest the relatively easy access to information distort the record to the negative.

Conditions for Russians may be a touch better here than in Kazakhstan but the pattern is the same: it is estimated that about one-third of the 900,000 Russians have left. Professors at the Russian University report the rise of abusive language in everyday remarks and note the purging of Russians from high-level jobs. As in Kazakhstan, Russian will not be designated the second official language, and Kyrgyz will be required in all official business by the year 2000. Akaev also has opposed dual citizenship.

Chinara Jakzpova, who has begun an independent newspaper, *Politika*, spoke to us about free press issues. She reports that independent papers pay higher prices (double) for paper and access to the government printing plant. Independent media also have a more difficult time getting access to official information. And all independent papers were closed down for a week before the January referendum. When Jakzpova published an article last September critical of the President, her apartment was robbed and her equipment stolen. She is convinced that the police were searching for evidence they believed she might have of government wrongdoing.

Nonetheless, there are five lively, independent newspapers which are flourishing: *Res Publica*, a political weekly; *Asaba*; *Delo N.*, a social-political weekly; *Politika*, a supplement to *Delo N.*; *Yuzhng*; and *Kurier*, a weekly for the Slavic population.

The Kyrgyz-American Bureau on Human Rights and Rule of Law was organized in early 1993 in response to Bishkek's acquiescence in the kidnapping by Uzbek authorities of an Uzbek dissident who was attending a human rights conference in Bishkek. Among the bureau's current concerns are the recently passed Interior Police Law and National Security Law, which expand the right of the police to search without a warrant, to wiretap without a judge's permission, and to confiscate communication and transportation equipment in emergencies. The bureau also is concerned by "massive" violations of people's rights, including police brutality and the denial of quick access to an attorney. Bureau officials report that the use of torture to secure confessions is "an everyday occurrence." While these measures appear to be aimed at ordinary criminals, there is potential for political abuse under a less democratic administration.

A third troublesome law, the Law on the Protection of State Secrets, has been passed by Parliament but not yet signed by the President. It defines state secrets so broadly that they include information on the economy, the conditions of highways, and sanitary conditions in the military. Bureau chief Natyala Abhova has asked Human Rights Watch to protest this law, which opens a loophole for state censorship.

## Uzbekistan

Uzbekistan is the most complicated and interesting of the Central Asian states we visited. To put it mildly, Uzbekistan does not encourage visitors like us. It is extremely difficult to get a visa—impossible at any location in the United States. Human Rights Watch personnel observing a trial were expelled in 1993, and subsequent requests for visas for Human Rights Watch personnel have been denied. I had been advised by a Human Rights Watch staff member that I could not get a visa, and even if I got in, there would be no one to talk to, since dissidents risked imprisonment for talking with foreigners. I felt challenged by that bleak picture and determined not to give in to a repressive regime. Simply gaining entry would be a victory of sorts, opening up some space in a similar fashion to what the New School faculty had done in the dark days of the Soviet regime in Eastern and Central Europe.

We learned from the U.S. State Department of a loophole that might bypass the visa requirement: a treaty among Uzbekistan, Kazakhstan, and Krygyzstan provides that a valid visa for any one country should allow a 72-hour transit period through the others. We did not know, of course, whether it would be honored at the border, and I had images of being turned back in the dead of night if we took the 12-hour overnight bus ride between Bishkek and Tashkent. Given the risk, it seemed best to travel by car during the day and as luck would have it, one of President Akaev's black Volvos was available for hire—only for U.S. dollars. Thus the great adventure evolved into a smooth, 7-hour drive through beautiful country in the comfort of the President's air-conditioned Volvo. We were not even stopped at the border. I took some pleasure in moving freely around Tashkent and traveling to Samarkand (in and out of Kazakhstan twice along the way) without a valid visa for Uzbekistan.

News reports that characterize the Karimov regime as "Brezhnev-style, Soviet authoritarianism" miss the nuances of the situation. To be sure, Karimov is in firm control, and the former Communists run the government. Parliament is not independent. The 1991 election was a sham—Karimov won 86 percent of the vote and 95 percent of the population voted. There is no free press; dissidents are harshly dealt with. The Birlik Democratic Movement and the ERK party it spawned have been banned.

But there is more space for independent thought today in Uzbekistan than existed in the former Soviet Union or its satellites when the New School began its work in the 1980s. Karimov's approach of gradual transition to free markets while maintaining tight political control is bound to fail, but not right away. The seeds for its failure come with the much sought-after foreign investment, the presence of international organizations such as the World Bank, and the willingness to allow foreign-run, nongovernment organizations like IREX and the Eurasia Foundation to operate. Through these organizations come faxes and E-mail as well as visitors like us. While Karimov controls television, radio, and print—even keeping out "liberal" news and programming from Moscow—he does not control the thousands of other daily contacts which bring information in. And the foreign press, such as it is in Central

Asia, is headquartered in Tashkent. We met with representatives of Reuters, the BBC, and the *Washington Post* (the only American correspondent based in Central Asia!), who operate more or less unharassed by the government.

Many of the nongovernment organizations are located in the same building, which is a beehive of activity containing IREX, PERDCA (Project on Economic Reform and Development), and others, with the Eurasia Foundation nearby. Idealistic young Americans (mostly from the Midwest) who staff these organizations told us that it is possible to work without too much hassle in Uzbekistan so long as you are careful not to challenge the government in a public way.

By all accounts, the Karimov government is reasonably popular and could win a fair election. As one American observer put it, "Democracy is a hazy concept, not a form of government familiar to Uzbeks, not something lost to be regained." Karimov has skillfully played upon fears generated by the Tajik civil war, which he portrays, too simply, as a reflection of a rising tide of Muslim fundamentalism.

Karimov did allow the ERK to mount a challenge in the December 1991 election which resulted in 85.9 percent of the votes for Karimov and 12.5 percent for his opponent, Mukhammad Salikh, who was later exiled. Since the election the ERK, which some leaders of Birlik never trusted as an authentic opposition, has been banned. The remaining three parties are all "safe:" Karimov's People's Democratic Party (former Communists), the Way of Independence, and Progress of the Nation. We are told there are only fifty members of Birlik active in Tashkent, perhaps more in the regions where the means of repression are not as well honed. No new opposition groups have appeared. We met with Abdurahim Polat (as the head of Birlik, Polatov now calls himself) in Istanbul, where he is in exile. He says there is no organized Uzbek diaspora working against Karimov and that he believes the only way to promote reform in Uzbekistan is for Moscow to pressure Karimov, an unlikely prospect to be sure. He told us:

I do not expect Yeltsin to help us now, because Karimov provides a suitable government for the Russians. They do not want to see another Elchibey* tilting to Turkey, and they want a buffer for Tajikistan fundamentalism. Uzbekistan needs a Gorbachev figure to emerge from within the government—the dissidents are not strong enough to break the deadlock.

Polat said there are such figures who understand that the time for dictatorship has passed and know that political reform must go hand in hand with economic development. He named the Mayor of Tashkent, Fazilbelkov Adhan, and, to our surprise, the Minister of Interior as potential progressive figures. His own prediction: it will be 5-10 years before Karimov (or his successor) is forced to reform. In the meantime, he predicts a gradual opening of space for free expression as people involved in business and international relations have more contact with foreigners.

A bright, even arrogant man, Karimov believes his own planning background equips him to manage the economy. And so far his record is better than that in Kazakhstan and Kyrgyzstan. Superficial signs in Tashkent suggest a prosperous country: more cars on the street, public spaces well maintained, less talk of economic crisis. Small enterprises employing under 50 people have been privatized, and the next tier, employing between 50 and 200, is now in the process of privatization. Early in 1994, Karimov struck a deal with Kazakhstan's Nazarbaev to form an economic union which allows for free circulation of goods, services, and capital between the two countries and provides for "coordinated policies" in credit and finance, budgets, taxes, customs, duties, and currency. In theory, the union is open to the other three Central Asian republics, but so far none has signed up.

While Kazakhstan has the lead in attracting foreign investment, in part because Karimov's Soviet-style bureaucracy is off-putting, there are some hopeful signs for Uzbekistan:

---

*Abulfaz Elchibey, the democratically elected President of Azerbaijan, was deposed by a coup in 1993, at the same time that we were in Baku.

Newmont Mining has signed a deal to process ore from the Muruntao Gold Mine, and South Korea's Daewoe and Germany's Mercedes Benz plan to build factories, while Britain's Meredith Jones is building a spinning mill near Samarkand. Our visit overlapped with a trade mission by the President of South Korea, which in turn followed a visit by Chinese Prime Minister Li Peng in April. Emerging from a meeting with Karimov at which he signed four trade agreements, Li said, "Now we want to build a new Silk Road to make our relations even more glorious." Returning the compliment, Karimov said, "We cannot overemphasize the role that China plays in this region in preventing separatist feelings and enhancing peace and stability."[3] We were told that President Clinton's collapse on renewing most-favored-nation trading status, despite its human rights difficulties, has stiffened Karimov's determination to pursue the China model and not be pressured by the threatened linkage of human rights to foreign investment.

By most accounts, however, Karimov will soon face a moment of economic truth that will test his mettle. Despite all these hopeful signs and the superficial prosperity visible in Tashkent, the underlying economic reality is less healthy: gross domestic product decreased for three consecutive years, falling 15 percent in 1992 alone, while inflation rose almost 500 percent in 1991.[4] Nearly 12 million people are out of work, and 45 percent of the population lives below the poverty line. According to Reuters correspondent James Kzngy, Uzbekistan is experiencing increasing deficits hidden by "cooked books." He believes that the decision to issue a new, convertible currency will require backup from international agencies, which in turn will subject Uzbekistan to International Monetary Fund controls. That will place pressure on the policy of gradual conversion to the free market and require a diminishment of the social safety net.

The search for a usable sense of national history which we discussed with Aron Brudney in Bishkek can also be observed in Uzbekistan. Despite the existence of ancient cultures, so clearly revealed in Samarkand, Uzbekistan does not have a long history as a modern independent state to draw upon as it seeks to establish a new national identity. In this respect, the countries of Central Asia face a more formidable challenge than the Baltic states or the former Soviet satellites of Eastern and Central Europe. The curious case of Tammerlane illustrates this point. A Mongol emperor who reigned over the region from 1370 to 1405, he has been appropriated by the Uzbek culture as an authentic national hero. Indeed, the statue of Lenin in the park in front of the Hotel Uzbekistan has been replaced with a statue of Tammerlane with Uzbek features.

I have already spoken of some human rights abuses—for example, the suppression of a free press and the banning of opposition parties. We were privileged to meet with two courageous dissident writers: Diloran Iskhahova and Vasila Inoiatova. A week earlier, both had tried to meet with U.S. Senator Arlen Specter but had been arrested and detained for 3 days outside of Tashkent. Not wishing to jeopardize them further, we sent a message through a third party indicating our availability to meet with them. Both responded that they would take the risk of meeting with us.

They decided to meet with us separately because they do not fully trust each other. Our effort to meet with Inoiatova in a park behind the American Embassy was initially thwarted by a violent thunderstorm. We then went to Iskhahova's apartment, entering under the watchful eye of two 24-hour surveillance details.

Iskhahova gave us a primer on the state of the opposition. It does exist but in a weakened form. Birlik still adds members, is active in recruiting students, but no longer holds the monthly meetings which had been broken up by the police. An opposition newspaper is printed in Kyrgyzstan and appears occasionally in Tashkent, but each issue sparks a new round of repression.

Iskhahova told us of her abortive attempts to meet not only with Senator Specter but also with the staff of visiting French President Mitterand and U.S. Ambassador Strobe Talbott. All the attempts had been prevented. "When my children see a report on television of upcoming visiting celebrities, they expect I will be arrested." When asked why she persisted, Iskhahova at first responded, "I don't know, I ask myself that question a lot." Then stiffening, she said, "But I am mad at what the government does to us—we are not a threat, yet they harass our families and have us fired from our jobs. We are like dogs barking at a caravan of thieves that passes by unaffected."

She went on to say that it was very important to be known in the West by name and that attention from international human rights groups offers a measure of protection. We went over the list of political prisoners previously identified by Human Rights Watch/Helsinki, to which she added another dozen names. All told, it is estimated there are at least forty political prisoners in Uzbekistan. She asked our help in drawing public attention to four prisoners whose lives she felt were in danger, especially two who were in poor health and in hard labor camps. I passed all the names along to Human Rights Watch.

Later we returned to the American Embassy to learn that Vasila Inoiatova had come there after the thunderstorm and was hiding in an office until the local Uzbek staff left. We were able to talk with her for an hour beginning at 6:30 in the evening. She told us a lengthy tale of harassment, including 7 days of being held incommunicado under a false name after she attended a human rights conference in Bishkek. As a protest she slit her wrist, causing the authorities to release her. She told of fierce pressure on Birlik/ERK members which had broken many dissidents and intellectuals into supporting Karimov. Since she has not bowed to that pressure, she has been subject to intense harassment, including late-night telephone calls telling her not "'to mess with the government or we will take you away,' which means kill me." She has refused a Ministry of Interior offer to "turn coat" and become an informer and as a result has no job and feels in constant danger for herself and her children. She reports that the police, sometimes drunk, barge into her home at night and ask for documents.

I asked her in face of all this why she sought to meet with

Senator Specter or with us. "They often harass me for nothing," she replied, "but if they attack me for meeting with a Senator, that is a great success—by making my problems public to the world I have done what is necessary so the world knows Karimov is not in complete control. Contact with foreigners—being known—gives us space to continue our work. If they do kill me," she concluded, "it will advance human rights in Uzbekistan."

We heard of an independent paper in Samarkand so we traveled there to meet with one of the founders, a young physicist at the university, Rafshan Sabirov, whose father chairs the Physics Department. With the help of a Peace Corp volunteer, Sabirov runs the Information Consulting Center, which works to build local nongovernment organizations (NGOs) and to link them with foreign NGOs. Here can be seen one of the paradoxes of Uzbekistan. Sabirov operates freely and had no qualms about meeting with us. His paper—called *Chance*—is the only independent paper in Uzbekistan and is actually printed by the government. It carefully avoids political material but does have cultural news and features aimed at Samarkand's large university community.

I asked Sabirov, who is about 30, whether he has colleagues in philosophy, history, and the social sciences who are independent-minded. To my surprise, he said there is a circle of young people—thirty to thirty-five in number—who meet every Saturday to talk about political and economic issues. They are free to be critical, he said, so long as none of their criticism is in print. This might be a group with which the New School could work, and I asked the Peace Corp volunteer to attend the Samarkand Circle and give me an assessment. In the meantime the Information Consulting Center is building an English language library at its office on the university campus. The library would be a good location for the journals that we help distribute.

Another possible setting for our work emerged from a surprising place: the new University of World Economy and Diplomacy, started by Karimov in February 1993 to bypass the conservative Tashkent State University and the Ministry of

Education. Karimov's Foreign Minister is the Rector. Students are selected on a competitive basis in journalism, international law, international relations, and economics. It is a 4-year undergraduate school (with some master's work available), now enrolling 600 students with an aim of 1,500 at full strength. About 40 percent of the students are not Uzbek. It already has ties with Duke and Georgetown universities and a major exchange agreement with Mississippi State, where ten faculty members will be studying under a USIA grant. The new university welcomes students from abroad. More than half its students speak English. They pay tuition and eventually will pay at a high enough rate to cover the full cost of the University's operation.

We met with economist Kamol Islamov, who is head of the University's Department of Foreign Affairs. He expressed interest in our Journal and told us the University was actively building its English language collection, aided by a recent shipment of 2,000 books from the Sabre Foundation. He also expressed interest in our Cracow summer institute. I warned him that our faculty was independent-minded and our students were encouraged to think critically. He said that would be no problem because his own students debated different models of economic and political development, evaluated the structure of government and the efficiency of the ruling bureaucracy, and critically commented on proposed government decrees.

Thus Uzbekistan is a more complicated situation than it appears at first glance. To be sure, the regime is more repressive and less reform-minded than its neighbors, Kazakhstan and Kyrgyzstan. Yet there is some space for independent thought, space that is bound to grow with economic development and foreign contact.

## NOTES

1. Economist, April 23, 1994
2. Economist, April 30, 1994
3. Economist, April 23, 1994
4. Economist, March 19, 1994

APPENDIX

# New School Chronology

*1919*
The New School for Social Research is founded by a group of scholars, including historian Charles Beard and economist Thorstein Veblen.

*1921*
Alvin Johnson, economist and *New Republic* editor, becomes director of the New School.

*1930*
Daniel Cranford Smith, a retired businessman, donates land on West 12th Street in Greenwich Village for the New School's first new building, designed by Joseph Urban.

*1933*
The University in Exile is established at the New School as a center for refugee scholars who were dismissed from teaching and government positions by totalitarian regimes in Europe.

*1934*
The University in Exile is converted into the Graduate Faculty of Political and Social Science.

*1936*
The New School grants its first academic degrees to students who had completed the master's program in the Graduate Faculty.

*1940*
The New School establishes a French faculty (later to become independent as the Ecole Libre des Hautes Etudes) with support and cooperation of the French and Belgian governments in exile.

*1940*

The Dramatic Workshop is established under the leadership of German dramatist Erwin Piscator.

*1942*

The Institute for World Affairs is organized to mesh theoretical research with real social problems on an international scale.

*1943*

The New School starts its first degree-granting undergraduate program for adults, the Senior College.

*1950*

Enrollment at the New School reaches 10,000.

*1956*

Construction starts on the eight-story Jacob M. Kaplan building on West 12th Street.

*1959*

The Middle States Association of Colleges and Secondary Schools grants the institution and its degree programs full accreditation.

*1962*

The New School establishes the Institute for Retired Professionals, the first major effort by an institution of higher education on behalf of senior students.

*1964*

J. M. Kaplan Center for New York City Affairs, the first teaching and research center to focus its attention on a single metropolitan area, is founded.

*1966*

The New School College is begun as an experimental undergraduate program of liberal arts study leading to a bachelor of arts degree.

*1968*

The Graduate Faculty moves to the four-story Albert List Academic Center on Fifth Avenue between 13th Street and 14th Street.

*1970*

Parsons School of Design, founded in 1896 by painter William Merritt Chase, becomes the third major academic division of the New School.

## 1975
The university creates a fourth academic division, the Graduate School of Management and Urban Policy.

## 1977
Parsons' Fashion Design Department moves into a five-story building in Manhattan's garment district at Seventh Avenue and 40th Street.

## 1978
The New School College, later to be renamed after philanthropist Eugene Lang, is rededicated with the establishment of its first full-time 4-year undergraduate program.

## 1980
Jonathan F. Fanton, a Yale-trained historian and vice president of the University of Chicago, is named seventh president of the New School.

## 1983
The New School grants an honorary degree to political philosopher Adam Michnik, Poland's leading intellectual, who has been imprisoned by his country's Communist regime. President Fanton and others travel to Warsaw to present the award personally.

## 1984
The Graduate Faculty launches the Center for Studies of Social Change, a research institute focusing on popular collective action, the emergence of capitalism, and the development of the national state.

## 1987
Under the wing of the Graduate School of Management, the New School creates the Community Development Research Center to conduct assessments of community based economic development in distressed urban and rural communities.

## 1989
Mannes College of Music, founded in 1916, is merged into the university as its sixth academic division.

## 1989
The New School establishes the East and Central Europe program to forge a permanent link with academics and intellectual

communities in those countries emerging out of the collapse of communism.

*1990*

The Environmental Simulation Center, a computerized three-dimensional modeling facility, finds a home within the Graduate School of Management.

*1991*

The World Policy Institute, dedicated to public policy research and discussion of U.S. and international economic and security issues, becomes part of the university.

*1993*

The Center on Ethnicity is established as a resource for scholars to investigate and discuss patterns of migration, xenophobia, and demographic shifts worldwide.

*1994*

The Actors Studio joins the New School to create a 3-year M.F.A. program in acting, directing and playwriting. In May of 1995, the program is renamed the School of Dramatic Arts and becomes the seventh major academic division of the University.

# STATISTICAL PROFILE OF THE NEW SCHOOL

Year established: 1919

*Major divisions and their founding dates:*
  Adult Division (The New School)—1919
  Graduate Faculty of Political and Social Science—1934
  Parsons School of Design (by merger, 1970)—1896
  Graduate School of Management and Urban Policy—1975
  Eugene Lang College (Rededicated, 1985)—1978
  Mannes College of Music (by merger, 1989)—1916
  School of Dramatic Arts—1995

## 1994-95 Statistics

|  | *Fall Enrollment* | *Percentage of Tuition* |
|---|---|---|
| Undergraduate | 3,100 | 60% |
| Graduate | 2,700 | 20% |
| Noncredit | 13,200 | 20% |
| Total | 19,000 | 100% |

| | |
|---|---|
| 1994-95 Degrees Granted | 1,200 |
| Alumni Degrees and Diplomas, all Divisions | 33,000 |

| | |
|---|---|
| Total Institutional Space | 880,000 square feet |
| Full-time Faculty and Staff | 650 |
| Part-time Faculty | 1,250 |
| Annual Budget | $115 million |
| Endowment | $52 million |
| Annual Contributions and Grants | $16.65 million |

# Index

Abbott, Berenice, 36, 64
Abhava, Natalya, 493
Abkahazia (Republic of Georgia), 411, 414, 422-23
    Russian involvement in, 426, 427
Abrahams, Trevor, 457
Abrams, Charles, 46
academic freedom, 192
    accreditation practices and, 211, 212
    Trnava University case and, 387-89, 441-42
    *see also* freedom of expression
Academy of Sciences (Kazakhstan), 485
accreditation of colleges and universities, 209-14
Acheson, Dean, 4, 70
Actors Studio, 507
Adhan, Fazilbelkov, 497
Adult Division (New School), 22, 48, 49
    curriculum reform in, 142
    distance learning at, 227
    internationalism of, 54
    liberal arts at, 225
Advisory Task Force on State Support for High Technology Research, 196

Afanasyev, Yuri, 262, 264, 265, 268, 424, 425, 431, 452
African-Americans
    doctorates awarded to, 200
    education of, 202
    at New School, 141, 142
African National Congress (ANC; South Africa), 458, 459, 462-63, 465-70, 474
Afrikaaner Volksfront (South Africa), 463-65
Akaev, Askar, 479, 487-90
Albania
    constitution and legal system of, 373-76
    decommunization in, 378
    ethnic tensions in, 379
    former political prisoners in, 371-72
    history of, 368-69
    new government of, 380-81
    political life in, 370
    political opposition in, 376-78
    press in, 378-79
Albanians
    in Serbia, 305, 380
    in Yugoslavia, 306
Alexander I (czar, Russia), 404
Alexander, Lamar, 211

Alexander, Neville, 468
Alia, Ramiz, 368-69, 375-76
Aliev, Haider, 409, 413, 417-19, 444-46
Alliance of Free Democrats (Hungary), 397, 398
Alliance for Social Democracy (Bulgaria), 357
Alliance of Young Democrats (Hungary), 397
Almaty State University (Kazakhstan), 485
alumni, 67
    of New School B.A. program, 59
    of Parsons School of Design, 48, 86
American Civil Liberties Union (ACLU), 117
American Revolution, 4
American School (Kyrgyzstan), 491-92
American University (Armenia), 430, 452
American University (Bulgaria), 452
Amsden, Alice, 473
Anastasiu, Calin, 449
Andrew W. Mellon Foundation, 448, 451
Ankara (Turkey), 338, 348
Antal, Jozsef, 397, 398, 400-402, 437-38
anti-Semitism, 401
apartheid, 99, 102-3, 193-94
    economic sanctions against, 468-69
    fall of, 460
Arato, Andrew, 395, 447
Aristotle, 41, 43
Armenia, 403-5, 409
    educational reform in, 430
    human rights in, 413-14
    Nagorno Karabakh conflict and, 419-22
    political life in, 410
    Yerevan, 405-7

Armenians
    in Azerbaijan, 417
    in Nagorno Karabakh, 419-20
Army War College, 116
Arnhold, Henry, 301
arts
    national policy on, 179-82
    public funding of, 171-74
    public funding of, in U.S. and in Europe, 175-76
    *see also* National Endowment for the Arts
Association of Former Political Prisoners (Albania), 368, 369
Atatosov, Georgi, 362
Audubon Society, 187
Azerbaijan, 405, 409, 444-46
    Baku, 408-9
    human rights in, 413-14, 416-19
    Nagorno Karabakh conflict in, 419-22
    political life in, 412-13

Bailsford, Henry, 51-52
Baku (Azerbaijan), 408-9, 417
Baltic nations
    draft resistance in, 326-27
    economic situation in, 440
    Fanton in, 319-23
    future of Soviet Union and, 335-37
    history of, 323-24
    independence movements in, 327-28
    new governments of, 325-26
    political life in, 324-25
    Russians in, 425-26
    Soviet destabilization of, 328-35
Barkley, Richard, 338
Barrows, Stanley, 175
Baruch College (City University of New York), 210-12
Baskin, Leonard, 59
Beard, Charles, 23, 35, 51, 123-24

Belgrade (Yugoslavia), 307
Bellah, Robert, 43
Bella Lewitsky Dance Foundation, 117, 167
Benton, Thomas Hart, 36, 64
Berisha, Sali, 368-72, 375-78, 380, 381
Berko, Michael, 387
Berlin (Germany), 176, 298, 303
Bernstein, Blanche, 47
Bernstein, Richard, 140
Berov, Lubin, 438
Bethe, Hans, 197
Bible, 26-27
Bishkek (Kyrgyzstan), 479, 483, 487
Bishkek International School of Management and Business (Kyrgyzstan), 492
Blanshard, Paul, 46
Blockmen (Albania), 374, 376
Blum, John Morton, 3, 5
Board of Trustees, *see* Trustees of New School
Boas, Franz, 36
Bogert, Carroll 424, 425
Bokov, Philip, 357
Bonn (Germany), 303
Bophuthatswana (South Africa), 464-65
Bosnia, 306, 310, 313
Botha, Pik, 462
Bowen, William, 199
Bratislava (Slovakia), 242, 382
Breslow, Ronald, 186
Brewster, Kingman, 7, 116
Brucan, Silviu, 274, 276, 278, 280, 281, 287, 288, 293, 296
Brudney, Aron, 489-90, 498
Buchanan, Patrick, 151, 179
Bucharest (Romania), 271-72, 274
  demonstrations in, 287, 290-96
  student movement in, 280
Bucharest, University of, 285

Budapest (Hungary), 396
Budlender, Geoffrey, 457
Bulgaria, 246-48
  under Berov, 438-39
  Fanton in, 354-55
  human rights in, 359-65
  political dissidents in, 249-51
  political life in, 355-59
  political prisoners in, 251-52
  transition to democracy in, 365-67
  Turkish minority in, 248-49
Bulgarian Socialist Party (BSP), 355-58, 360, 362-65, 438
Bundy, McGeorge, 204
Bundy aid program, 205-6
Bush, George, 120, 125, 180, 269, 322
Buthelezi, Mangosuthu G., 461, 463-65
Butler, Nicholas, 123
Butora, Martin, 448

Califano, Joseph, 8
Campeanu, Pavel, 282, 437, 440
Canada, 181
Cape Town (South Africa), 461
capital punishment, 363
*Caravan* (newspaper; Kazakhstan), 486-87
Carnogursky, Jan, 384, 385
Carter, Betty, 175
Carter, Rosalynn, 254
Cartner, Holly, 296
Catholic Party (Peoples Party; Czech Republic), 389
Caucasus, 403
  Abkahazia, 422-23
  Armenia, 403-4
  Azerbaijan, 405
  Baku, 408-9
  educational reform in, 429-32
  Georgia (Republic of), 404
  human rights in, 413-19, 444-46

Nagorno Karabakh conflict in, 419-22
political life in, 409-13
Russian destabilization of nations of, 427
Tbilisi, 407-8
Yerevan, 406-7
Ceausescu, Elena, 271, 275
Ceausescu, Nicolae, 271, 272, 273, 274, 275, 276, 277-8, 284
Cela, Kudret, 368
Celac, 283, 284
Celakovice (Czech Republic), 433
Celinski, Andrzej, 448
censorship
  agreement between New School and National Endowment for the Arts on, 166-67
  of controversial speakers, 121-22
  discriminatory harassment and, 119-20
  Fanton's letter to *New York Times* on, 131-33
  founding of New School as response to, 123-24
  National Endowment for the Arts and, 81-83, 117-18
  New School suit against National Endowment for the Arts on, 159-63
  public funding of arts and, 171-74
  reauthorization of National Endowment for the Arts (1990) and, 164-65
  in Turkey, 347
Center for New York City Affairs (New School), 47, 67
Centers for Advanced Technology, 190
Center for the Study of Social Change (New School), 260
Central European University (Budapest), 452
Chan, Patrick, 457

Charter 77 (Czechoslovakia), 241, 243, 394
Chase School (Parsons), 63
Chicago, University of, 7-8, 116
Children of Bohemia (Czechoslovakia), 242
China, 478
Chitac, Mihai, 294
Chomutov (Czechoslovakia), 242
Christian Democratic Union (CDU; Slovakia), 385
Christian Democratic Peoples Party (Hungary), 397
Christian Democratic Union (Czech Republic), 389
Circle of Independent Intellectuals (Czechoslovakia), 239
Citizens Initiative (Bulgaria), 250
*City Almanac*, 47
Civic Democratic Alliance (ODA; Czech Republic), 389
Civic Democratic Party (ODS; Czech Republic), 389
Civic Forum (Czechoslovakia), 325, 389
Civic Movement (OH; Czech Republic), 389
Clinton, Bill, 177, 498
  arts policies of, 179-81
Cocoran Gallery (Washington), 81
Cohen, Henry, 47
colleges and universities
  accreditation of, 209-14
  erosion of support for, 192-94
  national shortage of faculty for, 199
  private, importance of, 186
  students enrolled in (in New York State), 195
  Tuition Assistance Program for, 189-91
  *see also* higher education; universities
Columbia University, 123, 196, 197
Commission on Higher Education

of the Middle States Association, 209
Commission on Independent Colleges and Universities (CICU), 195
Committee on 273 (Bulgaria), 250
Committee for the Defense of Four (Yugoslavia), 310
Committee for the Defense of Religious Rights, Freedom of Conscience, and Spiritual Values (Bulgaria), 250
Committee for the Defense of Slovenia, 310
Committee for International Academic Freedom, 388
Communist Party
  in Baltic nations, 325, 329
  of Bulgaria, 251, 355, 359-61, 367
  of Czechoslovakia, 240, 241
  of Czech Republic, 389
  of Georgia (Republic of), 410
  of Kyrgyzstan, 488, 489
  of Latvia, 330, 331
  of Lithuania, 332, 334
  of Romania, 272, 277-79
  of Soviet Union, 259, 263, 264, 266
  of Yugoslavia, 310, 311
Community Development Research Center (New School), 186
Community News Service, 47
computers, at New School, 226-27
Conference on Security and Cooperation in Europe (CSCE), 414
  on Nagorno Karabakh, 419, 421, 422n
conscription (draft), 326-27
controversial speakers, 116-17, 120-22, 193
Copland, Aaron, 36
Cornea, Doina, 276
Cornell University, 197
cosmopolitanism, 149-51

Council of Europe, 247, 248
Cournaud, Andre, 196
Cràvecoeur, Hector St. John, 20
Croatia, 305, 308-11, 313, 315
Croats
  in Serbia, 315
  in Yugoslavia, 305, 306, 309
Croly, Herbert, 25, 51
Csurka, Istvan, 401
Cuomo, Mario, 201, 205, 206, 490
curriculum reform, 126-29
  in Eastern and Central Europe, 450
  at New School, 140-42, 228
Czechoslovakia, 382-84
  Czech Republic, 389-95
  dissident movement in, 239-46
  Fanton in, 233-37, 238-39
  lustration in, 360
  Slovakia, Republic of, 384-89
  "velvet revolution" in (1989), 321-22
Czech Republic, 383, 386, 389-95

Davies, John, 117, 167
Davis, Stuart, 36, 64
decommunization (lustration)
  in Albania, 378
  in Bulgaria, 354, 359-61, 439
  in Czech Republic, 392-93
de Klerk, F.W., 458, 465-66, 469, 474
Delores, Jacques, 315-16
Demirel, Suleyman, 338, 342-46, 351-52
Democracy Seminars (New School), 12, 429, 447-49
  Bulgaria meeting of (1992), 354
  Prague meeting of (1993), 433-43
Democratic Alliance (Albania), 370
Democratic Center (Bulgaria), 356
Democratic Charter (Hungary), 400-402
Democratic Convention (Romania), 439

Democratic Forum (Hungary), 437-38
Democratic Initiative (Czechoslovakia), 241-42
Democratic Labor Party (Lithuania), 334
Democratic Left (Slovakia), 385
Democratic Left Party (Turkey), 342, 343
Democratic Party (Albania), 368-70, 375
Democratic Party (South Africa), 465, 467, 468
Democratic Party (Yugoslavia), 314
Democratic Union of Hungarians in Romania, 439
Demsky, Gabor, 449
Denber, Rachel, 403
de Tocqueville, Alexis, 5, 185, 253-54
Dewey, John, 37, 51, 123-24
Dienstbier, Jiri, 389, 390, 392-93
Dinescu, Mircea, 274, 282, 285, 289
discrimination
 in American society, 139
 on campuses, 138
 New School in leadership against, 146
 racist incidents and, 145
 *see also* minority groups; racism
discriminatory harassment, 113-15, 118-20, 124
 New School policy on, 140, 142
 "political correctness" issue and, 125, 126
Discussion Club (Bulgaria), 249, 251
dissidents
 in Azerbaijan, 417
 in Bulgaria, 246-51
 in power, 390
 in Soviet Union, 255, 257
 in Uzbekistan, 494, 499-501
 in Yugoslavia, 310, 317
Djilas, Milovan, 305, 308, 315, 316, 318

doctorate programs (Ph.D.s)
 minority graduates of, 200
 underrepresented groups among, 141
 *see also* graduate education
draft resistance, in Baltic nations, 326-27
Durres (Albania), 372
Du Toit, Andre, 458

East Berlin (Germany), 298
East and Central Europe program (New School), 12, 271, 448-51
East Germany, 298-302, 304
Ecevit, Bulent, 342
Eco-Glasnost (Bulgaria), 246, 249-51
Edelman, Gerald, 196-97
education
 in arts, 180-81
 curriculum reform in, 126-29
 "political correctness" in, 125
 public school system, 49-50
 reforms in, in former Soviet Union, 429-32
 shortage of teachers and, 199
Education, U.S. Department of, 125
 accreditation of colleges and universities and, 209-12
Einstein, Albert, 39
Elchibey, Abulfez, 412-13, 416-22, 445-46, 497
elections
 in Albania, 368-70, 375, 379
 in Armenia, 410
 in Azerbaijan, 412, 417
 in Baltic nations, 325, 328
 in Bulgaria, 355-58, 363
 in Czech Republic, 389
 in Georgia (Republic of), 411
 in Kazakhstan, 480-81
 in Kyrgyzstan, 488-89
 in Latvia, 440
 in Romania, 278-79, 283, 289, 290, 439-40

in Russian Republic, 425
in Slovakia, 384-85, 441
in Slovenia, 310
in South Africa, 458, 463-68
in Turkey, 342
in U.S., of 1936, 467
in U.S., of 1948, 152
in U.S., of 1992, 151, 179
in Uzbekistan, 495, 496
English as a Second Language program (New School), 48-49
Environmental Defense Fund, 186-87
Erikson, Kai, 2
ERK (party; Uzbekistan), 495, 496
Estonia, 440
draft resistance in, 326-27
Fanton in, 319, 320, 322-23
foreigner laws in, 403, 425-26
future of Soviet Union and, 335-37
history of, 323-24
new government in, 325-26
politcal life in, 324-25
Soviet Union and, 327, 328
ethnic minorities, *see* minority groups
Eugene Lang College (New School), 50, 60-62, 67, 218
Army War College speakers at, 116
as liberal arts school, 224
European Economic Community (EEC), 340
Everan, Kenan, 342
Everett, John R., 1, 21

faculty
Middle States Association on diversity in, 210-11
national shortage of, 199
of New School, 66
of New School, post-World War I (1920s), 51-52
of New School, reduction in, 216
of New School, role in governance of, 221-23
training for, 200
of University in Exile, 95
Fakes, Grace, 175
Falk, Peter, 59
Fanton, Cynthia Greenleaf, 456
Fanton, Jonathan F.
on accreditation in higher education, 209-13
administrative influences on, 8
on aid to higher education in New York, 104-6
on controversial speakers, 116-117, 120-21
on cutbacks at New School, 215-21
on end of Cold War, 148
on erosion of image of higher education, 192-94
on faculty in New School's governance, 221-3
on freedom of expression, 131-33
on graduate education in New York, 195-202
on Higher Education Opportunity Program, 202-4
historical and literary influences on, 4-6
Inaugural Address of (1982), 19-27
on liberal arts at New School, 223-226
on Matsunaga art exhibition, 104-11
on national arts policy, 179-82
on National Endowment for the Arts, 81-4, 117-20, 159-63, 164-65, 166-67
on network of Parsons alumni, 85-89
on New School's characteristics, 31-34
on New School's founders, 35-37

on New School's growth, 45-50, 66-70
on New School's internationalism, 51-58
New School interview of, 6-7
on New York's Tuition Assistance Program, 189-91
on official statements by universities, 99-103
on pluralism, 151-54, 227-29
on political alienation in U.S., 73-78
on "political correctness," 123-30
on post-Cold War Europe, 149-51
on public funding of arts, 171-74
on public funding of arts, in Europe, 175-78
reappointed as president of New School, 214
on support for private institutions, 185-88
on theoretical thinking, 38-40
on training for arts, at Parsons, 63-65
on undergraduate education at New School, 59-62
on underrepresented groups in higher education, 137-43
on universities as sanctuary for dissent, 112-15
on University in Exile, 95-98
at Yale, 2-3
Fanton, Willard, 4
Farrakhan, Louis, 121
federal government
arts policy of, 179-82
decline in financial aid from, 218
funding of arts by, 171-74, 175-76
independent institutions supported by, 185-88
universities directly aided by, 194
Feldek, Lubomir, 387

Ferrari, Frank, 456-57
Filipescu, Radu, 296-97
financial aid
decline in federal and state funds for, 218
Higher Education Opportunity Program, 202-4
New School policies on, 219
in New York State, 200-201
Tuition Assistance Program, 189-91
to underrepresented groups, 141
*Finley* v. *National Endowment for the Arts* (U.S., 1993), 179-80
*Fiscal Observer*, 47
Fleishman, Joel, 8
Fokina, Ninel, 482-83
Ford Foundation, 448
France, 175-77, 181
Frank, Jean-Michel, 175
Frankfurt (Germany), 303
Frankfurter, Felix, 36
Freedom Alliance (South Africa), 463-65, 467
freedom of expression
for controversial speakers, 116-17, 120-22
discriminatory harassment and, 114-15, 118-20
Fanton's letter to *New York Times* on, 131-33
*Finley* case and, 179-80
founding of New School for, 123-24
fragility of, 144-45
in Georgia (Republic of), 416
Matsunaga art exhibition and, 104-11
National Endowment for the Arts and, 117-18
New School suit against National Endowment for the Arts and, 159-63

public funding of arts and, 171-74
stereotypes and, 83-84
Frei, Hans, 3
French Revolution, 253-54
Freshman Year Program (New School), 60-61
Frohnmayer, John, 160-61, 163, 164
Fromm, Erich, 36
Front for National Salvation (Romania), 276-82, 286, 288, 289, 439
Frost, Robert, 36
Fund for the Improvement of Post Secondary Education, 227
Fund for New Initiatives (New School), 220-21

Gabal, Ivan, 233, 236
Gabalova, Zdenka, 233
Gaitandjiev, Stefan, 356
Gambar, Isa, 417
Gamsakhurdia, Zviad, 410-11, 415
Gardner, John, 187-88
Gates, Robert, 298
Geneva 49 (organization, Estonia), 327
Geneva Convention (1949), 327, 414
Georgia, Republic of, 404, 409
 Abkahazia conflict in, 422-23
 human rights in, 413-16, 445
 political life in, 410-12
 Tbilisi, 407-8
Gerhart, John, 456-58
Germany, 304
 East Germany, 298-302
 funding for arts in, 176
 West Germany, 302-3
Gerwel, Jakes, 473
*glasnost*, 263, 335
Goldenweiser, Alexander, 46
Goldfarb, Jeffrey, 57, 434, 447
Goncz, Arpad, 398, 399, 401
Gorbachev, Mikhail, 244, 257, 259-64, 425, 490
 Baltic nations and, 319-22, 324, 328, 335-36
 conflict between Yeltsin and, 264-67
 future of, 268-70
 future of Soviet Union and, 337
 Lithuania and, 332-35
 in post-Soviet Russia, 424
Gorbunov, Anatolijs, 440
Gotsividze, Irakli, 416
graduate education, 195-200
 financial aid for, 200-201
 minority groups enrolled in, 199-200
 part-time students in, 201-2
Graduate Faculty of Political and Social Science (New School), 23-24
 accreditation reviews of, 212-13
 internationalism of, 52-53
 liberal arts at, 224-25
 New York links of, 48
 rebuilding of (1980s), 218
 as University in Exile, 12, 21, 95-98
Graduate School of Management and Urban Policy (New School), 25, 47, 67, 218, 223, 226, 473
Graduate School of Management and Urban Professions (New School), 25, 47, 218, 226
Graduate School for Social Research (Warsaw), 452
Graham, Martha, 36
Gray, Hanna, 7-8, 116
Gray, Thomas, 119
Greeks, in Albania, 379
Grigorievs, Alex, 440, 449
Group for Social Dialogue (Romania), 282-83, 285, 292, 296, 297
Gulf War (1991), 342
Gutmann, Amy, 112
Gypsies, 436

in Albania, 379
in Bulgaria, 363, 364
in Czech Republic, 393-94
in Hungary, 402
in Slovakia, 386

Hacker, Paul, 384, 385
Hajduk, Anton, 387-89, 441-42
Hajek, Jiri, 238-39, 389, 390
Hamidov, Iskandar, 417
Hamza, Gabor, 396-99, 402, 437
harassment, 112-15, 118-20, 124
 New School policy on, 140, 142
 "political correctness" issue and, 125, 126
Haraszti, Miklos, 449
Havel, Vaclav, 245, 383, 389-92, 435
 arrest of, 233
 Gorbachev's meeting with, 266
 as president of Czechoslovakia, 360, 384
 Trnava University appointment of, 388, 441
Haxhia, Maksim, 376-77
Heckscher, August, 48
Heidelberg, University of, 98
Heilbroner, Robert, 23
Helfer, Andreas, 303
Helms, Jesse, 82, 88, 106, 120, 171-73, 179
Helsinki Watch Committee, 12
 Abkahazia conflict and, 423
 Albania and, 368
 Baltic nations and, 319
 Bulgaria and, 246, 250, 360-61, 365
 Czech Republic chapter of, 393, 395
 Georgia (Republic of) and, 414-16
 Kazakhstan and, 486
 on Latvia and Estonia, 426
 Latvian chapter of, 440
 Romania and, 271
 Romanian chapter of, 283
 on Romanian election, 289
 Turkey and, 248, 338
 Yugoslavia and, 305
 *see also* International Helsinki Federation for Human Rights
Hercegovina, 306, 310, 313
Heuss Professorship, 52
higher education
 accreditation in, 209-14
 in Armenia, 430
 curriculum reform in, 126-29
 Eastern and Central Europe reforms in, 447-55
 erosion of public support for, 10, 192-94
 Higher Education Opportunity Program for, 202-4
 institutional aid for, 204-6
 in Kazakhstan, 484-86
 in Kyrgyzstan, 490-92
 part-time graduate students in, 201-2
 private, 11, 186
 in Russian Republic, 431
 in South Africa, 470-73
 students enrolled in (in New York State), 195
 Tuition Assistance Program for, 189-91
 undergraduate, at New School, 59-62
 in Uzbekistan, 501-2
 *see also* colleges and universities; universities
Higher Education Opportunity Program (HEOP), 142, 202-4
high schools, 49-50
 Freshman Year Program and, 60-61
Hill, Kenneth, 354, 361
Hirst, William, 450
Hispanics, education of, 202
Hofstadter, Richard, 5
Holmes, Oliver Wendell, 26
Hook, Sidney, 36
Hopkins, Harry, 172

Hoxha, Enver, 368, 369, 373, 375
Hoxha, Mrs. Enver, 368, 374-76
human rights
    in Albania, 370
    in Azerbaijan, 416-19
    in Bulgaria, 246-52, 354-55, 359-65
    in Caucasus, 413-14
    in Czechoslovakia (1989), 238-46
    in Czech Republic, 392
    in Georgia (Republic of), 414-16
    in Hungary, 400-402
    importance of Human Rights Watch for, 187
    in investment decisions, 444-46
    in Kazakhstan, 486-87
    in Kyrgyzstan, 492-94
    Moscow meeting on (1990), 253-58
    in Nagorno Karabakh, 420
    New School's concerns for, 57
    in Romania, 273, 284
    in Russian Republic, 426
    Schwarzenberg on, 436-37
    in Slovakia, 385-89
    in Soviet Union, 263-64
    in Turkey, 338, 342, 345-52
    in Ukraine, 429
    in Uzbekistan, 499-501
    in Yugoslavia, 312, 314
Human Rights Committee (Bulgaria), 246
Human Rights Foundation (Turkey), 345
Human Rights Watch, 187
    Moscow meeting of (1990), 253
    in Uzbekistan, 494
    Uzbekistan and, 500
Humm, Nancy, 475$n$
Humphrey, Doris, 36
Hungarian Democratic Forum (MDF), 397, 398
Hungarians
    in Romania, 280, 284, 289
    in Slovakia, 385
Hungarian Socialists, 397
Hungary, 395-402
    Democratic Forum in, 437-38
Hurwitz, Edward, 488
Husseinov, Surat, 413, 417, 419, 445
Hyak, Milos, 241

Iceland, 327
Iliescu, Ion, 439-40
    election victory of, 289, 290
    as Front for National Salvation leader, 276
    miners' demonstration and, 291, 293-96
    as Romanian president, 275, 277, 279, 280, 283, 286, 288
    youth's distrust of, 281
immigration and immigrants
    in Germany, 298-99
    in New York City, 58
Independence Now (Lithuania), 334
Independent Peace Movement (Czechoslovakia), 242
Independent Society for the Protection of Human Rights (Bulgaria), 250
Inkatha (South Africa), 461-64
Inoiatova, Vasila, 499-501
Inonu, Erdal, 338, 342, 343, 345, 350, 351
intellectuals
    in East Germany, 299-301
    in Romania, 282-83, 285-86, 289-90
    in Turkey, 340
    in Yugoslavia, 316-17
Interfront (Baltic nations), 325
International Committee on Academic Freedom, 442
International Ecological Forum, 354
International Helsinki Federation for Human Rights, 238, 246, 354

Moscow meeting of (1990), 253-58

*see also* Helsinki Watch Committee

international programs, 57

investments
　human rights in decisions on, 444-46
　in South Africa, 193
　stock ownership by universities, 100-101

Iskhahova, Diloran, 499-500

Islam
　in Kazakhstan, 483-84
　in Kyrgyzstan, 488
　in Turkey, 339

Islamov, Kamol, 502

Istanbul (Turkey), 338

Jakzpova, Chinara, 489, 493

James McDonnell Foundation, 450

Jarmalavicius, Ivozas, 332

Jazz Program, 218, 223

Jefferson, Thomas, 41-42

Jensen, Arthur, 116

Jews, 379, 401

Johannesburg (South Africa), 459, 461

John Lennon Peace Club (Czechoslovakia), 242

Johnson, Alvin
　European scholars rescued by, 11-12, 52, 95
　as first President of New School, 2
　at founding of New School, 51
　Jefferson as model for, 42
　on name of New School, 19, 35
　on New School's dedication to freedom, 130
　University in Exile established by, 21, 66, 96, 97
　vision for New School of, 36

Johnson, Samuel, 19

Jordan, Paulo, 462

Journal Project (New School), 451

Kallen, Horace, 36

Kaplan, Jacob M., 47

J.M. Kaplan Center for New York City Affairs (New School), 25, 47, 50

Karimov, Islam, 479, 495-98, 501-2

Kask, Peet, 322

Kaslan, Gilbert, 59

Katznelson, Ira, 33, 48, 448

Kazakhstan, 475-76
　higher education in, 484-86
　human rights in, 486-87
　political life in, 480-84
　Uzbekistan in economic union with, 497

Kazakhstan National University, 484-85

Kempel, Brian, 475$n$

Kennedy, John F., 5

Kenyon, Cecilia, 366-67

Keynes, John Maynard, 38, 40, 52

Kiev (Ukraine), 427-29, 431

Kis, Janos, 449

Kitovani, Tengiz, 423

Klaus, Vaclav, 384, 389-91

Klimova, Rita, 240, 390$n$, 392, 394, 448

Koch, Edward, 33

*Koha Jone* (newspaper; Albania), 377, 379

Kolarova, Rumyana, 437, 452

Kopliku, Bashkim, 368

Kosovo (Serbia), 305, 306, 312, 380

Koszeg, Ferenc, 449

Kovac, Michal, 441, 442

Kovalev, Sergei, 264, 269

Kovazko, Milan, 240

Kravchuk, Leonid, 428, 429

Krawchenko, Bohdan, 428, 429

Krbusek, Jaroslav, 241

Krol, Marcin, 449

Krotke, Wolfgang, 298

Kuchakov, Mahmut, 491

Kuchma, Leonid, 428
Kurczewski, Jacek, 448, 449
Kurds, in Turkey, 339, 349-51
Kuron, Jacek, 390, 448
Kyrgyz-American Bureau on Human Rights and Rule of Law, 493-94
Kyrgyzstan, 475-77, 487-90
   higher education in, 490-92
   human rights in, 492-94
Kyrgyzstan-Russian University, 492
Kzngy, James, 498

Laber, Jeri
   in Albania, 368
   in Czechoslovakia, 238, 239
   in Estonia, Latvia and Lithuania, 319
   in Romania, 271
   in Slovakia, 384, 387
   in Turkey, 338, 350
Lamar, Howard, 3
Landsbergis, Vytautas, 319, 322-23, 327, 332, 334
Lang, Eugene M., 9, 61
Lang, Jack, 176-77
Lang College (New School), *see* Eugene Lang College
Laski, Harold, 52
Latinos, at New School, 141, 142
Latvia, 440
   draft resistance in, 326-27
   Fanton in, 319-23
   future of Soviet Union and, 335-37
   history of, 323-24
   new government in, 325-26
   political life in, 324-25
   Russians in, 426
   Soviet Union and, 328-31
Latvian Way (party), 440
Lederberg, Joshua, 198
Lederer, Emil, 23
Leiss Sheriff, 82, 88
Lerner, Gerda, 59

Levin, Michael, 119
Lewitsky case, 117
Libardian, Girard, 420, 421
liberal arts, at New School, 223-26
Liberal Social Union (Czech Republic), 389
liberal studies, 225
Liberty Scholarship and Liberty Partnership programs, 202-4
Licht, Sonja, 305
*Lidove-Noviny* (Czechoslovakia), 243
Lindblom, C.E., 5
Li Peng, 498
List, Vera, 13, 156
Lithuania
   "attempted coup" in, 332-35
   draft resistance in, 326-27
   Fanton in, 319-23
   future of Soviet Union and, 335-37
   history of, 323-24
   new government in, 325-26
   political life in, 324-25
   Soviet Union and, 327-30
Longstreth, Bevis, 387
Lordkiparidze, Grigol, 414-15
Lovett, Robert, 2, 6
Lowe, Adolph, 23
Lukanov, Andrei, 362, 438
Lukasiewicz, Piotr, 448
Lundine, Stanley, 196, 202
Lundine Report, 196, 198
lustration, *see* decommunization

Maastricht Treaty, 176-77
Macedonians, in Yugoslavia, 306
MacIver, Robert, 47
Mack, Arien, 451
McNamara, Robert, 116, 193
Mamedov, Etibar, 413
Mandela, Nelson, 457, 458, 462-66, 468, 469, 471
Mangope, Lucas, 464
Mann, Thomas, 36, 98
Mannes, David, 54

Mannes College of Music
  internationalism of, 53-54
  merged with New School, 67, 218, 223
Mansbridge, Albert, 35
Manukian, Vazgen, 420, 421
Mapplethorpe, Robert, 81, 82, 174
Marga, Andrei, 449
Markovic, Ante, 309, 311-13, 317, 318
Martin Luther King Society (Hungary), 402
Masanov, Nurbulat, 481
Matsunaga, Shin, 83
  exhibition of art of, 104-11, 119, 131
Matynia, Elzbieta, 448
Mayer, Clara, 35
Mazilu, Dumitru, 275
Mbeki, Govan, 457, 473-74
McCarthyism, 126
Mead, Margaret, 36
Meciar, Vladimir, 383-88, 441-42
media
  human rights issues regarding, 436
  *see also* press
Media Studies, M.A. degree in, 67
Meksi, Aleksander, 368
Meltser, Igor, 486
Memorial (Soviet Union), 263
Merrifield, Bruce, 197
Mesic, Stipe, 305, 309, 315, 317
Metropolitan Information Service, 47
Meyer, Julie, 46
Michnik, Adam, 447, 449
Middle States Association of Colleges and Schools, 209-13
Milano, Robert, 220
Militaru, Nicolae, 275-76
*Miller v. California*, 117, 118, 166
Milosevic, Slobodan, 308-12, 314-15, 317, 318, 380
minority groups
  in Abkahazia, 422
  in Albania, 379
  in Azerbaijan, 405, 417
  in Baltic nations, 323, 426
  in Bulgaria, 248-49, 355, 361-65
  in Czech Republic, 393-95
  enrolled in colleges in New York State, 195
  in Georgia (Republic of), 404
  in higher education, 199-200
  Higher Education Opportunity Program and, 202-4
  in Hungary, 402
  in Kazakhstan, 475-76, 483, 486
  in Kyrgyzstan, 476
  in Latvia, 440
  in Lithuania, 334
  in Nagorno Karabakh, 420
  as part-time graduate students, 201
  in Romania, 280, 284
  in Soviet Union, 254-56
  in Turkey, 339, 349-51
  in Uzbekistan, 477
  in Yugoslavia, 305-9
Miszlivetz, Ferenc, 400-402
Mitchell, Wesley Clair, 19, 35
Mitterand, Franáois, 176-77
Mladina, 310
Mohyla Academy (Ukraine), 431-32, 452
Mokrzycki, Edmund, 449
Montenegrins, in Yugoslavia, 306
Morgan, Edmund, 3, 4
Morrison, Elting, 6
Moscow (Soviet Union; Russia), 424
  economy of, 260-62
  International Helsinki Federation meeting in (1990), 253
  refugees in, 427
Motherland Party (ANAP; Turkey), 342, 343
Movement for Civic Freedom (HOS; Czechoslovakia), 241

Movement for a Democratic Slovakia, 384-85
Movement for Rights and Freedom (MRF; Bulgaria), 355, 438
Moynihan, Daniel Patrick, 182
multiculturalism, 126-29
Mumford, Lewis, 36, 46, 64
Munteanu, Marian, 294
music, federal policies on, 181-82
Muslims, *see* Islam
Mutalibov, Ayaz, 412

Nagorno Karabakh (Azerbaijan)
    Armenian politics and, 410
    conflict in, 403, 409, 413, 419-22
    population of, 405
    Russian involvement in, 426
National Academy of Sciences (NAS), 198
National Democratic Party (Kazakhstan), 480
National Democratic Progressive Party (Romania), 279
National Endowment for the Arts (NEA), 88, 126
    agreement between New School and, 166-67
    budget of, 175-76
    *Finley* case and, 179-80
    funding for, 181
    in national arts policy, 181-82
    New School suit against, 10, 117-18, 159-63, 171
    public funding of arts by, 172-74
    reauthorization of (1990), 164-65
    restrictions on grants from, 81, 82, 145
National Endowment for the Humanities (NEH), 161
National Institutes of Health (NIH), 172, 197
National Liberal Party (Romania), 279, 288, 289, 291, 294
National Party (South Africa), 458, 459, 465-68
National Peasant Party (Romania), 279, 288, 289, 291
National Resources Defense Council, 186
National Salvation Committee (Lithuania), 332, 333
National Science Fellows, 197
National Science Foundation (NSF), 172
Nature Conservancy, 187
Nazarbaev, Nursultan, 444, 479-83, 497
networking, 85-86
Neumann, Vaclav, 240
Neustadt, Richard, 458
New College (Oxford, England), 20
New Deal, 172
Newport Harbor Art Museum, 167
*New Republic*, 51
New School for Social Research, 1-2
    accreditation reviews of, 209, 212-13
    admission to, 32
    Adult Division of, 22
    agreement between National Endowment for the Arts and, 166-67
    arts at, 64
    chronology of, 503-6
    commitment to freedom of, 130
    committee work at, 69-70
    cultural diversity at, 140-43, 153
    current status of, 8-9
    Czechoslovakia and, 246
    decline in enrollment at (1990-92), 215-16
    early history of, 35-36
    East and Central Europe program of, 12, 447-55
    faculty role in governance of, 221-23
    Fanton becomes President of, 7
    Fanton's interview for, 6-7

Fanton reappointed as president of, 214
financial status of, 217-21
former Soviet Union and, 429-30
founding of, 51-52, 123-24
goals of (1992), 216-17
Graduate Faculty of, 23-24
growth of, 66-68
history of growth of, 21
importance of theory at, 38-40
internationalism of, 52-58
Kyrgyzstan's universities and, 491
liberal arts at, 223-26
Matsunaga art exhibition and, 105-11, 131-33
National Endowment for the Arts sued by, 117-18, 159-63, 164-65, 171
in new assault on discrimination, 146
as New York City institution, 45 47
New York-oriented programs at, 47-50
official policy on apartheid of, 99-100
origins of name of, 19-20, 35
Parsons School of Design merged with, 65, 87
pluralism at, 227-29
policy on harassment of, 113-15, 119-20
responsibilities of Trustees of, 68-69
role of Trustees of, 9-10
Romania and, 282-83, 285-86
Russian Republic and, 431
South Africa and, 456, 471-72
statistical profile of, 507
technological capabilities of, 226-27
Trnava University and, 442
undergraduate college at, 22-23
undergraduate education at, 59-62
University in Exile established by, 95-98
urban environment of, 25-26
urban studies at, 46-47
New Union for Democracy (Bulgaria), 438
New York (State)
aid to private higher education in, 204-6
college and university students enrolled in, 195
financial aid for graduate education in, 200-201
Higher Education Opportunity Program in, 202-4
minorities in higher education in, 199-200
part-time graduate students in, 201-2
scientific research in, 196-99
Tuition Assistance Program in, 189-91
New York, City of, 25
immigrant populations of, 58
New School as institution of, 45-50
shortage of teachers in, 199
New York Commission on Independent Colleges and Universities, 10-11
New York School of Fine and Applied Arts (Parsons), 63-64
*New York Times*
Fanton on higher education in, 192-94
Fanton on human rights in investments in, 444-46
Niazov, Saparmurat, 479
Nichols Amendment, 312, 316
Nifadyev, Vladimir, 492
Ninidve, Tedo, 415-16
Niyazov, Saparmurat, 444
Nizich, Ivana, 305
Nkondo, Sankie, 457
Nkosi, Morley, 457

Nobel Prizes, 186, 196
nonprofit organizations, 185-88
North, Oliver, 341
North, University of the (South Africa), 471, 472
North Atlantic Treaty Organization (NATO), 340

Obroda (Renewal; Czechoslovakia), 241
obscenity
  agreement between New School and National Endowment for the Arts on, 166-67
  National Endowment for the Arts and, 117-18
  New School suit against National Endowment for the Arts on, 159-63, 171
  reauthorization of National Endowment for the Arts (1990) and, 164-65
Odom, William, 175
Omonia (Albania), 379
Orlov, Yuri, 254
Orozco, José, 36
Ozal, Turgut, 339, 342, 343

Palous, Jan, 448
Palous, Radim, 301, 449
Pan African Congress (PAC; South Africa), 465-68
Papazov, Boyan, 449
Parliament Committee (Bulgaria), 251, 252
Parsons, Frank Alvah, 63-64
Parsons School of Design, 21
  cosmopolitanism of, 175
  expansion of, 218
  Higher Education Opportunity Program at, 142
  history of, 63-64
  hundreth anniversary of, 85
  internationalism of, 53
  liberal arts at, 60
  Matsunaga art exhibition at, 83, 104-11, 119, 131
  merged with New School, 59, 66-67, 223
  as network, 86-89
  in service to New York City, 47-48
  study abroad programs of, 56
  technology at, 226-27
Pascu, Ion Mircea, 294, 296-97
Pashko, Gramoz, 368, 377
peer review accreditation, 210
Pen Club (Slovakia), 387
People's Congress (Kazakhstan), 480
People's Front (Latvia), 325, 331
*perestroika*, 268, 269, 277, 335
Petovar, Tanja, 305
Petrova, Dimitrina, 437
Petrusek, Miloslav, 449, 452
Pew Charitable Trusts, 448, 451
Pithart, Petr, 239, 394, 448
Pityana, Sipho, 472
Plesu, Andrei, 274, 282
pluralism
  in art, 173
  as international tendency, 151-52
  at New School, 227-29
Podkrepa (Bulgaria), 250
Polanski, Sol, 246
Polat, Abdurahim, 496-97
police brutality, 415-16
"political correctness," 10, 120, 123-30
political prisoners
  in Albania, 369, 371-72
  in Bulgaria, 250-52, 364
  in Czechoslovakia, 243
  in Romania, 284
  in Soviet Union, 256
  in Turkey, 345
  in Uzbekistan, 500
Pollack, Norman, 2-3
Popovic, Srdja, 305, 318

Popular Fron (Estonia), 325
Potter, David, 4-5
Pound, Roscoe, 36
Prague (Czech Republic), 382
    Democracy Seminar at (1993), 433-43
    Fanton in, 233-37
    political demonstrations in, 242-43
    "velvet revolution" in (1989), 321-22
press
    in Albania, 378-79
    in Bulgaria, 365
    in Georgia (Republic of), 416
    in Kazakhstan, 486-87
    in Kyrgyzstan, 493
    in Slovakia, 385-86
    South Africa portrayed in, 462
    in Uzbekistan, 495-96, 501
Prunskiene, Kazimiera, 332
public education, *see* education
public school system, 49-50
Puryear, Martin, 159

Qasim Khan, 476

Rabi, I.I., 197
Rabin, Yitzhak, 121
racism, 145
    in American society, 139
    apartheid, 99, 102-3, 193-94, 460
    freedom of expression and, 131-33
    increase on campuses of, 137
    in Matsunaga art exhibition, 105-7
    stereotypes and, 83-84
    *see also* minority groups
refugees, 436
Reich, Robert, 73
Reinschke, Kurt, 298, 300-301
Republican Party (Albania), 370
Republican Party (Czech Republic), 389, 391
research, 195-202

Revolutionary Left (Dev Sol; Turkey), 349
*Revolver Review* (Czechoslovakia), 242
Rhodes, Frank, 200, 202
Richards, Dickinson, 196
Ricoeur, Paul, 79
Riga (Latvia), 320, 321, 330, 331, 440
Robinson, James Harvey, 23, 35, 51
Rockefeller Foundation, 117
Rockefeller University, 186, 196
Rockwell, John, 176
Roman, Petru, 275, 288, 439
Romania
    antigovernment demonstrations in, 290-96
    election in (1990), 289-90
    Fanton in, 271-72
    following revolution, 287-89
    future of, 283-84
    human rights in, 284
    intellectuals in, 282-83
    new leadership of, 296-97
    political life in, 439-40
    provisional government in, 276-80
    revolution in (1990), 272-76
    scholarly life in, 285-86
    student movement in, 280-82
*Romania Libera* (newspaper), 291
Romania Mare Party, 439
Romanian National Unity Party, 439
Roosevelt, Franklin D., 5, 172, 467, 469
Roosevelt, Theodore, 64
Rorty, Richard, 76-77
Rose and Irwin Wolfson Center for National Affairs (New School), 55-56
Rous, Peyton, 196
Ruml, Jiri, 240
Russell, Bertrand, 36, 52
Russian Republic, 262, 265, 268, 423-27

Central Asian republics and, 479
educational reform in, 429-32, 431
Uzbekistan and, 497
*see also* Soviet Union
Russian Revival Party, 425
Russians
in Baltic nations, 425-26
in Kazakhstan, 483, 486
in Kyrgyzstan, 493
in Latvia, 440

Sabirov, Rafshan, 501
Sachs, Jeffrey, 486
Sadykov, Tokmohammed, 485
Sajudis (Lithuania), 325
Salikh, Mukhammad, 496
Salvemini, Gaetano, 51-52
Salzer, Felix, 54
Samarkand (Uzbekistan), 479-80, 495, 501
Sandton City (South Africa), 460-61
Saudargas, Algirdas, 327
Schapiro, Meyer, 36
Schenker, Heinrich, 54
Schiaparelli, Elsa, 175
Schlesinger, Arthur, Jr., 5
Schuller, Robert, 484
Schwarzenberg, Karl Johannes von
in Bulgaria, 238, 354
at Democracy Seminar (Prague), 435-37
at International Helsinki Federation Conference (Moscow), 254
in Romania, 271, 281
scientific research, in New York State, 196-99
Securitate (Romania), 271, 275, 284
Select Committee on the Future of Private and Independent Higher Education in New York State, 204-5
Seminar College (New School), 61, 67

senior citizens, 49
Serbia, 311, 313, 314, 380
Serbs
in Croatia, 315
in Yugoslavia, 305, 306, 308, 309
Shakespeare, William, 20
Shakhnazarian, David, 420, 421
Sharshnekeeva, Kamila, 491
Shashev, Jusenhaev, 490
Shevardnadze, Eduard, 283, 409-12, 416, 423, 444
Shockley, William, 116, 193
Sibl, Marijan, 313
Sigua, Tengiz, 411, 412, 422
Sigurimi (Albanian secret police), 378
Singer, Arthur, 8
Slapins, Andris, 321
Slobodnik, Dusan, 383-88
Slovakia, Republic of, 383-89
Trnava University in, 441-42
Slovak National Party, 385
Slovenes, in Yugoslavia, 306
Slovenia, 305-7, 310, 313, 316
Small Holders Party (Hungary), 397
Smith, Douglas, 354
Sobadigiev, Liubomir, 250
Social Democratic Party
of Albania, 370
of Czech Republic, 389
of Romania, 279
of Turkey (SHP), 342, 343, 350-52
Socialist Party (Albania), 370, 375
Socialist Party (Kazakhstan), 480
*Social Research*, 57, 447
Soderlund, Kurt R., 403, 475
Sofia (Bulgaria), 247, 354
Solomin, Leonid, 482, 483
Sora, Mihai, 274, 282
Soros, George, 401
Soros Foundation, 432, 475*n*
Sosa, Julie Ann, 199
South Africa, 193-94
apartheid in, 99, 102-3

current situation in, 457-62
economy in, 468-70
Fanton in, 456-57
future of, 473-74
higher education in, 470-73
political life in, 462-68
Sullivan principles on, 446
Soviet Union, 148, 253
Abkahazia and, 423
Baltic nations and, 319-22, 324, 326-37
dispute between Gorbachev and Yeltsin in, 264-67
ethnic groups in, 254-55
future of, 267-70
human rights concerns in, 255 57
Nagorno Karabakh and, 419
*perestroika* in, 277
political life in (1990), 258-64
Romania and, 283-84
Ukraine as part of, 428
Soweto (South Africa), 460
Specter, Arlen, 499, 501
Stalin, Josef, 419, 483
Stampp, Kenneth, 4
Stanculescu, Victor, 293
Stankevich, Sergei, 253, 256, 259-61, 424-27
Stanton, Louis, 118, 166-67
Staudinger, Hans, 23
stereotypes
in art, 83-84
in Matsunaga art exhibition, 105-7
Stern, Jan, 393
Steyn, Richard, 456
Stimson, Henry Lewis, 6, 73
stock ownership by universities, 100-101
Stoyanov, Sasho, 359
Strasky, Jan, 388
students
in Czechoslovakia, 241
enrolled in New York State, 195
graduate, in New York State, 198-99

graduate, part-time, 201-2
minority, 199-200
at New School, decline in enroll ment of (1990-92), 215-16
at New School, involvement by, 68-70
at New School, undergraduate, in 1969, 66
at Parsons School of Design, 85
in Romania, 278, 280-82, 289
in South African universities, 471
Tuition Assistance Program for, 189-91
study abroad programs, 56
Sulek, Antoni, 452
Sullivan principles, 446
Supreme Court (U.S.), 161-63
Suzman, Helen, 456, 467

Tabyshalieva, Anara, 483
Tajikistan, 427, 479
Talbott, Strobe, 499
Tallinn (Estonia), 320, 322
Tammerlane (emperor of Mogols), 499
Tashkent (Uzbekistan), 479, 495, 497
taxes
nonprofit organizations and, 185
private donations for arts and, 172, 174, 182
private universities exempt from, 192
value of charitable deductions on, 187
Taylor, Lance, 473
Taylor, Paul, 458
Tbilisi (Republic of Georgia), 407-8, 415-16
Tbilisi State University (Republic of Georgia), 416
teachers, 49
graduate education for, 200
shortage of, 199

Teodorescu, Alin, 282, 285
Ter-Petrossian, Levon, 410, 420, 422
terrorism, in Turkey, 349
Thatcher, Margaret, 269
Thomson, Virgil, 36
Tilly, Charles, 32, 260
Tirana (Albania), 369
Tito (Josip Broz), 307
Todorov, Antoni, 449
Tolerance (organization; Czech Republic), 393-95
torture, in Turkey, 338, 343, 345-48
Townes, Charles, 197
Transylvania (Romania), 280
Trnava (Slovakia), 388
Trnava University (Slovakia), 387-89, 441-42
True Path Party (Turkey), 342, 343
Truex, Van Day, 175
Truman, Harry S, 73, 152-53
trustees, boards of
    Middle States Association on diversity of, 209
    responsibilities of, 68-69
    role of, 9-10
    on South Africa, 194
    Vietnam War condemned by, 193
Trustees of New School
    cultural diversity encouraged by, 141
    diversity of views encouraged by, 121-22
    Eugene Lang College established by, 61
    on freedom of expression, 106-7
    on freedom of expression for controversial speakers, 116-17
    Fund for New Initiatives created by, 220-21
    "official" views of, 99-100
Tudjman, Franjo, 308-10, 314, 315, 318
Tugwana, Gabu, 456

Tuition Assistance Program (TAP), 189-91
    for graduate education, 200-202
Turk, Ahmet, 351
Turkey, 248, 478
    Fanton in, 338-39
    human rights in, 345-52
    international situation and, 339-41, 352-53
    political life in, 342-45
Turks, in Bulgaria, 248-50, 252, 355, 361-65
Turner, Frederick Jackson, 4-5
Tverenikov, 332
*22* (journal; Romania), 283

Ukraine, 427-29, 427-29
    educational reform in, 431-32
Ukraine Legal Foundation, 429
Ulysses S. Grant Foundation, 6
undergraduate education
    minority groups enrolled in, 199
    at New School, 22-23, 59-62, 66, 67
    at New School, liberal arts in, 225
    students enrolled in (in New York State), 195
    Tuition Assistance Program for, 201
    *see also* Eugene Lang College
Union of Democratic Forces (UDF; Bulgaria), 355-63, 365, 438
Union for Human Rights (UHR; Albania), 368, 370, 379
Union of National Unity of Kazakhstan (SNEK), 480-81
Union of Soviet Socialist Republics (USSR), *see* Soviet Union
United Nations' International Convenant on Civil and Political Rights (1966), 414
United States
    alienation in, 74

apartheid in South Africa and, 103
arts funding in, 81-83, 175-76
future of Soviet Union and, 337
intellectuals isolated from, 76-77
Romania and, 283-84
Turkey and, 340-41
voter participation in, 73
weak leadership in, 75
Yugoslavia and, 312
universities
as communities, 98
controversial speakers at, 120-22
division between faculty and administration in, 221
in Eastern and Central Europe, 447-55
in East Germany, 301
increase of racism on, 137
in Kazakhstan, 484-86
in Kyrgyzstan, 491-92
neutrality of, 68-69, 99-102
official positions taken by, 121-22
private, 11, 186
role of trustees of, 9-10
in Romania, 285-86
as "sanctuary of nonrepression," 112-15
in South Africa, 470-73
underrepresented groups in, 138-40
*see also* colleges and universities
University Committee on Equal Opportunity (New School), 142
University in Exile (New School), 12, 21, 162, 447-48
establishment of, 66
fiftieth anniversary of, 95-98
impossible outside of New York, 46
neutrality of universities and, 101

University in Exile Professorship, 52
University Scholars program, 141
University of World Economy and Diplomacy (Uzbekistan), 501-2
Urazhtsev, Vitaly, 425
Urban, Jan, 239, 241, 244, 251, 449
on breakup of Czechoslovakia, 383-84
at Democracy Seminar (Prague), 437
Urbanek, Zdenek, 390<bi>n<ei>
Urban Policy program, 228
Urban Reporting Project, 47
urban studies, 46-47
Ursu, Doru Viorel, 295
Uzbekistan, 475, 477-78, 494-502

Van Valkenburgh, Michael, 159
Veblen, Thorstein, 23, 51, 123-24
Vejvoda, Ivan, 305
Velcheva, Virgiana, 359
Videnov, Jan, 360
Vieru, Sorin, 282-84, 285
Vietnamese, 394
Vietnam War, 74, 193
Vilnius (Lithuania), 320-22, 332-33
Vlasceanu, Lapar, 295

Wagner, Herbert, 298, 302
Walesa, Lech, 390
Walzer, Michael, 4
Washington, Harold, 120
Watergate scandal, 74
Weisse, Hans, 54
Welfare Party (Fundamentalists; Turkey), 342, 343
Wessel, Karl Friedrich, 298-300
Western Cape, University of the (UWC; South Africa), 471-73
West Germany, 302-4
Westminster Theological Seminary, 210-12
Westmoreland, William, 116

Wildmon, Donald, 171, 179
Wilson, Francis, 456, 469
Wilson, Woodrow, 64, 75
Winthrop, John, 4
Wittels, Fritz, 51-52
Wolfe, Alan, 298, 304, 448
women, as part-time graduate students, 201
Woodward, C. Van, 5
Workers Party of Kurdistan (PKK; Turkey), 349-51
Works Progress Administration (WPA), 172
World Policy Institute, 218
Writers Union (Romania), 282
Wunderlich, Frieda, 46

Yale University, 192
   under Brewster, 7
   controversial speakers at, 116
   Fanton at, 2-3
Yazov, 332
Yeltsin, Boris, 152, 253, 260-64, 322, 334
   Abkahazia conflict and, 423
   conflict between Gorbachev and, 264-67
   Estonia and, 403
   ethnic Russians in Baltic nations and, 426
   performance of, 425
Yerevan (Armenia), 405-7
Yerevan State University (Armenia), 430
Yugoslavia, 148, 149, 305-7
   current situation in (1991), 307-12
   future of, 312-18
   human rights abuses in, 312

Zagreb (Yugoslavia), 307
Zapryanov, Anton, 250
Zekeidze, David, 415-16
Zeman, Rudolf, 240
Zhelev, Zheliu, 354, 355, 357-58, 360, 362, 365, 439
Zhirinovsky, Vladimir, 479
Zhivkov, Todor, 354, 355, 361, 362, 438
Zimbabwe, 458
Zimmerman, Friedrich, 301
Zimmermann, Warren, 305
Zog I (Ahmed Beg Zog; king, Albania), 368